YO-ARY-661

Commercial Property

Coverage Guide
Second Edition

Interpretation and Analysis

Bruce J. Hillman, J.D.
Michael K. McCracken, CPCU, ASLI

The
NATIONAL
UNDERWRITER
Company

Professional Publishing Group
P.O. Box 14367 • Cincinnati, OH 45250-0367
1-800-543-0874 • www.nationalunderwriter.com

This publication is designed to provide accurate and authoritative information in regard to the subject matter covered. It is sold with the understanding that the publisher is not engaged in rendering legal, accounting, or other professional service. If legal advice or other expert assistance is required, the services of a competent professional person should be sought. — from a Declaration of Principles jointly adopted by a Committee of the American Bar Association and a Committee of Publishers and Associations.

Copyright © 2001 by
THE NATIONAL UNDERWRITER COMPANY
P.O. Box 14367
Cincinnati, OH 45250-0367

All rights reserved. No part of this book may be reproduced in any form by any means without permission from the publisher.

Reproductions of and quotations from ISO insurance policies and forms in this book are the copyrighted material of Insurance Services Office, Inc. and are used with permission.

Reproductions of and quotations from AAIS insurance policies and forms in this book are the copyrighted material of The American Association of Insurance Services, Inc. and are used with permission.

International Standard Book Number: 0-87218-390-4
Library of Congress Control Number: 2001130418

Printed in The United States of America

Table of Contents

Coverage Scenario Index

Introduction: The Building and Personal Property Coverage Form 1

Property Coverage Forms 1
ISO Rules 2
Underwriting 3
Purpose of this Work 4

Chapter 1: The Insuring Agreement; Covered and Not Covered Property 5

Section A. Coverage 5
What is "Direct Physical Loss or Damage?" 5
Section A.1. Covered Property 6
Section A.1.a. Building Coverage 7
Section A.1.b. Business Personal Property 11
Meaning of Premises 11
A.1.c. Personal Property of Others 21
Section A.2. Property Not Covered 22

Chapter 2: Additional Coverages, Coverage Extensions and Optional Coverages 27

Section 4. Additional Coverages 28
4.a. Debris Removal 28
4.b. Preservation of Property 31
4.c. Fire Department Service Charge 31
4.d. Pollutant Cleanup and Removal 32
4.e. Increased Cost of Construction 34
Section 5. Coverage Extensions 35
5.a. Newly Acquired or Constructed Property 35
5.b. Personal Effects and Property of Others 37
5.c. Valuable Papers and Records—Cost of Research ... 38
5.d. Property Off-Premises 38

5.e. Outdoor Property 40
5.f. Nonowned Detached Trailers 40
Optional Coverages 41
Section G.1. Agreed Value 41
Section G.2. Inflation Guard 42
Section G.3. Replacement Cost 42
Section G.4. Extension of Replacement Cost to Personal
    Property of Others 46

Chapter 3: Covered Causes of Loss—Named Perils Forms 49

CP 10 10—Causes of Loss—Basic Form 50
CP 10 20—Broad Form Causes of Loss 60
Exclusions that Apply to Both Named Perils Causes
    of Loss Forms 62
Subsection B.2. Exclusions 69
Special Exclusions 70
Additional Coverage 70
Collapse 70

**Chapter 4: Special Covered Causes of Loss Form
    (CP 10 30) 73**

Similarities to Named Perils Forms 74
Open Perils Exclusions—Section B.2. 75
Losses that Happen over Time—Section 2.d. 76
Other Exclusions 81
Concurrent Causation Exclusions 85
Special Exclusions 87
Limitations 87
Limitations on Other Types of Property 91
Special Theft Limits 92
Additional Coverages and Limitation 92
Additional Coverage Extensions 92

Chapter 5: Conditions 95

Commercial Property General Conditions 95
Cancellation 95
Changes 96
Examination of Your Books and Records 96
Inspection and Surveys 96

Premiums 97
Transfer of Rights and Duties under This Policy 97
Commercial Property Policy Conditions 97
Concealment, Misrepresentation or Fraud................................. 98
Control of Property 99
Insurance under Two or More Coverages 100
Legal Action against the Insurer 100
Liberalization 100
No Benefit to Bailee 100
Other Insurance.. 101
Policy Period, Coverage Territory 101
Subrogation... 102
Other Relevant Provisions of the Commercial Property Policy ... 102
Limits of Insurance and Deductible... 102
Loss Conditions 103
Abandonment and Appraisal 103
The Insured's Duties in the Event of Loss 104
Loss Payment... 105
Recovered Property 108
Vacancy 108
Valuation 110
Additional Conditions 112
Coinsurance 112
Mortgageholders 114

Chapter 6: Builders Risk 117

Covered Property 119
Property Not Covered 120
Covered Causes of Loss 121
Additional Coverages 121
Coverage Extensions 121
Trees, Shrubs and Plants.. 122
Limits of Insurance 122
Deductible... 123
Loss Conditions 123
Additional Conditions 123
Builders Risk Coverage Options 124
Building Renovations 125
Builder's Risk Reporting Form 125
Separate or Subcontractors Interest 126
Collapse during Construction 126

Theft of Building Materials, Fixtures, Machinery, Equipment 126
Building Materials and Supplies of Others 127

Chapter 7: Other Coverage Forms 129

Leasehold Interest 129
What is Insured 129
Causes of Loss, Exclusions, and Limitations 130
Limits of Insurance 131
Loss Conditions 132
Cancellation 133
Schedule Form CP 19 60 134
Leasehold Interest Factors 135
Mortgageholders Errors and Omissions - CP 00 70 135
The Four Coverage Agreements 136
Coverage A - Mortgageholder's Interest 136
Coverage B - Property Owned or Held in Trust 138
Coverage C - Mortgageholder's Liability 139
Real Estate Tax Liability—Coverage D 140
Exclusions 140
Limits of Insurance 141
Additional Coverage—Collapse 142
Additional Conditions 143
Conditions Applicable to All Coverages 144
Definitions 147
Tobacco in Sales Warehouses 147
Covered Property 148
Additional Coverages 148
Coverage Extension 148
Exclusions and Limitations 149
Additional Conditions 149
Deductible 149
Loss Conditions 149
Definitions 150
Condominium Associations 150
Covered Property 150
Other Provisions 152
Commercial Condominium Unit-Owners 153
Property 154
Additional Coverages and Coverage Extensions 154
Limits and Deductible 154
Loss Conditions 155

Other Provisions 155
Legal Liability Coverage Form 155
Coverage 157
Coverage Extensions—Additional Insureds and Newly
    Acquired Organizations 158
Newly Acquired Property 158
Perils and Exclusions 159
Loss Conditions 160
Additional Conditions 161

Chapter 8: Commercial Property Endorsements 163

Additional Building Property, CP 14 15 163
Additional Covered Property, CP 14 10 163
Additional Locations Special Coinsurance Provisions, CP 13 20 164
Additional Property Not Covered, CP 14 20 165
Agricultural Products Storage, CP 13 30 166
Alcoholic Beverage Tax Exclusion, CP 99 10 167
Brands and Labels, CP 04 01 167
Broken or Cracked Glass Exclusion Form, CP 10 52 168
Burglary and Robbery Protective Safeguards, CP 12 11 .. 168
Condominium Commercial Unit Owners Optional
    Coverages, CP 04 18 169
Contributing Insurance, CP 99 20 169
Debris Removal Additional Insurance, CP 04 15 170
Deductible Limitation, CP 03 10 170
Distilled Spirits and Wines Market Value, CP 99 05 170
Earthquake and Volcanic Eruption Endorsement Form,
    CP 10 40 171
Earthquake Inception Extension, CP 10 41 172
Electrical Apparatus, CP 04 10 172
Flood Coverage Endorsement, CP 10 65 172
Functional Building Valuation, CP 04 38 173
Functional Personal Property Valuation-Other Than Stock,
    CP 04 39 175
Grain Properties—Explosion Limitation, CP 10 51 176
Household Personal Property Coverage, CP 99 92 176
Leased Property, CP 14 60 177
Legal Liability Coverage Schedule, CP DS 05 177
Loss Payable Provisions, CP 12 18 177
Manufacturers Consequential Loss Assumption, CP 99 02 178
Manufacturer's Selling Price (Finished Stock Only), CP 99 30... 178

Market Value Stock, CP 99 31 178
Molten Material, CP 10 60 179
Multiple Deductible, CP 03 20 179
Multiple Location/Premium and Dispersion Credit
    Application, CP 13 70 179
Newly Acquired/Constructed Property-Increased Limit,
    CP 04 25 179
Off-Premises Services-Direct Damage, CP 04 17 180
Ordinance or Law Coverage, CP 04 05 180
Outdoor Trees, Shrubs and Plants, CP 14 30 182
Outside Signs, CP 14 40 182
Peak Season Limit of Insurance, CP 12 30 183
Pier and Wharf Additional Covered Causes of Loss, CP 10 70 ... 184
Pollutant Cleanup & Removal Additional Aggregate
    Limit of Insurance, CP 04 07 184
Protective Safeguards, IL 04 15 185
Radio or Television Antennas, CP 14 50 186
Radioactive Contamination, CP 10 37 186
Report of Values, CP 13 60, and Supplemental Report
    of Values, CP 13 61 187
Spoilage Coverage, CP 04 40 187
Sprinkler Leakage Exclusion, CP 10 56 188
Sprinkler Leakage-Earthquake Extension, CP 10 39 188
Storage or Repairs Limited Liability, CP 99 42 188
Tentative Rates, CP 99 93 189
Theft Exclusion, CP 10 33 189
Utility Services - Direct Damage, CP 04 17 189
Vacancy Changes, CP 04 60 189
Vacancy Permit, CP 04 50 190
Value Reporting Form, CP 13 10 190
Vandalism Exclusion, CP 10 55 191
Watercraft Exclusion, CP 10 35 191
Windstorm or Hail Percentage Deductible, CP 03 21 191
Windstorm or Hail Exclusion-Direct Damage, CP 10 53 192
Windstorm or Hail Exclusion, CP 10 54 192
Your Business Personal Property-Separation of
    Coverage, CP 19 10 193

**Chapter 9: The Commercial Properties Program
    of American Association of Insurance Services (AAIS) .. 195**

Building and Personal Property Coverage Part 196

Covered Property 196
Property Excluded and Limitations 197
Additional Coverages 198
Supplemental Coverages 198
What Must Be Done in Case of Loss 200
Valuation 201
How Much We Pay 201
Loss Payment 202
Other Conditions 203
Special Causes of Loss Form 204
Additional Property Excluded and Limitations 205
Additional Coverages 206
Other Coverage Parts 206
Endorsements 207

Chapter 10: E-Issues under the Commercial Property Policy 209

What Today's Businesses Face 209
Insuring Intangible Assets 210
What Current Policies Say 212
Newly Developed Policies 213

Specimen Forms 217

Building and Personal Property Coverage Form 218
Condominium Association Coverage Form 231
Condominium Commercial Unit-Owners Coverage From 243
Builders Risk Coverage Form 253
Legal Liability Coverage Form 260
Leasehold Interest Coverage Form 263
Mortgageholders Errors and Omissions Coverage Form 267
Tobacco Sales Warehouses Coverage Form 277
Commercial Property Conditions 282
Causes of Loss - Basic Form 284
Causes of Loss - Broad Form 288
Causes of Loss - Special Form 294
Common Policy Conditions 301

Index 303

Coverage Scenario Index

Equipment Damaged by a Covered Peril—Spoilage
    Loss Consequential   6
Nonfunctioning Water Tower as Covered Property?   7
Lawn Tent as a Fixture?   9
Modular Office System as "Fixture"   12
Improvements and Betterments—Coverage Dependent on
    Term of Lease?   15
May the Exclusion of Excavation Costs be Applied
    to Debris Removal?   22
Excavation of Broken Water Pipe Covered?   23
Foundations as Property Not Covered   24
Outdoor Sprinkler System as Underground Pipes?   25
Debris Removal—Is Repair or Replacement Required?   29
Debris Removal Coverage and Coinsurance Provision   30
Debris Removal Coverage - Volunteer Expense   30
Fire Department Service Charge Coverage   32
Pollution Cleanup   32
Newly Acquired Location   37
Meaning of Locations You "Own, Lease, or Operate"   39
Replacement by Substitution - Commercial Property   44
Replacement Cost—Reconditioned Property   45
Is a gunshot an explosion?   50
Tractor Falling off Trailer—Falling Object or Vehicle Damage?   55
"Remodeling" as Vandalism?   57
Sinkhole Collapse under Commercial Property Form   59
Water Damage—Costs to Repair Leak Even if Building
    is Undamaged   62
Earth Movement Exclusion   64
Damage by Police Action   64
Power Failure vs. Power Surge   66
Application of the Mechanical Breakdown Exclusion   70
Heavy Construction and the Earth Movement Exclusion   75
Wear and Tear Exclusion—Damage to Shower Stall
Mechanical Breakdown Exclusion and Concurrent Causation   80
Repeated Seepage or Leakage   82
Steam Boilers—Condition or Event Inside   88
Water Damage and Boarded-Up Windows   88
Missing Property—No Physical Evidence   89

Marble Slab as Fragile Article   91
Property in Transit   93
Appraisal of a Loss   104
Valuation and Selling Price   111
Coinsurance Application in a Total Loss   113
Loss during Foreclosure   115
Value of the Building on the Completion Date   118
Need for Builders Risk on Renovations to Existing Building   127
Leasehold Interest—Terms in a Lease   131
Carpeting in Condominiums   151

Introduction

The Building and Personal Property Coverage Form

The principal contract for insuring the building and personal property exposures of commercial insureds is the Insurance Services Office (ISO) ***Building and Personal Property Coverage Form, CP 00 10*** (or, the commercial property policy). Introduced by ISO in 1985 as part of the development of simplified language insurance policies, the form has undergone several revisions. It currently exists—where approved—as the 12/2000 version; it is this edition of the form that is the basis of this book.

This book's in-depth analysis puts the policy into context with the rest of the ISO commercial property program and all its basic forms and permutations. In addition to the CP coverage form, this work treats the commercial property program's three causes of loss forms (basic, broad, and special); optional coverages; builders risk coverage form and options; and the other coverage forms comprising the ISO Commercial Property Program.

The building and personal property coverage form is one building block in the ISO commercial property program. Also, the commercial property program is one part of the protection available for commercial insureds. Property coverage usually must be combined with general liability, crime, fidelity, inland marine, workers compensation, and automobile coverages in order to adequately protect the interests of commercial insureds.

Property Coverage Forms

Virtually all types of commercial property are eligible for the building and personal property coverage form. Specialized versions of property coverage

1

forms exist for use with condominium and builders risk exposures. Other coverages, such as legal liability, value reporting, mortgage holders errors and omissions, tobacco sales warehouses, and leasehold interest are available through separate forms. Of course, coverage may be modified in many ways through the use of various endorsements.

The commercial property program adopts a modular format, in that a coverage form (such as the commercial property policy) must be combined with policy declarations, an appropriate causes of loss form (basic, broad, or special), two conditions forms (commercial property and common policy), and any desired endorsements to form a *coverage part*. A commercial property coverage part may be used as a monoline policy covering property only or combined with other commercial lines coverages (e.g., general liability, commercial auto, etc.) to form a commercial package policy.

ISO Rules

The rules for the commercial property policy are in the ISO Commercial Lines Manual (CLM) at Division Five—Fire and Allied Lines. A review of some of the basic rules is helpful in putting the form's use into context.

Policies may be written for a specific term, up to three years (i.e., for one year, two years, or three years), or on a continuous basis. It is of historic interest to note that property policies were commonly written for three, and even five, year terms, often with annual billing. During the inflationary period of the 1970s, annual policies became the standard. Today, longer term periods have returned.

Common policy conditions form IL 00 17 is used with all policies. This form contains six conditions that must be incorporated into any policy written under the program and that apply to all the policy's coverages. Most of these common policy conditions are restatements of provisions of the standard fire policy. The conditions included in IL 00 17 are cancellation, changes, examination of your books and records, inspections and surveys, premiums, and transfer of rights and duties.

The Commercial Property Conditions Form CP 00 90 is also attached to all policies, except when Mortgage Holder's Errors and Omissions Coverage Form CP 00 70 is the only form applicable to commercial property coverage. The CP 00 90 contains the following provisions: concealment, misrepresentation or fraud; control of property; more than one coverage applying to loss; legal action against the company; liberalization; no benefit to bailee; other insurance; policy period; coverage territory; and subrogation.

Interstate accounts may be written on the same policy. One policy may be written to cover locations in more than one state. The coverage may be property or business income and may cover on either a specific or blanket basis. Such a policy is subject to the rules of:

1. the state in which the insured's largest-valued location or headquarters is located; or
2. where the insurance is negotiated.

Where contributing insurance is an issue—where coverage is divided between two or more insurers on a percentage basis—contributing insurance endorsement CP 99 20 may be attached. This endorsement provides that the insurance company's liability on any loss shall not exceed it's percentage of total coverage. Simply stated, this means that if there are two policies covering a piece of property, one with a limit of $70,000 and the other with a limit of $30,000 ($100,000 total coverage), the first insurer would be liable for only 70 percent of the total of any loss.

Underwriting

ISO defines seven different types of construction: frame, joisted masonry, noncombustible, masonry noncombustible, modified fire resistive, fire resistive, and mixed. In addition to the construction of the building itself, the underwriter also looks at the floors, roofs, and partitions. The area of the building and any unprotected openings are also considered.

The use of firewalls between portions of a building can greatly reduce the rate for property insurance. The area between firewalls is a fire division. Fire divisions prevent the spread from one section of a building to another.

However, the lack of fire walls can have an adverse effect on the rate charged. Several years ago, a popular shopping mall in Ohio was remodeled. It had been a one-story structure, with two-story anchor stores at each of the corners. The one-story portion was divided by firewalls into several fire divisions, in effect creating several small exposure units.

The remodeling project added a second story over the one-story section. Unfortunately, the firewalls were not extended up and through the new second story, thus rendering them useless. The mall went from being several small fire divisions, to being one big fire division. Even though the mall has a sprinkler system and is masonry noncombustible construction, the rate for its property insurance increased substantially.

Occupancy refers to the use of the structure. A building that houses fireworks will certainly pay a higher rate for property insurance, than the office building next door.

Protection refers to the kind and quality of protection, both public and private, available to a structure. Private protection ranges from fire extinguishers and sprinkler systems to a private fire department. Only the biggest of companies (such as huge manufacturers) have their own fire departments.

Towns and cities receive a protection class code based upon several factors: the firefighting equipment; the training of the firefighters; the mix of full-time and volunteer firefighters; and the local water supply. Class codes range from one to ten, with one being the best and ten being a risk with no responding fire department within five miles.

Currently, no city in America has a class one rating. Classes two through five require all full-time firefighters. Classes six, seven, and eight can be a mix of full-time and volunteer. Class nine is typically all volunteer and class ten may or may not have any fire department at all. One issue that many older cities are facing is the downgrading of their fire protection class, due mainly to the aging of their infrastructure, specifically the water supply apparatus. As the cities get older, many are experiencing a drop in water pressure. Combine the lower water pressure with more and taller buildings and a problem arises in the efficacy of the fire fighting.

Exposure refers to external exposure of the building. In other words, what is next to the insured structure? In the above example, the office building next to the fireworks warehouse may pay a higher rate than a comparable office building in an office park elsewhere in the same city. The office building faces a greater chance of loss from fire at the fireworks warehouse.

Purpose of this Work

This book reviews and analyzes the CP 00 10, its three causes of loss forms, and optional coverages. Where relevant, other forms comprising the commercial property program are also included and analyzed.

This work is one of a number of books published by The National Underwriter Company reviewing and analyzing individual insurance forms. Other titles in the Coverage Guide series include: *Personal Auto, Homeowners,Personal Umbrella, CGL, Business Auto, Businessowners, Directors and Officers Liability,* and *Employment PracticesLiability, Workers Compensation and e-Coverage.* Additional forms and issues are treated in the *FC&S Bulletins.*

Chapter 1

The Insuring Agreement; Covered and Not Covered Property

Section A. Coverage

The core of the building and personal property coverage form, CP 00 10 is the insuring agreement and its description of what is, and what is not, covered property. The insuring agreement obligates the insurer to pay for "direct physical loss or damage to covered property at the premises described in the Declarations caused by or resulting from any Covered Cause of Loss."

What is "Direct Physical Loss or Damage?"

The promise to pay for direct physical loss or damage (to covered property) means that the policy responds to damage that is directly caused by an insured peril. Directly caused refers to a causal relationship between the event immediately responsible for the loss (the insured peril, e.g., fire, vandalism, windstorm, etc.) and the damage done to covered property (i.e., a building, structure, or business personal property).

For damage to be directly caused, the insured event (peril) must be immediately responsible for the damage. Fire lapping at a piece of furniture turning it to ash is damage directly caused.

Indirect or consequential losses arise as a consequence of a direct loss. A restaurant has a fire that cuts out all electricity in the building. Before the electricity can be restored, the food in the freezer thaws. The damage to the building by the fire is direct, but the food thawing is an *indirect* loss. It resulted as a consequence of the fire. The policy covers the damage to the building, but not the thawed food.

Equipment Damaged by a Covered Peril— Spoilage Loss Consequential

A building and its contents are covered under the commercial property policy with the special causes of loss form. Lightning struck a utility pole located off premises damaging a compressor attached to a walk-in refrigerator. Food stored in the refrigerator spoiled. The insurer pays for the damage to the compressor but denies coverage for the spoilage, claiming that it is a consequential loss. The insurance agent believes that the spoilage is covered because lightning, a covered cause of loss, was the proximate cause of the entire loss.

The spoilage loss is appropriately denied. Because of the lapse in time between the lightning damage and the spoilage, it is common to rule out coverage under the commercial property policy. In other words, lightning is the direct cause of the damage to the equipment, but is a remote cause of the food spoilage. Change in temperature caused the spoilage, not lightning striking the compressor.

The insured may choose the perils covered in his policy—basic, broad or special causes of loss form (see Chapters 3 and 4). Direct physical loss or damage means that consequential damage—damage flowing from, but not directly caused by the insured peril—is not covered by the commercial property policy. Consequential damage can be seen as *remote* or *indirect* damage; i.e., not directly causally related. Frequently cited examples of consequential damage are loss from depreciation, delay, deterioration, or loss of market. There is coverage available for most of these consequential losses, but not under the unadorned commercial property policy.

Section A.1. Covered Property

Coverage under the commercial property policy is for property (meaning there is no liability coverage) and includes buildings, the insured's business personal property, and personal property of others (in certain circumstances). A limit of insurance must be stated in the declarations for that type of property (i.e., for buildings and/or contents). This is because the commercial property policy can be written to cover only buildings or only contents (personal property). A limit has to be shown in the declarations for one or both for that type of property to be covered.

Section A.1.a. Building Coverage

The commercial property policy covers the buildings and structures shown in the declarations.

A basic tenet of insurance contract interpretation is that words and phrases in insurance policies are governed by their common dictionary definition unless specifically defined in the policy. For example, the commercial property policy contains only two defined terms, "stock," and "pollutant." Therefore, these two terms have the meaning that is specifically ascribed to them in the form; all other terms will be given a common usage meaning. So in the absence of a policy definition, if there is a common usage meaning that is more favorable to the insured than the meaning put forth by the insurer, the insured will be allowed the more favorable definition.

Building means the building or structure described in the declarations. As neither term is further defined in the policy, a common meaning will be implied. Inasmuch as the building or structure must be described in the declarations, not much argument can arise regarding what is a building or structure in terms of policy interpretation. The building or structure described in the declarations is the covered item of property.

However, the term structure is broader than the term building, and some items that might not readily suggest themselves as buildings might be named in the declarations, thereby affording coverage. This might include, among other items, swimming pools, garages, or semipermanent items such as a wooden floor covered by a tent that is used for events at a private club. The important point is that such items be listed in the declarations; not all structures are covered, only those listed. Failure to list all structures for which coverage is desired will result in no insurance recovery on loss to undeclared structures.

Nonfunctioning Water Tower as Covered Property?

An insured had an extensive fire at his hotel. On top of the hotel was a nonfunctional water tower valued at about $40,000.

The insurance company adjuster believes it should not have to include the cost of the water tower in the insurance settlement because it was not functional and therefore had no value. The agent believes that the insurer should pay the $40,000 cost to replace it because: 1) there could have been an alternate use for the tower; 2) the tower was a part of the building and did have a value even though at the time it was nonfunctional (and could have been considered decorative); and 3) when a company insures a structure, it insures the complete structure whether a portion of it is functional or not.

(scenario continues next page)

(continued from previous page)

The issue is how the tower should be adjusted.

The commercial property policy does not refer anywhere to functional or nonfunctional property. It only mentions covered and noncovered property. Covered property includes the building. The water tower, being attached to the building, qualifies as covered property.

If a coinsurance requirement is shown in the policy declarations, and if the insured has met the coinsurance requirement for insuring to value, the building, including the water tower, is covered to the full limit of the policy. If the insured has not met the coinsurance requirement, the penalty will apply, lowering the amount available to cover the loss and capping recovery.

The attempt to deny coverage for the tower due to its present nonfunctional state is analogous to denying coverage for an unused second story of a building. It would not be correct to reduce the value of a building due to the nonuse of a portion of that building. It is just as incorrect to reduce coverage for the loss due to whether or not the building structure is functional. The tower should be included in the insurance recovery.

The use of the singular (building or structure) rather than the plural (building*s* or structure*s*) does not mean that the policy cannot be used to cover more than one building or structure. Using the singular construction avoids confusion after policy inception in the event the insured builds additional buildings or structures that were not on the premises at the time of the original policy. The phrase "buildings or structures" might be interpreted (or misinterpreted) by insureds (and courts) as implying that *all* buildings and structures on the insured premises are covered, regardless of the qualifying language, "described in the Declarations."

The commercial property policy provides coverage under the building portion for five other classes or types of property:

1. **Completed additions.** If the insured has added onto the described building, the commercial property policy automatically covers that new portion. This coverage is beneficial to the insured by providing automatic coverage for new additions during the term of the policy. However, it can also lead to difficulty under the terms of the coinsurance clause if the overall amount of insurance is not adjusted to account for the increased values.

2. **Fixtures, including outdoor fixtures.** The commercial property policy also covers fixtures under the building limit. A standard desk-top dictionary says that a fixture is "something that is fixed or

attached ... as a permanent appendage or as a structural part." For example, a light mounted into a brick wall on the patio is a fixture; a table lamp on a pool side table attached to the wall only by its electric cord is not a fixture.

Lawn Tent as a Fixture?

A country club has a tent that it uses for outdoor events, such as receptions, dances, etc. This tent has permanent solid flooring to which the tent is attached. The tent is dismantled each year during the winter and stored.

The tent was damaged by fire, a covered cause of loss. The insurance agent maintains it is a fixture, and as such is covered under the commercial property policy's building coverage. The adjuster sees it otherwise, arguing that the tent is business personal property, and, as such covered under the contents coverage.

The tent is not a fixture. It is a structure. But not all structures are fixtures. It is not affixed to the building or to the realty, and therefore is not covered under the building coverage of the commercial property policy (unless it is listed in the policy declarations as a covered structure.

The tent is business personal property and qualifies for coverage under the contents section.

3.   **Permanently installed machinery and equipment.** The commercial property policy covers as part of the building permanently installed machinery and equipment. This includes drive-on scales, refrigerated lockers, pulleys, and the like. The policy does not define permanently installed, but install commonly means, "to set up for use or service," and permanently means, "continuing or enduring without fundamental or marked change; stable."

An item does not have to become a part of the building structure of the building for it to be considered permanently installed. For example, a refrigerated locker is permanently installed if it is set up for use in the insured's building with the intent that it should remain there as long as the insured is in business at that location.

Again, the issue is what is permanently installed? Analyzing the common usage meaning of permanent and install, it becomes apparent that some items of personal property used in a business can be covered under the building portion of the policy. Permanent, as stated above, means "continuing or enduring without fundamental or marked change; stable." And install means "to set up for use or service." Therefore, a computer assigned permanently for the use of an employee and which has been installed by setting it up for use or attaching (installing) it to a network could be covered under the buildings coverage portion of the policy, if that was more advantageous for the insured (this becomes important, for example, when contents limits have been depleted or exhausted, but building coverage limits have not). Under the same logic, a telephone system might be covered as building property.

Not all office equipment is installed, and therefore would not be eligible for building coverage consideration. For example: a desk sitting in an office lacks the element of installation, as would planters, tables, etc.

The insured must be careful in declaring values for limit-setting purposes. If the insured makes a claim for a computer under the building coverage, all permanently installed machinery and equipment must then be considered for coinsurance purposes. Carrying an adequate limit on the building, but not on business personal property might lead to serious coinsurance penalties in the event of a loss.

4. **Personal property used to maintain the building.** Personal property that the insured owns and uses to service or maintain the building or structure or its premises is covered under the building coverage section. The policy contains a nonexclusive list, by way of example, of what such equipment is: fire extinguishing equipment; outdoor furniture; floor coverings; and appliances used for refrigerating, ventilating, cooking, dishwashing or laundering. This category might include many other types of personal property, such as a golf cart used to carry items around the premises, lawn mowers, or snow blowers. The list is illustrative, not comprehensive.

5. **Additions under construction or alteration and repairs to the building or structure.** Further, so are materials, equipment, supplies, and temporary structures within 100 feet of the described premises, used for making additions, alterations, or repairs to the building or structure.

Note that this item appplies to in progress construction or alteration and is available only if no other insurance exists for the project. The commercial property policy's other insurance provision permits a pro rata or excess payment of loss if other insurance also exists. But other insurance cooperation does not apply to additions, alterations, or repairs in progress. Other insurance in this one special case rules out coverage of this property entirely under this form.

While the commercial property policy does not state that materials, supplies, and equipment must be owned by the insured, the insured must have an insurable interest in order for these items to be covered under the insured's commercial property policy. For example: a contractor leaves a backhoe on the premises with the keys in the ignition and it is stolen. The insured's commercial property policy would not respond, as the insured has no insurable interest in the property. If, however, the backhoe was leased to the insured and the insured was legally liable for it, the insured would have an insurable interest, and coverage would attach.

Section A.1.b. Business Personal Property

In addition to building property, the commercial property policy also covers business personal property of the insured. Business personal property is broadly described, and, in addition to other specified types of property, includes "all other personal property owned by you and used in your business." This broad characterization of property allows for a wide interpretation of what might be covered under the contents portion of the commercial property policy.

The commercial property policy covers business personal property that is located in or on the building described in the declarations; that is in the open; or that is in a vehicle within 100 feet of the described premises. *In the open* includes property in bales or otherwise stored in the open, as well as that stored in open sheds.

Meaning of Premises

The commercial property policy covers business personal property including property in the open within 100 feet of the premises. The question then arises: does premises include the land on which the building sits so that coverage extends to property in the open beyond the perimeter of the land or is premises limited to the building itself?

Premises includes the grounds, parking lot, and so on that are part of the property on which the building is located. Thus, coverage would apply to property that might be temporarily stored (within 100 feet) on an adjoining vacant lot awaiting movement onto the insured's property. In the absence of a more restrictive definition in the policy itself, the dictionary definition of premises, "a tract of land with the buildings thereon" or "a building or part of a building, usually with its appurtenances (as grounds)," applies. But grounds should not be thought of so broadly as to include any amount of acreage on which a building might be situated. The grounds are those that pertain to the service of the building.

Inasmuch as premises is a broader term than building, this provides coverage for property off the insured's premises, so long as the property is located within 100 feet of the premises. For example, the insured's business personal property in a car parked across the street from the insured's business is covered, so long as the car is parked within 100 feet of the insured's location.

The classes of business personal property covered by the commercial property policy are further outlined in seven clauses.

1.   **Furniture and fixtures.** Note that coverage for fixtures appears both under the building and business personal property sections of the commercial property policy. If the insured has purchased both coverages, fixtures are covered under either. However, the insured is free to call for coverage under whichever of the two items— building or property—yields the greater advantage, under the following circumstances:
       a.   if the business personal property is not insured for the same causes of loss as the building;
       b.   if it is subject to a different coinsurance requirement; or
       c.   if the limits under one or the other coverages are exhausted.

       Fixtures that are tenants' improvements and betterments (i.e., affixed to the realty and considered the landlord's property) are not included in this item in the tenant's policy. Rather, the tenant's use interest is covered under item number 6 (see below).

Modular Office System as "Fixture"

An insured suffered a loss due to a hurricane. The insured carried only building coverage, no contents protection.

(scenario continues next page)

(continued from previous page)

The insured had a modular office system custom designed and installed. The agent maintains that those panels which were mounted on the building's walls are fixtures, and therefore, covered under the commercial property building coverage. The independent adjuster maintains that since they can be removed and relocated to other areas they are furniture, and not covered.

The panels require a wall-mounting kit. In order to move the wall-mounted panels, the insured would have to call the manufacturer and request an installer at $45 per hour because the insured could not move the panels himself.

The issue is whether these panels can be covered as building items, or whether the insured would have to have contents coverage in order to recover for their damage.

The panels are fixtures for coverage purposes. The term fixture is not further defined in the commercial property policy, leaving its interpretation to the common lay meaning. A common usage dictionary defines fixture as "something that is fixed or attached (as to a building) as a permanent appendage *or as a structural part*"(emphasis added). The term is further defined as "an item of movable property so incorporated into real property that it may be regarded as legally a part of it."

Permanent does not mean that the item has to be so attached to the property as never to be removed. It means "continuing or enduring" and "stable."

Free-standing panels, however, if not installed in any way into the building, are not fixtures and would only be covered under the contents portion.

2. **Machinery and equipment**. Whereas the building coverage portion covers permanently installed machinery and equipment, the business personal property coverage is not so limited. Any machinery or equipment of the insured's is covered, regardless of the state of installment. Here again, the insured would have the discretion of covering this type of property either as building or contents, whichever is more favorable to the insured.

3. **Stock.** The commercial property policy covers the insured's stock. Stock is defined in the policy as "merchandise held in storage or for sale, raw materials and in-process or finished goods, including supplies used in their packing or shipping."

    The form clarifies, under the "property not covered" section, that stock of outdoor trees, shrubs, and plants is treated as any other stock and is not subject to the coverage limitations imposed by the outdoor property coverage extension (see Chapter 2). In other words, the limited coverage for trees and shrubs provided under the coverage extensions does not apply to trees and shrubs as stock—full business personal property limits are available.

One might question whether goods sold but not delivered are treated as the insured's business personal property or as the property of others. To determine the answer, the bill of sale provisions and the Uniform Commercial Code need to be examined. After ownership is established, the amount of coverage available and the value of the property must be determined.

If treated as the insured's business personal property the commercial property policy's valuation provision states that stock sold but not delivered is valued at the selling price less discounts and expenses the insured otherwise would have had. ABC Widget normally sells its product for $5 each. In a contract with XYZ for 10,000 widgets, ABC offers such a large quantity at $4 each. If a fire destroys those widgets while still at ABC, ABC's insurance policy will value them at $4 each—the normal selling price less the offered discount.

If considered the property of others, then the limit for property of others is available. If this coverage has not been purchased, then $2,500 of coverage is available under a coverage extension if a coinsurance provision of at least 80 percent or a value reporting symbol is shown in the declarations (see Chapter 2, Coverage Extensions).

4. **All other personal property owned by you and used in your business.** This broad statement means that personal property—of any kind—is covered property under the commercial property policy, subject to the requirements that it be owned by the insured and used in the insured's business. There is no requirement that the property be used exclusively in the insured's business. For example: a portable CD player used in both the insured's home and office would be covered as personal property used in the insured's business.

5. **Labor, materials, or services furnished or arranged by the insured on personal property of others**. This represents the value of the insured's business processes or operations where loss involves property of others that the insured has performed service or processes upon. For example: Bill owns a television repair shop. A fire occurs and damages a customer's set that was in for repairs. Bill's commercial property policy will cover the cost of the TV set plus the value of the materials and labor he put into it prior to the fire. If Bill gets $30 an hour for labor and has expended $50 in parts

and two hours labor to repair that set, the commercial property policy will pay him $110. The commercial property policy will also make payment to the customer for the value of the TV.

6. **Use interest as tenant in improvements and betterments.** When a tenant makes a permanent addition to a leased building, the improvements usually become part of the building and the property of the landlord. A new store front, installed by the tenant with the expectation of attracting more customers is a good example. The tenant, of course, has the right to use the improvement—new store front or whatever—for the term of the lease, but that is all.

Suppose a fire damages the improvements before the lease expires. The tenant has lost no property that belongs to him. The improvements belong to the landlord. What the tenant has lost is the use of the property and it is the right of use for the term of the lease that creates the tenant's insurable interest in the improvements. Or, put another way, it is the possible loss of use of the improvements in which the tenant has invested that represents the tenant's exposure.

Improvements and Betterments— Coverage Dependent on Term of Lease?

A building suffered lightning damage to a central air conditioning unit. The insured is a tenant, not the owner. The insured paid for the air conditioning unit five years ago.

The insured carries contents insurance, which includes the use interest in improvements and betterments. The insurance company initially declined the claim stating that the units were part of the building and, as there was no building coverage, there would be no recovery. The agent argued that the unit was an improvement and betterment. The company agreed with this, and also agreed that the cause of loss was a covered cause of loss.

The claim was denied on the basis that the tenant had no insurable interest in the improvement and betterment. The lease is an annual renewable lease. Nothing in the lease addresses the ownership of improvements and betterments. The lease was first executed in 1977 and renews automatically unless one party notifies the other within a certain time prior to the end of the annual period.

The insurance company based its position on the fact that when any lease renews, all improvements and betterments belong to the building owner. In other words, a tenant only has an insurable interest for the period of the lease, in this case one year.

(scenario continues next page)

(continued from previous page)

Improvements and betterments coverage would be severely impinged upon under the interpretation proposed by the insurance company. It would limit any coverage for improvements and betterments made by the tenant to a one year lease term, when in actuality, the building in question has been continuously leased for twenty years.

The form on its face belies this interpretation. It is the insured's use interest in improvements and betterments that is covered; further, an improvement and betterment is specifically stated to be fixtures made a part of the building the insured occupies but does not own and that were acquired or made at the insured's expense but cannot legally remove. Nowhere does this definition of improvements and betterments tie coverage to the duration of a lease. If there is a fixture that qualifies as an improvement and betterment and the insured's use interest is damaged, there is coverage.

Here, the insured acquired a fixture at his expense that was made a part of the building the insured occupies but does not own and which he cannot legally remove. His use interest in that fixture is damaged. Coverage applies.

The term improvements and betterments is one of elasticity and implies a substantial alteration, addition, or change to real property that enhances its value. The commercial property policy defines improvements and betterments as "fixtures, alterations, installations, or additions that are made a part of the building that is occupied but not owned by the named insured, and that the named insured acquires or makes at his expense but cannot legally remove." Coverage is automatic if the insured has an improvements and betterments exposure since business personal property is said to consist of, among other things, the named insured's use interest as tenant in improvements and betterments.

The definition of improvements and betterments is broad and generalized. Questions can and do arise as to whether, under given circumstances, particular work paid for by the tenant falls within its meaning.

For example, do repairs made on a permanent part of the building by the tenant constitute improvements and betterments? The answer seems to be no. *Modern Music Shop v. Concordia Fire Ins. Co.*, 226 N.Y.S. 630 (1928) provides a guide, though it involved an older form that referred simply to "the insured's interest in improvements and betterments." The court said, "These words imply and mean a substantial or fairly substantial alteration, addition, or change to the premises used and occupied by the insured, rising above and beyond and amounting to something more than a simple or minor repair."

In another case, *U.S. Fire Ins. Co. v. Martin,* 282 S.E.2d 2 (1981), the Virginia Supreme Court decided that air conditioners that the insured tenant had repaired but not installed were not within the meaning of improvements and betterments. The court reasoned that the tenant had not made the original expenditures for the air conditioners, that the expenditures were not later acquired by the tenant, and the expenses put out by the tenant were for repair only; therefore, there was no coverage under the terms of the policy.

The present definition and the court decisions in these two cases imply that an improvement must substantially change the building. A minor maintenance or repair task, such as painting the building, installing new locks on doors, etc., is not an improvement in the insurance meaning of the word. Tenants often agree to maintain the building or to undertake repairs or do these things voluntarily because the landlord refuses to do so. Such expense should probably be considered additional rent or a business cost, rather than an investment in improvements.

An important distinction is that between improvements and *trade fixtures.* The latter are installed by the tenant, often in such a way that they become a part of the building, but—either by express provision in the lease or by established custom—the vacating tenant removes them. Trade fixtures retain the character of personal property. Taking a store as an example, a new front installed by the tenant is an improvement, but counters, no matter how firmly they are attached to the building, are usually trade fixtures.

The commercial property policy sets out three methods (under section E.7.e Loss Conditions, Valuation) for determining recovery when improvements are damaged by an insured peril:

1) If the insured makes the repairs at his own expense (and is not reimbursed by the landlord), the commercial property policy covers the improvements at actual cash value, just as though the insured owned them. The policy requires that repairs be made promptly, but does not define what promptly is.

At least one court has held that the amount recoverable by the tenant for improvements is reduced by any amount that the tenant is reimbursed by the owner for the cost of the improvements. In *Atlanta Eye Care, Inc. v. Aetna Casualty and Surety Co.,* 364

S.E.2d 634 (1988), the insured was covered under a businessowners policy for improvements and betterments. The insured made improvements costing $19,000 to the leased property. The lease agreement, however, provided that the owner would reimburse the tenant $8,000, and this was done. After the property suffered a loss, the insurer paid all but $8,000 of the tenant's claim for improvements and betterments. Ruling in the insurer's favor, the court found that the coverage was correctly limited to those improvements for which the tenant had not been reimbursed.

2) If someone else (usually the landlord) repairs the improvements at his own expense for the use of the insured, the commercial property policy owes nothing. In this situation, the insured has suffered no loss and consequently should not recover anything. Where the insured has suffered temporary loss of business because of the damage to the improvements, the loss should be covered by business income coverage.

3) If the improvements are not repaired or replaced promptly, the insured tenant recovers a proportion of the original cost of the damaged improvements. The insurer determines the proportionate value by multiplying the original cost of the improvements by the number of days from the loss or damage to the expiration of the lease. Then, this amount is divided by the number of days from the installation of improvements to the expiration of the lease. If the insured's lease contains a renewal option, the expiration of the renewal option period becomes the expiration date for use in determining the amount recoverable. The lease option provision does not require that the tenant give notice to the owner, either verbally or in writing, of an intent to exercise the option.

The third situation is the one which most often presents difficulties. If neither the insured nor the landlord repairs or replaces the improvements promptly, and there is no definition of the word promptly, the commercial property policy pays an amount generally referred to as the unamortized portion of the investment. The simplest example of recovery under this situation is a tenant who has invested $10,000 in improvements at the beginning of a ten year lease. In effect, the tenant has bought the use of these improvements for ten years for $10,000. A fire destroys the improvements after five years, and the tenant loses half of the investment. If the improvements are not replaced, the third provision sets up the machinery for recovery of that lost half. Of course, when this third provision takes effect is open to question due to the lack of a time schedule. Does promptly mean 60 days, 90 days, 180 days, or more probably, depend on the particular circumstances surrounding the loss and its aftermath? If the damaged property is not repaired, there is nothing against which to measure promptly. The insured's loss of use is measured from time of loss.

When the insured or the landlord does not promptly repair or replace the damaged improvements, the basis for recovery under the policy is the original cost of the improvements, i.e., the amount the tenant had invested. Depreciation makes no difference. Neither does whether those improvements would cost more or less to replace at the time of loss than they actually cost to install matter. Actual cost of installation is the insured's investment. And that investment is what is lost—wholly or partially—if the improvements are destroyed and not restored.

Suppose an insured spent $10,000 on improvements at the beginning of November, 1997 under a lease running to the end of 2011. At the beginning of February, 1998, the improvements are destroyed and not replaced.

Under the formula for recovery in CP 00 10, the $10,000 is multiplied by 155 months, as that is the amount of time from the loss to the expiration of the lease. The resulting amount, $1,550,000, is divided by 170 or the amount of time from the installation of the improvements to the expiration of the lease. The recovery is $9,117.65.

Note that the original cost may be greater than the actual cash value of the improvements. If the insured must tear out a portion of the building in making the alterations or improvements, the original investment is the cost of the improvements plus the amount spent getting ready for them. For example, commercial property insured, Pat Tenant, spends $10,000 for improvements. But before these improvements could be made, Pat had to spend an additional $4,000 to remove the building front and inside wall. The total investment in improvements is $14,000, not $10,000. Then a fire occurs that totally destroys the improvements. If Pat chooses to replace the improvements, she will not have to redo the demolition work that she originally did. The commercial property policy, thus, ignores the $4,000 that she originally spent and her recovery is then the actual cash value of the improvements—replacement cost less depreciation, which might be more or less than $10,000. On the other hand, if Pat does not replace the improvements, the commercial property policy bases her recovery on the total original cost—$14,000, the cost of the demolition work plus the original cost of the improvements.

What if Pat has only a month-to-month lease? The commercial property policy still bases recovery on the provisions as set forth in the form. However, she has very little enforceable time of tenancy. If Pat replaces the improvements, she will recover their actual cash value, just as if under a lease with a long time to run. But if she does not replace them, her recovery will be very little, since the fraction arrived at by the procedure for the third situation will reflect only a small portion of the cost of the improvements.

Such was the situation presented to the New Hampshire Supreme Court in *Magulas v. Travelers Ins. Co.,* 327 A.2d 608 (1974). The insured had a two-year verbal lease, but he knew that as a tenant-at-will his legally enforceable tenancy was limited to thirty days. The owner had told him that the building, which he leased to use as a restaurant, might be demolished, but that it would not be demolished for at least two years. The insured relied on the likelihood of staying in the building for two years and made improvements of $20,000. Two months after the restaurant opened, it suffered a fire loss and the owner refused to rebuild. The insurer argued that the insured's interest in the improvements and betterments was limited to his legally enforceable right to have thirty days' notice before tenancy could be terminated. The court found that the insured's insurable interest in the improvements and betterments was not so limited, stating: "[The insured] expected to use the improvements for two years and should recover on the basis of that expectation despite the fact that his legally enforceable rental term was limited to thirty days."

However, if the insured has an option to purchase, his insurable interest in improvements and betterments is still bound by the unexpired term of the lease. Once the option to purchase is exercised, the improvements and betterments are transformed into building property in which the insured has an absolute interest, not merely a use interest.

7. **Leased personal property for which the insured has a contractual responsibility to insure**. One important point to note about leased equipment coverage is that the form provides coverage for leased equipment for which the insured has an obligation to insure. This provision allows the insured some flexibility by covering unplanned, short-term equipment leases under the business personal property.

However, the agent and the insured must carefully review lease terms and agreements. For example, Kevin has a commercial property policy and leases some equipment for sixty days. While Kevin had this equipment it was damaged. His lease imposes legal liability on him for the equipment. Since the lease does not contain an express requirement for Kevin to provide insurance, his commercial property policy provides no coverage under this provision. Remember that legal liability may be satisfied in ways other than by way of insurance.

A.1.c. Personal Property of Others

The final category of covered property in the commercial property policy is property of others in the insured's care, custody, or control. The same conditions as to the location of such property apply here as to the insured's own business personal property: the property must be on, in, or within 100 feet of the premises.

The commercial property policy automatically provides $2,500 of additional insurance for the property of others, by means of a coverage extension (see Chapter 2). The purchase of additional and specific personal property of others coverage is appropriate when the insured needs coverage of values in excess of this $2,500 amount. Bill has charge of $10,000 worth of personal property of others at his business. Bill's commercial property policy gives him coverage for the first $2,500 as an extension of business personal property (assuming 80 percent coinsurance is listed on the declarations). He should then purchase an additional $7,500 of coverage under personal property of others. Note carefully that the commercial property policy provides no coverage for the property of others, other than the $2,500 extension, unless the agent activates the coverage by the appropriate entry on the declarations page.

Any loss to property of others is adjusted for the account of the owner of the property.

Section A.2 Property Not Covered

The commercial property policy specifies sixteen classes of property as "Property Not Covered":

a.   **Accounts, bills, currency, deeds, food stamps or other evidences of debt, money, notes or securities.** The policy specifically exempts lottery tickets held for sale from the list of noncovered property, by stating that lottery tickets held for sale are not securities.

b.   **Animals.** However, the policy *does* cover animals belonging to others that the insured boards. It also covers the insured's own animals if they are held as stock and are inside of a building.

c.   **Automobiles held for sale.**

d.   **Bridges, roadways, walks, patios or other paved surfaces.**

e.   **Contraband, or property in the course of illegal transportation or trade.**

f.   **Cost of excavations, grading, backfilling, or filling.**

This provision may cause controversy between insured and insurer, as seen in the following examples:

May the Exclusion of Excavation Costs be Applied to Debris Removal?

An insured suffered a total fire loss to his business, insured on the commercial property form. The debris from the destroyed building fell into the foundation and heaped-up above ground level. The insurer stated that it was not responsible for removing the debris from within the foundation walls. Instead, the insurer claimed that its only responsibility was to pay for removal of debris above ground level, and to fill any remaining hole with dirt so as to level the surface. The adjuster cited provision 2.f. under "property not covered": "Covered property does not include... the cost of excavations, grading, backfilling or filling."

In this case, the insurer is mistaken in applying the exclusion of coverage for the cost of excavation to the debris removal provision. They are two distinct things. The commercial property policy does promise that the insurer will pay the cost to "remove debris of covered property caused by... a covered cause of loss." The fire was the covered cause of loss, and the resulting debris of the covered property is what must be

(scenario continues next page)

(continued from previous page)

removed from within the foundation walls. Nothing in the additional coverage limits what debris will be removed.

The cost of excavation exclusion, on the other hand, is found within a list of items that are either uninsurable, such as contraband, or should be insured elsewhere, such as automobiles held for sale. Further, "the cost of excavations" appears within the list of other items commonly associated with new construction, such as grading, backfilling or filling.

The debris removal additional coverage provision contains only one exclusion, and that is for the cost to extract pollutants from land or water, or to remove, restore, or replace polluted land or water. If the policy drafters wanted to apply another exclusion to this coverage, surely it would be included here.

Therefore, debris removal from within the foundation walls is covered by the commercial property policy.

Excavation of Broken Water Pipe Covered?

An insured's building suffered water damage from a broken underground water pipe. The damaged pipe led from the water main in the street to the insured's building. Naturally, the broken pipe had to be dug up to be repaired in order to avoid continued water damage to the building. The insurance company authorized payment for the water damage to the building, but refused to pay the cost of digging up the water pipe to repair it citing the commercial property provision stating that the cost of excavations, grading, backfilling, or filling is property not covered. The insurer cited this provision to say that the cost of excavating the pipe to repair it was not covered.

The commercial property policy says that covered property does not include the cost of excavation. The building is covered property, so its insured value does not include the cost of excavation. Excavation is a service that goes into the cost of constructing a building if the building is set in the ground. It is part of the cost of the building, as is the cost of painting it or the cost of cleaning up the construction debris once the building is finished.

The form drafters wanted to cover most costs involved in replacing a building destroyed by a covered cause of loss, but they did not want to cover the portion of the building's cost attributable to excavation.

However, to use policy language to exclude the cost of digging up a broken water pipe is an unwarranted stretch. By excavating, the insured is preventing further water damage to his building.

One of the insured's duties in the event of the loss as set out in the commercial property form is to "take all reasonable steps to protect the Covered Property from further damage by a Covered Cause of Loss." The form asks the insured to keep records of expenses incurred in arranging emergency repairs "for consideration in the settlement of the claim."

(scenario continues next page)

(continued from previous page)
Repairing a broken water pipe that causes water damage to an insured building is just the type of emergency repair that the form contemplates.

g. **Foundations of buildings, structures, machinery, or boilers,** if such foundations are below the lowest basement floor or the surface of the ground, if there is no basement.

Foundations as Property Not Covered

Under the property not covered section, the commercial property policy reads, "foundations of buildings, structures, machinery or boilers if their foundations are below: (1) the lowest basement floor; or (2) the surface of the ground, if there is no basement."

Some adjusters say that because of the use of "their foundations," instead of "the foundations," then machinery on a foundation with a top surface below ground level is not covered. If "the" had been used, then coverage would be effective as to machinery but not as to the foundation.

However, this is an incorrect position.

Only foundations are the subject of the commercial property policy's provision A.2.g regarding foundations as property not covered.

The entire clause goes back to the word foundation. Foundations of buildings, structures, machinery, or boilers are not covered property if the foundation is below the lowest basement floor or the surface of the ground, if there is no basement. The use of the word "their" rather than "the" does not affect coverage for the building, structure, machinery, or boiler. Those remain items of covered property, and are not included in the scope of property-not-covered.

h. **Land, including the land on which the property is located, water, growing crops, or lawns.** Land is generally an uninsurable item. This provision makes clear that the ground upon which the insured property is located is not covered. Water, such as water in a lake on the insured's property is also not covered. Some losses involving water might involve an on-premises leak in a water pipe that causes a sudden rise in the insured's water bill. While most losses of this type will be of amounts so small that they would never reach litigation, an argument can be made that the excess over the normal water bill is covered. Reading the term in context with the other enumerated items in the list (land, growing crops, lawns) it can be stated that the water referred to would be natural water (ponds, lakes, etc.).

i.   **Personal property while airborne or waterborne.**

j.   **Bulkheads, pilings, piers, wharves or docks.**

k.   **Property more specifically described in another coverage form.** For example, the commercial property policy covers equipment and machinery. If, however, the insured has a piece of machinery that is more specifically described (listed in the declarations) of another insurance policy (for example, an EDP form), the item is only covered for any excess amount of loss over the amount of more specific insurance.

l.   **Retaining walls, unless the retaining wall is part of a building.**

m.   **Underground pipes, flues, or drains.**

Outdoor Sprinkler System as Underground Pipes?

The policy is written on an open perils causes of loss basis, the special form. The insured has a sprinkler system in the yard which has pipes underground. The sprinkler heads extend about a quarter of an inch above ground.

A windstorm toppled a concrete-footed light pole, which, as it fell, uprooted the sprinkler pipes, damaging the sprinkler system. The insurer denied coverage for damage to the sprinkler system, as underground pipes are specifically property not covered. The insured argued that the loss should be covered, as a permanently installed fixture or equipment, or as personal property used to maintain the premises.

The commercial property policy may provide some coverage for the sprinkler system, although not as much as the insured would desire.

There is no coverage for the sprinkler system as permanently installed fixtures or equipment. That coverage is under the building or structure coverage and does not extend to such items that are not part of the building or structure. If the underground system extends from the building's plumbing it would ordinarily qualify as "building, including permanently installed fixtures." However, the commercial property policy specifies that underground pipes are property not covered.

The insured's argument that the sprinkler system is personal property used to maintain the premises appears to have merit; however, because a fixture to the realty normally cannot be removed without damage to the realty, the sprinkler system would be seen as real, not personal property. Even if considered personal property the exclusion of underground pipes prevails.

Therefore, any damage to the underground pipes is not covered. However, any damage to sprinkler heads or connecting pipes above ground would be covered.

n. **Costs involved in researching, replacing or restoring valuable papers and records.** However, a coverage extension does provide $2,500 coverage for such costs (see Chapter 2).

o. **Vehicles or self-propelled machines.** This category removes coverage from vehicles that are licensed for use on public roads or that are operated principally away from the insured premises. However, it makes an exception (thus providing coverage) for the following:

1. vehicles that the insured manufactures, processes, or warehouses (including autos);
2. vehicles held for sale (other than autos);
3. rowboats and canoes out of water at the insured premises; and
4. trailers.

Exception 4 is a change in the commercial property policy from the 1995 edition to the 2000 edition. The 2000 version of the policy provides a coverage extension for trailers that the insured does not own, but uses in his business. Thus, exception 4 applies only to the extent of the coverage extension. For more on this coverage extension, see Chapter 2.

p. **Grain, hay, straw, or other crops while outside of buildings.**

q. **Fences, radio or television antennas, including satellite dishes, and their lead-in wiring, masts, towers, signs (unless attached to buildings), trees, shrubs, or plants (other than stock).** The commercial property policy picks up limited coverage ($1,000) for such property under the coverage extensions section. See Chapter 2.

Chapter 2

Additional Coverages, Coverage Extensions and Optional Coverages

The 2000 edition of the commercial property policy gives the insured five additional coverages (up from four in the previous version); six coverage extensions (up from five); and four optional coverages (up from three). The additional coverages might be analogized to coverage for indirect losses; while the coverage extensions are just that—extensions of coverage that already exists in the policy. The optional coverages may be activated on the policy declarations, if appropriate or desired.

The five things covered as additional coverages all happen as a consequence of a direct loss, but are not direct physical damage as required by the insuring agreement. These types of losses are not directly attributable to the insured peril, but are nevertheless events for which insurance is provided: a covered loss leaves debris behind that must be removed; undamaged property must be moved to be protected; a nongovernmental fire department must be paid; pollutants that escape onto the premises as a result of an insured peril must be cleaned up; and building codes create increased rebuilding costs.

Section 4. Additional Coverages

4.a. Debris Removal

The first additional coverage is debris removal. After damage to covered property by an insured peril, often the expense to remove the debris is quite high. Since this expense is not a direct result of the peril (consequential, indirect damage), it is does not meet the requirement of direct damage in the insuring agreement. However, the additional coverage for debris removal provides money for the insured to remove debris.

The 2000 edition of the commercial property policy contains an entirely new and much longer description of how the coverage works and what it pays. It promises to pay the insured's expense to remove debris of covered property that results from a covered peril. The expenses must be reported to the insurer within 180 days of the date of loss.

Debris removal coverage, however, specifically does not pay to extract pollutants from land or water. Nor does it cover the expense to remove, restore, or replace polluted land or water.

The policy includes the amount spent for debris removal within the limit of liability for the covered property. That provision was in the Limits of Insurance section in the 1995 edition; it is now (in the 2000 edition) in the debris removal section.

The commercial property policy places a top limit on the amount of debris removal expense payable. That amount is limited to 25 percent of the total loss (insurance payment plus deductible). For example, Jim's Shoe Store is insured on a commercial property policy for $90,000, with a $500 deductible. A fire does damage in the amount of $50,000 (for a payment by the insurer of $49,500). Debris removal expense amounts to $10,000. In this case, the maximum debris removal expense payable is $10,000, because it is less than 25 percent of $50,000 (loss payable plus deductible). Therefore, the total loss payable is $59,500 ($49,500 direct damage plus $10,000 debris removal). Since the total loss is less than the limit of liability, the entire loss of $59,500 is payable.

In some cases, the basic debris removal coverage is not adequate. It might be that the sum of the direct damage plus debris removal is greater than the limit of liability. Or, the amount of debris removal might exceed 25 percent of the total loss. In that case, the policy provides an additional flat amount of $10,000 for debris removal.

Let's look at Jim's Shoe Store again. Everything is the same, except the fire loss is now more serious—$80,000 direct damage, with another $30,000 in debris removal expenses. The payment by the insurer for the direct damage is $79,500. Even though the initial calculation of debris removal is $20,000 (25 percent of $80,000) the policy will only pay $10,500. That brings the insurer's total payment for direct and indirect damage to the limit of liability, $90,000. Then, the policy pays the additional amount of $10,000 for debris removal. The total debris removal expense payable is $20,500, leaving $9,500 of debris removal expense uncovered.

If the insured chooses, he may purchase extra debris removal coverage on endorsement CP 04 15 (see Chapter 8).

Debris removal expense is payable only if the insured reports the expense in writing to the insurer within 180 days of the physical loss. In the 1988 and 1990 versions of the form, the insured was given 180 days from the date of the loss or from the end of the policy period, whichever was earlier. Now the expense must be reported within 180 days of the date of the loss.

Note that if the insured chooses not to replace the building, the $10,000 flat amount for debris removal is still payable. There is no requirement in the policy that the building be repaired or replaced before this coverage is available. The policy states that if the sum of the direct physical loss and debris removal expense exceeds the limit of insurance, or if the debris removal expense exceeds the 25 percent, then an additional $10,000 for each location in one occurrence is available. Neither here nor under the loss payment conditions is a requirement for repairing or replacing the building imposed on the insured. However, if the insured chooses not to replace the building, the loss settlement reverts to actual cash value.

Debris Removal—Is Repair or Replacement Required?

A small warehouse insured on the commercial property policy was completely destroyed. The insured does not intend to replace it and the insurer has agreed to an actual cash value settlement.

At issue is the additional $10,000 debris removal coverage, which will be needed when the building is completely demolished. The question is whether the building must be repaired or replaced before this amount can be paid.

(scenario continues next page)

(continued from previous page)

There is no requirement in the policy that the building be repaired or replaced before this coverage is available. The policy states that if the sum of the direct physical loss and debris removal expense exceeds the limit of insurance, or if the debris removal expense exceeds the 25 percent limit, then an additional $10,000 for each location in one occurrence is available. Neither here nor under the loss payment conditions is the requirement for repairing or replacing the building imposed on the insured.

Debris Removal Coverage and Coinsurance Provision

The debris removal examples, thus far, presume that the insured carries an adequate amount of insurance to meet the coinsurance requirement. But, what if that isn't the case?

A company adjuster is adjusting a loss on a building insured on form CP 00 10. There was both direct damage and debris removal expense. However, the property was underinsured, thus requiring a coinsurance penalty. The adjuster asked if she should apply the same coinsurance penalty to the debris removal payment as to the direct damage payment.

In this case, the adjuster should not apply a direct coinsurance penalty to the debris removal settlement. An indirect penalty already applies when the property is underinsured. The debris removal clause provides up to 25 percent of the amount paid for the direct loss, not 25 percent of the amount insured. With the coinsurance penalty applied to the direct loss settlement, the amount payable for debris removal is 25 percent of an already penalized amount.

Debris Removal Coverage - Volunteer Expense

What about a debris removal situation that seems a little different than the ordinary?

A church insured on form CP 00 10 sustained some damage from a fire. The insurance company paid $81,000 for the direct damage.

Instead of hiring a contractor to remove the debris, members of the church volunteered their services. While the volunteers were taking away the debris, the church provided them with meals.

The church then submitted the cost of these meals, asking to be reimbursed under the debris removal provision. The insurance company denied payment for the meals, stating that no coverage applied.

The agent's contention was that the insured kept the overall cost of debris removal down because of the assistance from the members of the congregation. To the agent, it seemed reasonable for the church to feed the volunteers.

Form CP 00 10 promises to pay the insured's "expense to remove debris of

(scenario continues next page)

(continued from previous page)

Covered Property caused by or resulting from a Covered Cause of Loss." It does not specify what costs it will pay. The only costs specifically not covered are expenses to remove pollutants from land or water, or the expenses to restore polluted land or water. Additionally, the policy does not specify by whom the work must be done.

In a typical situation, the company engaged to do the removal would charge an amount per hour. The insurer would then pay that company its fee. In this case, the fee is the expense to feed the volunteers. Such an expense seems well within the concept of the "expense to remove debris of Covered Property caused by or resulting from a Covered Cause of Loss."

4.b. Preservation of Property

After a loss, the commercial property policy requires the insured to protect any undamaged property from further damage (see Chapter 5). Even if the insured must move the undamaged property to another location, the commercial property policy provides protection against any direct physical loss during the move and for up to thirty days while it is temporarily stored at another location. This additional coverage is called preservation of property.

It is important to note that this promise of protection is against any direct physical loss. For an insured who must move any undamaged property, the policy provides protection for that property against loss or damage from perils such as flood, war, and nuclear, which are normally excluded. For example: Jim in the above story moves his undamaged shelving units (covered as "improvements and betterments") to a warehouse for safekeeping, after the fire. Unfortunately, there is a heavy rainstorm and the warehouse floods, ruining the shelving units. Jim's commercial property policy pays for the flood damage to these units, under this additional coverage.

4.c. Fire Department Service Charge

Sometimes an insured may have to agree up-front in a contract to pay for a fire department's service. Or, a local ordinance may call for such payment.

In either event, the commercial property policy pays up to $1,000 for such charges, with no deductible.

Note that this coverage in the commercial property policy differs from similar coverage in the homeowners policy. The homeowners policy does not cover this expense if the covered property is located within the limits of the city, municipality, or protection district that furnishes the protection. The commercial property policy does not restrict where the property may be located. Also, the commercial property policy pays this expense, if required by local ordinance. The homeowners policy does not mention this at all.

Fire Department Service Charge Coverage

The insured's building was in a rural area in Vermont. Town fire departments often have contracts with smaller towns, villages, or townships to provide service. The question is raised about the provision in the additional coverage that ties payment for fire department service charges to the insured's liability assumed by contract or agreement. In most cases, the only contract is between the local governments, and not between the individual property owner and a government entity. Is the insured covered in this instance?

Yes, the insured has coverage under such circumstances. No formal contract is required for coverage, since an agreement will suffice. According to *Webster's Ninth New Collegiate Dictionary*, an agreement is "an arrangement as to a course of action." Simply by being located in his town, the insured has made an agreement to abide by the local ordinances, regulations, and arrangements for payment of services. The insurance policy does not specify who the parties to the agreement must be. If all property owners of a particular town must pay for services passed down to them for services provided by an out-of-town fire department, coverage applies.

4.d. Pollutant Cleanup and Removal

The fourth additional coverage, pollutant cleanup and removal, provides an annual aggregate amount of $10,000 for such expenses. The policy provides coverage for land and water at the insured location. It responds if a covered peril causes the discharge, dispersal, seepage, migration, release, or escape of pollutants.

Pollution Cleanup

A mercury-vapor light fixture above a swimming pool exploded, releasing material into the pool which necessitated the draining, cleaning, and testing of the pool at a considerable expense. The agent believes that the commercial property policy with the special causes of loss form provids coverage for this loss in its entirety, less the deductible. He cited paragraph B.2.l of the commercial property policy—the exception to the pollution exclusion for loss resulting from a specified cause of loss.

The insurer agreed only to coverage provided under A.4.D. Additional Coverages—Pollution Cleanup and Removal, which limits coverage to $10,000.

(scenario continues next page)

(continued from previous page)

The agent's understanding of additional coverages is that they are there to be used if the standard coverage form does not provide adequate coverage to cover a given loss. He contended that additional coverage forms provide limited additional perils or additional amounts of coverage over and above that provided by the standard coverage form.

Because, in this particular case, the pollution was caused by one of the specified causes of loss (explosion), the damage arising out of that explosion should be covered in full. The $10,000 limit should apply only if the pollution was caused by a peril not in the list of specified causes of loss.

Dispersal or release of pollutants is excluded under the special causes of loss form unless that dispersal or release is itself caused by any of the specified causes of loss. Explosion, which is the cause of loss in this situation, is one of the enumerated specified causes of loss. Therefore, the pollution exclusion does not apply to this loss.

Additional coverages are available to an insured in the event that the basic policy, absent additional coverages, for one reason or another does not respond to the loss; for example, basic policy limits are expended and additional limits are needed for debris removal, preservation of property, etc. Generally, additional coverages provide additional perils and additional amounts of coverage over and above that provided by the standard form. If the basic coverage provided by the form is adequate or appropriate to the loss (not limited by amount or exclusion), the additional coverage is not reached and the loss is settled on the basis of the policy's basic coverage.

In this event, the pollution loss was caused by a specified covered peril, explosion. The pollution exclusion does not apply. If the pollution exclusion did apply, the additional limited coverage for pollution cleanup would have to be accessed. Inasmuch as the loss is not excluded by the basic policy, full policy limits are available.

The concept of annual aggregate is unusual in property insurance. What this means is that the limit for pollutant cleanup is limited to $10,000 each year. For example, an insured gas station suffers vandalism in January, which is the policy beginning month. As a result, some petroleum products are spread on the grass around the station. The cost to cleanup the ground is $8,000. If another pollutant event occurs before the end of the year, the insured would have only $2,000 of coverage available for pollutant cleanup. The limit is refreshed to $10,000 at the start of the next annual period.

The policy does not cover the cost of tests to monitor or assess the existence or effects of pollutants. However, it does cover such costs, if the testing occurs during the course of the pollutant removal.

4.e. Increased Cost of Construction

Often, after a loss, a commercial property insured must make sure that the repaired building meets current building or zoning laws. For example, an older warehouse has knob and tube wiring. It suffers damage from a fire. The local building code now requires the building's owner to rewire with Romex (circuit breakers). The cost for this upgrade is not covered by the 1995 commercial property policy, unless endorsed.

The 2000 edition of the commercial property policy adds increased cost of construction as the fifth additional coverage. It provides up to $10,000—above the limit of liability—for increased costs associated with the enforcement of building or zoning laws. The notes from ISO say that the purpose of this new coverage is "to respond in some measure to the situation where a building code requires some upgrades but not major construction changes." Of course, the insured may still purchase, via endorsement, coverage above this amount. Note, however, that this coverage applies only to buildings for which the insured has purchased the replacement cost optional coverage.

The additional coverage promises to pay for increased costs the insured incurs in order to comply with enforcement of an ordinance or law while the damaged property is being repaired or rebuilt. The law must regulate construction or land use at the described premises and must be in force at the time of the loss. If law required compliance prior to the loss and the insured did not comply, this coverage does not respond. As with debris removal, this additional coverage does not cover costs for pollutant removal.

The limit of liability for this additional coverage is the lesser of: 5 percent of the insurance on the building or $10,000. If the policy provides blanket coverage on several buildings, this coverage is limited to the lesser of $10,000 or 5 percent of the value of the damaged building.

The additional coverage for increased cost of construction has its own conditions. It does not pay for the increased cost until the insured actually replaces the damaged property. The insured may replace at the described premises or any other premises. However, if he chooses to replace at another premises, the policy pays only the amount it would have paid at the old premises for the increased construction costs. If the insured must relocate due to the dictates of a law, then the policy pays increased costs at the new location.

Section 5. Coverage Extensions

The policy also provides six coverage extensions which become operable under either one of the following conditions: a coinsurance percentage of 80 percent or more is shown; or a value reporting period symbol is used.

Except where specified otherwise, the coverage extensions apply to property located in or on the described building or in the open (or in a vehicle) within 100 feet of the described premises. Unlike the additional coverages, the coverage extensions are additional insurance, which represent increased limits of liability.

5.a. Newly Acquired or Constructed Property

The first coverage extension covers newly constructed or acquired property of the type already covered on the policy. If the insured is building a new building on the described premises, this coverage extension covers that building during construction. Remember that the commercial property policy covers additions to existing buildings under building coverage.

The policy also covers buildings at a different location that the insured acquires. Coverage for these buildings is subject to two conditions:

1.   They must be intended for similar use as the described building; or

2.   They must be intended for use as a warehouse.

The policy provides up to $250,000 coverage per covered building under this coverage extension. Note that this $250,000 coverage extension amount is available even if the insured carries less insurance on the declared building. For example, the insured's present building is insured for $100,000; however, a new building under construction on the same premises is, or will be, worth $500,000. If this building under construction suffers covered damage, the insured may collect up to $250,000, the limit of this coverage extension. He is not limited to the $100,000 he carries on the existing building. Note that this is a per building amount. It applies to a new building under construction on the described premises. It also applies, at the same time, to a building that the insured acquires at another location—as long as he intends to put that building to use in a similar manner as his existing building, or he intends to use it as a warehouse.

The second part of this coverage extension has been extensively revised in the 2000 edition of the commercial property policy. If the insured already carries coverage on business personal property, this extension gives the insured up to $100,000 coverage, regardless of the stated policy limit for personal property, for business personal property at a newly acquired location. This extension does not, however, apply to business personal property at fairs or exhibitions. The 2000 policy adds trade shows as another place where newly acquired business personal property is not covered.

While the 1995 edition of the form promised coverage for business personal property at any location the insured acquires other than fairs or exhibitions, the 2000 policy adds language to clarify the intent. It breaks down the coverage for newly acquired business personal property into three categories:

1. Business personal property, including newly acquired business personal property, at any location (with the exception of fairs, exhibitions, and trade shows).

2. Business personal property in newly constructed or acquired buildings at the described location.

3. Newly acquired business personal property at the described location.

The extension for newly acquired business personal property does not cover:

1. Business personal property of others upon which the insured is working.

2. Business personal property of others that the insured has temporarily in his possession while manufacturing or wholesaling.

The extension of coverage to newly acquired buildings and business personal property is good for thirty days. The thirty-day period begins when the insured acquires or begins to build the new property. It ends after thirty days, at policy expiration, or when the insured reports the values to the insurer, whichever is earliest. The additional premium due for the additional property is calculated from the date the construction begins or the insured acquires the property.

Newly Acquired Location

A risk insured under the commercial property policy was damaged by a tornado. After looking into the claim, the agent found that the insured had rented a second location. This location, used as a warehouse, had been obtained within thirty days prior to the loss. As of the date of loss, the location had not been added to the policy. The question is whether the location qualified for coverage as a newly acquired location.

However, the insurer then brought them into a discussion regarding the definition of acquired. The insurer contended that acquired means to buy and did not include the renting of property. A common dictionary definition of acquire is "to come into possession of: get." The issue is if acquire includes an element of control as opposed to outright ownership.

Absent a specific policy definition of the word," the insured is entitled to the most favorable common dictionary meaning. "To come into possession of" does not necessarily connote ownership; it is broad enough to encompass other forms of possession; e.g., renting, leasing, or even borrowing. Additionally, the policy uses the word acquired rather than purchased or bought or some other term meaning acquiring title. As acquiring is a broader term than purchasing, it is appropriate to include means of obtaining property other than acquiring ownership through purchase. This additional premises should be afforded coverage under the newly acquired property provision.

5.b. Personal Effects and Property of Others

The second coverage extension provides up to $2,500 for damage to the property of others. The first part of the extension provides coverage for the personal effects belonging to the named insured, its officers, directors, partners, employees, members, or managers. Recognizing the increased use of the limited liability company formation, members and managers were added to the 2000 edition. All perils of the policy apply to this personal effects and property of others, except theft.

The other part of this extension covers others' property that the insured has in his care, custody, or control. The limit of $2,500 represents goodwill coverage only, and is insufficient for an insured who regularly takes in property of others for servicing or processing. If the insured has a true care, custody, or control exposure, bailees coverage should be arranged. Theft is covered for this second class of others' property.

Note that the first part of this coverage extension provides much narrower coverage than the second. The policy limits coverage for employees, officers, directors, etc. to their personal effects. A standard desk-top dictionary says that personal effects are "privately owned items (as clothing and toilet articles) normally worn or carried on that person."

5.c. Valuable Papers and Records—Cost of Research

When a fire or other covered peril destroys valuable papers and records at a described location, several separate items must be considered in restoring such property:

1. The cost of blank paper, film, disks, etc.

2. The cost of actually transcribing or copying such papers and records from available duplicates.

3. If no duplicates exist, the cost of research and other expenses in reconstructing the records.

The third item, the expense of research involved in recompiling data, is the subject of coverage extension 5.c. The insured may apply up to $2,500 for such research costs following destruction of valuable papers and records by an insured peril. Without this extension, the commercial property policy covers only the first two items, new stock and transcription.

5.d. Property Off-Premises

The commercial property policy provides up to $10,000 coverage for property located away from the described premises. The policy lists three places where it covers such property:

1. A location the insured does not own, lease, or operate.

2. At a leased storage location, if the insured entered into the lease after the effective date of the policy.

3. At any fair, trade show, or exhibition.

The coverage provided by number 3 is new with the 2000 edition. Previous editions of the commercial property policy specifically eliminated property at fairs, trade shows, and exhibitions from this extension.

Note that this is not in-transit coverage, as property is not covered off-premises while in a vehicle. Further, the property (samples, usually) may not be in the control of any of the insured's salespersons, unless the salesperson has the property at a fair, trade show, or exhibition. The coverage for property held by a salesperson at a fair, etc. is new with the 2000 edition. Previously, this coverage extension did not apply to property in the care of a salesperson, regardless of where located.

Finally, the exclusion of coverage for stock has been removed. The 2000 edition also covers stock off premises, under this extension. The policy defines stock as "merchandise held in storage or for sale, raw materials, or in-process or finished goods, including supplies used in their packing or shipping."

Meaning of Locations You "Own, Lease, or Operate"

A commercial property insured went to a customer's location to answer a service call. While at the customer's shop, a piece of equipment leased by the named insured that was brought with him on the service call, fell off a ledge and was damaged to the amount of $2,900.

The question is whether coverage extension 5.d., property off-premises, applies to the damaged equipment. The insurer denied the claim under this provision, stating that the insured was operating at this location while making the service call.

The commercial property policy specifically includes, in the definition of business personal property, leased equipment for which the insured has a contractual responsibility to provide insurance. If the terms of the insured's lease required him to provide insurance for the damaged piece of property, the leased item would qualify as covered property.

The commercial property form's property off-premises provision allows the extension of coverage (up to $10,000) to apply to covered property that is temporarily at a location that the insured does not own, lease, or operate. Performing a service call at a customer's premises does not convert that premises to a location that the insured operates. The words own, lease, or operate connote a control feature that is absent in this instance. Simply coming onto a customer's premises to perform services does not turn control of that location over to the person coming in. The word operate must be viewed in relation to the other words in the provision and read in that context.

Therefore, the leased piece of equipment is covered for up to $10,000 under coverage extension 5.d.

5.e. Outdoor Property

The commercial property policy lists as property not covered a variety of outdoor property which may sometimes be found around a commercial enterprise. This extension restores coverage for direct damage and debris removal for loss to the following types of outdoor property (which are not covered under the basic commercial property policy): outdoor fences, radio and television antennas (including satellite dishes), signs (other than signs attached to buildings), and trees, shrubs, and plants (other than stock of trees, shrubs or plants).

This extension applies only if the loss is caused by fire, lightning, explosion, riot or civil commotion, or aircraft. The total amount available for direct damage and debris removal is $1,000 per occurrence, but only $250 for any one tree, shrub, or plant.

5.f. Nonowned Detached Trailers

The 2000 edition of the commercial property policy adds this sixth coverage extension. ISO explains: "Many insureds have goods delivered by truck and may be held responsible by the trucking company for damage to or theft of detached trailers left on the insured's premises for unloading and retrieval. In addition, insureds who rent detached trailers from others for storage purposes may be held responsible for damage to or theft of the trailers." The current commercial property policy provides no automatic coverage for such trailers. ISO has introduced this coverage extension to provide limited coverage on nonowned detached trailers.

The policy provides $5,000 of coverage (with larger amounts available) for nonowned trailers that the insured has on its premises. This additional coverage is excess over any other applicable insurance, whether or not it is collectible.

In order to qualify for this coverage, the nonowned trailer must meet three requirements:

1.   It must be used in the insured's business.

2.   It must be in the insured's care, custody, or control at the described premises.

3. The insured must have a contractual obligation to pay for damage to the trailer.

The coverage does not apply while the trailer is attached to a motor vehicle or while it is being hitched or unhitched. There is also no coverage if the trailer becomes accidentally unhitched from a motor vehicle.

Optional Coverages

The 2000 commercial property policy offers the insured four optional coverages: agreed value, inflation guard, replacement cost, and extension of replacement cost to personal property of others. As these are built into the form, no extra endorsements are required. Rather, when the insured wants to buy any of these, an indication is made on the declarations page.

Section G.1. Agreed Value

When the insured selects agreed value, this optional coverage provides for a predetermined amount to be paid in the event of a total loss to the described property. If the insured does not desire this option for the entire policy period, he may choose when to make this option effective and when to terminate it.

When the insured chooses this option, the coinsurance condition does not apply. However, the rules state that the insured must agree to carry an amount equal to 80 percent of the building's value; 90 percent for risks written on a blanket basis. Property written on a reporting basis is not eligible for agreed value, nor are builders risk policies.

The insured and agent must complete the statement of values endorsement, CP 16 15. Replacement cost values are used if the insured has purchased replacement cost coverage.

If the building is insured on an agreed value basis for $200,000 and it is a total loss, the insurer would simply write the insured a check for $200,000.

The insured may also choose to cover some or all of his contents on this basis.

Section G.2. Inflation Guard

As a protection against the effects of inflation, the insured may choose this optional coverage. Inflation guard automatically increases the designated property, either completed buildings or personal property, by a predetermined annual percentage. Inflation guard may be used on policies written either on a specific or blanket basis.

If there is a mid-term loss, the limit of liability is increased on a pro-rata basis, from either the effective date of the policy or the effective date of the last change in the limit.

The current edition of the commercial property policy contains the following example of how this coverage works:

> **If:**
> The applicable limit of insurance is $100,000
> The annual percentage increase is 8 percent
> The number of days since the beginning of the policy year (or last policy change) is 146
> **Then:**
> The amount of increase is $100,000 x .08 x 146/365, which equals $3,200

Section G.3. Replacement Cost

The insured may purchase replacement cost coverage on the following types of property:

1. Buildings and permanent machinery, fixtures, and equipment that are covered with the building.

2. Business personal property including furniture, fixtures, machinery and equipment.

3. Merchandise and stock if the including stock option is shown as applicable in the Declarations.

4. Tenants improvements and betterments. New to the 2000 edition is specific wording that for the purposes of replacement cost cover-

age, tenants improvements and betterments are not considered the property of others. Since these items become the property of the landlord, some confusion existed in the past about how to treat them in the event of a loss. This wording makes it clear that a tenant who has purchased this endorsement will receive replacement cost coverage for the improvements he has made to a building.

5.   Personal property of others if the extension of replacement cost to personal property of others is shown as applicable in the declarations (discussed below).

The policy specifies the following types of property as not eligible for replacement cost coverage:

1.   Personal property of others

2.   Contents of a residence

3.   Manuscripts

4.   Works of art, antiques or rare articles, including etchings, pictures, statuary, marbles, bronzes, porcelains and bric-a-brac

5.   Stock unless the insured indicates including stock on the declarations.

The insured may make a claim for the actual cash value (ACV) of the damaged property and request replacement cost within 180 days. By first making an ACV claim, the insured gets some money and may engage a contractor to start the work. The insured must make repairs or replacement as soon as reasonably possible. The insurer will not make a replacement cost settlement until the repairs or replacements are completed.

With the addition of coverage for tenant improvements and betterments, the optional coverage has added two conditions regarding paying replacement cost for these items:

1.   If the insured does not replace the improvements or if he does not replace them as soon as reasonably possible after the loss, the loss adjustment reverts to the valuation condition (Chapter 5).

2.   If someone else, such as the landlord, pays to repair or replace the improvements, the policy pays nothing.

The commercial property policy agrees to pay the least of these amounts:

1.   The limit of liability applicable to the damaged property.

2.   The cost to replace the property for the same use, with material of comparable material and quality.

3.   The amount the insured actually spends.

Provision 2, above, has been changed in the 2000 edition. The wording, "on the same premises" has been removed, because it caused some confusion in the past. Many interpreted this to mean that the policy required the insured to rebuild on the same location to receive replacement cost.

It was not meant as a restriction on where the insured could build. It was intended as merely a restriction on how much the insurer would spend.

The 2000 policy adds the following wording that clearly allows the insured to rebuild at a new location: "If a building is rebuilt at a new premises, the cost described in e.(2) above is limited to the cost which would have been incurred if the building had been rebuilt at the original premises."

For example: if the building costs $300,000 to replace at its current location, but the insured chooses to rebuild in another part of town where it will cost $350,000, he will receive only $300,000 from the insurer.

Replacement by Substitution - Commercial Property

What happens if the insured chooses to purchase and remodel an existing structure at another location? The following scenario is enlightening.

An insured whose building was heavily damaged by fire found another suitable structure which, after remodeling, would become a replacement for the damaged one. The insurance company agreed to pay the cost of the acquisition, but not for the cost of the improvements at the new site.

The values of the two sites, the old one and the substitute, were generally equivalent, as were the outbuildings. Thus, the transaction represented an even trade from that standpoint. So, in essence, what the insured was requesting of the insurer was to allow the him to spend the dollars improving the substitute site that would have been spent in repairing the original. Yet, the insurer balked at the transaction.

(scenario continues next page)

(continued from previous page)

When an insured chooses the optional replacement cost coverage, the commercial property policy stipulates three limits. It agrees to pay the least of the following: "1) The limit of insurance applicable to the lost or damaged property; 2) The cost to replace the lost or damaged property with other property: a) Of comparable material and quality; and b) Used for the same purpose; or 3) The amount you [the named insured] actually spend[s] that is necessary to repair or replace the lost or damaged property."

The third limitation opens the promise to replacement at any site. Consequently, if the third category expenditure is both less than the coverage limit and less or even equal to the price of repairs at the original site, then the conditions of the policy are met and the insured may make the move.

The word necessary might seem to be a curious entry in the third limitation. Since it is not defined in the policy so as to give the insurer a say about what may be thought of as necessary, that judgment seems to be left to the insured. And that is appropriate. The first limitation protects the insurer. It limits the insurer's payment to no more than the applicable limit stated in the contract. Whether the insured elects to repair the damage to the existing structure or move off site, the insurer's possible maximum loss is not affected.

Replacement Cost—Reconditioned Property

Another question arises about the meaning of comparable material and quality. The following scenario sheds light on this issue.

A commercial property insured elected the replacement cost option. Lightning destroyed the insured's computerized phone system to the extent it could not be repaired and had to be replaced.

The insurer located a used reconditioned phone system of the same make and model as that which was damaged and offered to purchase and install it. The insurer believed that this option met their policy obligation, since the policy states "at our [the insurer's] option, we will: . . . 2. pay the cost of repairing or replacing the lost or damaged property." The insured, however, insisted on a new phone system.

The commercial property policy states that the value of covered property (the phone system) will be determined at replacement cost (without deduction for depreciation). A reconditioned phone system is still a used phone system and, as such, is depreciated. The policy promises the insured that losses to covered property will be adjusted on a replacement cost basis. Note that replacement cost means new for old. The insured is entitled to a new phone system.

Replacement Cost - Reconditioned Property

What happens if the replacement cost of a building is less than its actual cash value (ACV)?

(scenario continues next page)

(continued from previous page)

The insured owned a building that was destroyed by fire. The building was insured on the commercial property policy. The actual cash value (ACV) of the building was $190,000 but the insured had it covered for replacement cost at $300,000. Rather than replacing the building at the same location, the insured got a good deal and bought another building at another location.

The new building was one-third larger than the destroyed building, yet it cost less. It cost $230,000 and the insured put $20,000 into it to make it usable for a total of $250,000. Since the building is one-third larger than the old building, the insurer wanted to pay only 75 percent of the cost of the new building, or $187,500. This figure was less than the ACV on the old building. The insurer claimed that the extra square footage in the new building is betterment and should not be paid for by them.

The insured questioned whether or not it is right for the insurance company to pay less than actual cash value when the insured was able to do everyone a favor. He negotiated a good deal at a cost that was under the replacement cost limit. Should the insured have been paid full replacement cost, actual cash value, or the value of the new building pro-rated for the number of square feet in the destroyed building?

This is one of the few examples of a replacement cost settlement on a commercial property loss paying less than an actual cash value settlement. Situations such as this are why the insured is given the chance to choose an actual cash value settlement even though the replacement cost option is in force.

Under paragraph e. of the replacement cost option, the insurer states that it will pay the least of three replacement costs: 1) the limit of the policy; 2) the cost to replace the property with property of comparable material and quality for the same use; or 3) the actual amount spent to replace the property at any location.

In this case, the third option applies and must be used. Since the replacement property was one-third larger than the original property, the cost of actually replacing the destroyed property's square footage is 75 percent of the cost of the new property (That is, 100 sq. ft. x 1.333 = 133 sq. ft.; but 100 sq. ft. = 75 percent of 133 sq. ft., because 133 x .75 = 100). Since the new property cost less per square foot to construct than the old property, the insured receives a lower settlement at replacement cost than if he had chosen the actual cash value valuation.

This is why the replacement cost option gives the insured the opportunity to choose an actual cash value settlement even though the replacement cost option had been activated. The framers of the policy realized that, in some cases, ACV would yield a larger settlement than replacement cost.

Section G.4. Extension of Replacement Cost to Personal Property of Others

New with the 2000 edition is the option for the insured to extend replacement cost coverage to the property of others. When the insured chooses this option, it deletes the reference to property of others as not being covered under the replacement cost option.

The insured must be subject to a written contractual obligation governing his liability for the property of others. If such an obligation exists, then the policy covers loss or damage to such property at the amount for which the insured is liable under such contract. The payment is limited to the lesser of the property's replacement cost or the limit of insurance.

Chapter 3

Covered Causes of Loss—Named Perils Forms

The perils covered by the commercial property policy (and several other of the insuring forms comprising the commercial property program) depend upon the insured's choice of three causes of loss forms. The insured may select from the basic (CP 10 10), broad (CP 10 20), and special (CP 10 30) causes of loss forms. The basic form covers for eleven basic perils; and the broad form adds three perils and one additional coverage, collapse.

Under previous commercial property programs, insureds had to purchase separate coverage for the glass in their buildings, form CP 00 15. As mentioned in the Introduction, that form is no longer in use. At the request of agents and insurers, ISO has agreed to simplify the underwriting process (and the policy) by writing coverage on glass under the forms and subject to the perils applicable to other property.

The special form (CP 10 30) is open perils, with coverage being defined by the exclusions. Form CP 10 30 is the subject of the next chapter. The insured selects one of the causes of loss forms and that form is attached to the commercial property policy.

CP 10 10—Causes of Loss—Basic Form

This form provides named perils coverage. Only those perils specifically included in the form are covered and loss or damage has to be directly caused by the peril. The insured perils under the basic form are:

Fire. The named peril forms do not limit the peril of fire in any way. However, courts have long held that fire means a hostile fire, one that has left its intended confines. Hostile fires are contrasted to the *friendly fire* doctrine. In its basic form (the one that continues to be applied by the majority of courts) the friendly fire doctrine provides that loss by friendly fires is not insured, and that a friendly fire is one which the insured intentionally kindles and which remains in the place it was intended to be. A hostile fire is one that is either not confined to the place intended or one not started intentionally. A minority of courts have expanded the idea of hostile fire to include those that they characterize as excessive, as when a thermostat or other part of a furnace malfunctions and damages either the heating device itself or some other property through extreme heat.

The distinction between friendly and hostile fires only applies to insureds who have purchased named perils coverage. In an open perils policy, the doctrine of friendly fire does not apply; coverage is not restricted to named perils, but is instead openly available unless a specific exclusion applies. Since open perils policies do not contain a coverage limitation that would grant coverage only in cases of hostile fires, both types of fires are covered.

Lightning. As with the peril of fire, the policy does not limit lightning in any way. From the earliest insuring forms, lighting has been an accepted corollary of the fire peril.

Explosion. Explosion is a broad term that the commercial property policy does not define. In these cases, the dictionary meaning is looked to: "the act of exploding;" "to burst forth with sudden violence or noise from internal energy" or "to undergo a rapid ... reaction with the production of noise, heat and violent expansion..." or "to burst violently as a result of pressure from within."

Is a gunshot an explosion?

The insured owns a gun shop covered on a commercial property policy with basic causes of loss, CP 10 10. While the store owner was cleaning a gun, it accidentally discharged, causing a large hole in one of the interior walls. The agent thought that the loss was covered as an "explosion," but the insurer disagreed, and denied the claim.

(continued on next page)

> *(continued from previous page)*
> The commercial property policy does not define the term explosion. It does, however include the explosion of gases or fuel in a furnace. It also excludes rupture of pressure relief devices. It does not specifically exclude gunshot from the definition of explosion.
>
> A definition of explosion is "a large-scale, rapid, and spectacular expansion, outbreak, or upheaval." That is what happened here and the damage to the shop's wall is covered.

Both named perils causes of loss forms exclude two types of explosion peril: operation of pressure relief devices and rupture due to expansion of the contents of any structure caused by water. Steam boiler explosion is also excluded under 2.d of exclusion section B in form CP 10 10 and under 2.b. in form CP 10 20.

Windstorm or Hail. Coverage for damage by windstorm or hail does not include the following:

1. frost or cold weather;
2. ice (other than hail), snow or sleet, whether driven by wind or not;
3. loss or damage to the interior or a building or structure (or the property therein) caused by rain, snow, sand or dust (whether driven by wind or not). In order for such a loss to be covered, the building or structure must first sustain wind or hail damage to the roof or walls through which the rain, snow, sand, or dust enters.

A subject of considerable argument and litigation has been the question of what is direct physical loss caused by or resulting from windstorm. Forms do not define windstorm and so the courts are often asked to do so within the circumstances of a particular case. The Arizona Supreme Court said that, "a windstorm is a wind of sufficient force to proximately cause damage to the 'ordinary condition of the thing insured.'"

The great majority of courts agree that the wind does not need to be the only cause of loss for a loss to be directly related to windstorm; the rule is that the windstorm must be the proximate cause or the efficient proximate cause of the loss. The minority of courts have followed the rule that any contributing cause to the damage must itself not be excluded by the policy.

Many courts have followed the rule that a direct loss from windstorm occurs when it is shown that the force or strength of the wind caused the damage. Some jurisdictions require that the winds be tumultuous and have the nature of a storm.

Some courts have addressed the issue of whether there is direct loss from windstorm when the damaged property was damaged was in poor physical condition. Generally, these courts have held that there is such a loss if the windstorm was the proximate cause of the loss.

The first part of the exclusionary language outlined above reaffirms the policy drafters' intent that damage by frost or cold weather is not equivalent to damage by windstorm or hail. However, if a windstorm during the winter months causes damage that is not equivalent to damage by cold weather, and as such, would be covered.

The policy makes clear that before there is coverage for windstorm or hail damage to the interior of a building, the exterior must suffer damage from wind or hail. Once wind or hail damages the exterior of the building, the policy covers the interior for damage caused by rain, snow, sand, or dust entering the structure.

Windstorm or hail is one of three causes of loss that may be removed from coverage of the commercial property program by endorsement (either CP 10 53 or CP 10 54). Insurers doing business in certain areas (such as the South Atlantic or Gulf coast) often refuse to write wind coverage or write it subject to high rates and large deductibles. In such areas, windstorm coverage is available through a catastrophe pool or similar facility administered by a governmental entity.

Endorsement CP 10 53 applies the exclusion only to the coverage parts providing direct physical damage coverage. Endorsement CP 10 54 also applies the exclusion to those coverage parts providing coverage for indirect losses: business income, extra expense, and leasehold interest.

Smoke. Smoke, like fire, is undefined in the policy. Many courts have followed a definition similar to this one from *Webster's Tenth New Collegiate Dictionary*: "the gaseous products of burning carbonaceous materials especially of organic origin made visible by the presence of small particles of carbon."

At one time, smoke damage referred only to sudden and accidental smoke from the faulty operation of a heating or cooking unit at the insured premises. Damage resulting from smoke from a fireplace was excluded. The current property forms cover sudden and accidental smoke damage from almost any source, except for agricultural smudging (i.e., the use of smudge pots to produce a smoky fire for protecting certain crops from frost, insects, etc.) and industrial operations. The commercial property policy excludes smoke damage from these sources because such operations represent constant or constantly recurring exposures. Damage is certain to occur, so there is no risk, just a certainty. There can be no insurance where there is no risk.

Courts usually apply a definition of smoke that requires a visible product of combustion. However, a 1979 case from Wisconsin, *Henri's Food Products Co. v. Home Insurance Co.,* 474 F. Supp. 889, held that the insured was covered for smoke damage when the outside of bottles of salad dressing stored in a warehouse were contaminated by the vaporization of agricultural chemicals also stored in the warehouse. The court did not discuss its reasoning in any depth, stating simply that it relied on *Words and Phrases*, and *Webster's Third New International Dictionary.* Perhaps the court relied on the inclusion of vapor among the dictionary definitions. This raises a question as to whether an ordinary person would understand all vapors to be smoke.

In 1991, the U.S. District Court in Pennsylvania disagreed with the Wisconsin Court's opinion. In *K & Lee Corporation v. Scottsdale Insurance Company,* 769 F. Supp. 870, that court held: "An unabridged comprehensive dictionary lists every conceivable usage of words, including those that are arcane, archaic, and obscure. While smoke may result from some chemical reactions, the common usage of the term refers to the products of combustion and, more importantly, to matter that is visible."

The term *industrial operations* raises another problem. A Georgia court of appeals ruled that the term did not to apply to what the court described as a small neighborhood bakery (*Georgia Farm Bureau Mutual Insurance Co. v. Washington,* 243 S.E.2d 639 [1978]). The insured was a dress shop owner whose merchandise was damaged by smoke that escaped from the faulty exhaust vent of the nearby bakery. The trial court held for the insured and the court of appeals affirmed with little comment. The trial court had held that exclusions and exceptions must be taken more strongly against the insurer, and that a layman's reasonable reading of words in an insurance contract, in their plain, ordinary and popular sense, prevails.

Other than the reference to agricultural smudging or industrial operations, the named perils forms cover smoke damage from any other source, as long as the damage is sudden and accidental. There are no other qualifications or limitations with respect to this peril. Thus, even when smoke originates away from the insured premises—at an adjacent building or even at a more distant location—smoke damage is covered.

Aircraft or Vehicles. This cause of loss covers damage done to covered property by physical contact with an aircraft or vehicle. This includes damage done by a spacecraft or a self-propelled missile. It also covers damage from objects that fall from an aircraft or are thrown up by a vehicle, though not thrown from a vehicle, as by a vandal.

There are many instances in which a vehicle can cause damage without coming into actual contact with the damaged property. From time to time, insureds report losses of the following nature: a truck pulling away from a building to which, unknown to the driver, a chain was attached; a vehicle hitting another object and propelling it into the side of a building; a vehicle shearing off a water hydrant with resultant severe water damage to property in a nearby building; and so on. Due to the peril's requirement of physical contact between the property and the vehicle, insurers often deny coverage.

However, courts have found coverage under the vehicle peril in situations where, for example, a boom fell off a crane and damaged an insured building. The court stating that "to exclude this loss because contact was only with the boom would be similar to excluding loss caused if a tractor-trailer loaded with piling jackknifed and the projecting piling, but not the trailer, damaged a building. The difference is simply one of degree." The case implies that in some instances, damage without actual physical contact by the vehicle would be covered, even where the policy states that coverage only applies in cases of physical contact.

On the other hand, a court held that no actual physical contact occurred while a truck pulled a cable through a doorway. In this case, a boiler on the cable damaged the building. The damage occurred when a barrel that supported a beam or upright to a beam was dislodged, causing the roof to sag about eight to ten inches. The insured argued that the term vehicle included every accessory piece of equipment attached to the vehicle. The court found that the term vehicle was not ambiguous and refused to apply the insured's definition to the construction of the policy. Perhaps the difference in interpretation between this case and other discussed earlier, was the nature of the equipment that caused the damage. Whereas a crane cannot be effectively operated without a boom, so that the boom is an integral part of the machine, a cable is more remotely related to the day-to-day operation of a truck. The question of relatedness to the vehicle is one of degree.

The form further states that damage by vehicles owned by the named insured or by vehicles operated in the course of the named insured's business is excluded.

Tractor Falling off Trailer— Falling Object or Vehicle Damage?

A lawn service, insured under the commercial property policy with broad causes of loss (CP 10 20) suffered damage to one of its lawn tractors. The tractor had been in the shop for repair and was being returned to the insured by the mechanic. The mechanic brought the tractor back to the insured and while turning into the insured's driveway, the trailer hit a pothole causing it to sway. The tractor fell off the trailer and onto the road, becoming damaged. The insurer denied coverage under the falling objects peril, stating that the object itself is not covered. The agent believed that the cause of the loss was the upset of the vehicle and therefore covered.

Vehicle damage is a named peril under either the basic or broad causes of loss form. The policy promises to cover direct physical loss to business personal property caused by vehicles. Losing control of the vehicle and dropping the property onto the road is a sure way of causing direct loss to that property.

Even though the mower became a falling object in its course from the trailer bed to the ground, it wasn't damaged by being an object in fall. The damage came when it hit, having been tossed from a vehicle.

Riot or Civil Commotion. The common definition of riot, although it may vary slightly among cases and commentators, can be stated as follows: "Any tumultuous disturbance of the public peace by three or more persons mutually assisting one another in execution of a common purpose by the unlawful use of force and violence resulting in property damage of any kind."

Black's Law Dictionary defines riot as follows: "A public disturbance involving an act or acts of violence by one or more persons, part of an assemblage of three or more persons, which act or acts shall constitute a clear and present danger of, or shall result in, damage or injury to the property of any other person or to the person of any other individual; or, a threat or threats of the commission of an act or acts of violence by one or more persons, part of an assemblage of three or more persons having, individually or collectively, the ability of immediate execution of such threat or threats, where the performance of the threatened acts or acts of violence would constitute a clear and present danger of, or would result in, damage or injury to the property of any other person or to the person of any other individual."

Generally, the courts have not found coverage where the damage was done by stealth or secretly, meaning that a riot must be more or less a public event. A federal appeals court ruled: "It is a clear doctrine of the common law that a stealthy act of destruction is not transformed into an act of riot because upon later discovery of the damage there is public disturbance," *(Providence Washington Insurance Co. v. Lynn,* 492 F.2d 979 [1974]).

The Supreme Court of Mississippi went further in the definition of riot by listing four necessary elements of a riot:

1.   unlawful assembly of three or more people (or lawful assembly that due to its violence and tumult becomes unlawful);
2.   acts of violence; and
3.   intent to mutually assist against lawful authority. . .
In addition, there must be some degree of:
4.   public terror. . . .
Without the element of public terror, any minor public disturbance could legally be a riot.

The meaning of civil commotion is more obscure than that of riot (and has received less attention from the courts). Some authorities doubt that it is possible to conceive of a case in which a loss would be paid as a civil commotion but would not be covered under a policy or endorsement referring only to riot. However, the drafters of current forms chose to retain both terms in spite of their intention to simplify policy language.

The case of *Hartford Fire Insurance Co. v. War Eagle Coal Co.,* 295 F. 663 (1924) is enlightening. The Eagle Coal Company was insured on an old property form that excluded loss or damage by civil commotion. The question here was this: does this exclusion bar recovery by War Eagle, whose property was blown up by union organizers? The United Mine Workers had been organizing in West Virginia, and the governor had declared martial law. The evidence showed conclusively that a conspiracy of five men blew up the mine property in furtherance of union activity. The insured proved that although there had been disturbances in the area, there had been no disorder at the mine or disturbances until the explosion and fire. The explosions and fire were started secretively at one in the morning. The insurer denied coverage, but the trial court held for the insured and the court of appeals affirmed.

The court quoted the following definition of civil commotion from the legal commentary in *Corpus Juris*: "An uprising among a mass of people which occasions a serious or prolonged disturbance and an infraction of civil order, not attaining the status of war or an armed insurrection. A civil commotion requires the wild or irregular action of many persons assembled together." The court said that since a serious issue of fact had been raised as to whether the property damage was a consequence of the civil commotion in the general area, or was due to the independent initiative of the conspirators, it would affirm the lower court's decision.

The policy specifies that these two events do constitute a riot or civil commotion: 1) acts of striking employees occupying the described premises, and b) looting at the time and place of a riot or civil commotion.

Vandalism. This peril covers the willful and malicious damage to or destruction of covered property. In prior editions of the commercial property policy, the peril was phrased as "vandalism and malicious mischief." Malicious mischief is no longer part of the name of this peril, although the definition remains the same as that of vandalism or malicious mischief in earlier forms—willful and malicious damage to or destruction of the insured property.

"Remodeling" As Vandalism?

The insured owned several commercial buildings that he rented to various tenants. A tenant notified the insured that they were vacating, but before he could inspect the dwelling in their presence, they left. When he went to the building, he found that the bathroom had been remodeled. Plumbing had been improperly installed, resulting in a leaking commode. The sink now drains onto the driveway. Doors were removed and shelves were installed. In a room used as an employee cafeteria, cabinets were removed and a large cabinet containing a built-in oven was installed. Additionally, the carpet was worn in several places and there were nail holes in the walls from pictures.

The insured had not inspected the building for seven years prior to discovering the loss. The agent thought that the loss should be covered as vandalism, but the insurer disagreed.

Although it may appear that the tenant made improvements to the property (the sink draining onto the driveway notwithstanding), the truth is that the insured suffered a loss that is not excluded under commercial property form. His property was vandalized in that the original state of the property has been defaced by the new additions. Though the prudent landlord might inspect the property on a regular basis, the commercial property policy contains no such requirement that he do so. If the insured had discovered the improvements the day after they had been made coverage would have applied. The lapse of time does not affect this.

(continued on next page)

(continued from previous page)

No coverage applied for the worn carpet and nail holes. These are normal wear and tear occurrences, and are expected (and therefore uninsurable) in a rental property.

Note, however, that the answer depends upon the terms of the lease. If the lease did not allow the tenants to make improvement to the premises, then vandalism has occurred; if the lease provided that the tenants could make modifications to the premises, then no vandalism occurred.

The 2000 edition makes a big change to the vandalism coverage in the named peril forms in regard to building glass. Previous editions excluded glass breakage caused by vandalism. An insured was required to purchase the broad form perils which added glass breakage as an additional coverage or to purchase the glass coverage form, CP 00 15. Now both named peril forms cover glass breakage from any of the named perils; treat glass as part of the building; and include glass coverage within the limit of liability for the building.

Building damage caused by the break-in or exit of burglars is covered, but other loss caused by or resulting from theft is excluded.

Under earlier forms of commercial property insurance, vandalism and malicious mischief coverage was optional. Under the current program, the insured may choose to exclude this coverage via endorsement CP 10 55.

Vandalism is one of six causes of loss (sprinkler leakage, glass breakage, water, vandalism, theft, and attempted theft) for which there is no coverage if the building where the loss occurs has been vacant for more than sixty consecutive days.

Sprinkler Leakage. Under earlier commercial property forms, an insured had to purchase this coverage separately, if desired. It is now automatically part of the policy and the insured may choose to exclude it via endorsement CP 10 56. Coverage is for leakage or discharge from an automatic sprinkler system, including the collapse of the system's tank, if there is one.

Automatic sprinkler system is a defined term within the context of the sprinkler leakage cause of loss. It refers to an automatic fire protective or extinguishing system. The definition includes sprinklers, nozzles, ducts, pipes, valves, fittings, tanks, pumps, and private fire protection mains. It also includes nonautomatic systems, hydrants, standpipes, and outlets supplied from an automatic system.

If the insured's building is covered property, then this cause of loss also pays to repair or replace damaged parts of the system. The policy does not specify what must cause the damage to the system. It only states that repair or replacement of damaged parts to the sprinkler system will be made if the damage is a result of sprinkler leakage or is directly caused by freezing. Therefore, damage to the system itself might be from an uncovered cause of loss, but if sprinkler damage results, the sprinkler damage is covered and any damaged parts to the system itself will also be replaced or repaired.

The policy also covers the cost of tearing out and replacing part of the structure in order to repair the system if there has been sprinkler damage that necessitates such tearing out or replacement.

The policy provides no coverage for damage from this peril if the building has been vacant for sixty or more consecutive days.

Sinkhole Collapse. Coverage for this exposure was previously available only by endorsement and only in certain regions of the country where sinkholes occur with some frequency. The provision defines sinkhole for coverage purposes: "[loss or damage caused by] the sudden sinking or collapse of land into underground empty spaces created by the action of water on limestone or dolomite." It is important to note that the source of the water that creates the sinkhole is immaterial.

Sinkhole Collapse under Commercial Property Form

The insured's building was covered by the building and personal property form with basic causes of loss. The building had a system of pipes that diverted water runoff from the roof into a retention basin.

One of those pipes broke and the water coming out of it eroded the underlying limestone. A sinkhole was created and part of building slipped into that sinkhole.

The insurer denied the claim, citing the exclusion for collapse into man-made underground cavities.

The commercial property form defines sinkhole collapse as the sudden sinking or collapse of land into underground empty spaces. The space is one created by the action of water on limestone or dolomite. The source of the water is not material to the definition.

Collapse into underground "man-made. . .cavities" is outside the definition of sinkhole collapse. Thus, collapse into a mine shaft or other man-made holes would not be covered.

This peril does not include the cost of filling the sinkhole itself nor does it include instances where the ground sinks or collapses into man-made cavities in the earth. This exposure is more appropriately the subject of mine subsidence coverage, which is available by endorsement.

Volcanic Action. Volcanic action coverage also was previously available only on an optional basis by endorsement. This peril is now part of the causes of loss forms and covers damage from the above-ground effects of a volcanic eruption—airborne blast and shock waves, ash, dust, particulate matter, and lava flow. It does not include the removal cost of volcanic ash or dust that has not physically damaged insured property. The earth movement exclusion precludes coverage for damage from the seismic effects of a volcanic eruption.

This cause of loss considers all volcanic eruptions occurring within a seven day period (168 hours) as a single occurrence. Prior to the 1988 revisions in the commercial property policy, this period was three days.

CP 10 20—Broad Form Causes of Loss

In addition to the above eleven named perils, the broad form causes of loss form (CP 10 20) adds coverage for falling objects; weight of snow, ice, or sleet; and water damage. It also provides one additional coverage, collapse.

Falling Objects. This peril covers damage by falling objects to the following kinds of covered property: buildings or structures and the inside of buildings or property within buildings only if the falling object first damages the roof or an outside wall. Damage by a dropped or falling object within a building, such as a chandelier falling on the table below it or a heavy object accidentally dropped on a piece of furniture, does not come within the scope of this peril.

This cause of loss does not apply to personal property in the open. Note, however, that under the aircraft/vehicles cause of loss (discussed above), there is coverage for damage by objects falling from aircraft. Therefore, if an object falling from an airplane damages personal property in the open, that damage is covered.

Weight of Snow, Ice, or Sleet. The weight of snow, ice, or sleet peril applies to all covered property other than personal property outside of buildings or structures. The 1995 form did not cover such damage to gutters and downspouts. That language has been removed, thus providing coverage in the 2000 edition for gutters and downspouts from the weight of snow, ice, or sleet.

Water Damage. This provision covers damage done by the accidental discharge or leakage of water or steam when any part of a system or appliance containing water or steam breaks or cracks. The 2000 edition enumerates the systems covered: plumbing, heating, air conditioning, or other. Water damage coverage does not encompass leakage or discharge from an automatic sprinkler system, which is the subject of coverage under a separate cause of loss (see above). Nor does it cover discharge from a sump, regardless of what causes the discharge. The form goes on to exclude overflow due to sump pump failure or the inability of the sump pump to keep up with the amount of water.

The most recent edition of the form also excludes coverage for damage done by water that comes out of roof drains, gutters, downspouts, or similar fixtures, or equipment. Although ISO says that this change to the policy represents no change in coverage, it may be argued that it represents a significant narrowing of coverage to the insured. What happens now when a roof drain gets clogged and cannot properly remove water from a roof? Under previous forms, the damage done would have been covered. This is not so under the 2000 version of the policy.

The peril also covers the cost of tearing out and replacing part of the building or structure to repair damage to the system or appliance if the building is covered property. For example, if the accidental discharge was from the sudden rupturing of a pipe in the insured's fire sprinkler system, and the system's pipes are within the insured's walls, the cost of tearing out and repairing the walls is covered. The defect that caused the loss or damage is not covered. That would eliminate coverage for the broken pipe itself, unless the damage to the pipe was by another covered cause of loss.

The form specifies that it does not cover damage from repeated leakage occurring over a period of at least fourteen days. There is no coverage for plumbing rupture caused by freezing unless: the insured maintains heat in the building or structure; or has drained the heating equipment and shut off its water supply. Earlier versions of commercial property forms imposed these last conditions on coverage for freezing losses only when the building was vacant or unoccupied. Broad form CP 10 20 makes no such distinction, imposing the conditions with respect to freezing losses regardless of the building's status. Coverage for water damage does not apply after the building has been vacant for sixty days.

Water Damage—Costs to Repair Leak Even if Building is Undamaged

A pipe burst under the concrete slab of a building insured under the commercial property policy with the broad form causes of loss attached. This break in the pipe caused a loss of water into the ground under the building. The insured and insurer disputed coverage for this loss. The insurer denied the insured's request for coverage for the cost of tearing out and replacing the concrete slab so the broken pipe could be fixed. The denial stated that the policy did not cover this loss because the escaping water ran into the ground and did not damage covered property.

The correct adjustment of the loss would have the commercial property policy covering the costs of tearing out and replacing the slab. The wording of the water damage peril does not require damage to covered property by water before such costs are covered. What it requires is that the damaged system be contained in covered property. In this case, the pipe is part of the system contained within the covered building.

Furthermore, the building coverage insuring agreement states that the insurer will pay for direct physical damage to covered property caused by or resulting from a covered cause of loss. Destruction of the covered property (the slab) resulted from the covered peril of accidental discharge. Digging up the slab was made necessary by the covered peril.

Exclusions that Apply to Both Named Perils Causes of Loss Forms

Section B of the basic and broad causes of loss forms contains the exclusions applicable to both forms. Section B contains three subsections. Subsection one is identical in both forms, with the following exclusions: ordinance or law; earth movement; governmental action; nuclear hazard; utility services; war and military action; and water. Each of these is treated in the following section.

The lead in language applies concurrent causation language to section B exclusions. The concurrent causation doctrine, which arose as a legal concept in the mid-1980s, holds that losses are covered if caused jointly by an excluded peril, such as flooding or earth movement, and some other peril not excluded by the policy, such as negligent construction. Under earlier cases, coverage was found where the nonexcluded peril played any role in the loss; under the efficient proximate cause doctrine, the nonexcluded peril must have been the predominant factor in the loss. Not all states have adopted the concurrent causation doctrine, but its development prompted Insurance Services Office (ISO) and insurers filing independent policies to alter property forms in an attempt to avoid recovery in concurrent causation situations.

An example of concurrent causation would be where earth movement causes damage to an insured structure. The commercial property policy specifically excludes such damage, but the insured claims that the cause of loss was actually a third party's negligence in preparing the soil under the house for construction, arguably a non-excluded peril under an open perils policy. Where the concurrent causation doctrine has been accepted, coverage would apply. Under the revised concurrent causation lead-in language, the damage would be excluded.

Ordinance or Law (formerly called Building Ordinance). This exclusion eliminates payment for losses arising out of the enforcement of building laws or ordinances, including those that may require the demolition of damaged structures. For example, a city's building code requires that any building undergoing substantial renovation or repair after a major loss must be equipped with facilities for handicapped access; or the building code might dictate additional safety features that were not part of the original building. Additionally, the law may require that a building not in conformance with current building codes that is damaged to more than 50 percent or so of its value may not be repaired, but must be demolished and rebuilt. If, for example, an insured building was determined to be a 60 percent loss, it could not be rebuilt, and the undamaged portion would have to be demolished. As demolition after loss is not a covered cause of loss, there would be no coverage for the cost of demolishing the undamaged portion and removing debris.

The ordinance or law exclusion precludes insurance payment under these forms for the cost of compliance with these requirements. However, the 2000 edition now provides a limited amount ($10,000) of coverage for the increased costs of construction incurred due to the enforcement of a building law. The insured may also purchase additional coverage via endorsement CP 04 05 (see Chapter 8).

Earth Movement. Both basic and broad causes of loss forms exclude all types of earth movement (earthquake, landslide, mine subsidence, etc.) other than sinkhole collapse. The basic and broad causes of loss forms specifically cover sinkhole collapse. The policy does cover any ensuing fire or explosion damage.

Generally, the term earth movement applies only to naturally occurring phenomena of a catastrophic nature (i.e., landslide or earthquake). For example, damage to an insured building done by the earth shifting as a result of seismic tremors is readily excluded under the commercial property policy with the basic or broad causes of loss form attached. However, suppose that the insured building is situated close to a highway on which heavy construction work is in process.

Earth Movement Exclusion

The insured's building was situated close to a highway on which the transportation department was doing some heavy reconstruction work. The pile driving sent tremors through the earth. The insured was concerned that his building might be damaged as a result. The agent asked if the earth movement exclusion would apply.

No, it would not. The earth movement exclusion relates to earth tremors caused by natural forces. The earth movement that might be brought on by an explosion as well as by the action of the pile drivers is a horse of a different color. The examples of earth movement listed in the exclusion (earthquake, landslide, mine subsidence, or earth sinking, rising, or shifting and volcanic eruption or explosion) provide all the support that is necessary for the notion that natural causes are the subject of the exclusion.

Because, in the majority of courts that have considered this issue, the earth movement exclusion relates to earth tremors caused by natural forces, this damage could not be excluded by the earth movement exclusion.

The earth movement exclusion also eliminates coverage for loss caused by volcanic eruption, explosion, or effusion. However, the policy does cover fire damage occurring as a result of these events. The policy also covers loss attributable to volcanic action—the above-ground effects of volcanic eruption, an insured cause of loss under the basic and broad forms.

Governmental Action. The policy does not cover seizure or destruction of covered property as an act of governmental authority. For example, if the police break down a door or damage walls in executing a search warrant or chasing a fugitive, exclusion will probably be validly applied, according to the one court that has decided the issue (see Damage by Police Action, below). It does however cover the destruction of property, when ordered to prevent the more general spread of fire, if the fire itself would be a covered cause of loss (for example, if fire authorities burn down a building in creating a fire break to prevent the spread of a wild fire.

Damage by Police Action

A health clinic covered under the commercial property broad form suffered unusual damage. A man who was trying to evade capture by the police ran into the clinic and proceeded to take hostages. Eventually, he was forced to surrender by the police who used tear gas and gunfire. In the process of capturing the fugitive, damage was done to both the building and personal property of the health clinic.

(continued on next page)

(continued from previous page)

The insurance company denied coverage under the governmental action exclusion. This exclusion eliminates coverage for loss or damage caused directly or indirectly by seizure or destruction of property by order of governmental authority.

Before examining the exclusion, the existence of a covered peril under form CP 10 20 must be addressed. The one that might apply is explosion. After all, exploding tear gas canisters contributed to the damage.

Once a named peril that covers the damage is found, then comes the analysis of the insurer's use of the exclusion for seizure or destruction of property by order of governmental authority.

The aim of the exclusion is to eliminate coverage for the intentional destruction of property by governmental authority because of some hazard that the property presents, such as when the government orders the destruction of vegetables that are infected with the Mediterranean fruit fly or a building burned down to create a firebreak. The type of loss occasioned by our scenario seems to be outside of the scope of the exclusion.

In this case, the destruction done by the police was incidental to the capture of the fugitive. Bullets that damaged equipment were intended to control the fugitive—they were not fired because the equipment posed any danger to people or property. One would not expect the police officer in charge to state that he or she ordered the destruction of property. For these reasons, the insured might have coverage under the policy.

Note, however, that a New Jersey court has held that damage done to an apartment by the police in conducting a duly authorized search, was properly excluded under the governmental authority exclusion. How insurance companies handle loss of this type may, in the end, be a matter of judgment or further legal proceeding.

Nuclear Hazard. The nuclear hazard exclusion of the commercial property policy eliminates coverage of loss by nuclear reaction, radiation, or radioactive contamination regardless of the cause. The policy does pay for any ensuing fire loss.

Radioactive contamination coverage may be purchased via form CP 10 37.

Utility Services. This exclusion applies to the failure of power or other utility service (e.g., water, gas, etc.) to the insured premises that occurs away from those premises. For example: a power plant's turbine suffers mechanical breakdown, which results in a shutdown of services or a power outage. That power outage results in food spoilage in the refrigerator at an insured's premises. The commercial property policy does not cover that food spoilage. The exclusion operates regardless of the failure's cause, that is, even if the failure is brought about by a covered cause of loss.

If damage to insured property on the premises from a covered cause of loss results from on-premises failure of power or other utility service, the resulting damage is covered. For example, if heat interruption causes pipes to freeze and rupture and either the broad or special causes of loss forms (CP 00 20 or CP 00 30, respectively) applies, there is coverage.

If, on the other hand, a lightning strike away from the insured premises knocks out the electrical power at the premises, consequential property damage on the premises is not covered. Two examples of such losses are: spoilage of refrigerated products or of property-in-process depending on continuous heat or cooling. Though lightning is a covered cause of loss, the underlying agreement is to pay for direct physical loss caused by a covered cause of loss. Lightning that strikes off premises and runs in on a line to cause lightning damage directly on premises is covered under these provisions.

Power Failure vs. Power Surge

The insured is covered under the commercial property form with broad form causes of loss. There was a cessation of power off-premises that stopped operations, but caused no damage. However, when power was restored, an abnormal power surge damaged insured property (the sudden return of power caused a piece of electronic equipment to explode). The insurer denied the claim due to the power failure exclusion in the broad form causes of loss form. The insured is arguing that power failure and power surge are different events and that the exclusion would not apply to these facts.

The usual meaning of the term failure, as found in a standard dictionary, is "an omission of occurrence or performance." Absent a specific definition of power failure in the policy, it is this definition that must be applied. Therefore, any damage caused by the cessation of power would qualify as damage caused by a power failure; however, damage caused by a surge of power is not an omission of occurrence or performance, and would not fall under the power failure exclusion, properly applied.

However, the insurer could have relied on the artificially generated power exclusion further down in the form. Exclusion 2.a. eliminates coverage for damage caused by or resulting from artificially generated electric current...that disturbs electrical devices, appliances, or wires. However, if loss or damage by fire results, that damage is covered.

War and Military Action. This exclusion applies to three related causes of loss: war (including undeclared or civil war); warlike action by any governmental military force; and acts of insurrection, rebellion, revolution, or usurped power. While no court decisions involving the exact language of the war exclusion clause in the current commercial property form have arisen at this time, there are decisions involving other, past war exclusion clauses that do permit some reliable conclusions.

The courts, following British precedent, seem to adhere to a strict doctrine of what constitutes war, allowing the exclusion to be applied only in situations involving damage arising from a genuine warlike act between sovereign entities. The two following examples taken from case law best sum up this idea that for there to be a war, sovereign or quasi-sovereign governments must engage in hostilities.

Where members of a political activist group from Jordan hijacked an aircraft over London and destroyed the aircraft on the ground while in Egypt, the resulting loss to the aircraft was not due to war within the meaning of the term as used in the exclusionary clauses of the "all risks" policies covering the aircraft. The court reasoned that since the activist group had never claimed to be a state, it could not be acting on behalf of any of the states in which it existed when the plane was hijacked, especially since those states uniformly and publicly opposed hijacking. The hijackers were agents of a radical political group and not a sovereign government. The court concluded that although war can exist between sovereign states, a guerrilla group or radical political group must have at least some incidence of sovereignty before its activities can properly be defined as war. *(Pan American World Airways, Inc. v. Aetna Casualty & Surety Company, 505 F.2d 989[1974])*.

In a similar case, a court ruled against the war risks exclusion for a claim brought by an insured hotel in Beirut, Lebanon. The hotel suffered shelling damage during the hostilities that took place there. The insurer argued that the conflict in Lebanon involved three clearly defined independent entities, each having the attributes of sovereignty or, at the least, quasi-sovereignty, and that therefore, the war exclusion could be applied to deny coverage. The court focused on the faction occupying the hotel at the time of the fighting and concluded that it was not a sovereign entity. The court further stated that even if the group could arguably possess the necessary sovereignty, it was not fighting with another sovereign government at the time of the damage, and therefore, the war exclusion clause could not be invoked by the insurer *(Holiday Inns, Inc. v. Aetna Insurance Company, 571 F. Supp. 1460 [1983])*.

Previous versions of these causes of loss forms specified that loss from the explosion of a nuclear weapon (intended or unintended) was considered an act of war, and not covered. This provision was removed when the commercial property program went to readable format.

Water. The water exclusion clause (which appears in all three causes of loss forms, basic, broad, and special) excludes loss caused by flood, surface water, water that backs up from a sewer or drain, and water underground.

Though the exclusionary language is quite broad, disputes continue to arise when the language is applied to particular loss situations.

Surface water has traditionally been excluded when it occurs naturally. Thus, water from a heavy rain that damages a building is not covered. In the 1953 Pennsylvania case *Richman v. Home Insurance Co. of New York,* 94 A.2d. 164, the court stated that surface water is commonly understood to mean water on the surface of the ground usually created by rain or snow which is of a casual or vagrant character. Surface water follows no definite course and has no substantial or permanent existence.

This understanding of the meaning of surface water may be seen in the more recent case of *Georgetown Square v. United States Fidelity and Guaranty Co.,* (1995). A retaining wall on the insured's property was damaged by water and water pressure from an underground pipe that drained water from the roof of a neighbor's building. The insurer denied the claim, based on a policy provision excluding coverage for damages resulting from flooding, which the policy defined to include run-off and surface water. The court, applying Nebraska law, found that surface water is water "which is diffused over the surface of the ground, derived from falling rains or melting snows, and continues to be such until it reaches some well defined channel in which it is accustomed to flow and does flow with other waters." The court further found that surface water and run-off both lost their characteristics as surface water when diverted into artificial channels.

Part three of the exclusion (water that backs up or overflows from a sewer, drain, or sump), was made considerably more restrictive with the addition of the words overflows and sump to the 1995 edition. Previous editions of the form did not address the issue of overflow. And by not specifically excluding water coming from a sump, it was left up to interpretation as to whether or not a sump is a sewer or drain or part of the plumbing system. At least one major insurer has not adopted the current version of ISO's wording in this instance and continues to treat water coming from a sump as an overflow of the plumbing system.

Part four of the exclusion eliminates coverage for water that seeps through underground portions of a building (hydrostatic water pressure) and for water that seeps through other openings, such as doors and windows.

If loss from fire, explosion, or sprinkler leakage results, the policy covers that loss, if caused by water, as described above.

New to the 2000 edition is a statement at the end of Subsection B.1 that the described exclusions apply regardless of how widespread a loss is. ISO says that they have added this language "for the purpose of making this point explicit."

Subsection B.2. Exclusions

Subsection B.2. of each of the causes of loss forms contains several more exclusions. Unlike the subsection B.1. exclusions, these do not apply "regardless of any other cause or event . . ." to defeat coverage by a covered cause of loss that happens to involve damage by the excluded cause of loss (concurrent causation).

The basic form has six exclusions in this part, while the broad form has four because two of the six things excluded by the basic form are covered perils in the broad form (sprinkler leakage and water damage).

Both forms exclude loss or damage from artificially generated electrical current. This eliminates coverage for damage done by power surges. However, both will cover loss or damage from an ensuing fire. For example, if a power surge causes a piece of office equipment to short, damaging the piece of equipment and causing a fire damaging other property, the fire damage is covered, but damage to the piece of equipment caused by the surge is not covered. Fire damage to the equipment is covered.

Both also exclude loss from explosion of steam boilers, steam pipes, steam engines, and steam turbines. If such an explosion causes a fire or combustion explosion, that damage is covered. This emphasizes the special nature of the exposure presented by boilers, heavy machinery, and equipment of that kind. Boiler and machinery coverage is a specialized line of coverage necessary for those insureds with boiler and machinery exposures.

Finally, both forms exclude mechanical breakdown, but will pay for any loss that results from a covered peril. Again, as in the other exclusions in B.2., this exclusion is not subject to the concurrent causation language. Therefore, if the mechanical breakdown leads to otherwise covered damage, there is coverage. For example: an air conditioning unit suffers a mechanical breakdown and causes the unit to catch fire, burning down the building. The loss to the building could not be denied based on the mechanical breakdown exclusion. The only excludable damage would be the damage to the air conditioner directly caused by the mechanical breakdown. All resultant damage would be covered. However, if the air conditioner were consumed in the fire, that would also be covered.

Application of the Mechanical Breakdown Exclusion

A retail business covered by the commercial property policy with the basic causes of loss form had a failure in a solenoid switch in the furnace, causing a fire. The adjuster denied the claim, basing the denial on the exclusion that reads, "we will not pay for loss or damage caused by or resulting from mechanical breakdown." He said that it was the mechanical breakdown of the solenoid switch that caused the loss.

The mechanical breakdown exclusion is there to prevent the insurer from paying for a maintenance claim. If the insured had found that the solenoid switch was defective, he could not then turn to his property insurer and expect payment for a new switch. That is the purpose of the exclusion

The only part of this claim that should be denied is the mechanically unsound solenoid switch itself. The policy does not respond to damage caused by mechanical breakdown. However, the resultant fire damage is covered. Damage to the solenoid is properly excluded as mechanical breakdown, but the fire damage claim that followed is payable, because it resulted from a covered cause of loss (fire).

Special Exclusions

The final exclusion section of both forms excludes certain losses where the following coverage forms are made a part of the policy: business income and extra expense, leasehold interest, and legal liability. These exclusions are treated in the chapters in this book dealing with those forms.

Additional Coverage

The basic causes of loss form adds no additional coverages. The broad form adds one, collapse. As mentioned earlier, these causes of loss forms no longer exclude or limit glass coverage in any way. Glass is treated as part of the building, subject to the same perils as the rest of the building.

Collapse

Some time ago, collapse was moved out of the perils section of the policy and set aside as an additional coverage. The broad form covers a building against collapse (caused by the perils in the policy) or glass breakage.

There has been a shift in this area of insurance law since the late 1980s. Prior to 1990, only a minority of jurisdictions adopted the liberal view that a collapse occurs when there is a serious impairment to the soundness of a building or a portion of a building. This viewpoint does not limit collapse to a complete falling down or reduction to rubble. This is now apparently the majority viewpoint.

For example, in *Royal Indemnity v. Grunberg*, 553 NYS2d 527 (1990), a New York appellate court wrote, "In the view of a numerical majority of American jurisdictions, a substantial impairment of the structural integrity of a building is said to be a collapse." This "substantial impairment of the structural integrity..." language has become the test of whether an insurable collapse loss has occurred. The building does not have to fall into rubble to have been said to be damaged by collapse; instead, if the building is in imminent danger of collapsing, coverage is triggered.

Because of the decision in the above case (and others) ISO has significantly changed the collapse additional coverage. It now includes a long definition of what collapse is and what it is not. Wording is now in place that says collapse is "an abrupt falling down or caving in." This falling down or caving in may be of a building or any part of a building. The result must be that the building cannot be occupied as intended.

The following three things are not collapse for the purposes of the commercial property policy:

1. A building that is only in danger of falling down.
2. A part of a building that is still standing, even if it has separated from the rest of the building.
3. Any building, or part thereof, that is still standing, even if it shows evidence of cracking, bulging, sagging, bending, leaning, settling, shrinkage, or explosion.

In addition to coverage for the perils of the policy, the form lists the following as covered causes of collapse: hidden decay; hidden insect or vermin damage; weight of people or personal property; weight of rain that collects on a roof; and use of defective materials or methods in the construction, remodeling, etc. of a building (but the collapse must occur during the construction, remodeling, etc.).

The 2000 edition adds a caveat to the hidden decay and insect damage causes. Under the new form, such decay or damage is not a covered cause of collapse if the existence of the decay or damage is known to an insured prior to a collapse. Under the previous wording, an insured may have known about the damage, but if it was hidden, the commercial property policy would cover resulting collapse.

If listed as covered property, the following are covered against collapse of a building insured under the policy: outdoor radio or television antennas (including satellite dishes) and their lead-in wiring, masts or towers; awnings, gutters, and downspouts; yard fixtures; outdoor swimming pools; fences; piers, wharves, and docks; beach or diving platforms or appurtenances; retaining walls; and walks, roadways, and other paved surfaces.

The policy covers personal property if it "abruptly falls down or caves in" — even if that is not the result of a building collapse. However, the collapse of the personal property must:

1.   be caused by one of the listed causes of collapse;
2.   be inside a building; and
3.   not be one of the items listed in the above paragraph (antennas, etc.).

The form goes on to point out that collapse of personal property does not include settling, cracking, shrinkage, bulging or expansion. Any payments for collapse are included within the limit of liability for the covered property.

Chapter 4

Special Covered Causes of Loss Form (CP 10 30)

The most popular causes of loss option among both agents and insureds is the special form (CP 10 30), which provides open perils protection. Open perils differs from named perils coverage in that, rather than having to bring coverage in under one of the designated perils covered by the policy, all direct damage to covered property is covered unless a policy exclusion applies. It offers the insured the broadest possible protection.

The special form was, at one time, referred to as the all risks form. However, the claim began being made in court that a policy touting all risks coverage should provide just that—coverage against all risks of loss, regardless of any exclusions or limitations. Some courts applied the reasonable expectations doctrine to the all risks form. This doctrine held that it was reasonable for the insured to expect coverage against any, and all, exposures, based on the policy language pledging to cover all risks. To counter this expectation, ISO adopted phrasing that eliminated the all risks construction. These revised policies have been called open perils forms to distinguish them from named perils forms. In the commercial property program, open perils coverage is designated as the special causes of loss form CP 10 30.

The last version of the CP 10 30 to use the word all in the perils section was the January, 1983 edition (when ISO was still using the nonsimplified versions of the commercial property forms). In October of 1983 (still in the nonsimplified versions), the word was dropped. That form insured against "risk of physical loss."

The current wording was adopted in the first readable version (November, 1985), which insured against "risks of physical loss unless the loss is excluded. . .or limited."

The special causes of loss form's insuring agreement (or statement of what are the covered causes of loss) is not defined by a listing of named or specified causes of loss insured by the policy. Instead, the form states that when Special is shown in the declarations, the causes of loss covered means, "Risks of Direct Physical Loss, unless the loss is excluded in the Exclusions section or limited in the Limitations section." Therefore, the scope of covered perils is not defined by what is listed as a covered cause of loss, but by what is excluded under the otherwise broad coverage of the policy.

This broad coverage has another advantage for the insured in proof-of-loss situations. Where it is the insured's obligation to prove a loss falls under the coverage of a named peril, it is the insurer's obligation to prove the applicability of an exclusion. Open perils coverage generally creates a situation where a loss may be assumed to be covered, unless the insurer can prove the applicability of a policy exclusion.

Similarities to Named Perils Forms

The first set of exclusions (policy section B.1.a. through B.1.g) in the special causes of loss form is more or less identical to those found in the basic and broad named perils forms: ordinance or law; earth movement; governmental action; nuclear hazard; utility services; war; and water. See Chapter 3 for a discussion of these exclusions pertinent to all causes of loss forms. The lead-in language applies the concurrent causation language developed to avoid covering losses where a nonexcluded peril operates in conjunction with an excluded peril to cause damage. The concurrent causation theory is first described in Chapter 3 and later again in this chapter.

Like the other two forms, the special form gives back coverage for losses from fire, glass breakage, and volcanic action caused by a volcanic eruption. Coverage for volcanic action is provided in the basic and broad forms as a named peril; in the special form, it is an exception to the earth movement exclusion.

Heavy Construction and the Earth Movement Exclusion

A building located near an under-construction highway was covered by a commercial property policy with the special causes of loss form attached. The reconstruction of the highway required pile driving. The tremors from the pile driving damaged the building. Initially, the insurer denied the claim citing the earth movement exclusion.

However, the earth movement exclusion relates only to earth tremors caused by natural forces. Most courts agree with the opinion expressed by the Pennsylvania court in *Rightly v. Lebanon Mutual Ins. Co.* (79 Del 319, 1993 C.C.H.4097), "the Court finds that the earth movement exclusion applies only to spontaneous, natural, catastrophic earth movement and not movement brought about by other causes."

Earth movement that might be brought on by an explosion or the action of a pile driver is another matter entirely. The examples of earth movement listed in the exclusion (earthquake; landslide; mine subsidence; or earth sinking, rising, or shifting; and volcanic eruption or explosion) provide all the support that is necessary for the notion that natural causes are the subject of the exclusion. The *ejusdem generis rule* (that items in a list must be viewed in context with each other) would apply.

Like the named perils form, the open perils form adds a provision that the described exclusions apply regardless of how widespread a loss is.

Open Perils Exclusions—Section B.2.

The second set of exclusions (policy section B.2.a. through B.2.m.) has traditionally been called the all risks or open perils exclusions. Some of the exclusions eliminate coverage for events that have been historically uninsurable, such as wear and tear or mechanical breakdown, which are occurrences that will happen over time with some certainty as opposed to sudden and accidental occurrences. Others exclude losses more appropriately handled by specialized coverages, such as the boiler explosion or employee dishonesty exclusions (which can be covered by boiler and machinery and fidelity coverages). Still others exclude exposures that, as a matter of underwriting policy (either due to the enormous potential economic consequences of the event or because of the morale hazard), the drafters of the commercial property policy decided against covering. Examples of such exposures include the release of pollutants or the voluntary entrustment of property (again, specialized coverage forms have been developed to handle these exposures).

Artificially Generated Electrical Current. As in the named perils forms, the special form also excludes damage done to electrical devices, appliances, or wires by artificially generated electric current. Artificially generated includes any manmade electrical current; therefore, a lightning strike on a building that damages electrical devices would not be subject to this exclusion and any ensuing fire damage resulting from artificially generated electric current is be covered.

Delay; Loss of Use; Loss of Market. This exclusion emphasizes the commercial property policy's intent to cover direct damage and not consequential losses. The listed items (delay, loss of use or market) are indirect losses that are the result of a covered loss, such as a restaurant losing customers, with the attendant revenue, while rebuilding after a fire. The insured may purchase business income and extra expense insurance to cover this exposure.

Smoke, Vapor or Gas from Agricultural Smudging or Industrial Operations. This is the same exclusion that appears in the named perils forms under the peril of smoke. The same comment is applicable: the commercial property policy does not pay for this type of damage because such operations represent constant or constantly recurring exposures. Damage is certain to occur, so there is no risk, just a certainty.

Losses that Happen over Time—Section 2.d.

Several exclusions of a similar nature are grouped together in section 2.d. of the special causes of loss form, listed as 2.d.(1) through 2.d.(7). These are causes of loss that are more or less uninsurable, in that, given time, the event will occur. A component will wear out or an inherent defect will eventually reveal itself as damage.

In this regard, the special form excludes loss or damage caused by:

1. wear and tear;
2. rust, corrosion, fungus, decay, deterioration, or a hidden or latent defect. In short any quality in property that causes it to damage or destroy itself (the inherent vice exclusion of earlier property form language);
3. smog
4. settling, cracking, shrinking, or expansion;
5. nesting or infestations of birds, insects, or rodents. The form also excludes damage due to the release of waste products or secretions;

6. mechanical breakdown. Though resulting elevator collision is covered;
7. with respect to personal property, marring or scratching, dampness or dryness of atmosphere, and changes in or extremes of temperature.

If any of these excluded events cause resulting damage from building glass breakage or from one of the specified causes of loss listed in definitions section F of the form (and reproduced in the next paragraph), that resulting loss is covered. For example, if mechanical breakdown in a piece of machinery causes a fire that destroys the machinery and damages the building, the resulting fire damage to both the machinery and building is covered (excluding any damage to the machinery that was directly caused by the mechanical breakdown).

Specified Causes of Loss (referred to in the paragraph above) means the following: fire; lightning; explosion; windstorm or hail; smoke; aircraft or vehicles; riot or civil commotion; vandalism; leakage from fire extinguishing equipment; sinkhole collapse; volcanic action; falling objects; weight of snow, ice, or sleet; or water damage.

The form further defines the meaning of specified causes of loss for the following perils:

1. Sinkhole collapse means the sudden sinking or collapse of land into underground empty spaces created by the action of water on limestone or dolomite. This cause of loss does not include the cost of filling sinkholes or sinking or collapse of land into mine shafts or other manmade underground cavities.
2. Falling objects does not include loss or damage to personal property in the open or to the interior of a building or structure, or property inside a building or structure, unless the roof or an outside wall of the building or structure is first damaged by a falling object.
3. Water damage means accidental discharge or leakage of water or steam as the direct result of the breaking or cracking of any part of a system or appliance containing water or steam.

Some of the excluded items in the list of "things that happen over time" need further examination.

There has been confusion regarding the application of exclusion 2.d.(1), wear and tear. For instance, a rusted-out pipe inside a wall bursts and causes water to leak into an office. An adjuster's initial reaction may be to deny the claim based on the wear and tear exclusion (after all, the damage was caused by the wear and tear on the pipe). However, the only property in this example that is not covered is the pipe itself. The damage done by the water as well as the cost to repair the damage to the wall necessary to remove and replace the leaking pipe is covered.

The purpose of the wear and tear, rust, etc. exclusion (sometimes referred to as the maintenance exclusion) is to avoid payment for things that the insured should pay for as a matter of course. In the above example, if the insured had discovered the rusted-out pipe before it actually burst and caused damage, he could not go to his insurer and expect the replacement of the pipe to be covered. That is the purpose of the wear and tear exclusion; to avoid insurance recovery for normal maintenance. However, once wear and tear causes a covered loss, then that loss is covered.

Wear and Tear Exclusion—Damage to Shower Stall

A commercial property insured owned an apartment complex. It was insured on a commercial property policy with special causes of loss.

One of the insured's tenants was a very large individual. This tenant stepped into the bathtub/shower enclosure, and due to his excessive weight, he cracked the floor area of the tub. During the shower, there was extensive damage to the apartment below. The crack required replacement of the shower/tub unit, as well as cleanup of the damage.

The insured apartment owner turned in a claim to the carrier for replacement of the shower unit, and repair of the ceiling in the apartment below. The carrier offered to pay for the ceiling damage, but denied coverage of the shower enclosure due to the wear and tear exclusion. The shower unit was six months old. Inasmuch as the unit was relatively new, and the damage sudden and accidental, the agent believed that coverage should apply.

The damage to both the ceiling and shower unit should be covered. The wear and tear exclusion does not apply to a loss of this type, particularly where the unit was almost new. The wear and tear exclusion is one of a number of exclusions in the commercial property's special causes of loss form that eliminate coverage for what are essentially nonfortuitous losses; i.e., losses that are certain to happen and as such are not appropriate subjects for insurance coverage. If you use something long enough, it will wear out. This is not an insurable event.

However, a sudden and accidental breaking of a six-month old shower unit by a very large individual is not wear and tear. It may be that the stall was not manufactured strong enough to hold this person, but that does not bring it under the nonfortuitous loss exclusions, such as wear and tear.

The exclusion of settling, cracking, shrinking, or expansion has raised different issues. Specifically, what is the difference between settling, cracking, shrinking, or expansion and collapse? Courts have decided in favor of both insureds and insurers.

A Florida appeals court found that collapse must be defined independently of the language of the settling exclusion in *Auto Owners Insurance Co. v. Allen,* 362 So.2d 176 (1978). The court held that restrictions on coverage contained in the exclusion do not limit the definition of collapse itself. The court stated, "The provision at issue here is clear in only one regard as to the meaning of collapse. Coverage is not provided for loss from 'settling, cracking, shrinkage, bulging or expansion' which is occasioned by other than a direct result of collapse of the building."

In one instance, a motel was in imminent danger of falling down when the claim was brought. While a trench was being dug next to the back wall of the motel in order to lay sewer pipe, sandy soil fell away from the footings supporting the wall. Rejecting the argument that the exclusion was specifically designed to avoid ambiguity by limiting the insurer's liability to cases where the building fell down, the court said: "We cannot accept this construction. If [the insurer] had intended to limit its liability as it argues, it would have been a simple matter to include in the policy a restriction of coverage to a flattened form or rubble. Other than the exclusion for [settling, etc.] there is no attempt to define what a collapse is or is not."

However, the Kansas Supreme Court had earlier held differently. In the case of *Krug v. Miller's Mutual Insurance Assn. of Illinois,* 495 P.2d 949 (1972), the Kansas supreme court determined that the term *collapse* was not ambiguous when qualified by the exclusion pertaining to settling, cracking, etc. Where collapse coverage is so qualified, the court determined that collapse does not take place unless more than settling, cracking, etc. has occurred.

Like the other causes of loss forms, the special form also has a mechanical breakdown exclusion. However, the 1990 edition of the special causes of loss form added a provision to this exclusion, carrying over to the 2000 version, clarifying that the exclusion does not apply to any resulting loss or damage caused by elevator collision.

Mechanical breakdown is another area that has caused much confusion over the years. When a piece of machinery breaks down, any ensuing loss from a covered peril should be paid. However, insurers have denied such losses citing the mechanical breakdown exclusion.

The purpose of this exclusion is the same as that for the wear and tear exclusionary provision. If a piece of machinery just stops working, the insured may not look to his insurer to repair it. However, if that machine breaks down and causes a covered loss, that loss should be paid.

Mechanical Breakdown Exclusion and Concurrent Causation

An agent insured a church on a commercial property coverage part with the special causes of loss form. Air conditioning units were damaged by freezing. The insurer-appointed engineer stated there were two causes of loss: 1) failure of the pump-down solenoid, which allowed the compressors to run during freezing conditions, eventually resulting in the freezing of the circulating chilled water system and the destruction of the system; and 2) a control rod did not close on the louver vent economizer system, which allowed the very cold outside air into the church. The engineer concluded that the failure of the system was due to the mechanical failure of these devices.

The insurer then denied the entire loss based upon the mechanical breakdown exclusion, stating that the concurrent causation language in the policy removed coverage for any damage resulting from mechanical breakdown.

The loss in question is not appropriately denied in its entirety for several reasons. First, the concurrent causation language of the ISO CP 10 30 (current edition) does not apply to the mechanical breakdown exclusion.

The lead-in language to section B. Exclusions, clause 2. reads differently ("We will not pay for loss or damage caused by or resulting from any of the following:"). This is not concurrent causation language; in fact, this was the original lead-in to both B. sections 1. and 2., which was changed because of the development of the concurrent causation doctrine.

The concurrent causation language does not apply to this second set of exclusions. Therefore, if mechanical breakdown causes damage not otherwise excluded to something other than the item that actually broke down, any subsequent damage is covered. In this case, the loss to the air conditioning system was not caused by mechanical breakdown, but instead was due to freezing resulting from the mechanical breakdown. The failure of the solenoid may have set the stage, but it did not cause the loss. Freezing did.

(scenario continues next page)

(continued from previous page)

The mechanical breakdown exclusion (B.2.d.[6]) does not apply to the entire damage described in this situation, but only to damage caused directly by mechanical breakdown, in this case, the pump-down solenoid. The rest of the damage done to the system did not occur as a result of mechanical breakdown, but instead was caused by freezing. Without the concurrent causation language of B.1., there is no reason to apply the mechanical breakdown exclusion to any damage other than the damage to the part of the system that failed.

By way of example of how the mechanical breakdown exclusion works, apply these facts to a peril other than freezing. Suppose that the breakdown of the solenoid caused heat to build up and the entire building burned down rather than damaging just the components of the air conditioning system. The insurer could not deny the claim for the fire damage due to the mechanical breakdown of the solenoid.

The purpose of exclusion B.2.d.(5) is, as indicated by its placement in the policy, to eliminate coverage for things that happen over a period of time, such as damage done by a bird that builds its nest in an attic or the long-term buildup of waste from nesting birds.

The current wording makes the purpose of the exclusion much clearer. The form now excludes "nesting or infestation, or discharge or release of waste products or secretions, by insects, birds, rodents or other animals." There is no intention to exclude sudden and accidental damage done by animals.

Other Exclusions

Explosion of Steam Boilers, Steam Pipes, Steam Engines or Steam Turbines. This exclusion applies to such equipment that the insured owns, leases, or operates. Ensuing loss from fire or combustion explosion is covered. Again, as in the basic and broad causes of loss forms, this exclusion reiterates the fact that boiler equipment and industrial type machinery is beyond the purview of the commercial property policy and is more appropriately covered by a boiler and machinery policy.

Continuous or Repeated Seepage or Leakage of Water. An exclusion of damage from continuous or repeated seepage or leakage of water over a period of fourteen days or more modifies coverage for plumbing discharge under special form coverage just as it does the named cause of loss of water damage in broad form CP 10 20. Some insureds have argued that the fourteen-day period should begin when the insured first discovers the leakage. Instead, it is damage caused by the undiscovered leak that the policy is specifically excluding. The fourteen-day period begins with the onset of the leakage and not when the insured discovers the leak or damage.

Repeated Seepage or Leakage

A commercial property insured found that the floors in his building were becoming soft. He investigated in the crawl space under the floor and found the problem. There was a leak in a hot water pipe which caused moisture damage to the floor above. The damage was calculated at $123,000. The adjuster denied the claim due to the special causes of loss form's exclusion of repeated seepage or leakage over a period of more than fourteen days. The insured could not hear or see the water leak and so had no way of knowing what was going on under the floor. The insured questioned the application of the exclusion, stating that the fourteen-day period should begin at the discovery of the leak or damage and not from the date of the beginning of the occurrence.

However, the exclusion is appropriately applied. This type of loss is the very type meant to be excluded by the commercial property policy's repeated seepage or leakage exclusion.

The fact that the insured could not easily make himself aware of the impending damage does not make it any the less a nonfortuitous loss or bring it outside of the clear language of the exclusion.

Water, Other Liquids, Powder or Molten Material. The policy does not cover damage by these substances if, due to freezing, they leak or flow from plumbing, heating, air conditioning, or other equipment (except fire protective systems). The exclusion applies unless the insured "do[es] [his] best to maintain heat in the building or structure; or drain[s] the equipment and shut[s] off the supply if the heat is not maintained." If the insured meets these conditions, the exclusion does not apply. Note that the form does not exclude all damage by water, other liquids, powder, or molten material. It only excludes damage by these items if caused by freezing; and only then if the insured has not maintained heat or drained and shut off the system.

Dishonest or Criminal Acts. This exclusion eliminates coverage for dishonest or criminal acts committed by the named insured, partners, employees, directors, trustees, or authorized representatives of the named insured, or anyone to whom the named insured entrusts covered property. The 2000 edition adds members, officers, and managers in order to recognize the limited liability company (LLC) form of organization. This exclusion applies whether the person committing the act does so alone or in collusion with others and regardless of whether the act occurs during working hours.

While it obviously excludes employee theft (a subject for fidelity coverage), it does not exclude loss from acts of destruction committed by such individuals. Therefore, the form does not cover an employee stealing office equipment; however, if an employee damages or destroys a photocopying machine as an act of revenge, the policy does respond to such damage.

At least one court has applied the exclusion to arson by a 50 percent shareholder and corporate officer. The case is *Minnesota Bond Ltd. v. St. Paul Mercury Ins. Co.*, 706 P.2d 942 (1985). In this case a partner with a 50 percent interest set the building on fire, hoping to collect the insurance so that she could pay a debt. The trial court originally refused to apply the exclusion to this case. That court held that the "context of a 'willful or dishonest act' is described by the remainder of the language in the exclusion, which speaks to unexplained or mysterious disappearance of property or the voluntary parting with titled possession of property as a result of a fraudulent scheme. This Court concludes that this exclusion is inapplicable to the factual situation in the case at bar and the motion for reconsideration is denied."

However, the Supreme Court of Oregon overturned that decision. It reached its decision without any discussion of the coinsured's position. In its reversal, the Oregon Supreme Court said, "Although it may have been unwise for this insured to purchase a policy with such a far-reaching exclusion as contained in exclusion No. 4, nevertheless that decision was made by the plaintiff corporation when it chose to insure its property under this policy. The exclusion is clear and unambiguous and fully applicable to this loss. There is no coverage for this loss under the policy."

This case, as was implied here, involved individuals who have such control over the corporation that their acts essentially constitute the acts of the corporation; where a regular employee (not an officer, director, or partner) commits an act of arson, the policy would respond.

Trick or Device. This provision eliminates coverage where the insured has been tricked out of the property. This exclusion applies if the insured or anyone to whom the property has been entrusted has been induced to part voluntarily with the property by fraudulent scheme, trick, device, or false pretense. This reiterates the intent of the commercial property policy to provide coverage for direct loss to property, and not fidelity or theft coverage (which is available under the crime insurance program).

In the typical trick or device loss, the insured is defrauded. For example: the perpetrator may come into possession of the property lawfully, as in trying out a piece of equipment, but does not return it. Another example of such a scheme would be where a customer pays for an item with a bad check or stolen credit card and obtains possession of the property. The insured cannot look to the commercial property policy for coverage in such situations. Only auto dealers have such coverage routinely available to them and, obviously, their exposure is high.

Rain, Snow, Ice or Sleet Damage to Personal Property in the Open. The commercial property policy covers personal property in the described building or structure or in the open within 100 feet of the described premises. The policy also covers personal property temporarily off premises at certain locations (see Chapter 2). This exclusion modifies this coverage and is another example of a nonfortuitous loss that the policy excludes. Personal property left out in the open in rain, snow, ice or sleet will become damaged. Risk management techniques other than insurance are more appropriate to this exposure (for example, bringing it inside). Property covered by a tarp retains its characteristic as property in the open, and would not be afforded coverage.

Collapse. The special form excludes collapse. However, the form gives back coverage for collapse under the Additional Coverages section (see below). However, if a collapse causes otherwise covered damage ("if collapse results in a covered cause of loss"), the resulting damage is covered. For example: a collapsing beam somehow causes a fire that damages equipment; the resulting damage is covered as damage by fire. There is no coverage for the building for the collapse damage (other than under the additional coverage for collapse, treated later), but the policy does cover the fire damage to the equipment.

Discharge, dispersal, seepage, migration, release or escape of pollutants. The pollution exclusion originally read "release, discharge, or dispersal of pollutants or contaminants." In 1986 this phrasing was replaced by an exclusion that removed coverage for loss or damage caused by or resulting from the release, discharge or dispersal of pollutants unless the release, discharge or dispersal is itself caused by any of the specified causes of loss. Resulting loss or damage by the specified causes of loss was covered.

The 1990 form revision modified this language by adding the words *seepage, migration*, and *escape* of pollutants as well, thus giving stronger emphasis to the exclusion of nonsudden pollution losses. This change was in accord with changes made in the 1990 ISO Building and Personal Property

Coverage Form (CP 00 10). The wording of the exclusion remains the same in the current (2000) version of the form.

The effect of this exclusion is to limit the pollutant cleanup and removal coverage of the forms in the commercial property program providing building and personal property coverage to those sudden and accidental occurrences brought on by the specified causes of loss; i.e., the broad form perils.

The 2000 form adds a new exception to this exclusion. The exclusion does not apply to damage to glass done by chemicals that are applied to the glass. This is part of the simplification of the glass coverage. Damage done by such chemicals was covered by the old glass form. Since that form has been removed, the policy now provides the coverage by means of this exception to the exclusion.

Neglect. The 2000 edition adds this thirteenth exclusion. It emphasizes the insured's responsibility to protect his property from further loss at the time of the initial loss.

Concurrent Causation Exclusions

The special form contains a third set of exclusions (designated 3.a., b., and c.) that preclude coverage under the doctrine of concurrent causation.

Concurrent causation is a legal doctrine developed in case law to find coverage despite common property policy exclusions such as earth movement or flooding.

For example: a third-party contractor is negligent in the preparation of the soil prior to the construction of an office building. After the building is completed and occupied, it suffers earth movement damage. While earth movement is excluded, under the doctrine of concurrent causation the building owner could claim that the loss was caused by the negligence of the contractor that prepared the soil. Without these exclusions, the claim would be payable, because third-party negligence is not an excluded peril.

To avoid unintended insurance recovery in concurrent causation situations, ISO included concurrent causation lead-in language to a number of exclusions and added a concurrent causation exclusion with three sub-parts. These include loss or damage caused by:

1.   weather conditions;
2.   acts or decisions (or failure to act) of individuals and groups; and
3.   faulty, inadequate, or defective planning, design, defective materials, or maintenance.

They do not defeat coverage for a covered cause of loss that happens to involve damage by the excluded cause of loss. For example, a building suffers flood damage because of negligent maintenance of a dam. The flood damage is excluded under the surface water exclusion; and the concurrent causation exclusion operates to defeat coverage for a claim of negligent maintenance. If the building also suffers vandalism as a result of the flood, that vandalism is covered because the policy does not exclude vandalism.

However, there is no coverage for ensuing losses caused by one of the three special exclusions if the ensuing losses fall under one of the excluded risks. Thus there would be no coverage if faulty construction (one of the special exclusions) caused natural subsurface water damage to the foundation.

The weather conditions exclusion only applies if weather conditions contribute in any way with a cause or event excluded in exclusion section 1 (ordinance or law, earth movement, nuclear hazard, utility services, war and military action, and water. For example, heavy rain causes a landslide which in turn damages an insured structure. The policy excludes earth movement and the claim should be denied. However, at court the insured argues that it was not earth movement that caused the damage to the house, but instead, the cause of damage was the rainfall (a weather condition). Prior to the adoption of the concurrent causation exclusions this argument sometimes prevailed. ISO adopted the concurrent causation exclusions to retain the original intent of the drafters to not cover damage by earth movement (or the other excluded causes of loss), regardless of what caused the earth to move.

The second of the concurrent causation exclusions eliminates as a cause of loss the acts or decisions (including the failure to act or decide) by any persons, groups, or governmental bodies. For example, governmental officials fail to act in a crisis, allowing a dam to overflow and damage insured property. Under a seminal concurrent causation case, the court allowed the (nonexcluded) peril of negligent decision-making to override the policy's flood exclusion and found coverage under these same facts. The current version of the commercial property policy eliminates this possibility.

Part c. of these exclusions eliminates coverage where the alleged cause of loss is inadequate planning, design, workmanship, etc. The form provides a lengthy list of items falling under this exclusion: 1) planning, zoning, development, surveying, siting; 2) design, specifications, workmanship, repair, construction, renovation, remodeling, grading, compaction; 3) materials used in repair, construction, renovation, or remodeling; or 4) maintenance.

All three parts (a.,b., and c.) of the exclusion are subject to the provision that if loss or damage by a covered cause of loss results from one these excluded perils, coverage applies to the resulting loss or damage. For example, if faulty workmanship in the electrical system of a building results in fire, the resulting fire loss is covered. Or, if earth movement causes a fire, the fire damage is covered. Or, if the failure of the fire officials to act in creating firebreaks causes a building to burn, the fire damage is covered.

Special Exclusions

The final exclusion section of the commercial property policy excludes certain losses for the following coverage forms: business income and extra expense; leasehold interest; and legal liability. These exclusions are treated in the chapters in this book dealing with those forms.

Limitations

Under this section (C), the form clarifies that it does not cover loss or damage to certain types of property. It places dollar limits on certain types of property and limits coverage on other types to the specified causes of loss.

Steam Boilers, Steam Pipes, Steam Engines or Steam Turbines. The policy does not cover these items for damage that results from a condition or event inside the equipment. As mentioned earlier, ensuing loss from fire or combustion explosion is covered.

Steam Boilers—Condition or Event Inside

A commercial property insured, covered for open perils, suffered the following loss. In January, water was seen coming out an unoccupied building and the fire department was notified. They turned off the water and requested the power company to turn off the power. The management company was notified a few days later, and on inspection, found the boilers had frozen and were damaged.

The insurance company denied coverage based on the limitation in the policy for loss or damage to steam boilers resulting from any condition or event inside such equipment. The agent believed that the event causing the damage was the power company turning off the power, something outside the equipment; and, therefore, not reached by this exclusion.

This interpretation is correct. The limitation in the policy concerns loss caused by a condition or event inside the equipment. The event which resulted in the loss occurred outside the equipment, namely, turning off the power. Further, there is an apparent unbroken chain of events from the power company turning off the power to the boilers being found frozen.

The limitations in Part C must be read in context. The limitations apply to items that should be separately insured, such as jewelry, and to losses that are foreseeable and therefore uninsurable. For example, if the boilers were damaged due to lime buildup, the loss could have been prevented through proper maintenance and is therefore not covered. The freezing loss was outside the insured's control, and is covered.

Hot Water Boilers or Other Water Heating Equipment. As with the equipment in the above paragraph, the special form does not cover these items for damage caused by or resulting from any condition or event inside the equipment other than an explosion. Therefore, explosion damage, regardless of whether the explosion is caused by an internal condition or event, is covered.

Building Interiors and Personal Property in a Building. The special form does not cover these items for damage done by: rain, snow, sleet, ice, sand, or dust, unless the building first sustains damage by an insured peril to its roof or walls through which the rain, snow, etc. enters. The form also covers such damage caused by the thawing of snow, ice, or sleet on the building.

Water Damage and Boarded-Up Windows

An insured's building covered by an ISO commercial property policy with the special causes of loss form suffered rain damage to an unoccupied second floor. The

(continued on next page)

(continued from previous page)

second story windows were boarded up years ago with plywood to prevent water entering through any broken panes.

Extremely heavy storms accompanied by heavy winds and wind-driven rain knocked loose the plywood boarding, resulting in water penetrating the window openings and damaging the insured's business personal property stored on the second floor.

The insurer denied coverage for the loss citing the following limitation on water damage: the building must first suffer damage to its roof or walls by a covered cause of loss through which the rain would enter. In supporting his denial, the adjuster compared the boarding being blown in to that of a window (the agent assumed he meant "windowpane") being blown open. The adjuster went on to state that coverage would not apply in this similar situation unless the window (pane) would be blown out or damaged.

According to a standard desk-top dictionary, a window is the opening in a wall, covered by a material, typically glass (the glass is called a windowpane). The agent's position was that the windows, including the boarding, are part of the wall, and that the material covering the openings is irrelevant. The wind is a covered cause of loss, and it damaged the wall by blowing out the window covering. He believed that this should trigger coverage for the damage to the insured's interior business personal property.

The CP 10 30 does not cover rain damage to the interior of a building unless, "The building or structure first sustains damage by a Covered Cause of Loss to its roof or wall, through which the rain . . .enters." It says nothing about windows. Even if we were to accept the insurer's contention that the boarded-up window is not a window it is still part of the building's wall. When the wind blew out the boards covering the opening the wall suffered damage from a covered peril. Then rain entered and did damage. The loss is covered.

Building Materials. The policy does not cover these items for theft, unless they are held for sale by the insured. The inventory at a lumber yard or hardware store, for example, is not covered by a builders' risk form. This limitation also does not apply to business income or extra expense coverage.

Missing Property. The policy does not pay for missing property if 1) the loss can only be documented because of an inventory shortage; or, 2) there is no physical evidence to show what happened to the property.

Missing Property—No Physical Evidence

A hospital insured under the special causes of loss form submitted a claim for a scientific video monitor used in the intensive care unit. Hospital officials claimed that the monitor was stolen.

(continued on next page)

The insurance company denied the claim based on the exclusion found in limitation of coverage 1.e., which says, "We will not pay for loss or damage to:. . . property that is missing, but there is no physical evidence to show what happened to it, such as a shortage disclosed on taking inventory."

The subscriber questioned how, in a premises that is open twenty-four hours a day for public service, one might find physical evidence of forcible entry?

The loss should be covered. The clause the insurance company relied upon to deny coverage does not apply in this case.

Limitation of coverage 1.e. does not require visible signs of forcible entry, which is a requirement for coverage under the peril of burglary in the crime policy. This limitation refers instead to the loss of property that could not be recognized except by reference to written records.

For example, if the hospital had a storage room filled with hundreds of monitors and one were stolen, that theft probably could not be recognized by physical evidence alone. The physical absence of one monitor out of hundreds could not be seen without counting the monitors and comparing the total to a known number.

In this case, the absence of the monitor could be immediately noticed by anyone familiar with the room. The monitor was there yesterday and it is not there today. It is physically missing, and the hospital does not have to rely on an inventory to know that it is gone. The physical evidence is the empty space where the monitor used to be.

The purpose of the limitation of the coverage in question is to prevent claiming theft when the loss might, in fact, be due to poor record keeping. The limitation is not intended to exclude theft, which might be thought of as the disappearance of property from a specific place during a specific time period.

Gutters and Downspouts. This limitation has been removed from the 2000 version, thus extending coverage for damage from the weight of ice, snow, or sleet to these items.

Transferred Property. There is no coverage for property transferred to an off-premises person or place on the basis of unauthorized instructions. This is similar to the trick or device exclusion and eliminates what is more appropriately covered under crime or fidelity policies.

Glass. As mentioned elsewhere, the 2000 commercial property policy treats glass as part of the building with no limitations on payment or perils. The $100 per pane or $500 per occurrence limit has been removed.

Limitations on Other Types of Property

The following types of property are covered only for loss or damage due to the specified causes of loss: valuable papers and records; animals; fragile articles; and owned builders equipment or tools.

The 2000 edition clarifies that the limitation on valuable papers and records also applies to records that exist on film, tape, etc. The new form also adds the specification that prepackaged software programs are not valuable papers and records.

The policy covers animals only if they are killed or if they must be destroyed.

Earlier editions stated that the limitation on fragile articles did not apply to glass that is part of a building. However, with the new treatment of building glass in the 2000 edition, that exception to the limitation is no longer necessary and has been removed. The current form also removes the exception for photographic or scientific instrument lenses, thus making them subject to the fragile articles limitation. Now, the only exceptions to the fragile articles limitation are glass and containers of property held for sale. Finally, the new form removes reference to "glassware" as a fragile article.

The limitation on owned tools does not apply to property located on or within 100 feet of the described premises, unless the premises is insured under the builders risk form; nor does it apply to business income or extra expense coverage.

Marble Slab as Fragile Article

An insured covered by a commercial property policy, with a special causes of loss form attached, had a marble slab resting on a platform. The platform collapsed and the marble slab broke into pieces. The insurer denied the claim due to limitation C.2.c. which eliminates coverage for breakage of fragile articles such as glassware, statuary, marbles, chinaware and porcelains unless damage is by one of the defined specified causes of loss. The issue is whether the limitation's specific reference to marbles places the marble slab in the fragile articles category, and precludes coverage for this loss.

The loss to the unrefined marble slab does not fall under the purview of the fragile articles limitation. The operative word in the provision is *fragile*, and the items listed in the exclusion are examples, not definitions. Although a delicate piece of marble artwork is a fragile article, a large block of marble is outside the limitation. Many things

(continued on next page)

(continued from previous page)

(such as concrete blocks or bricks) may be breakable given sufficient force. However, they would hardly be considered fragile articles.

Special Theft Limits

Special Theft Limits. The following items are subject to a special limit for any one occurrence of theft. The special limit shown for each category is the total limit for loss or damage to all property in that category, no matter the number of items involved.

a. $2,500 for furs, fur garments, and garments trimmed with fur.
b. $2,500 for jewelry, watches, watch movements, jewels, pearls, precious and semiprecious stones, bullion, gold, silver, platinum, and other precious alloys or metals. This limit does not apply to jewelry and watches worth $100 or less per item.
c. $2,500 for patterns, dies, molds, and forms.
d. $250 for stamps, tickets (including lottery tickets held for sale), and letters of credit.

The final policy limitation precludes coverage for the cost to repair any system from which any liquid or molten material escapes. Fire extinguishing equipment is covered for discharges or for loss caused by freezing.

Additional Coverages and Limitation

As does the broad causes of loss form, the special causes of loss form provides one additional coverage, collapse.

This additional coverage is exactly the same in both forms. For a complete discussion of collapse, see Chapter 3.

Additional Coverage Extensions

Form CP 10 30 provides three additional coverage extensions: property in transit; water damage, other liquids, powder or molten material damage; and glass.

The form allows the insured to extend coverage on business personal property in transit more than 100 feet from the described premises. The extension, however, does not apply to property in the care of the insured's salespersons. The property must be located in or on a vehicle that the named insured owns, leases, or operates within the coverage territory.

The policy covers property in-transit for the following named perils: fire, lightning, explosion, windstorm or hail, riot or civil commotion, or vandalism; vehicle collision, upset or overturn (but not contact with the roadbed); and theft of an entire bale, case, or package. Theft is covered only in the case of forced entry into a securely locked body or compartment of the vehicle. The insured must demonstrate that such a forced entry occurred; i.e., there must be visible marks of the forced entry.

The limit of liability for this additional coverage extension is $5,000. This amount is in addition to the limit of liability.

Property in Transit

An insured plumber's tools were stolen from his van while parked on his home driveway. The tools were valued at more than $2,000.

The agent contends that the insured is entitled to $1,000 under paragraph E.1.A. of commercial property special causes of loss form CP 10 30 as personal property in transit.

The claims manager denied coverage stating that the in-transit coverage is not designed for the insured's tools and business property; instead, that this is a coverage intended for the insured's goods while being shipped or delivered to another location.

The transit coverage under the commercial property policy applies to personal property of the insured in transit more than 100 feet from described premises, while in or on a motor vehicle. However, damage must be by one of the described perils. Loss caused by theft is only covered where theft is of an entire bale, case, or package. The vehicle or compartment must be locked and there must be visible marks of forced entry.

Therefore, tools left loose in the vehicle do not qualify. If all the tools were contained in a case, and that case was stolen by someone leaving visible marks of forced entry, coverage would then apply. If the tools were not packaged or in a case, there would be no coverage.

The second additional coverage extension applies in case of a covered loss due to water, other liquids, powder or molten material. The insurer agrees to pay the cost to tear out and replace any part of the building in order to repair the appliance or system from which the material escaped.

New with the 2000 edition is additional coverage extension 3, glass. When the insured suffers a loss to building glass, this coverage pays for temporary plates or other coverings "if the repair is delayed." The limit of insurance provided by this extension is included in the limit of liability.

Chapter 5

Conditions

Commercial Property General Conditions

Common policy conditions form IL 00 17 of the ISO commercial property program contains six conditions that must be incorporated into any policy written under the program and that apply to all the policy's coverages. Most of these common policy conditions are restatements of provisions, modified in varying degrees, that have been standard features of property policies since the advent of the standard fire policy.

Cancellation

The named insured may cancel the policy at any time by notifying the insurer. The notification may be that the insured's copy of the policy is returned or a lost policy release is signed. Because the insured requests the cancellation, the return premium will be calculated at rates less than pro rata.

The insurer may also cancel the policy at any time with the appropriate written notice mailed to the insured. Cancellation for nonpayment requires a ten-day notice; any other reason, thirty days. When the insurer cancels, the return premium is figured on a pro-rata basis.

It is important to note that the policy calls for cancellation notices (either to or from the named insured) to be to or from the *first named insured* (the person or entity whose name appears first on the policy).

Cancellation is one area that varies greatly from state to state. Each individual state's Amendatory Endorsement should be checked to discover the exact cancellation provisions applicable in that state. This information is contained in the National Underwriter Company's *Cancellation and Non-Renewal Handbook*.

Changes

This condition stipulates that any changes in the terms of the policy can be made only by endorsement issued by the insurer. Any change requests by the insured must be by the first named insured.

Examination of Your Books and Records

This condition gives the insurer the right to audit books and records of the insured relating to the policy. The examination or audit may be made during the policy period or any time within three years after the policy period ends.

It does not allow the insurer to go randomly through the insured's records. Rather, the insurer may only examine the records that relate to the policy. Such related records may involve finances, safety, inventory, and so on.

Inspection and Surveys

This condition gives the insurer the right to conduct inspections, surveys, and reports. It also allows the insurer to make recommendations relating to insurability and premiums to be charged. It does not impose any obligation on the insurer to carry out such inspections and surveys.

It is also not meant as a warranty from the insurer that the insured's operations are safe or healthful. Nor does it warrant that the insured is in compliance with legal requirements that may pertain to those operations. This disclaimer also applies to any rating, advisory, or similar organization making inspections under the policy.

The inspection and surveys condition was called into play in Spring 1977. Over the Memorial Day weekend of that year, the Beverly Hills Supper

Club in Northern Kentucky burned, killing 165 people. As the investigation proceeded, it was discovered that the property insurer, the Kentucky Property Insurance Placement Facility, had just recently inspected the building. Based on this inspection, some plaintiffs' attorneys attempted to hold the insurer and Insurance Services Office (ISO) liable for the deaths and injuries sustained in the fire. The courts, however, did not allow the suit to go forward. (The cause of the fire was eventually determined to be due to faulty aluminum wiring.)

Premiums

This condition specifies that the first named insured is responsible for paying the policy premium. It also calls for any return premiums to be sent to the first named insured.

Transfer of Rights and Duties Under This Policy

The final common policy condition requires the insurer's written consent in order to transfer the insured's rights and duties under the policy to another person. The only time the written consent of the insurer is not needed is upon the death of a named insured. When a named insured dies, his or her rights and duties are transferred to the named insured's legal representative. In such cases, the legal representative exercises the deceased insured's rights and duties while acting as legal representative. Until a legal representative is appointed, rights and duties of the deceased insured with respect to the deceased insured's property pass to anyone having proper temporary custody of that property. Such individuals might include a spouse, a partner, or a corporate officer.

Commercial Property Policy Conditions

In addition to the common policy conditions, the commercial property policy contains form CP 00 90, *Commercial Property Policy Conditions*. Those conditions are

1. Concealment, Misrepresentation or Fraud
2. Control of Property
3. Insurance Under Two or More Coverages
4. Legal Action Against Us (the insurer)
5. Liberalization

6. No Benefit to Bailee
7. Other Insurance
8. Policy Period, Coverage Territory and
9. Transfer of Rights of Recovery Against Others to Us (subrogation).

Each of these is discussed individually below.

Concealment, Misrepresentation or Fraud

This condition voids coverage if, at any time (pre- or post-loss), the named insured commits a fraudulent act relating to the policy. Misrepresenting the use or occupancy of the building (representing the property as a pharmacy when in reality it is an illegal methamphetamine lab, for example), or misrepresenting the value of destroyed equipment to boost insurance recovery is fraud. Such an act, before or after loss, voids coverage. Note that *void* does not mean that the policy is canceled or suspended, but that a contract between the insurer and insured never existed. In other words, a bargain was never struck, due to the misrepresentation or fraud of the party.

The policy is also void if the named insured or any other insured intentionally conceals or misrepresents a material fact about the coverage, the covered property, a claim under the policy, or the named insured's interest in the property.

Therefore, fraud of any type by the named insured related to the policy voids coverage. Concealing or misrepresenting material facts by the named insured or any other insured also voids coverage.

The phrase *any other insured* was added in 1988. Note that the language does not void the policy only for the person committing the misrepresentation or concealment. It is possible, therefore, that the act of any insured could void the policy as to all other insureds, including the named insured. A number of courts have interpreted the language *the insured* under the concealment, fraud, or neglect provisions of the standard fire policy as applying only to the individual insured guilty of the fraud, giving coverage to other innocent insureds.

However, other federal court decisions have interpreted language similar to the ISO *any other insured* phrase in certain fire policies as unambiguously precluding coverage to innocent, as well as guilty, insureds. In *Employers Mutual Casualty Company v. Tavernaro,* 4 F. Supp. 2d 868 (1998), Mr. and Mrs. Tavernaro owned a business covered on a businessowners policy (with the same wording as the commercial property policy). Mr. Tavernaro set the building on fire and Mrs. Tavarnaro attempted to collect the insurance proceeds as an *innocent coinsured.* The court concluded that "the language clearly precludes recovery by either party in this case."

Control of Property

This condition protects the insured from the acts of others. It provides that acts or neglect by any person which are not under the direction or control of the named insured will not affect coverage. For example, if an employee of the named insured causes intentional damage the damage will be covered, despite the intentional acts exclusion (i.e., the intentional act is not imputed to the insured).

In view of the comments in the last paragraph of the preceding section regarding who can be an insured under the commercial property policy, it seems a moot point, but the language of the control of property condition leaves open the question of whether an innocent insured's coverage remains unaffected by the acts of another insured when those acts involve concealment, misrepresentation, or fraud. No cases on point were found and it remains to be seen how the courts will interpret the language of the two ISO conditions concerning fraud and control of property. Inasmuch as it seems improbable that there can be an insured other than the named insured in the commercial property policy, no case could have arisen that might be litigated.

The language of the second part of the control of property condition states that a breach of any condition at one or more locations does not affect coverage at any location where the breach does not exist at the time of loss. For example, a breach of the vacancy condition at one premises will not spill over to affect coverage at a second insured location.

Additionally, as there is no specific exemption regarding the fraud, misrepresentation, or concealment condition, it is reasonable to assume that the second part of the control of property condition applies equally to the fraud provision. If an employee of the insured commits fraud in connection with a claim, that will not bar the insured from recovering under the policy.

Insurance Under Two or More Coverages

In the event that more than one of the commercial property policy's coverages applies to a loss, this condition prevents double payment. It limits the amount of payment to the actual amount of loss or damage. For example, a piece of business equipment might be covered under both the building and contents section of the commercial property policy. The insured cannot recover under both to effect a double recovery. However, if the amount of coverage left under one section is insufficient to pay the entire loss, it could be paid under either or both sections, up to the actual amount of loss or damage.

Legal Action Against the Insurer

If the insured wishes to bring suit against the insurer, he or she must first fully comply with all the policy terms. The insured must bring the suit within two years following the loss or damage (note that this is not two years after a formal denial of the claim). Earlier policies that incorporated the standard fire policy language gave the insured one year in which to bring suit.

Liberalization

The commercial property policy provides that if the insurer liberalizes the policy (i.e., broadens or adds coverage) without any corresponding premium increase, the revisions automatically apply to the insured's unrevised policy. This provision applies to any liberalizations adopted by the insurer during the policy term or forty five days prior to the inception date.

For example: the current version of the commercial property policy provides $250,000 for a newly acquired or constructed building. If an insurer changes its policy to provide $300,000, without increasing the premium, then all existing policyholders would receive the $300,000 coverage.

No Benefit to Bailee

The commercial property policy is intended to protect the insured's property; there is no insurance under the policy for the benefit of others to whom insured property may be entrusted. If the insured owns a clothing store and has some of the clothing sent out to be dry cleaned, the dry cleaner is responsible for the clothing while it is in his care. If the clothing is damaged while at the dry cleaner, the dry cleaner cannot look to the clothing owner's commercial property policy for coverage. While the commercial property policy insurer may eventually settle with its own insured, it would still retain the right to enter into proceedings against the dry cleaner to recover the insurer's payment and would make no payment to the insured or the bailee for the benefit of the bailee.

Other Insurance

While this condition does not prohibit an insured from carrying more than one property policy—and, in fact, states that the insured may have other insurance subject to the same plan, terms, conditions and provisions—it spells out how a loss is handled in such a situation.

If the insured has more than one policy that covers the same plan, terms, conditions, and provisions, then any loss will be split pro rata by limits.

As an example, the XYZ company's headquarters is insured for $1 million with two policies covering the same plan, terms, conditions, and provisions. ABC Insurance has a policy for $750,000; DEF Indemnity has a policy for $250,000. If the XYZ building suffers a $400,000 fire loss, the payments would be split as follows: ABC - $300,000; DEF - $100,000. It is important to note that the insured would be responsible for two deductibles under this scenario.

The second part of this condition makes the commercial property policy excess over any other policy that does not cover the same plan, terms, conditions, and provisions. Note that the commercial property policy is excess even if the insured cannot collect from the other insurer.

Policy Period, Coverage Territory

The commercial property policy covers losses that commence during the policy period, which is shown on the declarations page of the policy. The loss must also commence within the coverage territory: the United States (including territories and possessions); Puerto Rico; or Canada.

Subrogation

This condition defines the insurer's subrogation rights when it makes a payment under the policy. Many times an insurer will, in order to expedite the claim process, pay its insured for property that was damaged by someone else. This condition then allows the insurer to pursue the ultimate wrongdoer to recover the amount it paid to the insured.

The subrogation condition also preserves the rights of the insurer when it comes to third parties, such as a bailor or mortgagee. When it comes to getting money back from the ultimate wrong doer, the insurer is first in line (at least for the amount it paid).

At any time *prior to a loss* an insured may waive, in writing, possible recovery rights against anyone. However, once a loss has occurred the insured may waive those rights against only: another insured; a business that the insured owns or controls (or owns or controls the insured); a tenant of the insured.

Other Relevant Provisions of the Commercial Property Policy

While not designated as conditions, there are several provisions in the commercial property policy (the building and personal property coverage form) that operate as conditions.

Limits of Insurance and Deductible

The policy clearly states that the most it will pay is the limit of liability as shown on the declarations page.

The limits section goes on to indicate that the amounts of insurance under all coverage extensions are in addition to the policy limits. The same applies to the additional coverages of Fire Department Service Charge and Pollutant Cleanup and Removal. The section also provides $1,000 coverage for outdoor signs attached to buildings.

This section concludes by putting the additional coverage of Preservation of Property within the policy limits. Debris Removal was included here, as well, but the new Debris Removal additional coverage now describes the maximum payable under that coverage (see Chapter 2).

The deductible provision has been rewritten to more clearly show how the deductible applies. If a loss happens, the insurer first applies the coinsurance condition or agreed value option to arrive at the adjusted amount of loss. The deductible then applies to that adjusted amount.

Loss Conditions

In addition to the common policy conditions and the commercial property conditions, the commercial property policy contains a set of conditions that operate in case of a loss.

Abandonment and Appraisal

The first loss condition is abandonment. The insured may not simply abandon damaged property to the insurance company. The insurer has the right to the salvage value of property for which it makes total payment, but cannot be compelled to take damaged or destroyed property.

The second loss condition, appraisal, provides a method to settle differences between insured and insurer regarding the valuation of damaged property or the amount of the loss. In this event, each party selects its own appraiser. Then, the two appraisers select an umpire. If the appraisers cannot agree on an umpire, they may request that the umpire be chosen by a judge of a court having jurisdiction. The appraisers then separately value the property and set the value of the loss. If the appraisers are unable to agree, the matter goes to the umpire. A decision to which any two agree (either both appraisers or an appraiser and the umpire) is binding on both parties.

The condition goes on to state that each party must pay its own appraiser. The costs of the umpire and of the appraisal process are shared equally.

The condition ends with these words: "If there is an appraisal, we will still retain our right to deny the claim." The inclusion of this statement helps the insurer avoid the implication that by participating in the appraisal process, there is an implied agreement to pay the claim. It also prevents the insured from claiming that entering the appraisal process keeps the insurer from denying the claim further on down the road.

Appraisal of a Loss

A commercial property insured suffered a major fire loss. The insured first hired a public adjuster to help him. They submitted a proof of loss and awaited the insurer's decision. When the insured and the insurer could not agree on the amount of the loss, the dispute was submitted to appraisal, as outlined in Loss Condition 2.

The appraisers reached a decision favorable to the insured. At that point, the insurer decided that it wanted to go back and readjust the claim. The agent asked if the insurer was allowed to do that.

Once a claim goes through the appraisal process and an amount is set, the insurer no longer has the options it once had. The language clearly says that the decision of any two of the three (appraisers and umpire) will be binding on all parties.

An insured must submit a proof of loss, so that the insurer may investigate the claim. That was already done in this case.

The policy says, in Loss Condition 4, that the insurer will pay a loss within thirty days after receiving the proof of loss and an appraisal award has been made. In this case, the appraisal award was made. The insurer cannot now go back and decide to settle the claim in a different manner.

The Insured's Duties in the Event of Loss

The policy lists eight things that an insured must do in the event of loss or damage under the policy. It also specifies the right of the insurer to examine the insured under oath, without any other insured being present. The policy specifies that the insured must:

1. Notify the police if a law was broken.
2. Send the insurance company a notice of loss that includes a description of the property. (This description does not have to be writing but it must be given promptly.)
3. Provide a description of how, when, and where the loss or damage took place. This must be done as soon as possible.
4. Protect the covered property from any further damage and keep track of costs for emergency and temporary repairs to do so. This includes separating damaged from undamaged property, if feasible. The insured must document expenses incurred in preserving the property from further loss. Such documentation is necessary for consideration in the settlement of the claim. These expenses, if paid, are subject to the limit of insurance.
    Note that the insured must protect the covered property from any further damage, not just damage from a covered peril. However, the insurer is

not liable for subsequent loss or damage resulting from any uncovered cause of loss.

5.   Compile an inventory of damaged and undamaged property if the insurer so requests.

6.   Allow the insurer to inspect the property, including the insured's books and records. The insurer may also take samples of damaged and undamaged property. Comparing these types of property helps in the investigation of a loss.

7.   Submit a signed, sworn proof of loss if requested.

8.   Generally cooperate with the insurance company. Cooperation includes submitting to questions under oath. It also includes allowing the insurer to examine the insured's books and records. Any insured answering such questions in writing must sign his or her answers.

The current edition of the form states that the insurer may examine the insured under oath (a term that courts have held encompasses both oral and written examination). The insurer may examine insureds separately and out of the presence of other insureds. Following *USF&G v. Hill,* 722 S.W.2d 609 (1986), in which a Missouri appellate court found the insurer's right to examine insureds separately had to be made explicit in the policy or else the insurer had no such right, this language was added to the form.

Loss Payment

After a covered loss, the insurer has four options for settlement. The insurer will settle using one of the following four options:

1.   **The value of the property.** Previous editions of the commercial property policy did not define the word *value*. The 2000 edition adds the reference that the insurer will determine the value of the damaged property "in accordance with the Valuation Condition" (see below).

2.   **The cost to repair or replace the damaged property.** The 2000 edition reiterates the policy ordinance or law exclusion by specifically eliminating any insurance recovery for any extra costs due to the operation of building or zoning laws. The policy may have been made clearer here with a reference to the newly added additional coverage of increased cost of construction (see Chapter 2).

3.   **The insurer may take the property at an agreed or an appraised value.**

4. **The insurer may actually repair, rebuild, or replace the property with that of "like kind and quality."** This option also excludes any extra costs due to the operation of building laws. Again, a reference to the newly added additional coverage of "increased cost of construction" (see Chapter 2) would be helpful.

Within thirty days of receipt of the sworn proof of loss, the insurer must advise the insured which option it chooses. Whichever option is chosen, the insurer will never pay the insured more than the insured's financial interest in the property.

Property of others is also subject to the same four options above. However, the insurer deals directly with the owner of the property in the insured's stead. Again, the insurer owes the owner of the property no more than his financial interest in it.

Sometimes the owners of damaged property may bring suit against the insured. The insurer promises to defend such suits at its own expense.

Once the insurer receives the signed, sworn proof of loss and reaches an agreement with the insured regarding the value of the property, the loss will paid within thirty days. Reaching an agreement on the value includes the award of an appraisal.

As mentioned earlier, actual cash value (ACV) can have many meanings. In actual usage, it has come to have three:

1. **Fair market value**, which is usually described as the price a willing buyer would pay to buy property from a willing seller in a free market.

2. **Replacement cost less depreciation**, which is generally accepted to mean the cost to replace property at the time of the loss minus its physical depreciation.

3. The **broad evidence rule** which involves a judicious application of either one or two to the unique circumstance of the claim, whichever is more favorable to the insured.

State laws vary considerably on the definition. In California, ACV means "fair market value" *Cheeks v. California Fair Plan,* 61 Cal. App. 4th 423 (1998). In *Cheeks* the Court admonished insurers: "If it [the insurer] wants to determine actual cash value on the basis of replacement cost less depreciation, all it has to do is say so in the policy." Courts in Pennsylvania have taken the entirely opposite view that ACV means replacement cost (*Judge v. Celina Mut. Ins. Co.* 449 A.2d 658 [1982]).

Fair market value, replacement cost, and *depreciation* are all fairly common and have commonly accepted meanings. They have been used over and over in establishing the value of damaged property.

The broad evidence rule, on the other hand, tries to bring other factors into consideration. *McAnarney v. Newark Fire Insurance Co.,* 159 N.E. 902 is a leading case on this question. The case involved the fire destruction of an old brewery that could not be used because of the National Prohibition Act. The building apparently had no other economic use, and the owner had advertised it for sale, unsuccessfully, for a fraction of the amount of insurance carried. In striking a compromise between the insured and the insurer, the court said ". . . Where insured buildings have been destroyed, the trier of fact may, and should, call to its aid in order to effectuate complete indemnity, every fact and circumstance which would logically tend to the formation of a correct estimate of the loss. It may consider original cost and cost of reproduction; the opinions upon value given by qualified witnesses; declarations against interest which may have been made by the insured; the gainful uses to which the buildings may have been put; as well as any other reasonable factor tending to throw light on the subject." In so reasoning, the court decided on a value between replacement cost less depreciation and the market value of the building.

The most important point regarding the broad evidence rule was quoted in the McAnarney case. The court said that "every fact and circumstance which would logically tend to the formation of a correct estimate of the loss," including the economic value of the property, should be considered in determining the actual cash value.

Valuing business personal property may be less difficult, because the value of the contents is not tied to the value of the land (as with a building). The problem with using replacement cost less depreciation is that business personal property is often diverse; is acquired over a period of time; and depreciates at various rates. Often receipts are unavailable.

Market value is also not a reliable guide. Few businesses would want their fairly new office furniture replaced with similar furniture that had been rented to others.

Another problem for businesses is the value of stocks of merchandise and raw materials. These items usually do not suffer depreciation. In such a case, the proper measure of recovery is the cost of replacing them at the current market value, less any salvage value. (Merchandise that has become shopworn and has deteriorated in value should, of course, be subject to depreciation.) Here again, the measure of recovery might be more or less than the original cost. It should be remembered, however, that the standard of recovery is the cost to the insured, not the price at which he or she expects to sell it to customers. (Rules in most states permit use of a market value or selling price clause which converts, for some insureds such as manufacturers and retailers, finished stock from actual cash value to selling price less discounts and unincurred expenses. Form CP 99 30 provides for valuation based on selling price, less any applicable discounts and expenses, for all completed stock (not just finished stock that is sold but not delivered, as in the building and personal property coverage form).

Recovered Property

This condition provides a method for loss readjustment in case stolen property is recovered. Here, the insured has the option to return the amount of any claim payment in return for the original item. Note that the insurer cannot require the insured to return the payment and take back the recovered property. Recovery expenses and any necessary repairs to the property are borne by the insurance company up to the applicable limit of liability.

Vacancy

The current version has two parts. The first defines building for both an owner-occupant and a tenant. The second describes the manner in which losses to a vacant building are handled.

The form defines building for a tenant as that portion rented or leased to the insured. The tenant's portion is vacant when it does not contain enough business personal property to conduct normal business.

The 2000 edition turns some of the language around, for a clearer picture of what is considered a vacant building. The policy says that a building is vacant if the insured does not rent at least 31 percent of the floor space to others, or if the insured does not use at least 31 percent of the floor space for his own operations.

Under earlier editions of the form, a building with the furniture and fixtures of a business—but from which the stock had been removed—would be considered vacant since customary operations are not possible without stock. In the 2000 edition, a building containing fixtures, fittings, and business personal property would still be considered vacant if it were being underutilized. This vacancy provision could cause problems for inner-city insureds, where a storefront operation is the only going concern in a multiple story building. Despite the going concern on the first floor, if less than 31 percent of the building is unrented or not used for customary operations, the building is considered vacant.

Prior to 1995, only buildings under construction were exempt from the vacancy provision. The 1995 version added buildings under renovation and this exception remains in the 2000 edition. Before this wording was added, adjusters tended to apply the exemption only to new buildings, because that is the implication of the word construction. *Webster's Third New International Dictionary* defines construction as "the act of putting parts together to form a complete integrated object: Fabrication." Insureds argued that the exposure was the same, and oftentimes that was probably true. However, the times when the building and personal property coverage form applies—by coverage extension—to a building under construction are rare and are limited by the provisions of the form (thirty days). An existing structure, on the other hand, can now be subjected to renovation at any time with no requirement of notice to the insurance company, since it will not be considered vacant. However, the insured must be careful of a coinsurance problem if much value is added prior to notifying the insurer.

The second part of the vacancy condition describes how losses are handled when the building has been vacant for more than sixty consecutive days (or longer, if so endorsed). There is no coverage for damage from any of the following causes of loss: vandalism; building glass breakage; water damage; theft or attempted theft; or sprinkler leakage (unless steps have been taken to protect the system against freezing). The policy covers loss from a covered peril in a vacant building at a reduction of 15 percent.

Valuation

The commercial property policy typically covers loss to covered property at actual cash value. The does, however, provide five exceptions:

1. If the insured meets the coinsurance requirement, the policy covers any loss under $2,500 at replacement cost. However, the following building items are still subject to ACV adjustment: awnings, floor coverings, appliances, outdoor equipment and furniture. The 1995 form added that replacement cost does not include any extra cost due to the operation of building laws. Again, a reference to the additional coverage, increased cost of construction, would be helpful here.

2. The policy covers stock at its selling price less any applicable discounts and normally incurred expenses. If the insured sells widgets at $100 each, and offers a discount of 2/10,net 30 (2 percent discount if paid within ten days, entire amount due within thirty days), with $10 in shipping expense, the recovery on the $100 item might be $88 ($100 selling price less 2 percent discount minus shipping fee of $10). Trade and business practice, along with examination of books and records, determines the actual valuation.

3. The policy agrees to replace damaged glass with safety glass if required by law.

4. Tenants improvements and betterments are adjusted at ACV, if repairs are made promptly. Note that the policy does not define promptly.

    If the insured does not make repairs promptly to his improvements and betterments, the insurer offers a proportional settlement via the following formula (example below). The original cost of the improvement times the number of days from: 1) the loss to the lease's expiration, or 2) the expiration of the renewal option period if applicable. The amount computed is then divided by the number of days from the installation of the improvement to the expiration of the lease or the expiration of the renewal option period. The inclusion of renewal option periods addresses the long standing question of whether such periods should be considered during loss settlement calculations to provide a better restitution for an insured's use interest in a damaged improvement. Assume a tenant holds a one-year lease for a commercial building that expires on July 31. The lease contains a one-year renewal option. On March 3, the tenant installs paneling costing $1,500. A fire occurs on June 2 that causes damage so extensive that the insured closes the business permanently. Had no loss occurred, the tenant would have stayed in business and exercised the renewal option.

Without taking the renewal option period into consideration, the insured stands to receive a $600 payment for the improvement ($1,500 x 60/150 = $600; where 60 equals the days from loss to lease expiration and 150 equals the days from improvement installation to lease expiration). When the renewal option period (365 days) is included in the calculation, the result of the proportional loss settlement is $1,238—[$1,500 x (60 + 365/150 + 365)] = $1,238—a significant difference.

These formulas come into play only if the insured does not make the repairs promptly, thus disqualifying him from an actual cash value recovery. The insured receives nothing from the insurer if someone other than the tenant (the landlord, for instance) repairs damaged improvements.

5. Valuable papers and records (whether written, electronic, or magnetic) are valued at the cost of the blank materials for reproducing the records plus the labor costs for transcribing or copying them from duplicates. The 2000 form provides up to $2,500 under a coverage extension for the cost to research and restore records when no duplicates exist. This provision does not contemplate replacing any prepackaged software programs. Instead, an actual cash value settlement applies to these items.

Valuation and Selling Price

A load of nonalcoholic beer was damaged when the load shifted during transit. The insured's customer made a claim against the insured for replacement of the shipment and a dispute over the value of the beer ensued.

Even though the buyer of the beer was to pay $4,300 for it, the replacement cost for the damaged goods to the insured was $10,260. It is standard practice in that industry to reduce the price on one product and increase prices on other products in order to maintain (or increase) profit margins.

The insurer took the position that it would pay the smallest of the following: replacement cost or actual cash value at the time of the loss. They state that at the time of the loss, the value was the selling price, $4,300.

However, just because the insured sold the beer for less than it cost him does not reduce the value of the beer to that amount. For example, you may buy a $150,000 house for $75,000, but the value remains at $150,000.

What needs to be established is the ACV of the beer. The insured needs to demonstrate that this practice of selling certain items for less than their cost to him is a standard business practice in this industry. In the absence of fraud, the insurer owes the amount that the insured paid for the beer.

Additional Conditions

The commercial property policy contains two additional conditions: coinsurance and mortgageholders.

Coinsurance

The principle of coinsurance has long been a source of confusion for insureds (and even for many in the insurance business). This principle says that in exchange for a reduced rate, the insured must agree to maintain a specified relationship between values and amount of insurance (e.g., 80 percent).

For example, a building with a value of $1,000,000 must be insured for at least $800,000. If the insured agrees to carry this amount of coverage, he may get a rate of fifty cents per thousand dollars of coverage. However, if he chooses to carry only $500,000, that rate might jump to seventy five cents or a dollar.

The building and personal property coverage provides three examples actually written into the insuring contract. The commercial property policy explains the mechanics of coinsurance with a step-by-step description. It also examines the ramifications of a coinsurance penalty. Examples show the effects of coinsurance computations in three different situations: where limits are inadequate; where limits are adequate; and where a blanket limit exists.

Since 1986, every version of the coinsurance provision found in commercial property form CP 00 10 applies the deductible after the calculation of the coinsurance penalty. The wording in the 2000 policy has been rearranged to emphasize this point. Prior to 1986, the forms applied the deductible prior to the calculation of the coinsurance penalty, a manner more advantageous to the insured.

The following is an example of the interaction between the deductible and the coinsurance clause: Two insureds each have a $50,000 loss under policies with a $250 deductible. Insured A is in compliance with the coinsurance requirement and recovers $49,750 ($50,000 minus $250). Insured B is underinsured and must accept 25 percent of the loss as a coinsurer. Insured B will collect $37,500 (75 percent of $50,000) less the $250 deductible for a net recovery of $37,250. Had insured B been covered under a pre-1986 commercial property form, he would have collected $37,316 (75 percent of $49,750). Subtracting the deductible before calculating the coinsurance penalty makes a difference of $66 for the insured.

Coinsurance Application in a Total Loss

At a seminar covering the ISO Building and Personal Property Form, CP 00 10, the following problem on coinsurance was presented:

A building with a replacement cost of $85,000 and an actual cash value of $70,000, suffered a total loss from fire. It was insured for replacement cost with a limit of liability of $50,000. The policy contained a $250 deductible and an 80 percent coinsurance requirement. Following the example included in the coinsurance clause of form CP 00 10, these steps were used to determine the insurer's liability under the policy:

(A) If the building is replaced:
   (1) the $85,000 replacement value of the building times 80 percent (.80) = $68,000, the amount of insurance needed to satisfy the coinsurance requirement;
   (2) $50,000/$68,000 = 73.5 percent of the loss is payable by the insurer;
   (3) 73.5 percent (.735) times $50,000 (total amount of the covered loss) = $36,750;
   (4) $36,750 - $250 deductible = $36,500, the portion of the loss at replacement cost paid by the insurer.
(B) If the building is not replaced:
   (1) the $70,000 actual cash value of the building times 80 percent = $56,000, the amount of insurance needed to satisfy the coinsurance requirement;
   (2) $50,000/$56,000 = 89.3 percent of the loss payable by the insurer;
   (3) 89.3 percent times $50,000 (total amount of the covered loss) = $44,650;
   (4) $44,650 - $250 deductible = $44,400, the portion of the loss at ACV paid by the insurer.

An attendee at the seminar believed the insured should receive the full limit of insurance minus the deductible, because ISO's provision for the total amount of covered loss should refer to the full amount of a loss insured by a covered peril, and not to the limit of insurance provided under the policy.

ISO says that it has always intended to apply the deductible to the adjusted amount of a loss, i.e. after the application of any coinsurance penalty or the agreed amount provision. The wording in the 2000 edition clarifies this intent.

While ISO introduced into the text of the simplified form some examples of how the coinsurance clause operates, they did not include an example like the one

(scenario continues next page)

(continued from previous page)

in this seminar; i.e. one that shows a loss in excess of both the limit of insurance and the amount payable after application of the coinsurance penalty.

Step three of the coinsurance provision says, "Multiply the total amount of the covered loss before the application of any deductible by the figure determined in step two." The seminar leader has interpreted the total amount of the covered loss to be the limit of insurance—$50,000—producing the anomaly of a $7,900 higher recovery for ACV than for replacement cost.

This is incorrect. The fire loss is a covered loss and the total amount of the covered loss is $85,000 at replacement cost or $70,000 at ACV. If these numbers are substituted for the $50,000 figure in step three, the result for both examples is $62,500. The $250 deductible is then subtracted from this amount (not from the $50,000 limit of insurance as the subscriber suggests), leaving $62,250. As this is more than the limit of insurance, a fifth step must be added to the computation—apply the lower of the amount payable under step four or the limit of insurance—in this case the $50,000 limit of insurance.

So the insurer should pay the $50,000 limit of insurance for either the replacement or the ACV loss.

The rewording of the coinsurance clause in the 1986 and subsequent ISO building and personal property forms is less precise than the previous wording. With the current wording, it might be reasonable that any loss exceeding the policy's limit is not covered by the policy; therefore, the total amount of the covered loss cannot be more than the policy limit. However, a more favorable reading (to which the insured is entitled because it is a) more favorable and b) supported by a lengthy tradition of coinsurance application) is that a covered loss is one reached by a covered peril and the total amount is just that—the total amount of the loss that is covered by the policy regardless of whether covered in full. ISO's old general property form (CF 00 11) shows the intent that the coinsurance clause apply to the amount of the total loss more clearly by saying that the company "shall not be liable for a greater proportion of any loss to the property covered . . ."

The coinsurance clause is designed to invoke the penalty only on partial losses. This intention would be forfeited by applying the coinsurance penalty to the policy limit.

Mortgageholders

This condition spells out the rights and duties of any mortgagees or trustees (here referred to as mortgageholders) that are named on the declarations.

In the event of a claim, any listed mortgageholder receives payment for losses as interests may appear. However, the insured must be in compliance with all coverage terms. Even if foreclosure proceedings or similar actions have begun on a building that suffers a loss, a mortgageholder may collect a loss payment.

Further, even if the insurer denies a claim to the insured (due to the insured's actions or lack of compliance with the terms for coverage), the mortgageholder may still collect. The mortgageholder must pay any premium due and submit the appropriate proof of loss.

Additionally, a mortgageholder must notify the insurance company of any known change in ownership, occupancy, or increase of hazard. When these conditions are satisfied, all terms of the building and personal property coverage form become applicable to the mortgageholder.

If partial claim payment is made to a mortgageholder (and not to an insured), the following occurs: the insurance company inherits a proportion of the mortgageholder's rights under the mortgage based on the extent of claim payment; and the mortgageholder still retains subrogation rights and may attempt to recover the full amount of the claim.

The insurance company may, at its option, pay the mortgage holder the full amount of the principal and interest on the mortgage in exchange for transfer of the mortgage to the insurance company. In this case, the insured continues mortgage payments, but to the insurance company instead of the original mortgageholder.

If the insurer cancels the policy, it must send written notice to the mortgageholder thirty days before the effective date of cancellation. If the cancellation is due to nonpayment of premium by the insured, then notice to the mortgageholder is only ten days. In the event of nonrenewal, the insurer must also send a ten-day notice to the mortgageholder.

Loss During Foreclosure

A large warehouse was insured for over a million dollars. The mortgageholder foreclosed on the property. Shortly after the foreclosure, a fire did nearly $700,000 in damage to the warehouse. The agent wondered about the insurer's obligation to the mortgageholder.

The amount of the loss does not determine the insurer's obligation to the

(scenario continues next page)

(continued from previous page)

mortgageholder; the amount of debt still owed on the property does. That amount is the mortgageholder's insurable interest.

The insurer's obligation to the named insured owner is the value of the loss limited to the former owner's insurable interest. If the owner of the building has complied with all the policy conditions, then the insurer owes the loss to the named insured and the mortgageholder as their interests may appear. The amount of each of their interest is a legal matter and best left to the lawyers.

Chapter 6

Builders Risk

Buildings under construction are not eligible for standard treatment under the commercial property policy. Due to the different exposures faced by a building under construction, such as an increased risk of theft and vandalism, different rates and forms must be used. Form CP 00 20, the Builders Risk Coverage Form combined with one of the causes of loss forms covers buildings under construction. It also covers: additions and alterations; foundations; temporary structures; materials and supplies owned by the insured; and on a limited basis, building materials and supplies of others.

All buildings under construction are eligible for the builders risk coverage form. Even some buildings that, once occupied, are not eligible for the commercial property policy because of use occupancy may still be covered on the CP 00 20 while under construction. Such exposures include: boarding or rooming houses (one to four units), farm properties, and dwellings.

Builders risk coverage is written for a minimum one-year term to cover a new building or structure under construction or an existing structure undergoing additions, alterations, or repairs. The rules state that policy inception should begin no later than the date that construction starts above the level of the lowest basement floor or if there is no basement, the date construction begins. The rules permit pro-rata cancellation when construction is completed, whether or not insurance on the completed structure is rewritten with the same company or companies. If the policy is canceled before the structure is completed, the general cancellation provisions found in the common policy conditions apply.

Blanket insurance, covering more than one building or structure, is subject to the rating rules for such coverage. This is useful for housing projects and other large risks with several units being erected at the same time.

A builders risk policy is written for the completed value of the insured building. This amount should include the value of all permanent fixtures and decorations that will become part of the building. The rules include the following warning: "Contract price does not necessarily equal the full value at completion." The rates contemplate the fact that the insurer does not face the total amount of exposure for the entire policy term.

While not described as a coinsurance penalty, the builders risk form does penalize the insured in the event of a loss when the limit of liability is inadequate. The policy calls for a reduction in loss payment by the percentage the customer is underinsured. If the building has a completed value of $200,000, but is only insured for $100,000, any loss payment will be reduced by 50 percent.

The builders risk insured with more than one location may choose to cover all locations on a blanket basis. The countrywide rules contain a formula for calculating the blanket average rate.

Value of the Building on the Completion Date

The builders risk coverage form (CP 00 20) has what amounts to a 100 percent coinsurance clause based on the value of the building on its completion date. But it is not always clear what comprises the completed building's value. More specifically, assume an insured is constructing a building that has a great deal of asphalt blacktop and a sizable volume of poured concrete in the footings and base slabs. The insured might not feel that these items should be included in the amount of insurance, although they are included in the contract price of the building.

The following is an example of why these items need to be insured. Keep in mind that these items will be excluded upon completion.

The builders risk coverage form applies to the building described in the policy declarations while in the course of construction. It does not contain the exclusion of foundations below the lowest basement (or, lacking a basement below the surface of the ground) found in the building and personal property coverage form. In fact, the builders risk form explicitly states that it covers foundations: "1) Covered Property ... Building Under Construction, meaning the building or structure described in the declarations while in the course of construction, including: a) Foundations; b) The following property: . . . 3) Your building materials and supplies used for construction; provided such property is intended to be permanently located in or on the building . . or within 100 feet of its premises; . ."

(scenario continues next page)

(scenario continued from previous page)

Unlike the case with a completed structure, there is a time during the course of construction when the footings and slabs the insured would like to exclude are exposed to loss. For instance, fire or wind could destroy the forms before the concrete is poured and cause a legitimate builders risk loss.

If construction has not yet begun—and insurance should certainly be in place before construction begins—the insured and the underwriter might agree to write an endorsement eliminating coverage for foundations, materials, and supplies connected with them in exchange for an appropriate reduction in the amount of insurance.

If construction is beyond the foundation stage, the insured has had the protection of the insurance while it was needed and there would be no justification for eliminating foundation values from the completed building value.

The same can be said for the asphalt blacktop. The builders risk form affords coverage for building materials and supplies used in construction provided the materials are to remain permanently in or on the building or structure described in the Declarations or within 100 feet of its premises. Perhaps the reason insureds generally decline this type of coverage is that the risk of damage or loss to the materials seems low. Instead, insureds often prefer to carry the risk themselves. Again, if the underwriter agrees, the value of the blacktopping might be removed from the completed value of the building in a preconstruction agreement, if the insured is willing to accept an endorsement excluding coverage of materials and supplies used in that operation.

Covered Property

The builders risk form covers direct loss or damage to covered property. The list of covered property is short, compared to the commercial property policy, because the property covered by the commercial property policy is being put to its intended use, while a builders risk policy covers property under construction.

The builders risk form covers the building under construction (as described in the Declarations) and its foundation. The form also provides coverage for the following: fixtures and machinery; equipment used to service the building; and the insured's building materials and supplies used for construction. The insured must "[intend that these items] be permanently located in or on the building" or within 100 feet of the premises.

The form does not define the phrase *in the course of construction*; therefore common usage will prevail. According to *Webster's Third New*

International Dictionary, construction is "the act of putting together to form a complete integrated object: Fabrication."

However, in *Patton v. Aetna Insurance Co.*, 595 F. Supp. 533 (1984), the court expanded the meaning. The court ruled that the term includes activities related to, but prior to the commencement of construction. The case concerned a builders risk policy issued to cover a building scheduled for renovation. A fire destroyed a large portion of the building. At the time of the fire, only preparatory work towards the renovation had been done by the insured. This included removing the furnace and lattice work, unhooking the gas and plumbing lines, and engaging in discussions with contractors regarding the lowering of the building. A United States district court in Mississippi determined that since the insured and the insuring company understood that renovation of the house was intended, it was reasonable to interpret construction to mean alterations of any type, whether additions or removals. As a result, the activities of the insured were considered "construction" and thereby covered under the provisions of the builders risk policy.

Note that there is no coverage for business personal property. Nor is there any coverage for the property of others. The builders risk form does, however, provide an additional coverage in the amount of $5,000 for material and supplies owned by others.

Temporary structures built on the premises are covered property if there is no other insurance on them. Such structures include: cribbing, scaffolding, and construction forms. (As a matter of interest, the term "cribbing" comes from the same root word as "corncrib" and connotes a structure built for storage.)

Property Not Covered

As with the property covered section, this section is also rather short as compared to the commercial property policy. Again, much of the property indicated as not covered under the commercial property policy is property that would only be present at a business already in operation.

The form specifically excludes land and water. It also excludes the following items (but coverage may be bought back via endorsement): lawns, trees, shrubs, plants; radio or television antennas, including lead-in wiring, masts or towers; and detached signs.

Although the builders risk form excludes land and water, it provides the same additional coverage for pollutant cleanup as does the commercial property policy. The form provides $10,000 of annual coverage for the costs to extract pollutants from land or water at the described premises. The word pollutants is defined, as in the commercial property policy: "any solid, liquid, gaseous or thermal irritant or contaminant, including smoke, vapor, soot, fumes, acids, alkalis, chemicals and waste. Waste includes materials to be recycled, reconditioned or reclaimed."

Covered Causes of Loss

As mentioned above, the builders risk form is combined with one of the causes of loss forms: CP 10 10; CP 10 20; or CP 10 30. For a discussion of these forms, see Chapters 3 and 4.

Additional Coverages

The builders risk form provides four additional coverages: debris removal, preservation of property, fire department service charge, and pollutant clean up and removal. These coverages are the same as provided in the commercial property policy. For further discussion, see Chapter 2.

Coverage Extensions

The builders risk form provides two coverage extensions: building supplies and materials of others; and sod, trees, shrubs, and plants.

The first extension pays up to $5,000 per location for material and supplies owned by others. The insured may purchase a higher amount of this coverage by making an entry on the policy declarations. This is an additional amount of insurance and applies at each described premises. These losses are settled for the account of the owner of the property. This coverage extension applies when the property of others is in the insured's care, custody, or control; and is located in or on the described building or within 100 feet of the premises.

In order for this extension to apply, the insured must intend to make the property a permanent part of the building (i.e., air conditioning or heating equipment), thus precluding coverage for the builder's machinery and equipment used in the construction. Builders risk coverage form CP 00 20 was released in 1986 with no separate item of coverage for builders machinery, tools, and equipment as found on the previous builders risk forms. According to explanatory information from ISO, the provision was deleted because broader coverage is available to builders and contractors through inland marine policies.

However, the current edition of the form provides limited coverage for builders' machinery, tools, and equipment, when special causes of loss form CP 10 30 is attached to the builders risk coverage form. The property must be owned by or entrusted to the insured. The coverage appears in item 3.d. under the limitations section C) of the special causes of loss form. It provides coverage against the specified causes of loss to builders' machinery, tools, and equipment.

Trees, Shrubs and Plants

Sod, trees, shrubs, and plants not covered under the builders risk policy. However, coverage extension b.—new with the 1995 version—provides limited coverage for these items. It covers such items for the perils of fire, lightning, explosion, riot or civil commotion, and aircraft. Coverage is limited to $1,000 per occurrence, regardless of the type or number of items lost, with a limit of $250 for any one tree, shrub, or plant.

Limits of Insurance

The limits of insurance as shown on the declarations page apply to the covered property on a per occurrence basis. One sublimit applies: $1,000 per outdoor sign per occurrence.

The amounts payable under the coverage extensions—building supplies and materials of others and sod, trees, shrubs, and plants—apply in addition to the limit of liability. Likewise, two additional coverages are outside the limit of liability: fire department service charge and pollutant clean up and removal.

The amounts payable under the other two additional coverages, debris removal and preservation of property, are included in the limit of liability. The debris removal provision contains the same $10,000 extra amount payable under certain conditions as in the commercial property policy.

Deductible

The deductible applies after any deduction required by the additional condition, need for adequate insurance (see below).

Loss Conditions

The following builders risk loss conditions are exactly the same as those found in the commercial property policy: abandonment, appraisal, duties in the event of loss or damage, and recovered property.

The 2000 edition adds wording to the loss payment condition. It now specifies that the insurer determines the value of covered property in accordance with the applicable terms of the valuation condition. The only valuation method used is actual cash value (ACV). Remember that the policy does not define ACV.

The vacancy loss condition, found in the commercial property policy, is not present in the builders risk form because any building under construction is usually vacant. The rates for builders risk contemplate this increase in exposure.

Additional Conditions

The 2000 builders risk form contains four additional conditions (down from five in previous versions): mortgageholders, need for adequate insurance, restriction of additional coverage—collapse, and when coverage ceases.

The mortgageholders condition is the same as that found in the commercial property policy.

The additional condition, *need for adequate insurance*, resembles the coinsurance condition of the commercial property policy and operates in the same fashion. It serves to penalize the insured in the event of a loss if he does not insure the building to 100 percent of its completed value. The policy calls for a reduction in loss payment by the percentage the customer is underinsured. If the building has a completed value of $200,000, but is only insured for $100,000, any loss payment will be reduced by 50 percent.

The broad and special causes of loss forms include collapse as an additional coverage. One of the covered causes of collapse is use of defective material or methods in construction, remodeling or renovation if the collapse occurs during the course of the construction, remodeling or renovation. The builders risk form eliminates this covered cause of collapse. Thus, the builders risk policy provides no coverage for collapse caused by the use of defective material or methods.

The builders risk coverage form says that coverage ceases when one of the following first occurs:

a.   the policy expires or is canceled;
b.   the property is accepted by the purchaser;
c.   the named insured's interest in the property ceases;
d.   the named insured abandons the construction with no intention to complete it;
e.   unless the insurer specifies otherwise in writing:
      (1)   ninety days after construction is complete; or
      (2)   sixty days after any building described in the Declarations is:
             (a)   Occupied in whole or in part; or
             (b)   Put to its intended use.

Builders risk rates do not contemplate the increased exposures of an occupied premises. However, the policy does not define occupied. In the past, courts have often held that a building is not considered occupied until it is put to the practical and substantial use for which it was designed. This definition of occupied, then becomes synonymous with a building being put to its intended use. The builders risk policy has employed the current policy language since 1985.

The previous edition of the builders risk form covered property in transit for $5,000 if subject to special causes of loss, CP 10 30. The previous edition of form CP 10 30 only covered this property for $1,000. This additional coverage has been removed from the builders risk form because the CP 10 30 now provides this coverage in the amount of $5,000.

Builders Risk Coverage Options

The builders risk program has six optional endorsements to modify the basic form. They include: Building Renovations; Builders' Risk Reporting Form; Separate Or Subcontractor's Interests; Collapse During Construction; Theft of Building Materials, Fixtures, Machinery, Equipment; and Building Materials And Supplies of Others.

Building Renovations

When renovations are made to existing buildings, builders' risk coverage may be amended to exclude the value of existing realty. This endorsement, Builders Risk Renovations (CP 11 13), changes the definition of covered property. Instead of insuring the building under construction, this endorsement covers renovations under construction. It provides coverage only for the value of building improvements, alterations, or repairs under construction. Unlike the CP 00 20, the CP 11 13 does not cover foundations. It does cover fixtures, equipment used to service the building, and building materials. These last three items must be intended for use in the building or within 100 feet of the premises. This endorsement adds to property not covered: the value of buildings or structures existing prior to construction of the improvements, alterations or repairs.

This endorsement also modifies the condition need for adequate insurance. Recall that this condition acts like a 100 percent coinsurance clause, in that it requires insurance in the full amount of the completed value of the structure. Since a completed structure already exists, that condition becomes impractical. Instead, form CP 11 13 requires the insured to carry 100 percent of the value of the improvements, alterations, or repairs at the described premises. When using this endorsement, the condition *when coverage ceases* does not apply.

Builders' Risk Reporting Form

The insured may choose to report the monthly values of the building under construction using endorsement CP 11 05. It requires the insured to choose a date when values will be reported each month. This choice must be made within thirty days of coverage inception.

If the insured does not make the required reports (on form CP 11 06), the policy provides for two different penalties. Being late with a report relegates loss adjustment to the last reported value. If the insured does not file any reports, then the building is valued at ACV as of the inception date.

Endorsement CP 11 05 removes the condition "need for adequate insurance." However, it still calls for losses to be adjusted by the proportion of values last reported to the ACV of the property at the time of loss. Total loss payment is still limited to the limit of liability—even if the reported values exceed that amount.

Because the values at risk change, the premium changes as well. The initial premium is based on the ACV of the property at policy inception. Then, the insurer makes adjustments based on the reported values.

Separate or Subcontractors Interest

The insured may also choose to cover or exclude the interests of other contractors or subcontractors. The exclusion endorsement is CP 11 14. This endorsement adds to the definition of property not covered the value of the installation that the contractor makes at the described location. Such value includes: labor, materials, and supplies. The endorsement also removes such an installation from the requirements under need for adequate insurance.

Endorsement CP 11 15 covers the interests of other contractors or subcontractors. It does just the opposite of what is described in the previous paragraph. It adds labor, materials, and supplies to the definition of *covered* property, and specifies that the installation described is the only item to which the condition "need for adequate insurance" applies.

Collapse During Construction

If the insured chooses broad or special causes of loss coverage, the builders risk form removes coverage for collapse during construction. Endorsement CP 11 20 restores this coverage for an additional premium. The rates for this coverage are published in the multistate pages. However, if the policy covers an architect, engineer, or building trade contractor as an insured or additional insured, the rate is increased five times.

Theft of Building Materials, Fixtures, Machinery, Equipment

Endorsement CP 11 21 covers, for theft and attempted theft, building materials, fixtures, machinery and equipment, that are intended to become a permanent part of the building if they are located within 100 feet of the building. The amount of insurance shown on this endorsement is separate from the amount of coverage shown on the Declarations as applicable to the building. The minimum deductible for this form is $1,000 and applies separately from the deductible under the builders risk policy.

In order for coverage to apply, there must be a watchman on duty during the hours when construction is not being conducted. If no watchman is on duty, there is no coverage.

The endorsement defines what does *not* constitute theft or attempted theft:

1.   dishonest or criminal acts by the named insured; any of the named insured's partners, employees, directors, trustees or authorized representatives; any contractors or subcontractors or their respective employees; or anyone to whom the property is entrusted.

2.   voluntary parting with any property by the named insured or anyone else to whom the property is entrusted, if induced to do so by any fraudulent scheme, trick, device or false pretense.

3.   property that is missing, where the only evidence of loss or damage is a shortage disclosed on taking inventory, or other instances where there is no physical evidence to indicate what happened to the property.

Building Materials and Supplies of Others

For an additional premium, the insured may choose to increase the coverage provided for these items. The basic amount is $5,000. The increase is indicated on the declarations page.

Need for Builders Risk on Renovations to Existing Building

The question has been asked, when, if at any time, would a builders risk policy need to be written in conjunction with a commercial property form on an existing building undergoing remodeling or renovation?

For a building owner, there is no reason to have separate builders risk coverage applying in conjunction with a standard commercial property policy on renovations to an existing covered building.

The standard commercial property form covers additions under construction, alterations, and repairs to the building or structure. It further covers materials,

(scenario continues next page)

(continued from previous page)

equipment, supplies, and temporary structures, on or within 100 feet of the described premises used for making additions, alterations, or repairs to the building. Note, however, that coverage for these items applies only if not covered by other insurance. Therefore, if the owner bought separate builders risk coverage on such a project, there would be no coverage under the commercial property form.

The policy, however, covers property owned by the insured. There would be no coverage, for example, of equipment or tools of a contractor unless the tools could be said to be in the care, custody, or control of the insured (and therefore covered as personal property of others).

Chapter 7

Other Coverage Forms

In addition to the coverage parts already discussed, the commercial property program offers these others: Leasehold Interest, Mortgagee E&O, Tobacco in Sales Warehouses, Condominium Associations, Condominium Commercial Unit-Owners, and Legal Liability. The glass coverage form (CP 00 15) available in previous versions has been withdrawn.

While these forms are similar to the commercial property policy, they have been modified to meet the particular needs of the entity being covered. Those modifications are the subject of this chapter.

Leasehold Interest

Often the tenant of a building may have a favorable lease. However, if property at the location suffers damage, the tenant may lose the advantage of that favorable lease (the leasehold interest). Note that the form refers to "property" and not to "covered property." Thus, the damage leading to the payment may be to the building (owned by someone else) or to the insured's property located in the rented location. Leasehold interest insurance (form CP 00 60) protects the tenant from this possibility. A building owner, on the other hand, would look to his business income coverage to pay his rental income in case of covered loss to the property.

What is Insured

The form defines four types of leasehold interest: tenants lease interest, bonus payments, improvements and betterments, and prepaid rent. Tenants lease interest may take one of two forms:

1.   The tenant occupies the premises under a favorable lease. The leasehold interest is the difference between the actual rental value of the premises and the rent payable for the unexpired term of the lease.
2.   The tenant sublets all or part of the premises. The leasehold interest is the profit the tenant-insured receives through subleasing for the unexpired term of the sublease.

For the second type of leasehold interest, an insured may pay an up-front bonus to obtain a favorable lease. If the bonus is nonrefundable, the monthly leasehold interest on such cash bonus is the original cost of the bonus divided by the number of months remaining in the lease at the time the bonus was paid. For example, if the bonus paid at the inception of the lease is $5,000 and the lease is for three years, the monthly leasehold interest is $138.89 ($5,000 divided by 36). A bonus does not include rent, whether or not prepaid, or security.

Third, if a tenant makes improvements to the premises, the unamortized portion of payments for those improvements represents a leasehold interest. The monthly leasehold interest in the improvements and betterments is the original cost of the improvements and betterments divided by the number of months remaining in the lease at the time of installation. If the installation of the improvements and betterments increases the rental value of the premises, the monthly leasehold interest is the increase in rental value divided by the number of months remaining in the lease at the time of installation.

For example: an insured currently leases his retail outlet for $1,000 per month. In the third month of the lease, he adds improvements and betterments to the store that result in an increase in the rental value of $6,000 per year. This insured's increase in monthly leasehold interest would be calculated: $6,000 divided by 9 months, or $666.

The final type of leasehold interest is prepaid rent. If the insured has prepaid rent and it is not refundable, the unamortized portion is insured. However, this does not include the customary rent due at any rental period (monthly or otherwise).

Causes of Loss, Exclusions, and Limitations

For these items, the leasehold interest form refers to the appropriate causes of loss form. In order for leasehold interest to be payable, property at the insured premises must suffer direct damage by a covered cause of loss.

Each of the causes of loss forms contains an identical special exclusions section regarding the leasehold interest coverage form. There are two provisions.

1. The building ordinance or law exclusion does not apply to claims for leasehold interest. Therefore, if zoning prohibits rebuilding, the leasehold interest loss is covered.
2. There is no coverage if the insured cancels the lease; if there is a suspension, lapse, or cancellation of any license that causes the cancellation of the lease; or from any other consequential loss.

Thus, leasehold interest applies if a lease is cancelled due to the operation of building laws, so long as a covered cause of loss causes the physical damage to the building. However, other consequential loss is not covered.

Leasehold Interest—Terms in a Lease

Terms in a lease can have an appreciable effect on insurance and warrant close review and attention when advising an insured on proper coverage. Any questions should be addressed with a leasing professional. For example, an insured with a lease that is totally silent on both continuing rents and cancellation of the lease may have a problem. If damage to property at the described premises (from a covered cause of loss) leads the insured to cancel his lease, there is no coverage. Note that there is a special exclusion in the causes of loss form used with the leasehold interest coverage form that prevents coverage where the insured cancels the lease ("we will not pay for any loss caused by: (a) your canceling the lease.").

Therefore, the insured cannot cancel the lease and turn to the policy for recovery. A lease that is absolutely silent on the matter of cancellation can prove troublesome to the tenant for many reasons, particularly where the tenant has a lease on untenable premises with no contractual provision to protect him or her. Again, the advice of a leasing professional should be sought.

In short, the leasehold interest coverage form will not respond where the insured cancels the lease. Where the lease is favorable, the insured will not want it cancelled, and should be further protected with business income and expense coverages to maintain business income in the event the leased premises are unusable for some period.

Limits of Insurance

The policy describes separate limits of insurance in section C for tenants lease interest and bonus payments, improvements and betterments and prepaid rent. *Tenants lease interest*, the most the insurer will pay because of the cancellation of a lease, is the net leasehold interest (the present value of the insured's gross leasehold interest). Gross leasehold interest is the difference between the rent the insured actually pays and the rental value of the premises. This amount decreases automatically each month. The amount of net leasehold interest at any time is the gross leasehold interest multiplied by the leasehold interest factor for the remaining months of the lease. For any period of less than a month a proportionate factor is used. The leasehold interest coverage policy always contains a table of leasehold interest factors.

With regard to bonus payments, improvements and betterments, and prepaid rent, the most the insurer will pay because of the cancellation of a lease is the net leasehold interest. A proportionate share of the monthly leasehold interest applies to periods of less than a month. After cancellation, if the landlord allows the tenant to stay under a new lease or other arrange-ment, the insurance covers the difference in rent between the canceled lease and the rent under the new arrangement.

Loss Conditions

The loss conditions of the leasehold interest form are similar to those in the commercial property policy. However, because the leasehold interest form does not cover tangible property, the provisions have been modified to eliminate property abandonment, the inventory requirement, recovered prop-erty, and valuation.

The insurer promises to pay for covered loss within thirty days after receipt of the sworn proof. In return, the insured must comply with all terms of the leasehold interest coverage part and an agreement must be reached on the amount of loss or an appraisal award cannot be made.

The first portion of the vacancy clause specifies that it applies only to the area actually leased to the insured. The insured's suite or unit is vacant "when it does not contain enough business personal property to conduct customary operations." A building under construction is not considered vacant.

If the insured subleases the premises to someone else, the vacancy clause applies somewhat differently. If the sublet building has been vacant for more than sixty consecutive days before the loss, there is no coverage for leasehold interest loss caused by: vandalism, sprinkler leakage (by freeze rupture in spite of the insured having protected the system against freezing), building glass breakage, water damage, theft, or attempted theft. Any other covered loss is paid with a reduction of 15 percent. If there is no sublease agreement at the time of loss, the policy will not pay any leasehold interest loss.

Cancellation

Section E of the leasehold interest form contains an additional condition relating to cancellation. This cancellation provision supersedes the cancellation clause of the common policy conditions form.

The difference between the two cancellation provisions is in the method provided for computing return premium. Because the amount of leasehold interest decreases steadily from inception to expiration, the daily earned premium is greatest early in the policy term. Cancellation must be computed based on the higher average net leasehold interest between inception and the date of cancellation, rather than the lower average leasehold interest for the full original term of the policy, the basis of the original premium. Only the difference between original premium and the earned premium for this higher average amount of insurance is returnable. As in the common policy conditions, the refund may be more favorable if the insurer, rather than the insured, cancels.

CLM rule 65 sets out the steps for premium determination and computation of earned premium at cancellation:

Actual rental value of premises (per month):	$2,000.00
Deduct actual rent paid (including taxes, insurance, janitor or other service which tenant pays as part of the rental consideration):	$1,000.00
Tenant's gross leasehold interest (per month). (Unexpired term of lease 7 1/2 years or 90 months to be written under a 3-year policy; rate $1.00 for 3 years and interest rate of 10 percent):	$1,000.00
Compute net leasehold interest at inception date of policy by multiplying gross leasehold interest of $1,000.00 as shown above by 64.0474 (the factor shown opposite 90 months), which gives the limit of insurance:	$64,047.00

Compute net leasehold interest at expiration date of policy after 36 months have elapsed by

multiplying monthly gross leasehold interest of $1,000.00 as shown by 43.7379 (the factor shown opposite 54 months) which gives:	$43,738.00
Add face amount at inception to amount at expiration:	$107,785.00
Divide by two to find average amount of liability for policy term:	$53,893.00
Which at the rate of $1.00 (per $100 of insurance) produces a premium of $538.93:	$539.00

In order to cancel the above example after one year, it is necessary to compute the average limit of insurance and compute the earned premium. In order to do this, use the following procedure:

Limit of insurance:	$64,047.00
Ascertain net leasehold interest at date of cancellation after 12 months have elapsed by multiplying gross leasehold interest of $1,000.00 as shown above by 57.9116 (the factor shown opposite 78 months), which gives:	$57,912.00
Add face amount at inception to amount at date of cancellation:	$121,959.00
Divide by two to find average amount of liability for the time policy has run:	$60,979.50
Which at the foregoing rate of $1.00 (per $100 of insurance) produces a premium of $609.80:	$610.00
If cancellation is pro rata, retain 1/3 of $610.00 or $203.33 rounded to $203. Deduct that amount from the original premium of $539 and return to insured:	$336.00

If cancellation is at the insured's request, return 90 percent of $336, or $302.

Schedule Form CP 19 60

Along with leasehold interest form CP 00 60, a leasehold interest schedule (CP 19 60) applies. This form shows the necessary information about the lease and the way the amount of leasehold interest insurance is developed. The schedule has spaces to enter the following: the inception and expiration dates of the lease, the number of months remaining at inception of the policy, and the percentage of interest that applies.

The schedule also shows the amount of gross leasehold interest, monthly leasehold interest, net leasehold interest at policy inception, and premium. Commercial Lines Manual (CLM) rule 65 sets out the steps for premium determination.

Leasehold Interest Factors

A table of leasehold interest factors, used in determining the tenant's net leasehold interest, is attached to each leasehold interest policy. Form CP 00 60 states that the tenant's net leasehold interest is the amount that, placed at the applicable interest rate, would provide the insured with the equivalent of the gross leasehold interest for each month of the unexpired lease term. ISO provides a series of endorsements (CP 60 05 through CP 60 15) for interest rates ranging from 5 to 15 percent.

The appropriate form, reflecting the current level of interest rates, is selected. The interest rate should be selected carefully in consultation between agent and insured. If interest rates change dramatically during the course of the policy, a rewrite should be considered. If for example, form CP 60 10, showing a ten percent interest rate is selected, ten percent is also entered in the interest space on form CP 19 60. The table shows interest factors for months numbered from 1 to 400. These factors are used to compute the amount of net leasehold interest coverage for tenant's lease interest at inception, throughout the policy term, for cancellation, or to determine the amount of loss payable under the policy if the lease is canceled due to a covered cause of loss.

Mortgageholders Errors and Omissions - CP 00 70

Mortgageholders E&O (CP 00 70) covers a lending institution or other mortgage servicing agency against losses arising out of the insured's failure to have proper insurance in force to protect the mortgaged property. Such a lack of insurance is usually the result of a mistake in the mortgagee's office procedure. A policy might be misfiled, for example, and subsequently expire without being renewed. If a fire destroys the property and the mortgagor is unable to continue payments, the institution holding the mortgage would have nothing but ruins upon which to foreclose.

Mortgageholders errors and omissions insurance covers lenders against both direct damage and legal liability losses that may arise out of error or accidental omission in its customary mortgage-handling procedures. It offers four coverage agreements: A and B deal with property coverage, while C and D describe liability coverage. The form itself lists the applicable causes of loss under the provisions for each individual coverage so that no separate causes of loss form needs to be attached.

The ISO Commercial Lines Manual (CLM) specifies that the commercial property conditions form (CP 00 90) is not to be used with form CP 00 70. Instead, the form itself includes a modified version of those commercial property conditions that apply in addition to the common policy conditions of form IL 00 17. The rules also specify that no causes of loss form is attached; rather, each coverage agreement is subject to a different set of perils.

The declarations page indicates the estimated number of mortgages that the insured will own or service during the policy period. The policy is to cover one named insured only and may not be endorsed to the names of servicing agents or other interests.

The Four Coverage Agreements

The four different coverages in this form are:

1. Coverage A - Mortgageholder's Interest
2. Coverage B - Property Owned or Held in Trust
3. Coverage C - Mortgageholder's Liability
4. Coverage D - Real Estate Tax Liability

Coverage A - Mortgageholder's Interest

A mortgageholder protects its interest in mortgaged property in one of two ways:

1. It requires the borrower to obtain insurance; or
2. It purchases its own insurance.

If the borrower obtains the insurance, then the mortgageholder is added as an additional insured under the policy. Coverage A promises to pay for loss of the insured's mortgageholders interest. The form defines this interest as the insured's "interest, as mortgageholder, in real or personal property, including your interest in any legal fiduciary capacity." It protects the insured against loss arising from errors and accidental omissions by the insured or a representative in requiring, procuring, or maintaining valid insurance to protect its interest.

Covered property for coverage A may be real property (such as a building where a business is conducted), or personal property secured in connection with that real property. Such personal property might include the contents of a business purchased as a going concern; for example, an existing dry cleaner with all the attendant machinery. Coverage A applies during and after the named insured's foreclosure. It also applies to property sold under an agreement whereby the named insured retains title (such as a conditional sales agreement).

Coverage A lists property not covered as: accounts, bills, currency, deeds, evidences of debt, money, notes, or securities. The form specifies that food stamps are evidences of debt (and excluded) and that lottery tickets held for sale are not securities (and not excluded). The form also states that land (including the land where the property is located), water, growing crops, or lawns are not covered property.

Covered causes of loss under coverage A are those that the named insured customarily requires mortgagors to insure. This may range from named perils to unspecified risk of physical loss (open perils). Whatever is customarily required by the mortgageholder is the rule of thumb. In the event of a dispute over what the named insured customarily requires its customers to insure, the common policy conditions, IL 00 17, contains the examination-of-your-books-and-records provision. By allowing the insurer to examine the mortgageholder's records, what it customarily requires can be readily ascertained.

The form specifies that the causes of loss do not include losses insured under mortgage loan guarantee insurance—insurance that protects the mortgageholder in the event that the mortgagor defaults (often called private mortgage insurance or PMI)—or under title, life, health, or accident insurance policies.

Coverage A extends to losses arising from mortgages owned by others and serviced by the named insured, as if the named insured owned the mortgageholder's interest. This servicing by the named insured must be done through a written contract. Losses are payable jointly to the named insured and the mortgageholder.

Coverage B—Property Owned or Held in Trust

While coverage A protects the insured against loss to property on which it has loaned money, coverage B protects the insured against loss to property it actually owns or in which it has a fiduciary interest.

Coverage B pays for loss to covered property if the loss is not otherwise insured. The absence of insurance must be due to error or accidental omission in the named insured's customary procedure in procuring valid insurance payable to the named insured as owner or trustee. If an insured buys both coverage A and coverage B, recovery under both coverages may be possible. For example, coverage A includes real property "during and after your foreclosure." Since coverage B covers property owned by the insured, a property that has been foreclosed on would fall under both coverages, allowing the insured to collect any remaining balance under B if the limits under A prove inadequate. However, the limits of coverage A and B cannot be combined to collect an amount greater than the insured's loss.

Property-not-covered is identical to that under Coverage A, just above.

While the covered causes of loss under Coverage A are quite broad (whatever the named insured normally requires its customers to purchase), the perils under Coverage B are limited to: fire, lightning, explosion, windstorm or hail, smoke, aircraft or vehicles, riot or civil commotion, sinkhole collapse, and volcanic action. These are the same perils (with two exceptions) as found in the basic causes of loss form CP 10 10. For a further discussion of these perils, see Chapter 3.

The exceptions to the perils mentioned above are vandalism and sprinkler leakage. There is no insurance under Coverage B for damage from these perils; presumably because the insured lender actually owns this often vacant property, these perils become much more of a risk to the insurer.

The additional conditions in form CP 00 70 state that Coverage B protection ends on the earlier of 1) ninety days after the date that the insured acquires the property or the insured's fiduciary interest begins, or 2) the day that other insurance is obtained.

Coverage C - Mortgageholder's Liability

In some cases, a mortgageholder may decide to purchase insurance on a mortgaged property, instead of having the customer purchase it. For those instances, the insured lending institution needs Coverage C.

Like the previous coverages, this protects the lender from damages due to errors or omissions in obtaining insurance. However, this time the insurance is purchased for the benefit of the mortgagor. Coverage C is similar to Coverage A in that the perils covered are those that the lender normally requires its customers to purchase. There are exclusions, including losses insured under mortgage guarantee insurance policies or programs or title, life, health or accident insurance policies. Collapse coverage is limited, as discussed under Additional Coverage—Collapse, below.

If the insured, in its capacity as a mortgageholder, mortgage fiduciary, or mortgage servicing agency, has agreed with the mortgagor to procure and maintain insurance against loss, thereby relieving the mortgagor of those responsibilities, and then fails to obtain such insurance, Coverage C will pay the legal obligations that subsequently may befall. The duty to defend is also included under Coverage C, although this duty ends when the Coverage C limit is used up in settlements or judgments.

In addition to the limits of liability shown, Coverage C provides supplemental payments for:

1. All expenses of the insurer.
2. Cost of bonds.
3. Expenses incurred by the insured at the request of the insurer, including loss of earnings of up to $100 per day.
4. Costs taxed against the insured in the suit.
5. Pre- and post-judgment interest.

Coverage C extends to additional insureds, such as the named insured's partners, executive officers, trustees, directors, managers, and stockholders. They are covered only in their capacity as such. Newly acquired organizations (other than partnerships, joint ventures, or limited liability companies) are automatically insured. Coverage for newly acquired organizations is limited to ninety days from the date of acquisition. The policy specifies that it does not apply to errors and omissions that occurred before the insured acquired the organization.

Real Estate Tax Liability—Coverage D

Some mortgages are set up so that the lending institution pays the real estate taxes on the property. This arrangement may be for the convenience of the borrower, who then makes monthly payments toward the tax, rather than two large payments per year. Or, it may be that the lender has some concerns about payment of the taxes and it may take the responsibility itself. With the proliferation of home mortgages now available with little money as a down payment, lenders routinely require that they collect and pay the real estate taxes via an escrow account until the owner's equity in the home reaches 20 percent.

Problems can arise in such an arrangement if the lender does not pay the taxes. In such a case, the property owner may suffer damages. These damages are insured by Coverage D. The policy limits the amount payable to not more than 15 percent of the limit of insurance for damages in connection with any single mortgage. Explanatory information from ISO states that this limit is expressed as a percentage rather than a dollar amount in order to reflect that property values, upon which real estate taxes are based, usually affect the amount of insurance selected by the mortgagee and thus the revised computation will be more accurately tied to the mortgagee's insurance needs. The 15 percent limit also corresponds to the requirements for real estate tax errors and omissions liability coverage of the Federal National Mortgage Association (Fannie Mae).

Exclusions

The following exclusions apply to all coverages under form CP 00 70: ordinance or law; earth movement; governmental action; nuclear hazard; off-premises power failure; war; and water damage. These exclusions apply "regardless of any other cause or event that contributes concurrently or in any sequence to the loss" (the concurrent causation wording).

The policy excludes damage from the "discharge, dispersal, seepage, migration, release or escape of 'pollutants,'" without the concurrent causation wording. However, if the lender customarily requires its customers to insure the property under the special causes of loss form (CP 10 30), pollution losses caused by one of the specified causes of loss defined in the policy are covered. Following the language that has been added to other forms in the commercial property program, pollutants are defined as "any solid, liquid, gaseous or thermal irritant or contaminant, including smoke, vapor, soot, fumes, acids, alkalis, chemicals and waste." The meaning of waste includes materials to be recycled, reconditioned, or reclaimed.

Losses caused by artificially generated electrical current are excluded, but resulting fire loss is covered. Also excluded is any event that occurs thirty or more days after a lender knows that an error or omission may have occurred.

The policy excludes loss or damage caused by or resulting from the insured's failure to maintain title insurance. This exclusion has been broadened to exclude coverage for the insured's failure to obtain, maintain, or properly process, mortgage guarantee, life, or health or accident insurance.

New with the 2000 edition is the *neglect* exclusion. This exclusion removes coverage if the insured does not use reasonable means to protect property from further loss.

The final set of exclusions, also introduced to avoid coverage under the concurrent causation doctrine, corresponds to exclusions already found in the special causes of loss form (CP 10 30). Excluded as part of this group are loss or damage caused by or resulting from collapse (except as modified by the additional coverage for collapse); weather conditions; acts or decisions (and the failure to act or decide) of individuals or groups; and faulty, inadequate, or defective 1) planning, zoning, development, surveying, siting; 2) design, specifications, workmanship, repair, construction, renovation, remodeling, grading, compaction; 3) materials used in repair, construction, renovation, or remodeling; or 4) maintenance—in regard to any property, whether on or off the described premises. However, if loss or damage by a covered cause of loss results from one these excluded events, coverage applies to the resulting loss or damage.

Limits of Insurance

In the event of a covered loss, the most the insurer will pay is the amount shown on the policy declarations, subject to certain limitations. Under Coverage A (Mortgageholder's Interest) or Coverage B (Property Owned or Held in Trust) loss payable is the least of the following:

1. The amount that would have been payable by the borrower's property insurance if the lender had made sure it was in force. The mortgageholders E&O policy reduces this payment by the amount of any other insurance payable to the lender.

2. The amount that would have been payable under policies that the lender should have obtained, but failed to do so.

3. The amount of the lender's mortgageholder's interest.

For Coverage C (Mortgageholders Liability), the insurer's limit of liability is shown on the declarations page. For Coverage D (Real Estate Tax Liability), the insurer's limit of liability is 15 percent of the amount of insurance as shown on the declarations page. This limit applies on a per mortgage basis.

Additional Coverage—Collapse

Collapse coverage applies under CP 00 70 for any building covered by the form or any building containing property covered by the form. The provision that collapse must be a coverage that the lender requires of its customers is no longer contained in the form. Collapse is covered if due to any of the following:

a. The specified causes of loss or breakage of building glass
b. Hidden decay
c. Hidden insect or vermin damage
d. Weight of people or personal property
e. Weight of rain that collects on a roof
f. Use of defective material or methods in construction, remodeling, or renovation if the collapse occurs during the course of the construction, remodeling or renovation

As mentioned in Chapter 3, collapse coverage has been changed. The policy now defines collapse as "an abrupt falling down or caving in." The falling down or caving in may be of a building or any part of a building. The result must be that the building cannot be occupied as intended.

The 2000 edition adds a caveat to the hidden decay and insect damage causes. Under the new form, such decay or damage is not a covered cause of collapse if the existence of the decay or damage is known to an insured prior to a collapse. Under the previous wording, an insured may have known about the damage, but if it was hidden, the commercial property policy would cover resulting collapse.

As with the other causes of loss forms, personal property must be located inside a building to be covered for collapse. The collapse must be due to one of the covered causes of collapse.

The causes of loss forms exclude certain types of property from collapse coverage: outdoor antennas, gutters, yard fixtures, pools, fences, piers, etc. No such limitation exists in the mortgageholders E&O form. Thus, these types of property are covered for collapse without having to be first damaged by a collapsing building.

Additional Conditions

Form CP 00 70 contains one additional condition that applies only to coverage A, four additional conditions that apply to coverage B, and two additional conditions that apply to coverages C and D.

The insurer may, in concert with other insurers on the risk, pay the lender the full outstanding amount of any mortgage, even if that amount is greater than the amount of the loss. Then, the insured lender must assign the mortgage and all other securities pertaining to it to the insurance company.

In the event of loss or damage under coverage B, the insurer reserves the choice of four options for itself. It can either:

1. pay the value of lost or damaged property;
2. pay the cost of repairing or replacing the lost or damaged property (prior to the 1988 form revision, if repairs left the property with a reduced value, the repair cost figure included an amount to cover the diminution in value);
3. take all or any part of the property at an agreed or appraised value; or
4. repair, rebuild, or replace the property with other property of like kind and quality.

In any case, the policy restricts the insured's recovery to its financial interest in the covered property. Furthermore, the value of lost or damaged property is determined at actual cash value as of the time of loss or damage.

If either the insured or insurer recovers lost property, it must notify the other party. However, the option of whether the insured takes back the property remains with the insured. If the insured chooses to take the property back, he must repay the insurer the amount of the claim. The insurer, on the other hand, agrees to pay recovery expenses and to pay for repairs to the property (up to the limit of liability).

As mentioned under the discussion of coverage B, the protection ends on the earlier of 1) ninety days after the date the insured acquires the property or the insured's fiduciary interest begins, or 2) the day that other insurance is obtained.

Coverages C and D (Mortgage Holders Liability and Real Estate Tax Liability) have two additional conditions: bankruptcy and separation of insureds. Even if the insured declares bankruptcy, the insurer is still obligated under Coverages C and D. The separation condition clarifies that the policy applies separately to each insured except for the limits of liability.

Conditions Applicable to All Coverages

The following conditions apply to the entire policy, though some apply differently to different portions:

1. **Abandonment.** As with other property policies, no property may be just abandoned to the insurer.

2. **Appraisal (Coverages A and B Only).** As with other property policies, the mortgageholders E&O form sets up a procedure for settling differences regarding the value of a loss. If the parties cannot agree, each hires its own appraiser and the two appraisers then hire an umpire. After reviewing the facts, the decision of any two of the three is binding on all parties.

3. **Duties in the Event of Loss.** Because this form covers both property and liability, different conditions exist for the different coverages. In the event of a loss under the property coverages (A and B), the insured must do the following:

    (a) Notify the police in the event of a crime
    (b) Give prompt notice to the insurer
    (c) Protect the property from further damage and keep a record of expenses in connection with this activity (Although anything spent by the insured in this regard does not increase the limit of liability, the insurer will not pay for subsequent losses from perils not covered. The insured must also separate the damaged and undamaged property for inspection by the insurer)
    (d) Provide the insurer with inventories of both the damaged and undamaged property
    (e) Allow the insurer to examine his/her books and records; and permit the insurer to take samples of damaged and undamaged property for testing and analysis

(f) Submit a signed, sworn proof of loss within sixty days of request by the insurer (Prior to the 1991 edition, the policy required a statement of loss. The current wording emphasizes the need for "proof.").

(g) Cooperate with the insurer.

Finally, the policy gives the insurer the right to examine any insured under oath about the claim. The 1991 version changed this right from "to question" to the right "to examine" the insured "while not in the presence of any other insured." Courts have held that the term examine encompasses both oral and written questioning, and the right to isolate the insured from others was made explicit after a Missouri Appellate Court ruled that the insurer had no such right without an explicit provision.

In the event of a claim under coverages C or D, the insured must:

a.   give the insurer prompt notice of the claim or suit,

b.   send the insurer copies of all correspondence and other papers in connection with the claim,

c.   authorize the insurer to obtain any necessary information,

d.   cooperate with the insurer,

e.   assist the insurer in enforcing its right of subrogation,

f.   give a signed statement of facts regarding the claim.

Finally, the insured may not make any payment or assume any obligation without the consent of the insurer.

4.   **Insurance Under Two or More Coverages.** As mentioned earlier, it's possible that more than one of the form's coverages may apply. In this case, the insurer still pays no more than the actual amount of the loss.

5.   **Legal Action Against Us.** Under coverages A and B, no one may bring a suit against the insurer unless all terms of the policy have been met. No suit may be brought later than two years after the insured discovers the error or omission.

As with Coverages A and B, under Coverages C and D no one may bring a suit against the insurer unless all terms of the policy have been met. Also, the policy prohibits anyone from joining the insurer in a suit against the insured.

After an agreed settlement or actual trial resulting in a judgment against the insured, suit may be brought to recover the amount due. The form defines an agreed settlement as a settlement and release of liability signed by all parties.

6. **Liberalization.** If within the forty-five days prior to the policy's inception the insurer adopts a policy provision that broadens coverage without an additional premium, that provision automatically applies.

7. **Loss Payment.** Once the insured submits a proof of loss and the parties reach an agreement or an award is made in arbitration as to the amount of the loss, the insurer will pay the loss within thirty days.

8. **Other Insurance.** The policy shares pro rata with other insurance containing the same plan, terms, conditions and provisions. However, it is excess over any other type of insurance—*whether or not* the insured can collect on the other policy.

9. **Policy Period, Coverage Territory.** The policy period condition identifies coverage under the mortgageholders coverage form as occurrence-based. It specifies that coverage applies to loss or damage, claims or suits (including arbitration proceedings) arising from an event that "occurs during the policy period shown in the Declarations." Therefore, even if an error or accidental omission happens outside the policy period, this coverage applies as long as the loss or damage occurs within the policy period.

    This form specifies the territory by limiting the location of the mortgaged property to the United States, its territories and possessions, and Puerto Rico.

10. **Transfer of Rights of Recovery against Others to Us.** The insured transfers any rights to recover from another under all coverages to the insurer, to the extent of the insurer's payment. In addition, the insured must do nothing to impair the insurer's rights.

    Under coverages A and B, the insured may—prior to any loss—waive his or her rights against another party if the waiver is in writing. The insured may make a post-loss waiver against any of the following:

    a. Someone else covered by the policy
    b. A firm that owns or controls the insured
    c. A firm that the insured owns or controls
    d. The insured's tenant.

11. **Vacancy.** The insurance does not cover damage to buildings that have been vacant for more than sixty days prior to the loss. It also does not cover suits arising out of such buildings. The policy defines a vacant building as one where at least 31 percent of its square footage is not

rented and used by the tenant to conduct normal operations; or where at least 31 percent of the square footage is not used by the building owner.

12. **Your Duties.** In addition to the specific duties after a loss, the insured has other, ongoing duties. This condition requires the insured to make every reasonable effort to procure and maintain valid insurance (i.e., either a valid policy or other evidence of insurance) on the mortgaged property. In the case of Coverage D it requires the insured to make prompt payment of real estate taxes on behalf of the mortgagor.

Definitions

The policy concludes with the definitions of five terms. Pollutants, specified causes of loss, and suit are defined the same as in the commercial property policy.

Mortgageholder's interest is what the policy protects—the lienholder's (named insured) interest in mortgaged property. *Valid insurance* refers to what must be missing in order for the mortgageholders E&O policy to be activated.

Tobacco in Sales Warehouses

The tobacco sales warehouse coverage form (CP 00 80) is an annual reporting form that covers direct physical loss of or damage to tobacco in sales warehouses. The tobacco warehouse and any other business personal property must still be covered on form the commercial property policy CP 00 10.

Because tobacco is stored in a warehouse only long enough to be sold at auction and shipped, the policy term is different from other property policies. The coverage applies only at the described premises and begins at 12:01 A.M. of the fifteenth day before the opening of the regular auction season. It ends at 12:01 A.M. of the fifteenth day following the official closing date of the regular auction season. The length of the auction season varies according to local custom.

The tobacco sales warehouses form requires the insured to report tobacco sales at each location and to pay premium on the amount of sales reported. These reports must be filed within thirty days of the close of the auction season. Reports may be in any format provided they are in writing.

Covered Property

As mentioned above, tobacco in the described warehouse is the only type of property covered by this form. The tobacco may be "leaf, loose, scrap and stem." It may either be the tobacco of others of which the insured has care, custody, or control or it may be tobacco that the insured has purchased and is holding for resale. The tobacco is covered for whatever causes of loss the insured chooses (basic, broad, or special).

The form specifies types of property not covered:

a.   Growing crops or water.
b.   Tobacco insured elsewhere that is more specifically described.
c.   Tobacco outside buildings or structures.
d.   Tobacco while waterborne.
e.   Contraband or property in the course of illegal transportation or trade.

Additional Coverages

The tobacco in sales warehouses form provides the following additional coverages: debris removal, preservation of property, fire department service charge, and pollutant clean up and removal. These are the same as the additional coverages in the commercial property policy.

A conflict could theoretically arise under the additional coverage of preservation of property. For example, a fire occurs at a tobacco warehouse located next to a river. The insured must move the undamaged tobacco away in order to protect it. If the insured moves the tobacco onto a boat and the boat sinks, a possible conflict exists.

This is because the definition of covered property excludes tobacco that is waterborne. However, the additional coverage of preservation of property provides thirty-day coverage for any direct physical loss or damage to the tobacco while it is being moved or stored at another location. Would this include the tobacco being temporarily stored on the boat? If an insured is in this position, it would be wise for his agent to clarify the matter prior to any loss.

Coverage Extension

As in the commercial property policy, the tobacco in sales warehouses form provides $10,000 coverage for property off-premises.

Exclusions and Limitations

These are described on the appropriate causes of loss form.

Additional Conditions

Although this section is near the end of the form, some of the previous provisions make reference to its terms, hence its discussion here.

Reports of Value: As mentioned, the tobacco in sales warehouses form is a reporting form. The policy requires a report within thirty days of the close of the auction season containing the following information: the total weight in pounds of the tobacco that the insured sold or resold during the season and the total price per pound.

Premium Adjustment: The insurer then bases the final premium for the policy on the information contained in these reports. It then charges an additional premium or makes a refund.

Need for Full Reports: While not labeled a coinsurance penalty, the policy operates to penalize the insured in the event the report does not equal 100 percent of the values at risk. In this case, the reported value is divided by the actual value at risk. That figure is then multiplied by the amount of the loss to arrive at a final payment.

For newly acquired locations (those acquired after the last report of values), the values at all locations are divided by the values at risk at all locations (including the new locations) and then multiplied by the amount of the loss to arrive at a final payment.

Deductible

The deductible condition is the same as that in the commercial property policy with one exception. The policy applies the deductible after any deduction calculated under the "need for full reports."

Loss Conditions

The loss conditions of form CP 00 80 are the same as in the commercial property policy, except for the valuation clause. Damaged tobacco is valued at the average price for similar grades and types. The average is based on the sale price on the day of the loss, two days prior to the loss, and two days following the loss.

The prices are those at the warehouse nearest to where the loss occurs. Total sales are divided by total number of pounds sold to arrive at an average price. The final price is determined by subtracting the following from the average price: any unearned warehouse charges, unearned auction fees, and unpaid government taxes.

Definitions

The only word defined is *pollutants*. It is the same definition as in the commercial property coverage form: "any solid, liquid, gaseous or thermal irritant or contaminant, including smoke, vapor, soot, fumes, acids, alkalis, chemicals and waste. Waste includes materials to be recycled, reconditioned or reclaimed."

Condominium Associations

Even though condominiums are typically occupied by their owners as a residence, the building (being owned in common by all unit-owners) must be insured on a master policy. For property that is owned by condominium associations (the buildings, the clubhouses, pools, etc.), ISO has form CP 00 17.

Form CP 00 17 is very similar to CP 00 10 in most respects. It has been modified to better fit the needs of the condominium association. This discussion centers on those differences.

Covered Property

Like the commercial property policy, the condominium association form covers items such as the building, completed additions, permanently installed equipment, etc. The commercial property policy covers appliances used for refrigerating, ventilating, cooking, dishwashing, or laundering. The condominium association form limits coverage to those items not contained within individual units. This places the responsibility for insuring such items on the unit-owner—the person who actually owns the equipment.

Form CP 00 17 adds a sixth class of covered property, consisting of certain items within individual units *if the condominium association agreement or bylaws requires the association to insure such property.* This property consists of:

1. fixtures, improvements and alterations that are a part of the building or structure; and

2. appliances, such as those used for refrigerating, ventilating, cooking, dishwashing, laundering, security or, housekeeping.

The important wording here is "if the agreement requires . . ." When writing coverage for a condominium association, it is always important to review the association agreement and the bylaws to be certain about whose responsibility it is to insure various items.

Carpeting in Condominiums

Many claims departments have problems adjusting losses to carpeting, wallpaper, and paint inside a condominium unit under form CP 00 17. The belief is that if the condo documents (master deed and bylaws) require the association to insure, for example, all units, common elements and "limited common elements," the CP 00 17 would pick up coverage for carpet, wallpaper and paint. Although association agreements vary, typically "limited common elements" are outside of the building, but serve only one unit. These include porches, sidewalks leading to the door, areas between privacy fences, and the like.

In many losses, the damage is confined to a single unit and it is necessary to replace vinyl or carpet and padding because of the buckling of the sub flooring. Confusion (not to mention frustration) occurs in trying to determine which policy covers the damage.

The HO-6 (condominium unit-owners) policy contains a statement making it excess over any recoverable insurance held by the association. The CP 00 17 is specific that it is primary and not contributing. There is some question regarding the interaction with the HO-6 in the case of a large deductible on the CP 00 17. Specifically, if the damage is under the amount of the deductible on the CP 00 17, would the HO-6 become primary?

At one time condo unit-owners were considered to have purchased air space and everything from bare walls out was considered the owner's responsibility to insure. Now the condo association master policy may cover individual unit owners' fixtures, improvements, and alterations that are part of the building structure so long as the association agreement requires it. Improvements and alterations that are part of the building include (but are not limited to) paint,

(scenario continues next page)

> *(continued from previous page)*
>
> wallpaper, lighting fixtures, counters, etc. There is also coverage for appliances such as dishwashers.
>
> Coverage for carpeting follows the same logic. If wall-to-wall carpeting is included in the mortgage, it is part of the realty and thus falls under the improvements and alterations that are part of the building structure. If not so designated, then generally where carpet is laid over an unfinished floor it is considered part of the building and would be covered as such. If the carpet is laid over a finished floor, and its removal would not materially damage the floor, courts have generally considered it contents. Coverage would therefore be found under the HO-6.
>
> If the unit-owner receives no payment from the association policy because the loss is under the deductible, then the unit owner's coverage becomes primary. The purpose is to prevent double payment for a loss, not to prevent payment for a claim.

The coverage for business personal property is more limited on the condo association form than on the commercial property policy. Like the CP 00 10, the CP 00 17 covers:

1. The insured's interest in the labor, materials, or services that the condo association furnishes or arranges on personal property of others.

2. Leased personal property which, via contract, is the insured association's responsibility to insure.

3. Personal property of others in the condo association's care, custody, or control. Such property must be located in or on the building described in the declarations or in the open (or in a vehicle) within 100 feet of the described premises.

The unique provision of the CP 00 17 is that, in addition to covering the personal property owned by the association, it also covers personal property owned indivisibly by all unit-owners (such as pool furniture). The form goes on to specify that property belonging to a unit-owner is not covered.

The property not covered is the same as in form CP 00 10.

Other Provisions

As with the CP 00 10, the CP 00 17 covers the property for whatever causes of loss form is attached. The condominium association form provides the same additional coverages: debris removal, preservation of property, fire department service charge, pollutant cleanup and removal, and increased cost of construction (see Chapter 2). CP 00 17 also provides the same extensions of coverage as does CP 00 10: newly acquired or constructed property, personal effects and property of others, valuable papers and records—cost of research, property off-premises, outdoor property, and nonowned detached trailers (see Chapter 2). The limits of insurance provision also reads the same in both forms (see Chapter 6).

The loss conditions are the same in both forms with three exceptions. Often, a condominium association appoints an insurance trustee to handle claims with its insurer. If that is the case, then the insurer agrees to pay the trustee.

The second difference addresses the issue of a unit-owner's insurance. If a unit-owner has insurance on property that is also covered by the association policy, the association policy is primary and does not contribute with the unit-owner's policy. The unit-owner's policy then becomes excess coverage.

The final difference is that the insurer agrees *up-front* to waive any subrogation rights against any unit-owner. In other commercial property forms, it is a simple matter for a building owner to waive subrogation rights against a tenant after a loss. The condo association form *requires* such a waiver.

The condominium association form has the same two additional conditions as does the commercial property policy: coinsurance and mortgageholders.

The final two sections contain identical optional coverages (agreed value, inflation guard, replacement cost, and replacement cost for personal property of others, see Chapter 2); and a definition of pollutants: "any solid, liquid, gaseous or thermal irritant or contaminant, including smoke, vapor, soot, fumes, acids, alkalis, chemicals and waste. Waste includes materials to be recycled, reconditioned or reclaimed."

Commercial Condominium Unit-Owners

ISO provides for the needs of the commercial condominium unit-owner under a separate coverage form, CP 00 18. The form is available for business or professional firms that own commercial condominium units. The form closely follows building and personal property coverage form CP 00 10, but is modified to fit the needs of commercial condominium unit owners. In addition, ISO has provided an optional endorsement, form CP 04 18, offering loss assessment coverage and miscellaneous real property coverage.

The following is a discussion of the current form, with differences from the previous form and the CP 00 10 noted.

Property

The first difference between the CP 00 10 and the CP 00 18 is that the condominium unit-owners form has no provision to cover any building property (other than coverage on building fixtures, improvements, and alterations owned by the unit owner). It begins with "your business personal property."

Property not covered includes fixtures, improvements, and alterations that are a part of the building, and appliances "such as those used for refrigerating, ventilating, cooking, dishwashing, laundering, security, or housekeeping," when the condominium association agreement requires that such property be insured by the association. Note that this provision is an absolute exclusion —unlike the provision of form HO 00 06 (covering owner occupied condos used as a residence) where the unit owners coverage is excess over the association coverage in the same situation — and it applies even when the association insurance is not properly written and does not, in fact, provide the coverage required by the agreement.

Additional Coverages and Coverage Extensions

The unit-owners form offers these additional coverages, just as does the commercial property policy: debris removal, preservation of property, fire department service charge, and pollutant cleanup and removal. The similar coverage extensions are: newly acquired property, personal effects and property of others, valuable papers and records-cost of research, property off-premises, outdoor property, and nonowned detached trailers.

Limits and Deductible

The limits of insurance and deductible provisions of the CP 00 18 are the same as in the commercial property policy.

Loss Conditions

The loss conditions of form CP 00 18 duplicate those in the commercial property policy, with one addition, condominium association insurance. The unit-owner's policy is excess of such other insurance. It is not intended to contribute with the other policy.

Other Provisions

Finally, these provisions of the CP 00 18 are identical to those in the commercial property policy: additional condition-coinsurance, and the optional coverages of agreed value, inflation guard, replacement cost, and replacement cost for the property of others.

The terms *pollutants* and *stock* are defined terms in the unit-owners policy as they are in the commercial property policy.

Legal Liability Coverage Form

The legal liability coverage form (CP 00 40) covers the insured's legal liability for loss or damage to real and personal property of others. The property must be in the insured's care, custody, or control, and the damage must be caused by an insured peril. It also covers loss of use of the property and provides defense coverage. The loss to covered property must be caused by accident, thus eliminating coverage for intentional damage brought about by the insured. The loss must be caused by an insured peril, as indicated on the appropriate causes of loss form.

The coverage can be applied to commercial property—mercantile or manufacturing, building or contents—in the care, custody, or control of the insured. However, form CP 00 40 cannot be used for a contractor while working on a building. A contractor needs a commercial general liability (CGL) policy to protect him while working on a building. However, such a policy still excludes damage to work performed. The CGL covers the contractor for damage done to a part of the building not directly being worked on.

Manual rules state that the declarations (or legal liability coverage schedule form CP DS 05) must include a precise description of the insured's business operations, location, and the property of others for which the insured may be legally liable. In actual practice, it is most often written for the tenant of a commercial building, where the tenant is—by lease terms—responsible for damage to the building.

Legal liability coverage may be written under a separate policy or included as a separate item in the same policy with property coverages.

The declarations page must indicate a definite description of the insured's business operation and location, a description of the property of others for which the insured may be legally liable, and separate limits of liability that apply for this coverage on or in each building.

The amount of insurance is usually based on replacement cost of the property, though consideration should also be given to the fact that coverage contemplates protection for the insured's liability as respects loss of use as well as damage or destruction of the property itself. Thus, the lessee of a building that has a replacement cost of $100,000 and earns $2,000 per month in rental fees might purchase fire legal liability insurance with a limit of $112,000—replacement cost plus rent for a maximum of six months of reconstruction. Obviously, a good deal of speculation and investigation is involved in the final selection of the amount of coverage. What are the chances of the building being totally destroyed, what are the prospects for speedy reconstruction, what does the lease have to say about continuation of rent payments while the building is shut down, and so on?

Note that tenants of multi-occupant buildings purchase fire legal liability coverage (in the CGL policy) on *that part of the building* in their care, custody or control. Coverage for their liability as respects the remainder of the building is properly the subject of general liability insurance—with attention to the matter of adequate property damage limits.

Many times the named insured under the form may be required to add different entities as additional insureds under the policy. Such entities may include someone buying the building under a land contract; co-owners of the premises, with respect to their liability as such; and mortgagees, assignees, or receivers. Most may be added without an extra premium charge. However, adding the following additional insureds require a surcharge of 25 percent: 1) general lessees, managers, or operators of premises in policies covering tenants or lessees of such premises; and 2) employees other than executive officers or partners in policies covering their employers. A general lessee of a multi-tenant building cannot purchase a policy and include the interests of each of the tenants as additional insureds. However, each of the tenants can purchase a policy in which the interest of the general lessee is covered as an additional insured.

The following may not be added as additional insureds at any time: 1) contractors or subcontractors in policies covering tenants or lessees of premises and 2) tenants, lessees, concessionaires, or exhibitors, in policies covering general lessees, managers, or operators of premises.

Coverage

The insuring agreement of form CP 00 40 requires the insurer to "pay those sums that the insured becomes legally obligated to pay as damages because of direct physical loss or damage, including loss of use, to covered property caused by accident and arising out of any covered cause of loss." The phrase *legally obligated* is used to emphasize that the insurance is in no way direct coverage. The policy does not cover damage to the property; it covers the insured's responsibility (following the damage) as imposed by law. Naturally, the insurer will use whatever legal defenses are available to the insured in resisting the assessment of responsibility. The policy reserves the insurer's right to investigate and settle any claim or suit.

This leads to the second aspect of fire legal liability coverage. The insurer has the right and duty to defend any suit seeking damages and will bear the cost of defending a suit against the insured. A suit is defined as including an arbitration proceeding. Payment of legal expenses is in addition to the limit set forth in the policy.

The insurer agrees to pay the cost of defense attorneys and court costs. The amount payable for these expenses is limited only by the provision that the insurer's obligation to defend ends when the insurer has paid the limit in payment of judgments or settlements. In other words, the insurer must pay whatever the insured's legal expenses are (even if they exceed the policy limit) until a judgment or settlement is reached and the amount of the limit has been paid out in the judgment or settlement.

The form also agrees to make the following supplemental payments in addition to the limit of liability:

1.   All expenses that the insurer incurs.
2.   The cost of bonds to release attachments.
3.   All reasonable expenses incurred by the insured at the insurer's request.

This includes actual loss of earnings up to $250 a day because of time off work.

4.   All costs taxed against the insured in the suit.
5.   Prejudgment interest awarded against the insured.
6.   All interest on the full amount of any judgment that accrues after entry of the judgment.

Coverage Extensions—Additional Insureds and Newly Acquired Organizations

If the named insured is a partnership or corporation, partners, executive officers, trustees, directors and stockholders are additional insureds while acting within the scope of their duties. The 2000 edition adds the managers of a limited liability company. Other employees may be named as additional insureds by endorsement, subject to an additional premium charge equal to 25 percent of the policy premium. Coverage under this extension does not increase the limit of insurance.

If the policy is appropriately endorsed, it is permissible (with two exceptions) to include others as insureds. The exceptions: a policy issued to a tenant or lessee may not also cover the insurable interest of a contractor or subcontractor, and a policy issued to a general lessee (one who leases an entire premises and sublets to others) or manager may not include the interest of a tenant, concessionaire or exhibitor.

The legal liability form covers newly acquired organizations within the applicable limit of insurance, for legal liability arising out of direct physical loss that occurs after the insured acquires or forms the organization. The meaning of insured includes any organization (other than a partnership, joint venture, or LLC) that the insured newly acquires or forms and over which the insured maintains ownership or majority interest, provided there is no other insurance available to that organization. This extension of coverage runs for ninety days after the acquisition or formation of the organization, unless the policy expires first.

Newly Acquired Property

Form CP 00 40 allows for limited automatic coverage for property (building and personal) that comes under the insured's care, custody, or control during the policy period. In order for a building to be covered by this provision, it must be intended for similar use to the one described in the declarations or for warehouse use. Coverage under the extension ends at the earliest of: policy expiration; thirty days after the insured acquires care, custody, or control; or the insured reports values to the insurer. Additional premium is charged and payments under the newly acquired property extension are in addition to the limits of insurance.

Coverage for a total loss of all newly acquired covered buildings arising out of one accident is limited to $250,000 at each building. The building limit can be increased by adding endorsement CP 04 25.

Newly acquired personal property must be either at a location owned by or in the care, custody, or control of the insured at the time of loss. There is no provision for adding newly acquired property that is in the insured's care, custody, or control at fairs or exhibitions. Total coverage for loss to this personal property resulting from one accident $100,000 at each building. Endorsement CP 04 25 cannot be used to increase this limit.

Perils and Exclusions

Under the legal liability form, any of the three causes of loss forms used with the commercial property program may be employed: basic form CP 10 10, broad form CP 10 20, or special form CP 10 30. However, CP 10 30 may *not* be attached when coverage is provided for personal property of others in the insured's care, custody, or control, or warehouse risks involving personal property. Presumably, these ineligible risks involve *business personal property* of others. However, the rules do not specify that limitation.

Since most (if not all) of the perils covered (extended coverage, vandalism and malicious mischief, or the *open perils* of form CP 10 30) typically involve either acts of God or acts of others, insureds sometimes question the logic of including these perils in their legal liability protection. Some would argue that the likelihood of their becoming legally involved seems remote. Nevertheless, the chance is there and it may be just as expensive to defend a groundless suit as any other kind. The cost of defense and coverage, contrasted with the normally very slight expense of adding these perils, is usually enough to persuade the insured in their favor. And, of course, the extended coverage perils of smoke, vehicle damage, and explosion are clearly valid items for inclusion in the legal liability contract.

Both the basic and broad form causes of loss forms exclude damage from a vehicle owned or operated by the named insured in the course of business. Employees are outside the scope of the exclusion except with respect to vehicles owned by the insured.

In relation to legal liability coverage, all three causes of loss forms contain a contractual liability exclusion. This exclusion provides that the insurer will not "defend any claim or 'suit', or pay damages that [the insured is] legally liable to pay, solely by reason of [the insured's] assumption of liability in a contract or agreement."

Certain exclusions in each of the causes of loss forms do not apply to the legal liability coverage form. The exclusions that do not apply are: ordinance or law, governmental action, nuclear hazard, power failure, and war and military action. The nuclear hazard exclusion of the applicable causes of loss form is replaced by one that pertains only to the legal liability coverage form. Unlike the generally applicable nuclear exclusion, the exclusion used with the legal liability form does not provide coverage for resulting loss or damage by fire.

The reason for specifically stating that some of the other exclusions do not apply is less clear. For example, just as damage by war is beyond the insured's control, so are many causes of earth movement; yet the earth movement exclusion is left fully intact. However, the elimination of the ordinance or law exclusion and governmental action exclusions is more significant. If the insured negligently damages a building to such a degree that a building ordinance requires its complete demolition, the total liability would not be covered without the elimination of the ordinance or law exclusion. Similarly, if the insured accidentally causes an unsafe condition on the premises that results in seizure and destruction of the property by local authorities, the insured would not receive full liability coverage without the elimination of the governmental action exclusion. For example, the insured negligently rents his building to someone operating a drug lab. If it is destroyed by the police in a raid, the insured would receive no coverage without the elimination of this exclusion.

Loss Conditions

Since the CP 00 40 covers liability, the loss conditions read more like those of the CGL than those of the commercial property policy. The form imposes the following conditions on the insured in the event of a loss:

1. Duties
    a. Notify the insurer of how and when the accident occurred and the names of any possible witnesses.
    b. Provide the insurer with prompt notice of any claim or suit.
    c. Send copies of any demands, summons, etc. to the insurer.
    d. Authorize the insurer to obtain any necessary information.
    e. Cooperate with the insurer.
    f. Assist the insurer in the enforcement of its subrogation rights.
    g. The insured may not, except at his own expense, make any settlement or offer any payment.

2. Legal Action Against the Insurer—no one may join the insurer in a suit against the insured and no one may sue the insurer under this form until all terms have been met.

3. Other Insurance—this policy responds pro rata with other like insurance.

4. Subrogation—the insured must do nothing to impair the insurer's subrogation rights. If the insurer requests, the insured must bring suit to help enforce those rights.

Additional Conditions

There are four conditions that apply in addition to the commercial property conditions:

1. Amendment of commercial property conditions: the only commercial property conditions that apply to the legal liability form are:
    a. Condition A., Concealment, Misrepresentation or Fraud;
    b. Condition C., Insurance Under Two or More Coverages; and
    c. Condition E., Liberalization.

2. Bankruptcy of the insured does not relieve the insurer of its obligations.

3   Policy period, coverage territory: the policy period is shown on the Declarations page and the territory is the United States, Canada, and Puerto Rico.

4. Separation of insureds: the insurance applies separately to all insureds, except for the limits of liability.

Chapter 8

Commercial Property Endorsements

ISO offers many endorsements to tailor the commercial property coverage form to the needs of the insured. This chapter reviews alphabetically the endorsements that change the policy.

Additional Building Property, CP 14 15

Business personal property items that are owned but not permanently installed may be designated as building items on this endorsement. See Chapter 1 for a discussion of issues related to business personal property coverage under the building section of the form.

Additional Covered Property, CP 14 10

The insured may purchase coverage for certain excluded items of property (both building and personal property) on this endorsement. Coverage applies only to those items scheduled on the endorsement and only at the premises designated. This endorsement adds coverage for certain building items, generally at the building rate (unless special class rates apply—see CLM rule 30). The following may be added to building coverage: cost of excavations, grading, backfilling, or filling; certain foundations; underground pipes, flues, or drains; bulkheads, pilings, piers, wharves, or docks; fences; freestanding retaining walls; bridges, roadways, walks, patios, or other paved surfaces.

CLM rule 30 allows for the following types of business personal property (that the CP policy otherwise excludes) to be covered:

163

1.   vehicles or self-propelled machines (including aircraft and watercraft) and
2.   animals.

For vehicles to be covered, they must be licensed for road use and operated principally away from the described premises. The insured may not manufacture, process, warehouse or hold any of these vehicles for sale. The endorsement also adds coverage for animals.

Note that the endorsement only adds these items as covered property under the CP 00 10. That form limits personal property coverage to that property on or within 100 feet of the described premises. The coverage is for physical damage only and is not as broad as coverage under the comprehensive coverage of a commercial auto policy or an open perils inland marine policy.

Additional Locations Special Coinsurance Provisions, CP 13 20

Some insureds may want to make use of multiple location average rating, but their personal property values at each location do not fluctuate enough to warrant use of value reporting form CP 13 10. Endorsement CP 13 20 extends business personal property coverage to include personal property at all reported, acquired, and incidental locations. It does not cover property at fairs or exhibitions.

CLM rule 35 says that the following types of property are eligible for this endorsement:

1.   Merchandise and stock (raw, in process, or finished) that the insured owns;
2.   All business personal property that the insured owns;
3.   Personal property owned by others in the care, custody, or control of the insured.

The CLM also specifies that property subject to the following rating schedules is ineligible for this endorsement:

1.   Petroleum Properties Schedule;
2.   Petrochemical Plants Schedule;
3.   Public Utility Electric Generating Stations Schedule;
4.   Public Utility Natural Gas Pumping Stations Schedule; and
5.   Rating Plan for Highly Protected or Superior Risks.

The endorsement applies a coinsurance percentage (at least 90 percent is required) to an overall limit of insurance. The overall limit is the sum of the total values from each individual location, including any reported, acquired, and incidental locations. It is shown in the Declarations or on the Reported—Acquired—Incidental Locations Schedule, CP DS 04. The average rate and premium are derived from the overall limit. It is not a blanket limit; however, each location possesses its own individual limit. A sample loss settlement is included on the endorsement to clarify the use of the overall limit.

Additional Property Not Covered, CP 14 20

The insured may choose to exclude items of building or business personal property by scheduling them on this endorsement. CLM rules 30 and 31 describe the types of property that may be excluded:

Building items that may be excluded:

a.   Awnings or canopies of fabric or slat construction,including their supports;
b.   Brick, metal, stone, or concrete chimneys or stacks that are not part of a building; or metal smokestacks;
c.   Crop silos;
d.   Swimming pools, diving towers or platforms;
e.   Waterwheels, windmills, wind pumps or their towers;
f.   The value of improvements, alterations or repairs (including labor, materials and supplies) being performed by a named individual or organization; (This includes existing real property that will be demolished or permanently removed in the course of making the improvements, alterations or repairs) and
g.   Any other type of property for which more specific property damage coverage is available.

Business personal property items that may be excluded:

a.   Personal Property contained in safes or vaults;
b.   Contents of crop silos;
c.   Glass which is not part of a building or structure;
d.   Metals in ingots, pigs, billets, or scraps;
e.   Ores, gravels, clay, or sand;
f.   Property of others;
g.   Property stored in open yards;

h.   Signs inside the premises;

i.   Vending machines or their contents;

j.   Any other type of property for which more specific property damage coverage is available;

k.   The following types of property contained within a condominium unit and covered under CP 00 18 whether owned by the Condominium Association or by the unit-owner, unless the Condominium Association Agreement requires the Condominium Association to insure this property:

1)   Fixtures, improvements, and alterations that are part of the building and

2)   Appliances.

Agricultural Products Storage, CP 13 30

Insureds who store grain (such as grain elevator operators) may cover it with endorsement CP 13 30, Agricultural Products Storage. This endorsement covers grain or grain products on the premises and part of stock at a manufacturing, warehousing, processing or finishing plant. Rice, flaxseed, beans, soybeans, seeds, or seed grain are also eligible.

The addition of this endorsement amends the property not covered provision of the property coverage forms pertaining to grain, hay, straw, or other crops outside of buildings. If such property is harvested and not in storage, it is covered under CP 13 30.

This form does not cover agricultural products stored at fairs or exhibitions or in transit; nor does it cover storage or elevator charges or unpaid customs duties on agricultural products.

In case of loss to covered property in terminal grain elevator plants, payment is made jointly to the named insured and anyone else with an established interest in the property. Such interest may be established by ownership, having a pledge for property, or holding or having a pledge for warehouse receipts. For losses to property stored at other locations, all liens, storage tickets, and warehouse receipts must be satisfied and released before payment occurs.

The endorsement values damaged or destroyed agricultural products at the market value of the covered property less any unincurred expenses such as commissions, loading and unloading charges, and freight. Loss to other commodities (those commodities for which market value is inappropriate) is figured at actual cash value of the property as of the time and place of the loss.

Alcoholic Beverage Tax Exclusion, CP 99 10

This endorsement has two purposes:

1. It excludes the value of taxes and custom duties paid on alcoholic beverages if the beverages suffer damage from a cause of loss other than theft. These taxes and custom duties are refundable under law when the beverages are damaged by a cause of loss other than theft.

2. When theft is a covered peril (as it is only under special causes of loss form CP 10 30), endorsement CP 99 10 includes the value of taxes and custom duties in the loss valuation. The insured cannot receive government reimbursement for such costs in the case of theft and therefore needs insurance protection.

A special theft limit may be scheduled at each covered location under business personal property, stock only, or personal property of others.

The distilled spirits and wines market value endorsement, CP 99 05, also excludes the value of taxes and duties, so endorsement CP 99 10 does not need to be added for that purpose when endorsement CP 99 05 applies. However, if the insured has theft coverage under the special causes of loss form, endorsement CP 99 10 may be used in conjunction with CP 99 05. The addition of both endorsements allows for valuation at market value with different limits for theft versus causes of loss other than theft.

Brands and Labels, CP 04 01

When an insurer takes the salvage of damaged property, an attempt to sell the salvaged property is made in order to recoup some of its payment. Such a situation, however, might place the insurer in direct competition with its customer, since the customer is still trying to sell new, undamaged merchandise.

The brands and labels endorsement provides the original manufacturer with two options in this situation:

1. He or she may stamp such merchandise as salvage material.
2. The insured may remove the brands or labels, if doing so does not damage the merchandise.

Prior to the CP 2000, the activities described above were to be at the insured's own expense. The newest endorsement adds a provision that the insurer will now cover such expenses within the limit of liability that applies to the covered property.

Broken or Cracked Glass Exclusion Form, CP 10 52

The broken or cracked glass exclusion endorsement identifies, at policy inception, any broken or cracked glass on the insured premises. It clarifies that no coverage applies for damage caused by or resulting from the existing cracks. It also eliminates coverage for damage done by the extension of these cracks. The insured may identify the existing damage either via a diagram of the glass or by a written description of the damage. Since the commercial property policy now covers glass, the endorsement refers to the *commercial property coverage part* rather than to the *glass coverage form*.

Burglary and Robbery Protective Safeguards, CP 12 11

Burglary and Robbery Protective Safeguards endorsement identifies safeguards (previous editions used the word systems) that protect the insured's property from burglary and robbery. According to rating procedures in the CLM, such devices warrant rate credits.

Previous editions of this endorsement referred to Underwriters Laboratories (UL). They also classified the various systems using the UL system. The 2000 edition removes any reference to Underwriters Laboratories. ISO says it did this because the classification system in the older form is now obsolete, and because there are many organizations that evaluate alarm systems.

The current endorsement refers to only four different types of systems:

1.   "BR-1" [for 'burglary and robbery'] Automatic Burglary Alarm, protecting the entire building, that signals to:
     (1) An outside central station or
     (2) A police station.

2.   "BR-2" Automatic Burglary Alarm, protecting the entire building, that has a loud sounding gong or siren on the outside of the building.

3.   "BR-3" Security Service, with a recording system or watch clock, making hourly rounds covering the entire building, when the premises are not in actual operation.

4.   "BR-4" The protective safeguard described in the Schedule.

The previous version of the endorsement required the insured to notify the insurer immediately in the event of any malfunction of the protective systems (burglar alarms, gongs, security services) at the premises. That requirement no longer appears. Rather, the insured is told that he must maintain the protective devices and/or services listed in the Schedule.

The insured must also give notice of any failure to maintain such systems. If the insured does not make the notification, or maintain the systems in working order, the theft coverage is suspended.

Condominium Commercial Unit Owners Optional Coverages, CP 04 18

The owner of a commercial condominium unit may purchase either of the additional coverages, loss assessment or miscellaneous real property, on this endorsement. In the event of loss to property that all unit-owners hold in common, the association may assess each owner a share of the loss. Such an assessment may include a portion of the master insurance policy's deductible. The association may also assess a portion of the loss itself if there is either no insurance or inadequate insurance. The endorsement covers all assessments, up to the limit of liability. However, it limits payment for the insured's share of any deductible to $1,000.

Depending on the terms of the association agreement, bylaws, and condominium declaration, the unit-owner may also need to insure some or all of the real property in the condominium. Endorsement CP 04 18 offers miscellaneous real property coverage for such property in the insured's unit only. This coverage is excess over the association coverage on the property, whether the insurance is collectible or not.

Contributing Insurance, CP 99 20

If the insured has coverage with more than one company, the contributing insurance endorsement clarifies the amount for which the insurer is liable.

The endorsement indicates the company's percentage of the total of all contributing insurance. The endorsement also shows the property and coverages to which it applies and the total limits for all contributing insurance.

Debris Removal Additional Insurance, CP 04 15

Debris removal additional insurance provides an additional amount of insurance for debris removal expenses incurred due to loss or damage to covered property from a covered cause of loss. The endorsement increases the $10,000 limit that the policy currently provides to the amount shown on the endorsement.

Deductible Limitation, CP 03 10

The deductible limitation endorsement allows the insured to select an annual accumulation amount for the deductible. The insurer agrees not to subtract any more than this amount for all losses the insured has in any one policy year. Losses that are less than 10 percent of the deductible do not count towards this annual figure. After the annual accumulation amount is reached, the insured must notify the insurer of any loss of more than $250. The insurer deducts $250 for such losses. Form CP 03 10 does not apply to any earthquake deductible.

Distilled Spirits and Wines Market Value, CP 99 05

This endorsement changes the valuation of distilled spirits and wines from actual cash value to market value. Such items may be either the insured's stock or the property of others in the insured's care. The insured schedules on the endorsement the locations to which the endorsement applies.

The endorsement defines five categories of distilled spirits:

1. Bottled winery products—wine that is either in a bottle or unbottled. If not bottled, it must be irreplaceable and it must be of the kind that the insured would normally bottle or have in his possession.
2. Bulk wine—anything other than bottled wine.
3. Irreplaceable bulk distilled spirits—the endorsement says that these are aged in wood, not replaceable, and held by the insured for sale to others.
4. Older bulk distilled spirits—irreplaceable bulk spirits that have reached a certain age.
5. Younger bulk distilled spirits—irreplaceable bulk other than older bulk spirits.

Valuation for distilled spirits is essentially market price at the time and place of loss less any discounts and expenses the insured otherwise would have had.

The form divides wines into two categories:

1.   bottled winery products—valued at the price they would have been sold as case goods and
2.   bulk wine—valued at the lesser of:
      a.   the price it could have been sold for; or
      b.   the market price of replaceable bulk wine of like kind and quality.

Values exclude federal taxes, discounts, and expenses the insured otherwise would have had, but include state, county, and local taxes.

Certain insureds covered by the special causes of loss form (CP 10 30) may want to add endorsement CP 99 10 when this endorsement is used (see above). For insureds with other types of stock subject to market value, another endorsement, CP 99 31, is available (see below).

Earthquake and Volcanic Eruption Endorsement Form, CP 10 40

Up until 1999, this endorsement was known as causes of loss-earthquake form. The insured may purchase earthquake and volcanic eruption coverage via this endorsement. It covers as one occurrence all shocks or eruption that occur within a 168-hour time period.

The insured may choose specific or blanket earthquake coverage. When choosing specific coverage, the declarations page must indicate the property to which the earthquake coverage applies. Even if the insured chooses blanket earthquake coverage, there may be some buildings he or she does not wish to cover. In that case, the declarations should, again, reflect the property to which the coverage applies.

Typically, the deductible for earthquake coverage is a percentage of the limit of liability applicable to the covered property. The deductible is calculated separately for and applies separately to:

1.   Each building, if two or more buildings sustain loss or damage;
2.   The building and to personal property in that building, if both sustain loss or damage;
3.   Personal property at each building, if personal property at two or more buildings sustains loss or damage;
4.   Personal property in the open.

Because a building made of masonry veneer is more likely to sustain heavy damage in an earthquake, the endorsement does not include the value of the veneer when calculating the deductible or applying the coinsurance condition. This limitation does not apply if the building's exterior is less than 10 percent masonry veneer or if the description of the premises specifically includes masonry veneer. Note that the limitation does not apply to stucco.

Earthquake Inception Extension, CP 10 41

Use of this endorsement avoids a coverage gap when an expiring policy and new policy both include earthquake coverage. The endorsement specifically covers damage that occurs on or after the inception of the new coverage if the damage is caused by earthquake shocks or volcanic eruptions that began within seventy two hours before the new policy takes effect.

Electrical Apparatus, CP 04 10

This endorsement modifies the electrical apparatus exclusion. That policy excludes damage caused by artificially generated electrical currents. However, it makes an exception allowing coverage for any resulting fire damage.

Endorsement CP 04 10 extends this exception to include coverage for damage to electrical equipment or devices from resulting explosions. It also covers damage by electricity after the fire or explosion. In order for such coverage to apply, the fire must continue even after the electrical current is turned off. Unless a higher amount is shown on the declarations, coverage under this endorsement is subject to a $1,000 deductible.

Flood Coverage Endorsement, CP 10 65

For the first time, the property program now allows flood coverage to be endorsed to a policy. In order to provide flood coverage in excess of that on a National Flood Insurance Program (NFIP) policy, the agent adds this endorsement and the flood coverage schedule, CP DS 65. The CP DS 65 allows for specific or blanket limits. It also shows the limits and deductibles applying at each location. The insured may choose to blanket several items of covered property, several different coverages (such as property and time element), or several different premises.

The rules state that the following are ineligible for this coverage:
1. property subject to the builders risk form;
2. certain property as defined in the following Federal Statutes:
    a. The Coastal Barrier Resources Act and
    b. The Coastal Barrier Improvement Act.

The endorsement itself even defines those properties in number two, above, as property not covered.

The endorsement defines flood as:

1. "The overflow of inland or tidal waters;
2. The unusual or rapid accumulation or runoff of surface waters from any source; or
3. Mudslides or mudflows which are caused by flooding as defined in C.2. above. For the purpose of this covered cause of loss, a mudslide or mudflow involves a river of liquid and flowing mud on the surface of normally dry land areas as when earth is carried by a current of water and deposited along the path of the current."

Many times another peril, such as fire, accompanies a flood. The limits of insurance section specifies that the limit shown on the DS 65 is the most the endorsement will pay and that the limits cannot be stacked.

The endorsement applies as excess over any NFIP coverage. It also is excess of any NFIP coverage that *should be* in place. If the insured is eligible for NFIP coverage, but does not purchase or maintain it, the ISO endorsement only pays in excess of the maximum amount available under the NFIP. For an additional premium, the insured may purchase a waiver of this requirement.

Functional Building Valuation, CP 04 38

Insureds may add this endorsement to the commercial property or the condominium association coverage form to provide an alternate method of valuation for building property. It provides for the replacement of a scheduled building with similar property that performs the same function but is less costly. The endorsement also provides building ordinance coverage at no charge.

The coinsurance condition does not apply. However, the rate for this coverage is 30 percent above the rate charged for buildings subject to the 80 percent coinsurance rule.

If the insured chooses to repair or replace the building, the insurer pays the least of four different amounts. The first choice is the limit of liability. If the building suffers a total loss, the insurer pays the cost to replace the building on the same site with one that is functionally equivalent. If the insured must rebuild on a different site, the endorsement pays to build on that different site.

In the event of a partial loss, payment by the insurer has two components:

a.   the cost to repair or replace the damaged portion in the same architectural style with less costly material (if available) and

b.   the amount the insured spends to demolish the undamaged portion of the building and to clear the site.

The insurer's fourth option is to pay the amount that the insured actually spends to repair or replace the building with less costly material (if available). The insured must contract for the repairs within 180 days of the loss, unless the insured and insurer agree otherwise.

If the insured does not select repair or replacement (or does not do so within the 180 day time period), the endorsement pays the smallest of

a.   The limit of liability.

b.   The "market value" (not including the value of the land) at the time of loss. The endorsement defines market value as, "the price which the property might be expected to realize if offered for sale in a fair market."

c.   A modified form of actual cash value (the amount to repair or replace on the same site with less costly material and in the same architectural style, less depreciation).

Unlike former endorsement CP 04 35, this endorsement and the manual rules do not specifically exclude functional replacement cost coverage for certain fixtures and personal property used to service the premises. The previous form and rules excluded these items because they are subject to rapid depreciation. The current endorsement does not exclude this property. Therefore, items such as awnings or floor coverings; appliances for refrigerating, ventilating, cooking, dishwashing or laundering; or outdoor equipment or furniture (treated as building property under the property coverage form) can be valued at functional replacement cost. Functional replacement cost coverage may be more favorable for such items than actual cash value.

In the event of other insurance using the same type of valuation, form CP 04 38 responds on a pro-rata basis. Coverage is excess when other insurance covering the loss is not subject to the same plan, terms, conditions (such as valuation), and provisions.

Like the Ordinance or Law endorsement, CP 04 05, the CP 04 38 adds a section that provides for proportionate loss payment when the property suffers damage from both a covered and an uncovered peril.

Functional Personal Property Valuation-
Other Than Stock, CP 04 39

Similar to endorsement CP 04 38 (discussed immediately above), the CP 04 39 provides an alternate method of valuation for business personal property. It is used when an item of personal property cannot be replaced with the same type of property (as when the damaged property is technologically obsolete), or when actual cash value would be inappropriate because the item depreciates quickly in value.

Coinsurance does not apply to this endorsement and blanket insurance is not allowed. The rate is 25 percent above that for personal property written with 80 percent coinsurance. Any items scheduled on this endorsement should be excluded from coverage under the CP policy.

Note that the insured may cover the property for more or less than its actual cash value. For example: a metal stamping plant uses an older piece of machinery with an actual cash value of $50,000. The closest thing available today is one that costs $100,000. Using endorsement CP 04 39, the insured could choose a limit of $100,000 to cover the cost of the new machinery.

The situation is the same when the values are reversed. An insured suffers a fire loss to the central computer. That computer (purchased two years ago) has an actual cash value of $50,000. However, due to advances in technology, the same computer may now be purchased for $30,000. Using endorsement CP 04 39, the insured may cover this computer for $30,000.

The insured must contract for repair or replacement within 180 days of the loss (a time period that may be altered by consent of the insurer and the insured). If the insured does so, the insurer pays the least of the following amounts under functional replacement cost:

1.   the endorsed limit;
2.   the cost to replace, on the same site, with the most equivalent property available; or
3.   the amount the insured spends to repair or replace the property.

If the insured chooses not to repair or replace (or does not do so within the 180 day time period), the insurer pays the smallest of:

1.   the limit of liability;
2.   the "market value" at the time of loss;
3.   the amount to repair or replace with material of like kind and quality, minus an allowance for physical deterioration and depreciation.

The endorsement defines market value as: "the price which the property might be expected to realize if offered for sale in a fair market."

Grain Properties—Explosion Limitation, CP 10 51

The grain properties—explosion limitation endorsement restricts the peril of explosion found in the basic and broad causes of loss forms (CP 10 10 and CP 10 20). It specifies that if a grain elevator or processing plant building or structure ruptures or bursts as a result of a change in temperature, the resulting damage is not covered as part of the explosion peril.

Household Personal Property Coverage, CP 99 92

This endorsement extends the definition of covered property to include household personal property that belongs:

1.   to the insured;
2.   to a member of the insured's family; or
3.   to a domestic employee of the insured.

It also covers household personal property for which the insured is legally liable. This includes property purchased through installment plans.

The insured may extend up to 10 percent of the applicable limit to such property away from the premises. According to explanatory information from ISO, this endorsement applies only to owner-occupants of three and four family dwellings.

Leased Property, CP 14 60

The insured may need to insure personal property that he leases. If he chooses not to include such property under the commercial property policy, this endorsement covers it. The leased property must be specifically described on the schedule. Any property covered by this endorsement should not be included when calculating a value for the insured's personal property or the property of others.

The insured may choose to have losses under this endorsement covered for an agreed value. However, unlike the optional agreed value coverage available in the property forms, coinsurance provisions still apply. This endorsement allows the insured to select a valuation other than actual cash value (such as replacement cost) on an item-by-item basis for leased property.

Legal Liability Coverage Schedule, CP DS 05

The legal liability coverage schedule is used in conjunction with form CP 00 40, legal liability coverage form (see Chapter 7). It describes:

a.   the insured's location and occupancy;
b.   the property to which coverage applies; and
c.   the limits of insurance.

Loss Payable Provisions, CP 12 18

When someone other than the named insured has an insurable interest in the covered property, form CP 12 18 protects that interest in one or more of the following three ways:

1.   **Loss payable**—this is very similar to loss payable provisions in other policies. Under this provision, any losses payable are payable to the insured and a named loss payee as their interests may appear. Under this provision, the loss payee has no further rights than does the insured.

2.   **Lender's loss payable**—like a mortgage clause, this provision establishes separate rights of the loss payee and insured. Even if the insured breaches any policy condition, the loss payee will still collect on a covered claim. This provision is used when a mortgage holders clause is not applicable. The insured and loss payee may document the loss payee's interest in the property by written instruments such as:

a.   warehouse receipts;
b.   a contract for deed;
c.   bills of lading;
d.   financing statements; or
e.   mortgages, deeds of trust, or security agreements.

   3.   **Contract of Sale**—this clause protects the duplicate interests of the insured and another party with whom the insured has entered into a contract for the sale of covered property. The endorsement amends the definition of the word *you* to include the loss payee.

There is no additional premium charge for use of endorsement CP 12 18.

Manufacturers Consequential Loss Assumption, CP 99 02

As with other consequential loss endorsements, this one covers indirect damage. It covers the reduction in value of physically undamaged stock in the process of being manufactured. Such a reduction in value must result from covered direct loss to other unfinished stock. The rate for this coverage is 25 percent above that for business personal property. When the policy does not break out stock from other personal property, the increase factor is 15 percent.

For coinsurance purposes, the value of stock in process at the insured location includes the additional value that it represents in stock at other locations. The minimum coinsurance amount is 80 percent.

Manufacturer's Selling Price (Finished Stock Only), CP 99 30

This endorsement amends the method at which loss to stock is adjusted. It provides for valuation based on selling price less any applicable discounts and expenses for all completed stock. Unlike the commercial property policy, such adjustment is not limited to finished stock that is sold but not delivered.

Market Value Stock, CP 99 31

Market value stock endorsement also amends the method by which loss to certain types of stock is adjusted. It covers stock subject to market value. Such stock is defined as the "kind that is bought and sold at an established market exchange where the market prices are posted and quoted." Stocks of wines and distilled spirits are not eligible for this endorsement (see CP 99 05 above).

The endorsement agrees to set the value of such stock at the market price less any applicable discounts and expenses.

Molten Material, CP 10 60

The molten material endorsement adds as a covered peril, the accidental discharge of molten material from equipment. It also covers damage done by the heat released from the discharged molten material. It applies only to the basic (CP 10 10) or broad (CP 10 20) causes of loss forms, because the special form (CP 10 30) contains no exclusion of this cause of loss.

The endorsement excludes:

1. loss of or damage to the discharged material;
2. the cost to repair any defect that caused the discharge; or
3. the cost to remove or recover the discharged material.

Multiple Deductible, CP 03 20

The multiple deductible endorsement allows the insured to schedule different deductible amounts at different locations. It also allows the choice of different deductibles for the perils of wind or hail and theft.

Multiple Location/Premium and Dispersion Credit Application, CP 13 70

Insureds use this endorsement for calculating a provisional premium for use with a reporting form or for determining a multiple location average rate.

Newly Acquired/Constructed Property-Increased Limit, CP 04 25

The policy automatically provides an extension in the amount of $250,000 for newly acquired/constructed property. This form increases that limit. It must be written for the same causes of loss as the underlying policy and it must apply to all policies providing coverage on the same building property.

Off-Premises Services-Direct Damage, CP 04 17

This endorsement provides coverage for damage to covered property caused by an off-premises interruption of utility service. The utility interruption must be caused by a covered peril to any of the following (when so indicated on the endorsement):

1. Water supply services—damage to pumping stations or water mains.
2. Communication supply services—damage to property that provides these services, including telephone, radio, microwave or television services. Examples of covered property include:
    a. Communication transmission lines, including fiber optic transmission lines;
    b. Coaxial cables; and
    c. Microwave radio relays, except satellites.
3. Power supply services—damage to property that supply electricity, steam or gas to the described premises:
    a. Utility generating plants;
    b. Switching stations;
    c. Substations;
    d. Transformers; and
    e. Transmission lines.

Coverage for damage to overhead transmission lines is available under numbers 2 and 3 by indicating in the appropriate box on the endorsement.

Ordinance or Law Coverage, CP 04 05

The ordinance or law coverage endorsement responds if the enforcement of any building, zoning, or land use law results in added costs that are not covered as direct loss. The insured indicates on the declarations which of three distinct coverages is desired:

1. **Coverage A, Loss to the Undamaged Portion of the Building**—covers the loss of value to the undamaged portion of the building caused by the enforcement of certain ordinances or laws. Such laws require demolition of a building after it suffers a certain percentage of direct damage. They also

regulate construction, repair, zoning, or land use (such as laws that do not allow the same type of land use upon rebuilding as the insured had before the loss). For coverage to apply, the ordinance or law must be in force at the time of loss (a requirement that does not apply to Coverages B and C). However, there is no coverage if the insured was required to comply with an ordinance and failed to do so. Coverage A is not an additional amount of insurance but merely an extension of the existing policy limit. Thus, recovery is limited to the lesser of actual cash value or the building coverage limit if replacement cost coverage does not apply. Replacement cost will not apply if an insured chooses not to repair or replace, or if the insured did not buy the coverage.

The insured must purchase coverage for at least 80 percent of the property's replacement cost value if the insured has added Coverage C (see below), or 80 percent of actual cash value if Coverage C is not included. Since coverage C requires that the underlying policy include the replacement cost option, the rules effectively require insurance equal to 80 percent of the property's replacement cost when Coverage C is selected.

2. **Coverage B, Demolition Cost Coverage**—if the insured must demolish the undamaged portion of the building, this coverage pays the cost of that demolition. It also pays to clear the site of undamaged parts of the property. The CP 04 05 limits the amount of debris removal coverage to the lesser of the amount actually spent to demolish and clear the site or the coverage B limit. Coinsurance does not apply to Coverage B.

3. **Coverage C, Increased Cost of Construction**—if the insured actually repairs or replaces the building (either at the same or another location), Coverage C pays the increased cost of construction at the same premises or the coverage C limit (whichever is less). Note that the coverage does not require replacement at the same location. It only limits payment to the cost to replace *at that location*. If the insured chooses to rebuild elsewhere, the loss payment is figured on the cost to rebuild at the original location.

However, if the ordinance or law requires relocation to another location, coverage C pays the lesser of: the increased cost of construction at the *new premises* or the applicable limit. The form limits the time to rebuild to two years. However, that limit may be extended by another two years.

The 2000 edition adds an extensive description of "proportionate loss payment." Many losses involve damage from both covered and uncovered perils. When a building suffers damage from both a flood and a fire, the CP policy covers only the fire damage. The new wording on the CP 04 05 emphasizes that any increased costs due to the operation of building laws will be covered on a proportionate basis for damage from the covered perils only.

The 2000 edition also adds a statement that clarifies that the endorsement responds only to the minimum requirements of that law. It specifically excludes costs of "recommend actions" in excess of what the law actually requires.

Outdoor Trees, Shrubs and Plants, CP 14 30

The policy provides up to $1,000 coverage, subject to a limit of $250 per item for outdoor trees, shrubs, and plants. It covers these items only for the perils of fire, lightning, explosion, riot or civil commotion, or aircraft.

This endorsement increases the coverage on these items and expands it to make them subject to the perils of the policy. The insured may choose to exclude loss caused by vehicles.

Even with *open perils* coverage, this endorsement still does not cover damage to trees, shrubs, and plants from ice and snow, insects, or animals. The 2000 edition of the CP 14 30 adds three exclusions. It does not cover outdoor trees, shrubs, and plants for loss from the following:

1. Dampness or dryness of atmosphere;
2. Changes in or extremes of temperature; or
3. Rain, snow, ice or sleet."

Trees, shrubs, and plants that the insured grows for commercial purposes are not eligible for this coverage. Neither is standing timber.

Outside Signs, CP 14 40

The commercial property policy provides $1,000 coverage for signs attached to buildings. Signs not attached to buildings are described as property not covered.

The ISO CLM says in rule 30 that this endorsement is used to provide coverage for outside signs attached to buildings. The basic policy already provides $1,000 on these items. The schedule on form CP 14 40 has a place to fill in a new limit of liability for each sign.

The CP 00 10 covers signs attached to building for damage from these perils: fire, lightning, explosion, riot or civil commotion, or aircraft. As with the CP 14 30, this endorsement provides more coverage and expands the applicable causes of loss to those the insured has selected for the rest of the policy.

The following information regarding the covered signs is scheduled on the endorsement:

a.   location;
b.   materials from which they are constructed;
c.   individual limits;
d.   coinsurance percentage;
e.   applicable causes of loss form; and
f.   additional premium.

The 2000 edition of this endorsement clarifies that the $1,000 limit in the basic policy no longer applies. When the insured chooses the CP 14 40, he has just the sign coverage provided on the endorsement. Any unscheduled signs, however, remain subject to the $1,000 limit of liability and the limited causes of loss in the coverage extension.

As the CP 14 30 does with trees, shrubs, and plants, the CP 14 40 adds exclusions specific to outside signs. It adds the same three as the CP 14 30 and a fourth to eliminate marring or scratching.

Peak Season Limit of Insurance, CP 12 30

Some businesses experience seasonal fluctuations in the value of business personal property. This endorsement addresses that issue by providing increased coverage during designated periods of time.

The insured chooses:

1.   the property that increases in value;
2.   the amount of the increase; and
3.   the applicable time period.

Reporting form policies are not eligible for this endorsement. Also, the time period(s) indicated must not extend beyond the expiration date of the policy (the anniversary date if payable in annual installments).

Pier and Wharf Additional Covered Causes of Loss, CP 10 70

Piers and wharves are covered property, only if added to the policy via endorsement CP 14 10 (see above). They face unusual exposure to certain causes of loss, not covered by the basic or broad causes of loss forms. This endorsement extends those causes of loss forms to cover loss caused by:

a.   floating ice or
b.   collision of any vessel or floating object.

All pier and wharf structures are eligible for this endorsement, except floating structures or equipment not incidental to a fixed pier or wharf. As mentioned, this endorsement is not used with the special causes of loss form, CP 10 30. See below for explanation of the procedure to override the watercraft exclusion, CP 10 35.

Pollutant Cleanup & Removal Additional Aggregate Limit of Insurance, CP 04 07

The policy provides an aggregate amount of $10,000 to cover the costs of pollutant cleanup and removal. The commercial property policy provides coverage if a covered cause of loss causes the discharge, dispersal, seepage, migration, release or escape of pollutants. This endorsement increases that annual aggregate amount.

The minimum deductible for this endorsement is $1,000, but it should not be less than the largest direct damage deductible for any of the locations shown on the endorsement. Note that this deductible is independent from the direct damage deductible.

Endorsement CP 04 07 does not come into play until both the underlying amount of $10,000 and the scheduled deductible are exceeded. For example: an insured fuel oil distributor suffers an oil spill. This insured purchased CP 04 07 in the amount of $35,000 with a $5,000 deductible. Earlier in the year, he used $7,000 of the policy's coverage to pay for another oil spill.

If the current spill involves cleanup charges of $40,000, payment by the insurer is calculated as follows:

$40,000   Cleanup charges
- 3,000   Amount of coverage remaining under CP policy
<u>- 5,000</u>   Deductible on endorsement CP 04 07
$32,000   Payment by insurer under the CP 04 07

Protective Safeguards, IL 04 15

As a condition of writing a risk, an insurer may require the installation of protective safeguards or the use of some other type of security device. This endorsement identifies the fire protection safeguards that exist on the insured's property. Such devices fall into one of the following five categories, as enumerated on the endorsement:

P-1 Automatic Sprinkler System, including related supervisory services, meaning:
(1) Any automatic fire protective or extinguishing system, including connected:
      (a)   Sprinklers and discharge nozzles;
      (b)   Ducts, pipes, valves and fittings;
      (c)   Tanks, their component parts and supports; and
      (d)   Pumps and private fire protection mains.
(2) When supplied from an automatic fire protective system:
      (a)   Non-automatic fire protective systems; and
      (b)   Hydrants, standpipes and outlets.

P-2 Automatic Fire Alarm, protecting the entire building, that is:
    (1)   Connected to a central station; or
    (2)   Reporting to a public or private fire alarm station.

P-3 Security Service, with a recording system or watch clock, making hourly rounds covering the entire building, when the premises are not in actual operation.

P-4 Service Contract with a privately owned fire department providing fire protection service to the described premises.

P-9 The protective system described in the Schedule.

The endorsement also clarifies the insured's duties with respect to the maintenance of such systems. The insured must:

1. keep the systems in operation and
2. notify the insurance company if they are not working properly.

If the insured does not notify the insurer, coverage is suspended. If an automatic sprinkler must be shut down due to breakage, leakage, freezing conditions, or the opening of sprinkler heads, the insured has forty-eight hours to restore the systems before they must notify the insurer.

Radio or Television Antennas, CP 14 50

The CP policy provides $1,000 coverage for these items, but only for limited causes of loss. This endorsement provides an additional amount of coverage, as well as expanding coverage to the perils of the policy. Use of this endorsement removes antennas from the outdoor property coverage extension and adds them as covered property.

As does form CP 14 30, this endorsement subjects antennas to the same three additional exclusions.

Radioactive Contamination, CP 10 37

This endorsement extends coverage for loss caused by sudden and accidental radioactive contamination or resultant radiation damage to the described property. Such damage must arise from material used or stored on the described premises.

The endorsement provides two types of radioactive coverage:

1. *Limited* — the radioactive contamination must be caused by a covered cause of loss.
2. *Broad* — does not require that the radioactive contamination be caused by a covered cause of loss.

The location and type of property must be scheduled on the endorsement and the type of coverage desired. However, only broad form coverage may be elected if the insured has special causes of loss, CP 10 30.

The endorsement describes three instances where the coverage does not apply:

1. If the described premises contains a functioning nuclear reactor.
2. If the described premises contains any new or used nuclear fuel intended for or used in such a nuclear reactor.
3. If the radioactive material causing the contamination is not located at the described premises.

Report of Values, CP 13 60, and Supplemental Report of Values, CP 13 61

These endorsements are used for submitting reports of property values according to the provisions of CP 13 10, the value reporting form (see below). The CP 13 60 no longer refers to itself as an endorsement. ISO says that the word endorsement implies a change to the policy and the CP13 60 makes no changes. Thus, they now call it a report.

Spoilage Coverage, CP 04 40

The insured may choose to extend direct coverage for spoilage of perishable stock via this endorsement. The endorsement offers coverage for loss or damage caused by:

a. "Breakdown or Contamination:
1. Change in temperature or humidity resulting from mechanical breakdown or failure of refrigerating, cooling or humidity control apparatus or equipment, but only while such equipment or apparatus is at the described premises; and
2. Contamination by the refrigerant.
b. Power outage, meaning change in temperature or humidity resulting from complete or partial interruption of electrical power, either on or off the described premises, due to conditions beyond the insured's control."

If the insured chooses breakdown or contamination coverage, he must keep a refrigeration maintenance agreement in force. If the insured voluntarily terminates the agreement, the coverage is suspended at that location.

This endorsement has a deductible separate from the rest of the policy. The insured may select to value the property at selling price. In that case the insurer determines the value of the property at selling price less any discounts and expenses.

Sprinkler Leakage Exclusion, CP 10 56

An insurer or an insured may wish to exclude sprinkler leakage coverage from some items of property. The declarations indicates such property. Note that if a covered cause of loss results, that damage is covered.

This endorsement may be used with any of the causes of loss forms. On the basic and broad forms, sprinkler leakage is excluded, unless caused by a covered cause of loss. Also under the broad form, this endorsement deletes sprinkler leakage as a covered cause of collapse.

It also makes the following changes to the special form, CP 10 30:

1. It eliminates coverage for damage done by liquids, powder, etc. that leak or flow from plumbing, heating, air conditioning equipment, etc., unless the insured:
    a. does his/her best to maintain heat in the structure; or
    b. drains the system and shuts off the supply if the heat is not maintained.
2. It agrees to pay for damage to fire extinguishing equipment, if the damage was caused by freezing and the insured:
    a. does his/her best to maintain heat in the structure; or
    b. drains the system and shuts off the supply, if the heat is not maintained.
3. It removes leakage from fire extinguishing equipment from the definition of specified causes of loss.

Sprinkler Leakage-Earthquake Extension, CP 10 39

This endorsement adds sprinkler leakage loss or damage caused by earthquake or volcanic eruption as covered causes of loss. It is not necessary to use the endorsement with causes of loss-earthquake form, CP 10 40, since that form already includes sprinkler leakage coverage.

Storage or Repairs Limited Liability, CP 99 42

This clause modifies the term Actual Cash Value as it relates to personal property of others in the valuation condition. In the event of a covered loss to such property, the insurer pays the lesser of:

1. the property's actual cash value; or
2. the value shown on the receipt the insured issued to the owner before the loss.

Tentative Rates, CP 99 93

Used only on specifically rated property, this endorsement states that the premium rates for the commercial property coverage part are tentative and that the insurer will adjust the premium once the rates are determined. If the policy is a renewal, the previous specific rate may need to be changed due to materially changed conditions. The endorsement provides that premium adjustment is effective from the renewal date once the rates are promulgated.

Theft Exclusion, CP 10 33

If an insurer or insured wishes to exclude theft from a policy subject to special causes of loss (CP 10 30), this endorsement is attached. With this endorsement attached, there is no coverage for theft. However, it does agree to cover:

1. Loss or damage due to looting at the time and place of a riot or civil commotion; or
2. Building damage caused by the breaking in or exiting of burglars.
3. Any damage caused by a resulting covered cause of loss.

Utility Services - Direct Damage, CP 04 17

This endorsement provides coverage for loss or damage to covered property that resulting from off-premises interruption of water, communication, or power supply services, if a covered cause of loss damages any of the properties furnishing these services. The insured may elect to cover one or all of the three exposures.

The current form allows the insured to extend coverage for losses resulting from damaged transmission lines listed under both communication and power supply services to lines that are overhead.

This coverage is subject to the limit of liability for the covered property.

Vacancy Changes, CP 04 60

The policy says that a building is vacant when at least 31 percent of its square footage is not rented or being used. This endorsement allows that percentage to be reduced to as low as 10 percent. In its explanatory material ISO says, "This new endorsement provides a tool to recognize risks where a lower level of occupancy is sufficient in averting the hazards associated with vacancy."

Vacancy Permit, CP 04 50

The commercial property policy covers a vacant building for sixty days. After sixty days of vacancy, there is no coverage for loss from: vandalism, sprinkler leakage, building glass breakage, water damage, and theft or attempted theft. Also, after sixty days of vacancy, the policy reduces payment for any other covered claim by 15 percent. If the insured desires coverage for a longer period, this endorsement must be attached.

Coverage for direct physical loss or damage applies only to the locations and for the permit periods scheduled on the form or on the declarations. (The insured may also exclude vandalism or sprinkler leakage as covered causes of loss during the vacancy for a reduction in premium.)

Endorsements CP 04 50 and 04 60 may not be written on the same risk.

Value Reporting Form, CP 13 10

The purpose of the value reporting form is to allow an insured who has property that fluctuates in value, to be fully protected at all times and to pay a premium based on the values actually at risk—provided the insured reports values correctly and promptly and maintains a sufficient limit of insurance to cover the highest value at any one time. In other words, if the insured lives up to the policy requirements; he or she:

1. will have complete and automatic coverage;
2. will avoid the dangers of both underinsurance and overinsurance on the property; and
3. will be spared the necessity of increasing and decreasing amounts of insurance as values move up and down.

The policy indicates how often reports of value must be made to the insurer: daily, weekly, monthly, quarterly, or by policy year. For daily, weekly, monthly, or quarterly reporting, the first report must be made within sixty days of the end of the first reporting period. Subsequent reports must be made within thirty days of the end of each reporting period. A policy with an annual reporting period requires the report to be made within thirty days of the end of the period. At policy expiration, the insurer charges either an additional premium or tenders a refund, based on the average of the insured's reports of value.

The value reporting form contains a 100 percent coinsurance requirement. The insured must report specific insurance on any items. The insurer then subtracts the specific insurance from the values reported when computing the final premium.

If the insured does not submit the necessary reports, the policy calls for two types of penalty. The first is if the insured does not submit an initial report. In that case, any loss payable is reduced by 25 percent. If the insured fails to submit subsequent reports, any loss is adjusted based on the value last reported.

Vandalism Exclusion, CP 10 55

For a reduction in premium, the insured may choose to exclude vandalism. Also, adding this endorsement may make an otherwise unacceptable risk into an acceptable one to some insurers.

Although the endorsement excludes vandalism, it does cover any resulting loss that is not excluded. The endorsement also deletes vandalism from the list of specified causes of loss.

Watercraft Exclusion, CP 10 35

This endorsement excludes damage by watercraft to the following types of property:

1. Retaining walls that are not part of a building;
2. Bulkheads; or
3. Pilings, piers, wharves or docks.

This endorsement may only be used with special causes of loss, CP 10 30.

Windstorm or Hail Percentage Deductible, CP 03 21

This endorsement allows the insured to choose a deductible for the perils of wind or hail, apart from the deductible that applies to all other perils. The available deductibles are 1 percent, 2 percent, or 5 percent of covered property. Note that the wind or hail deductible applies to all loss caused by windstorm or hail regardless of any other cause or event that contributes concurrently or in any sequence to the loss or damage.

In addition to applying regardless of what else happens to the covered property, this deductible also applies separately to:

a.   Each building, if two or more buildings sustain loss or damage;
b.   The building and to personal property in that building, if both sustain loss or damage;
c.   Personal property at each building, if personal property at two or more buildings sustains loss or damage;
d.   Personal property in the open.

Windstorm or Hail Exclusion-Direct Damage, CP 10 53

An insurance company or an insured may desire to exclude certain property, identified in the declarations from coverage for these perils.

This endorsement modifies the causes of loss forms to eliminate payment for loss caused directly or indirectly by windstorm or hail, regardless of any other cause or event that contributes concurrently or in any sequence to the loss or damage.

It also excludes damage done by rain, snow, or dust resulting from a windstorm. However, any resulting loss that is not excluded is covered.

The endorsement goes on to also exclude wind or hail damage as a covered cause of collapse and as a specified cause of loss. It also removes wind and hail as a covered cause of loss for property in transit.

Windstorm or Hail Exclusion, CP 10 54

The windstorm or hail exclusion extends the wind or hail exclusion to also apply to indirect losses covered under the following: business income coverage forms; extra expense coverage form; and leasehold interest.

Your Business Personal Property-Separation of Coverage, CP 19 10

The various categories of business personal property (stock, contents except stock, machinery and equipment, furniture, fixtures, tenant's improvements and betterments) may be assigned individual limits of insurance by using this endorsement. It also functions as a way to exclude certain types of personal property, since any categories not listed with an individual limit of insurance are not covered at the specified locations. Care must be taken that in specifying a limit on one class of property at a scheduled location (e.g., stock), so that coverage is not inadvertently voided at that location on another category (e.g., all business personal property except stock).

Chapter 9

The Commercial Properties Program of American Association of Insurance Services (AAIS)

The other major rating bureau that offers a commercial property program is the American Association of Insurance Services (AAIS). Located in Wheaton, Illinois, AAIS was formerly known as the Transportation Insurance Rating Bureau (TIRB).

Although the AAIS program is similar to that of ISO, there are some differences. This chapter highlights those differences.

While ISO does not specify what risks are eligible (or ineligible) for their commercial property program, AAIS does. AAIS lists the following as eligible risks: habitational, mercantile, nonmanufacturing, and warehousing properties. The underwriting guide goes on to describe the following as not eligible for the AAIS commercial properties program: manufacturers and processors, farm operations, and dwellings. However, AAIS does have other programs for such risks (commercial output program, farm properties program, and dwelling properties program).

In addition to the building and personal property coverage part (CP-12), AAIS offers the following coverage parts: builders risk (CP-14 or CP-15);

condominium buildings (CP-19); condominium unit coverage (CP-21); personal property coverage part - reporting form (CP-25); earnings coverage (CP-60); extra expense coverage (CP-69); and income coverage (CP-70). This chapter examines the differences between AAIS and ISO in the primary form, the building and personal property coverage part, and in the most popular causes of loss form, special perils.

Building and Personal Property Coverage Part

Covered Property

The AAIS form covers essentially the same building property as does the ISO form. In addition to the described building, the CP-12 covers:

1. completed additions;
2. fixtures, machinery, and equipment that are a permanent part of the building; and
3. outdoor fixtures.

Note that ISO separates fixtures from machinery and equipment and does not require that fixtures be permanent. However, use of the word permanent may be redundant, as the definition of fixture implies permanence.

The fourth item in the list of items covered as building is personal property that the insured owns and uses to maintain or service the building. In addition to fire extinguishing apparatus, floor coverings, and various appliances, AAIS adds air conditioning equipment to the list of examples. This clarifies that window-unit air conditioners are covered as part of the building.

The fifth and last category of building coverage is additions, alterations, and repairs to the building. Also covered are the materials and supplies used to make the alterations. The policy covers these things only if they are not covered elsewhere.

AAIS has simplified their coverage for business personal property. Instead of a list of the types of personal property covered, the AAIS policy says that it covers the named insured's business personal property in the buildings and structures described. Like ISO, the AAIS form also covers:

1.   the insured's interest (labor, material, and services) in the property of others;
2.   the insured's use interest in improvements and betterments that he or she makes to a rented building; and
3.   leased personal property for which the insured is obligated to provide insurance.

The final category of covered property is property belonging to others in the insured's care, custody, or control. As with ISO, the AAIS policy automatically provides $2,500 coverage for property of others as a supplemental coverage. Without indicating on the declarations, the AAIS policy provides only the $2,500 coverage for property of others.

Property Excluded and Limitations

While similar to the ISO property not covered section, this portion of the AAIS form also refers the reader to a section called supplemental coverages. It is there that coverage for some excluded items is restored.

The AAIS policy lists the following types of property as either excluded or limited in some fashion:

1.   **Animals**—like ISO, the policy covers animals of others that the insured boards or animals belonging to the insured that he holds for sale. Unlike ISO, the AAIS policy does not require animals held for sale to be located in buildings.
2.   **Antennas, Awnings, Canopies, Fences, and Signs**—AAIS covers these items under supplemental coverages (see below). This portion is more restrictive than ISO, because ISO places no limit on awnings or canopies.
3.   **Contraband**.
4.   **Foundations, Retaining Walls, Pilings, Piers, Wharves, or Docks**— unlike ISO, AAIS does not include bulkheads as property not covered. Also, AAIS does not further define foundations as those of buildings, structures, machinery or boilers.
5.   **Land; Water; Growing Crops or Lawns; Cost of Excavation, Grading, of Filling; Paved Surfaces; or Underground Pipes, Flues, or Drains**—although the meaning of paved is fairly clear, ISO shows the following as examples: bridges, roadways, walks, patios. AAIS adds driveways and parking lots, but does not specify patios.
6.   **Money and Securities**—ISO also excludes deeds, while AAIS does not mention that item.

7. **Property More Specifically Insured**.
8. **Trees, Shrubs, and Plants**—AAIS covers these items under supplemental coverages (see below).
9. **Valuable Papers and Records—Research Cost**—AAIS covers these items under supplemental coverages (see below).
10. **Vehicles, Aircraft, and Watercraft**. The AAIS policy makes an exception for (thus providing coverage):
    a. vehicles the insured manufactures, processes, warehouses, or holds for sale (other than autos held for sale).
    b. rowboats or canoes that are at the described premises and not in the water.

The ISO policy excludes personal property while airborne or waterborne. AAIS has no such provision.

Additional Coverages

The AAIS building and personal property coverage part contains the following additional coverages:

1. **Debris Removal**—the policy covers debris removal for up to 25 percent of the amount spent for the direct damage. This amount is included in the limit of liability. Unlike ISO, AAIS makes no mention of the deductible, thus limiting the insured's coverage for debris removal to 25 percent of the paid loss. The AAIS policy provides an additional $5,000 of debris removal when the total loss exceeds the limit of liability, or when the 25 percent is not adequate.
2. **Emergency Removal**—this is like ISO's preservation of property provision, but AAIS covers the moved personal property for ten days (ISO's policy covers for thirty days).
3. **Fire Department Service Charges**—$1,000. AAIS specifies that this amount is additional insurance, while ISO is silent on the matter.
4. **Pollutant Clean Up and Removal**—$10,000. Again, AAIS specifies that this amount is additional insurance, while ISO is silent on the matter.

Supplemental Coverages

AAIS offers several supplemental coverages that are comparable to ISO's coverage extensions. These coverages are available only if a coinsurance percentage of 80 percent or more is shown on the declarations. Unless otherwise indicated, all of these supplemental coverages represent additional amounts of insurance.

These coverages are available only when a limit is shown for either building or business personal property:

a.   **Antennas, Awnings, Canopies, Fences, and Signs**—$1,000 coverage for loss caused by fire, lightning, aircraft, riot or civil commotion, or explosion. AAIS specifically includes antenna masts, towers, and lead-in wiring. The $1,000 includes direct damage and debris removal.

b.   **Property Off-Premises**—$5,000 for property temporarily off-premises. ISO offers $10,000 and no longer excludes stock (merchandise held for sale); AAIS does not exclude stock from this supplemental coverage. This supplemental coverage does not apply to property:
     1. in a vehicle;
     2. in the care of the insured's salespersons; or
     3. at a fair or exhibition.

The following coverages are available only when a limit is shown for building property:

a.   **Increased Costs - Ordinance or Law**—up to $5,000 for each described premises to cover such costs. ISO's policy now offers $10,000 coverage in the basic policy.

b.   **Newly Acquired Buildings**—this coverage applies to buildings that are either built or acquired during the policy period. It is broader than ISO's. Unlike the ISO policy, AAIS does not restrict coverage for buildings being constructed to on the described premises. The limit available under AAIS an amount equal to 25 percent of the current building limit, with a maximum of $250,000.

c.   **Trees, Shrubs, and Plants.** The AAIS policy covers these for $1,000, subject to a maximum of $250 for any one tree, shrub, or plant. It provides coverage for these items for the perils of aircraft, civil commotion, explosion, fire, lightning, or riot.

The following coverages are available only when a limit is shown for business personal property:

a.   **Condominium Units**—if the described premises is a condo, AAIS provides up to 10 percent of the limit (maximum of $20,000) for fixtures, improvements, and alterations. This amount is included in the limit of liability. ISO has no similar coverage.

b.   **Extra Expenses**—$1,000 to cover extra expense incurred in order to continue business, after a covered loss. ISO offers this coverage only as part of the business income and extra expense form.

c.   **Personal Effects**—$500 for personal effects owned by the named insured or his officers, partners, or employees. The per person limit is $100. ISO offers up to $2,500 per described premises with no per person maximum.

d.   **Personal Property - Acquired Locations**—thirty-day coverage for personal property at acquired locations. AAIS provides this coverage in the amount of 10 percent of the business personal property limit, with a maximum of $100,000. This coverage does not apply to property at fairs or exhibitions.

e.   **Personal Property of Others**—$2,500 coverage. Unlike ISO, the AAIS policy also covers this property for the peril of theft.

f.   **Property in Transit**—$1,000 coverage for property in vehicles that the insured owns, leases, or operates. This coverage is available only with the special causes of loss form under the ISO program. The AAIS policy requires visible marks of forced entry.

g.   **Valuable Papers and Records-Research Cost**—$1,000 coverage (ISO, $2,500).

What Must Be Done in Case of Loss

The AAIS policy lists the following loss conditions:

a.   **Notice**—prompt notice must be given to the insurer or the agent. ISO makes no mention of agent.

b.   **Protect Property**.

c.   **Proof of Loss**—while ISO merely says that the proof of loss must "[contain] the. . .information" that the insurer requests, AAIS spells out what must be included in the proof.
1.   time, place, and circumstance of loss;
2.   other policies that might cover the loss;
3.   the insured's interest in the damaged property as well as the interests of any others;
4.   changes in the title or occupancy;
5.   detailed estimates for repair or replacement of the covered property;
6.   plans and specifications of buildings or structures;
7.   detailed estimates of income loss and expenses; and
8.   inventory of damaged and undamaged property. AAIS does not require an inventory of the undamaged property if the loss is less than $10,000 or less than 5 percent of the total limit.

d.   **Examination Under Oath.**

e.   **Records**—these must be produced if the insurer requests.

f.   **Damaged Property**—must be available for inspection.

g.   **Volunteer Payments**—the insured must not make any voluntary payments, except at his own expense. This provision does not appear in ISO's policy.

h.   **Abandonment.**

i.   **Cooperation.**

Valuation

The AAIS form specifies that if replacement cost is not shown on the declarations page, then all losses are adjusted at actual cash value (ACV). This provision then goes on to describe seven other valuations.

1.   **Limited Replacement Cost**—as with ISO, if the building meets the coinsurance requirement and the loss is less than $2,500, replacement cost applies.

2.   **Glass**—safety glass is used when required by law.

3.   **Merchandise Sold**—at selling price less all discounts and unincurred expenses. ISO refers to this as stock sold but not delivered.

4.   **Valuable Papers and Records**—the cost of blank materials and the labor to transcribe the records; same as ISO.

5.   **Tenant's Improvements**—at ACV if repaired within a reasonable time. If not repaired, the value is based on a portion of the original cost new. This provision is the same as ISO.

6.   **Pair or Set/Loss to Parts**—neither of these clauses appears in ISO's policy.

7.   **Replacement Cost**—this is an option, as with ISO. AAIS specifies that replacement cost does not apply to objects of art, rarity, or antiquity, or to property of others. It also does not apply to paragraphs two through six, above.

How Much We Pay

This section details six things that determine the amount of loss payable.

1.   **Insurable Interest**—ISO calls this financial interest.

2.   **Deductible**.

Unlike ISO, the AAIS form applies the deductible before the application of the coinsurance penalty. This formula results in a more favorable result for the insured. (See below.)

3.   **Loss Settlement Terms**—the AAIS policy agrees to pay the lesser of the following:
     a.   the value of the property, as described in the valuation provision;
     b.   the cost to repair, replace, or rebuild with materials of like kind and quality; or
     c.   the limit applicable.

4.   **Coinsurance**—the principle is the same as in ISO. To figure a loss divide amount of insurance carried by amount required and multiply by the amount of the loss. The difference from ISO comes in where the deductible is applied. ISO applies it after application of the coinsurance penalty; AAIS applies it before the coinsurance penalty. AAIS's method is more favorable to the insured, as shown in the following example:

     Value of the property: $2,000,000
     Coinsurance percentage: 80%
     Amount of Insurance Carried: $1,000,000
     Deductible: $10,000
     Amount of loss: $ 400,000

     ISO Method:
     Step 1: $2,000,000 times 80% = $1,600,000 (amount required)
     Step 2: $1,000,000 divided by $1,600,000 = .625
     Step 3: $ 400,000 x .625 = $250,000
     Step 4: $ 250,000 - $10,000 = $240,000 (payment by the insurer)

     AAIS Method:
     Step (1): $2,000,000 x 80% = $1,600,000 (amount required)
     Step (2): $1,000,000 divided by $1,600,000 = .625
     Step (3): $ 400,000 - $10,000 = $390,000
     Step (4): $ 390,000 x .625 = $243,750 (payment by the insurer)

5.   **Insurance Under More Than One Coverage**—same as ISO.
6.   **Insurance Under More Than One Policy**—same as ISO.

Loss Payment

     The AAIS policy provides the insurer with the same four options as does ISO:

1.   Pay the value of loss;
2.   Pay the cost of repairing or replacing the loss;
3.   Rebuild, repair, or replace with property of equivalent kind and quality, to the extent practicable; or

4.   Take all or any part of the damaged property at an agreed or appraised value.

The insurer agrees to advise the insured of its intentions within thirty days of receipt of the proof of loss.

Payment for the insured's losses are adjusted with the insured unless another loss payee is named in the policy. A covered loss is payable thirty days after:

1.   the insurer receives a satisfactory proof of loss is received;
2.   the amount of loss has been agreed to in writing; an appraisal award has been filed with the insurer; or
3.   a final judgment has been entered.

Payment for loss to property of others may be adjusted with the insured on behalf of the owner or directly with the owner.

Other Conditions

The AAIS policy is subject to four additional conditions:

1.   **Appraisal**—very similar to ISO's condition, but the AAIS policy imposes certain time limits. After the demand for the appraisal, each party has twenty days to give the name of its appraiser to the other. The appraisers then have fifteen days to select an umpire, or either party may then submit the umpire choice to a court.
2.   **Mortgage Provisions**—this is called mortgageholders in ISO.
3.   **Recoveries**—this is called recovered property in ISO. This condition is very similar to ISO, with one exception. If the insurer's payment for the original loss is less than the agreed loss because of a deductible or other limiting term in the policy, the AAIS policy calls for any recovery to be prorated between the insurer and the insured.
4.   **Vacancy-Unoccupancy**—the AAIS policy imposes one of two penalties on the insured if a building is vacant for more than sixty consecutive days. It also imposes a penalty if the building is unoccupied for the longer of sixty consecutive days or the usual or incidental unoccupancy period for the described premises. The penalties are:
    a.   No payment at all for loss from theft, attempted theft, glass breakage, sprinkler leakage, vandalism, or water damage; and
    b.   Any other loss payable is reduced by 15 percent.

Special Causes of Loss Form

The AAIS Special Perils Part (CP-85) is very similar to ISO's CP 10 30, special causes of loss. A brief review follows.

The AAIS form opens with three additional definitions: sinkhole collapse; specified perils; and volcanic action. The definitions of sinkhole collapse and specified perils are the same as in ISO, but ISO includes sinkhole collapse within the definition of specified perils. Volcanic action is the same as in ISO, but ISO includes it within the earth movement exclusion.

The AAIS form covers risks of direct physical loss subject to the following exclusions:

1. **Ordinance or Law**.
2. **Earth Movement or Volcanic Eruption**.
3. **Civil Authority** (Governmental Action in ISO).
4. **Nuclear Hazard**.
5. **Utility Failure** (Utility Service in ISO)—AAIS goes on to also exclude "reduced or increased voltage, low or high pressure, or other interruptions of normal services."
6. **War**—like ISO, but AAIS adds that the discharge of a nuclear weapon, even if accidental, is an act of war.
7. **Water**—AAIS's form contains two differences from ISO. It does not include mudslide or mudflow as types of water damage; and AAIS does not exclude water that backs up or overflows from a sump. This second difference is a significant benefit to the policyholder, who under an ISO form does not even have the opportunity to buy-back coverage for sump-pump overflow. (That option is available in the ISO homeowners program.)

The above seven items are excluded regardless of other causes or events that contribute to or aggravate the loss (concurrent causation language).

The following exclusions also apply, but any subsequent loss is covered, if not excluded elsewhere:

1. **Animals**—the only subsequent losses that are covered must be caused by a specified peril or glass breakage.
2. **Collapse**, except as provided in the additional coverage.
3. **Contamination or Deterioration**—this includes "corrosion, decay, fungus, mildew, mold, rot, rust, or any quality, faulty, or weakness in

property that causes it to damage ot destroy itself." As with ISO, subsequent losses caused by a specified peril or glass breakage, are covered.

4. **Criminal, Fraudulent, or Dishonest Acts**—as with ISO, losses caused by such acts of the insured, partners, directors, etc. are not covered. AAIS adds the category of "others who have an interest in the property." Thus, such acts committed by, for instance, the mortgagee, might cause a loss not to be paid.

5. **Defects, Errors, and Omissions**—in things such as land use, design, construction, workmanship, etc. Any ensuing loss not excluded is covered.

6. **Electrical Currents.**

7. **Explosion**—of steam boilers, steam pipes, steam turbines, or steam engines owned or operated by the insured.

8. **Freezing**—of water, other liquids, powder, or molten material.

9. **Increased Hazard**—not contained in ISO.

10. **Loss of Use**—includes loss of market.

11. **Mechanical Breakdown.**

12. **Neglect**—to save covered property at the time of a loss or when covered property is endangered by a covered peril.

13. **Pollutants.**

14. **Seepage**—AAIS adds seepage or leakage of steam.

15. **Settling, Cracking, Shrinking, Bulging, or Expanding**—AAIS adds bulging to this list.

16. **Smog, Smoke, Vapor, or Gas.**

17. **Temperature/Humidity.**

18. **Voluntary Parting.**

19. **Wear and Tear.**

20. **Weather.**

Additional Property Excluded and Limitations

1. **Animals**—are covered only if their death or destruction is caused by a specified peril or glass breakage. ISO covers animals if they are killed or their destruction is made necessary.

2. **Boilers.**

3. **Building Materials**—are covered only if held for sale by the insured.

4. **Furs**—covered for $2,500 per occurrence of theft

5. **Glass Breakage**—$100 per pane, $500 per occurrence. For loss by the specified perils, the policy provides unlimited glass coverage (other than for loss by vandalism).

6. **Glassware/Fragile Articles**—breakage is covered only if caused by one of the specified perils.

7. **Gutters and Downspouts**—not covered for loss due to weight of ice, sleet, or snow.

8. **Interior of Buildings**—not covered for damage from rain, snow, sleet, ice, or dust unless the exterior first suffers damage from a specified peril; or the loss is caused by thawing.

9. **Sub-Limits on Certain Types of Property**—theft of jewelry, watches, jewels, pearls, precious stones, and metals is limited to $2,500 per occurrence; theft of patterns, dies, molds, models, and forms is also limited to $2,500 per occurrence; theft of tickets, stamps, or letters of credit is limited to $250 per occurrence. ISO also limits theft of furs to $2,500 per occurrence, but AAIS's policy does not contain such a limitation.

10. **Builders Machinery, Tools, and Equipment**—same as ISO.

11. **Missing Property**—same as ISO.

12. **Personal Property in the Open**—same as ISO.

13. **Transferred Property**—same as ISO.

14. **Valuable Papers and Records**—same as ISO.

Additional Coverages

The AAIS policy has two additional coverages:

1. **Collapse**—same as ISO for the causes of collapse. However, the AAIS form does not define collapse nor does it limit collapse by defining what is not collapse.

2. **Tearing Out and Replacing**—same as ISO.

Other Coverage Parts

In addition to the building and personal property coverage part, AAIS offers the following:

1. Builders Risk - Completed Value
2. Builders Risk - Reporting Form
3. Condominium Building Coverage Part
4. Condominium Unit Coverage Part
5. Personal Property Coverage Part - Reporting Form
6. Earnings Coverage Part
7. Extra Expense Coverage Part
8. Income Coverage Part
9. Basic and Broad Form Perils
10. Earthquake Perils

Endorsements

The following endorsements are available under the AAIS commercial property program:

1. Household Personal Property.
2. Income Coverage from Dependent Locations - Separate Limits.
3. Income Coverage from Dependent Locations.
4. Seasonal Leases.
5. Tuition Coverage.
6. Expanded Restoration Period - Extra Expense.
7. Radioactive Contamination - Limited Coverage. The contamination must be caused by a covered cause of loss.
8. Radioactive Contamination - Broad Coverage.
9. Utility Interruption - Property Damage.
10. Utility Interruption - Time Element.
11. Alcoholic Beverages Valuation.
12. Automatic Increase.
13. Brand or Label Permit.
14. Condominium Buildings Exclusion - Entire Units.
15. Condominium Buildings Exclusion - Improvements.
16. Condominium Loss Assessment Coverage.
17. Condominium Units Exclusion.
18. Pollutant Clean Up and Removal Coverage. This endorsement provides for coverage above the $10,000 in the policy.
19. Contributing Insurance.
20. Debris Removal Coverage.
21. Deductible Schedule.
22. Electric Utility Coverage - $1,000 Deductible.
23. Loss Payable Options.
24. Manufactured Stock Valuation.
25. Market Price Valuation - Stock.
26. Market Price Valuation - Distilled Spirits.
27. Market Price Valuation - Wines.
28. Ordinance or Law Extension - Increased Cost of Construction.
29. Ordinary Payroll Exclusion.
30. Ordinary Payroll Limitation.
31. Peak Season Increase.
32. Perils Exclusion.
33. Electronic Information.
34. Increased Restoration Period - Ordinance or Law.

35.   Power, Heat, and Refrigeration Exclusion.
36.   Property Excluded.
37.   Report of Values.
38.   Resident Agent Countersignature.
39.   Specific Insurance.
40.   Sprinkler Leakage Earthquake Extension.
41.   Storage or Repairs Valuation.
42.   Theft Exclusion.
43.   Vacancy or Unoccupancy Permit.
44.   Spoilage Coverage.
45.   Outdoor Signs.
46.   Antenna Coverage.
47.   Water Damage - Backup of Sewers and Drains.
48.   Functional Replacement Cost.
49.   Market Value.
50.   Trees, Shrubs, and Plants.
51.   Alcoholic Beverages Manufacturers - Finished Stock.
52.   Explosion Limitation for Grain Risks.
53.   Explosion Limitation for Public Utility Gas Risks.
54.   Protective Devices.

Chapter 10

E-issues under the Commercial Property Policy

What Today's Businesses Face

"We are heading at blinding speed into a completely new world built on a foundation of information and communication technology. Change— driven by technology and put in motion across society—will be the biggest risk of all to manage." That provocative quotation comes from Scott K. Lange, former risk manager for Microsoft, and is contained in *E-Risk, Liabilities in a Wired World*, published by the National Underwriter Company.

Today, a business's only property may be intangible—its customer records, services, accounts, trademarks, brands, patents, and copyrights. Mr. Lange writes that such assets are often of far greater importance than the traditional tangible assets disclosed on balance sheets. Intangible property is the fuel of e-commerce.

Because of the growing importance of intangible assets and the challenges of cyber-security, protecting this type of property has become a major challenge facing agents, insurers, and risk managers. The traditional insurance mechanism for protecting tangile property has to be reevaluated in light of the e-business world. This new world of e-coverage is the subject of another National Underwriter Company book, *e-Coverage Guide*, by Leo L. Clarke and Martin C. Loesch, partners in TechRisk.Law, a technology-oriented law firm, with contributions by other experts in the area. *E-risk* and *e-Coverage* are dedicated to the exposures and coverages in this fast-developing area of insurance. This book will simply raise the issues dealt with in more detail in those two works.

Insuring Intangible Assets

This country's founding fathers recognized the right of individuals and companies to protect their intellectual property. Article I, Section 8 of the Constitution says: "Congress shall have power to promote the progress of science and useful arts, by securing for limited times to authors and inventors the exclusive right to their respective writings and discoveries."

In order to properly protect these assets, they must be adequately and fully described for the insurer. Insurers have developed specialized applications for e-property. The authors of *E-Coverage* describe the problem as follows: "The primacy of intellectual property makes risks in e-space difficult to pin down, hard to value, and challenging to describe. The ease through which the primary products of tech companies can be changed also creates a moving goal post." They go on to ask: "How can an insurer write an insurance policy that takes ten months to design, draft, and approve on a product that has fundamentally changed three or four times since work on designing the insurance policy began?"

One problem faced by insurers is how to value such assets. Traditional property can be appraised and a value set. Such property and the things that happen to it usually can be seen. *E-Coverage* points out: "Instead of physically appraising a building, insurers must grapple with the following questions:

- What is the value of a concept?
- What is the value of research and development?
- What is the value of a name?
- What is the value of customer service?
- What is the value of advertising?
- What is the value of speed to market?
- What is the value of a reputation?''

A simple example will suffice. What happens when an employee's laptop computer is stolen? Did the company lose just the value of the physical laptop? What about the value of the data stored on the laptop? And how does one quantify it? Is it the cost to recreate the data or the cost of losing the information?

Some courts have decided that in view of the language in current policies, damage to data is not damage to tangible property and thus not covered. In one case, a manufacturer of hardware lost the battle in court when trying to prove that defective hard drives had caused ensuing damage to tangible property(*Seagate Technology, Inc., v. St. Paul Fire & Marine Insurance Co.*). The basic holding is that the typical property insurance policy only responds to actual physical damage to a company's hardware or equipment.

The problem known as Y2K became a nonevent on January 1, 2000. But up until that time there was much concern on the part of businesses and their insurers. The following discussion of Y2K from *e-Coverage Guide* is illustrative of the problem and how insurers have traditionally dealt with such problems.

"Much time, effort, pain, and press were given to the specter of the Y2K dilemma as it was expected to touch every industry, company, office, and home that utilized any aspect of technology.

"Since insurance is a reactionary industry, it was not unusual that little was done when warnings of date-related issues initially were reported. Was this because the industry didn't realize (at least five years before Y2K) the impact that technology had on virtually every aspect of business? Was it that the industry didn't understand the impact of date-related issues? When did agents, brokers and underwriters really begin to discuss these exposures with their customers?

"When the issue of insurance coverage for a potential Y2K event finally came to the forefront, many insurance companies placed language on policies almost as an afterthought. Y2K exclusions on reinsurance and reinsurance treaties also seemed to be an after thought. Some carriers and reinsurers just began to issue final decisions on their Y2K positions in mid to late 1999. By then, insurers were in a panic to take a position on Y2K.

"Besides placing Y2K and date-related exclusions on practically all types of policies, Y2K questionnaires were required by many insurers. Removing the Y2K exclusion from a policy was like trying to move a mountain to some carriers. Agents and brokers were sometimes left scrambling to replace a customer's coverage because the incumbent carrier just wasn't comfortable with the customer's Y2K identification and remediation process.

"Questions about the validity of these exclusions also arose, at least partially because they were attached so late in the game. Questions arose over what the date of occurrence—if there were one—would be: the date of installation, the date of purchase, or the actual turn of the clock at 12:01 a.m. January 1, 2000? Questions arose over what would or would not be covered and the definition of tangible property. Many of these questions have been left unanswered because there were very few incidents to test policy interpretation.

"The most lasting effect of the Y2K nonevent is the memory of panic that insurers seemed to feel in 1999. This memory continues to affect many insurers' views of technology risks. They escaped one potential disaster, but why risk courting others in an industry where so much is unknown? At the very least, Y2K should have pointed out the need to close the timing gap between insurance and technology as risks emerge and are identified."

What Current Policies Say

The 2000 version of the commercial property coverage form promises to pay for "direct physical loss or damage to covered property at the premises described in the Declarations caused by or resulting from any Covered Cause of Loss." In the traditional sense, property has always meant tangible property. However, that use of the word—and insurers' narrow interpretation of it—is coming under heavy fire. The interpretation of the word property has implications both for direct damage policies and business income policies. Remember that a business income policy requires damage to property at the described premises before coverage applies. If data is not property, can there be a business income loss?

In one case, *American Guarantee & Liability Insurance Co. v. Ingram Micro, Inc.*, 2000 U.S. Dist. LEXIS 7299 (D. Ariz. April 18, 2000) the judge termed such use of the word property as "archaic." In that case, Ingram Micro lost data when its computers were shut down to due a power outage. Because the only property damaged was the data, the insurer denied payment for any direct loss and for any business interruption loss. The insurer claimed that the only thing lost was data. In addition to his description of the policy interpretation as archaic, the judge went on to say, "At a time when computer technology dominates our professional as well as personal lives, the Court must side with Ingram's broader definition of physical damage."

The problem is that the standard property policy protects against a range of standard perils. In this new world, insureds face not only direct damage to their property, but interruption of their services. Such losses may involve a hacker getting into a company's records or Web site. E-mail may be stolen; access to the Web site may be severely limited. All of this costs the insured money, but where is such loss covered in the traditional property policy? The answer is that the traditional property policy offers very little coverage in this area.

Newly Developed Policies

As a result of the confusion surrounding e-property, insurers have developed new policies to protect it. Generally, these policies fall into one of the following three categories:

- Third-party liability
- Prosecution or abatement
- First-party liability/loss

Because it is not within the purview of this book to examine third-party issues, this discussion is limited to the first-party issues surrounding e-property. Such specialty coverage is available, but it is generally limited and subject to strict underwriting requirements. Such a policy pays the insured for the value of its intellectual property when a patent is stolen or a trade secret is misappropriated.

Many patents are issued each year to small businesses. Often these businesses have few, if any assets and not much spare cash. How can they protect their patents? How can small businesses take on the big guys, if one of those big guys infringes a patent?

A fairly new type of insurance policy is aimed at these small businesses. It provides money for *offensive litigation* once the policyholder discovers its patent has been infringed. The policyholder must document the infringement to the insurer. When the insurer is satisfied that infringement has taken place, it then provides the policyholder with up-front money to finance its litigation against the infringer. Knowing that the patent holder has access to resources to finance litigation, the infringer may be more cooperative in reaching a settlement.

Because the area is so new, there are no admitted companies currently writing first-party property coverage for e-assets. However, there are several excess and surplus lines carriers who do. These policies protect against damage from:

1. unauthorized access to a company's Web site
2. unauthorized code (a virus) being put into a company's system
3. denial of service (for example, the flooding of a site with thousands of e-mail messages, making it difficult or impossible for the company to use the site
4. denial of access (in this scenario, the wrong doer redirects traffic away from the insured's Web site, thus causing the loss of business).

Although many businesses are grateful for these new policies, it sometimes can be more difficult to collect under them than the insured would like. In order to collect, the policies typically say that the act must be malicious. If the attacker cannot be caught, malice cannot be shown. In *e-Coverage*, Kevin Barnes says: "In the *love bug* virus attacks, the alleged developers and releasers of the virus were quick to say that it was just a school project that got away from them; they hadn't meant any harm. There could be a problem triggering coverage in such a situation if malice must be proven."

It is not within the purview of this text to do a review of such policies. For a in-depth look at them, please see the *E-Coverage Guide*, available from The National Underwriter Co.

The last issue to examine is valuation. What these policies protect is the insured's revenue stream from his operations. As with business income policies, they settle based on actual loss sustained. Under these forms, the insured must only make an estimate of any business income losses and insure accordingly. The problem is in the adjustment of claims. The insured will not realize what the settlement is until the claim has been adjusted.

In many businesses the Web site and other e-operations do not earn a profit. In that case, the net loss on the web site operation may offset any potential recovery under a business income form. Because there are no physical items to rebuild after a web site attack, the typical site is only down for a few hours or days. Thus, the amount of income lost may appear small.

The difficulty in choosing e-coverage and the responsibility of the broker or agent is summarized by Kevin Barnes in *E-Coverage:* "A careful review of policy language is needed when selecting coverage and a carrier to provide that coverage. Most agents will likely choose two or, perhaps, three carriers to use, so the initial choice is critical. Despite the fact that many carriers have been reluctant to formally design products for this market, the insurers that offer coverage tend to change their forms frequently. Additional coverage to address a special exposure may be available by endorsement or through manuscript wording.

"It is important, however, to consider whether the chosen carriers can offer the breadth of coverage needed. Can they write the accounts for a fair price and with deductibles that provide more than just catastrophe coverage? As technology risks change, accurately assessing the risks is the first step toward designing a comprehensive insurance program. Is the cost and manner in which the assessment work is done acceptable? What does the carrier offer in this area?"

Specimen Forms

ISO Forms

Form Name	Form No.	Page
Building and Personal Property Coverage Form	CP 00 10 10 00	218
Condominium Association Coverage Form	CP 00 17 00 00	231
Condominium Commercial Unit-Owners Coverage Form	CP 00 18 10 00	243
Builders Risk Coverage Form	CP 00 20 10 00	253
Legal Liability Coverage Form	CP 00 40 10 00	260
Leasehold Interest Coverage Form	CP 00 60 06 95	263
Mortgageholders Errors and Omissions Coverage Form	CP 00 70 10 00	267
Tobacco Sales Warehouses Coverage Form	CP 00 80 10 00	277
Commercial Property Conditions	CP 00 90 07 88	282
Causes of Loss—Basic Form	CP 10 10 10 00	284
Causes of Loss—Broad Form	CP 10 20 10 00	288
Causes of Loss—Special Form	CP 10 30 10 00	294
Common Policy Conditions	IL 00 17 11 98	301

BUILDING AND PERSONAL PROPERTY COVERAGE FORM

Various provisions in this policy restrict coverage. Read the entire policy carefully to determine rights, duties and what is and is not covered.

Throughout this policy the words "you" and "your" refer to the Named Insured shown in the Declarations. The words "we", "us" and "our" refer to the Company providing this insurance.

Other words and phrases that appear in quotation marks have special meaning. Refer to Section **H.** ⊐ **Definitions.**

A. Coverage

We will pay for direct physical loss of or damage to Covered Property at the premises described in the Declarations caused by or resulting from any Covered Cause of Loss.

1. Covered Property

Covered Property, as used in this Coverage Part, means the type of property described in this Section, **A.1.**, and limited in **A.2.**, Property Not Covered, if a Limit of Insurance is shown in the Declarations for that type of property.

a. Building, meaning the building or structure described in the Declarations, including:

(1) Completed additions;

(2) Fixtures, including outdoor fixtures;

(3) Permanently installed:

   (a) Machinery and

   (b) Equipment;

(4) Personal property owned by you that is used to maintain or service the building or structure or its premises, including:

   (a) Fire extinguishing equipment;

   (b) Outdoor furniture;

   (c) Floor coverings; and

   (d) Appliances used for refrigerating, ventilating, cooking, dishwashing or laundering;

(5) If not covered by other insurance:

   (a) Additions under construction, alterations and repairs to the building or structure;

   (b) Materials, equipment, supplies and temporary structures, on or within 100 feet of the described premises, used for making additions, alterations or repairs to the building or structure.

b. Your Business Personal Property located in or on the building described in the Declarations or in the open (or in a vehicle) within 100 feet of the described premises, consisting of the following unless otherwise specified in the Declarations or on the Your Business Personal Property ⊐ Separation of Coverage form:

(1) Furniture and fixtures;

(2) Machinery and equipment;

(3) "Stock";

(4) All other personal property owned by you and used in your business;

(5) Labor, materials or services furnished or arranged by you on personal property of others;

(6) Your use interest as tenant in improvements and betterments. Improvements and betterments are fixtures, alterations, installations or additions:

   (a) Made a part of the building or structure you occupy but do not own; and

   (b) You acquired or made at your expense but cannot legally remove;

(7) Leased personal property for which you have a contractual responsibility to insure, unless otherwise provided for under Personal Property of Others.

c. Personal Property Of Others that is:

  (1) In your care, custody or control; and

  (2) Located in or on the building described in the Declarations or in the open (or in a vehicle) within 100 feet of the described premises.

However, our payment for loss of or damage to personal property of others will only be for the account of the owner of the property.

2. Property Not Covered

Covered Property does not include:

a. Accounts, bills, currency, deeds, food stamps or other evidences of debt, money, notes or securities. Lottery tickets held for sale are not securities;

b. Animals, unless owned by others and boarded by you, or if owned by you, only as "stock" while inside of buildings;

c. Automobiles held for sale;

d. Bridges, roadways, walks, patios or other paved surfaces;

e. Contraband, or property in the course of illegal transportation or trade;

f. The cost of excavations, grading, backfilling or filling;

g. Foundations of buildings, structures, machinery or boilers if their foundations are below:

  (1) The lowest basement floor; or

  (2) The surface of the ground, if there is no basement;

h. Land (including land on which the property is located), water, growing crops or lawns;

i. Personal property while airborne or waterborne;

j. Bulkheads, pilings, piers, wharves or docks;

k. Property that is covered under another coverage form of this or any other policy in which it is more specifically described, except for the excess of the amount due (whether you can collect on it or not) from that other insurance;

l. Retaining walls that are not part of a building;

m. Underground pipes, flues or drains;

n. The cost to research, replace or restore the information on valuable papers and records, including those which exist on electronic or magnetic media, except as provided in the Coverage Extensions;

o. Vehicles or self-propelled machines (including aircraft or watercraft) that:

  (1) Are licensed for use on public roads; or

  (2) Are operated principally away from the described premises.

This paragraph does not apply to:

  (a) Vehicles or self-propelled machines or autos you manufacture, process or warehouse;

  (b) Vehicles or self-propelled machines, other than autos, you hold for sale;

  (c) Rowboats or canoes out of water at the described premises; or

  (d) Trailers, but only to the extent provided for in the Coverage Extension for Non-Owned Detached Trailers.

p. The following property while outside of buildings:

  (1) Grain, hay, straw or other crops;

  (2) Fences, radio or television antennas (including satellite dishes) and their lead-in wiring, masts or towers, signs (other than signs attached to buildings), trees, shrubs or plants (other than "stock" of trees, shrubs or plants), all except as provided in the Coverage Extensions.

3. Covered Causes Of Loss

See applicable Causes of Loss Form as shown in the Declarations.

4. Additional Coverages

  a. Debris Removal

    (1) Subject to Paragraphs **(3)** and **(4),** we will pay your expense to remove debris of Covered Property caused by or resulting from a Covered Cause of Loss that occurs during the policy period. The expenses will be paid only if they are reported to us in writing within 180 days of the date of direct physical loss or damage.

Copyright, Insurance Services Office, Inc., 1999
CP 00 10 10 00   □

(2) Debris Removal does not apply to costs to:

(a) Extract "pollutants" from land or water; or

(b) Remove, restore or replace polluted land or water.

(3) Subject to the exceptions in Paragraph **(4)**, the following provisions apply:

(a) The most we will pay for the total of direct physical loss or damage plus debris removal expense is the Limit of Insurance applicable to the Covered Property that has sustained loss or damage.

(b) Subject to **(a)** above, the amount we will pay for debris removal expense is limited to 25% of the sum of the deductible plus the amount that we pay for direct physical loss or damage to the Covered Property that has sustained loss or damage.

(4) We will pay up to an additional $10,000 for debris removal expense, for each location, in any one occurrence of physical loss or damage to Covered Property, if one or both of the following circumstances apply:

(a) The total of the actual debris removal expense plus the amount we pay for direct physical loss or damage exceeds the Limit of Insurance on the Covered Property that has sustained loss or damage.

(b) The actual debris removal expense exceeds 25% of the sum of the deductible plus the amount that we pay for direct physical loss or damage to the Covered Property that has sustained loss or damage.

Therefore, if **(4)(a)** and/or **(4)(b)** apply, our total payment for direct physical loss or damage and debris removal expense may reach but will never exceed the Limit of Insurance on the Covered Property that has sustained loss or damage, plus $10,000.

(5) Examples

The following examples assume that there is no coinsurance penalty.

Example #1

Limit of Insurance	$ 90,000
Amount of Deductible	$ 500
Amount of Loss	$ 50,000
Amount of Loss Payable	$ 49,500
	($50,000 - $500)
Debris Removal Expense	$ 10,000
Debris Removal Expense Payable	$ 10,000
($10,000 is 20% of $50,000)	

The debris removal expense is less than 25% of the sum of the loss payable plus the deductible. The sum of the loss payable and the debris removal expense ($49,500 + $10,000 = $59,500) is less than the Limit of Insurance. Therefore the full amount of debris removal expense is payable in accordance with the terms of Paragraph **(3)**.

Example #2

Limit of Insurance	$ 90,000
Amount of Deductible	$ 500
Amount of Loss	$ 80,000
Amount of Loss Payable	$ 79,500
	($80,000 - $500)
Debris Removal Expense	$ 30,000
Debris Removal Expense Payable	
Basic Amount	$ 10,500
Additional Amount	$ 10,000

The basic amount payable for debris removal expense under the terms of Paragraph **(3)** is calculated as follows: $80,000 ($79,500 + $500) x .25 = $20,000; capped at $10,500. The cap applies because the sum of the loss payable ($79,500) and the basic amount payable for debris removal expense ($10,500) cannot exceed the Limit of Insurance ($90,000).

The additional amount payable for debris removal expense is provided in accordance with the terms of Paragraph **(4),** because the debris removal expense ($30,000) exceeds 25% of the loss payable plus the deductible ($30,000 is 37.5% of $80,000), and because the sum of the loss payable and debris removal expense ($79,500 + $30,000 = $109,500) would exceed the Limit of Insurance ($90,000). The additional amount of covered debris removal expense is $10,000, the maximum payable under Paragraph **(4).** Thus the total payable for debris removal expense in this example is $20,500; $9,500 of the debris removal expense is not covered.

b. Preservation Of Property

If it is necessary to move Covered Property from the described premises to preserve it from loss or damage by a Covered Cause of Loss, we will pay for any direct physical loss or damage to that property:

(1) While it is being moved or while temporarily stored at another location; and

(2) Only if the loss or damage occurs within 30 days after the property is first moved.

c. Fire Department Service Charge

When the fire department is called to save or protect Covered Property from a Covered Cause of Loss, we will pay up to $1,000 for your liability for fire department service charges:

(1) Assumed by contract or agreement prior to loss; or

(2) Required by local ordinance.

No Deductible applies to this Additional Coverage.

d. Pollutant Clean Up And Removal

We will pay your expense to extract "pollutants" from land or water at the described premises if the discharge, dispersal, seepage, migration, release or escape of the "pollutants" is caused by or results from a Covered Cause of Loss that occurs during the policy period. The expenses will be paid only if they are reported to us in writing within 180 days of the date on which the Covered Cause of Loss occurs.

This Additional Coverage does not apply to costs to test for, monitor or assess the existence, concentration or effects of "pollutants". But we will pay for testing which is performed in the course of extracting the "pollutants" from the land or water.

The most we will pay under this Additional Coverage for each described premises is $10,000 for the sum of all covered expenses arising out of Covered Causes of Loss occurring during each separate 12 month period of this policy.

e. Increased Cost Of Construction

(1) This Additional Coverage applies only to buildings to which the Replacement Cost Optional Coverage applies.

(2) In the event of damage by a Covered Cause of Loss to a building that is Covered Property, we will pay the increased costs incurred to comply with enforcement of an ordinance or law in the course of repair, rebuilding or replacement of damaged parts of that property, subject to the limitations stated in **e.(3)** through **e.(9)** of this Additional Coverage.

(3) The ordinance or law referred to in **e.(2)** of this Additional Coverage is an ordinance or law that regulates the construction or repair of buildings or establishes zoning or land use requirements at the described premises, and is in force at the time of loss.

(4) Under this Additional Coverage, we will not pay any costs due to an ordinance or law that:

(a) You were required to comply with before the loss, even when the building was undamaged; and

(b) You failed to comply with.

(5) Under this Additional Coverage, we will not pay any costs associated with the enforcement of an ordinance or law which requires any insured or others to test for, monitor, clean up, remove, contain, treat, detoxify or neutralize, or in any way respond to, or assess the effects of "pollutants".

 Copyright, Insurance Services Office, Inc., 1999 CP 00 10 10 00 ☐

(6) The most we will pay under this Additional Coverage, for each described building insured under this Coverage Form, is $10,000 or 5% of the Limit of Insurance applicable to that building, whichever is less. If a damaged building is covered under a blanket Limit of Insurance which applies to more than one building or item of property, then the most we will pay under this Additional Coverage, for that damaged building, is the lesser of: $10,000 or 5% times the value of the damaged building as of the time of loss times the applicable coinsurance percentage.

The amount payable under this Additional Coverage is additional insurance.

(7) With respect to this Additional Coverage:

(a) We will not pay for the Increased Cost of Construction:

(i) Until the property is actually repaired or replaced, at the same or another premises; and

(ii) Unless the repairs or replacement are made as soon as reasonably possible after the loss or damage, not to exceed two years. We may extend this period in writing during the two years.

(b) If the building is repaired or replaced at the same premises, or if you elect to rebuild at another premises, the most we will pay for the Increased Cost of Construction, subject to the provisions of **e.(6)** of this Additional Coverage, is the increased cost of construction at the same premises.

(c) If the ordinance or law requires relocation to another premises, the most we will pay for the Increased Cost of Construction, subject to the provisions of **e.(6)** of this Additional Coverage, is the increased cost of construction at the new premises.

(8) This Additional Coverage is not subject to the terms of the Ordinance or Law Exclusion, to the extent that such Exclusion would conflict with the provisions of this Additional Coverage.

(9) The costs addressed in the Loss Payment and Valuation Conditions, and the Replacement Cost Optional Coverage, in this Coverage Form, do not include the increased cost attributable to enforcement of an ordinance or law. The amount payable under this Additional Coverage, as stated in **e.(6)** of this Additional Coverage, is not subject to such limitation.

5. Coverage Extensions

Except as otherwise provided, the following Extensions apply to property located in or on the building described in the Declarations or in the open (or in a vehicle) within 100 feet of the described premises.

If a Coinsurance percentage of 80% or more or, a Value Reporting period symbol, is shown in the Declarations, you may extend the insurance provided by this Coverage Part as follows:

a. Newly Acquired Or Constructed Property

(1) Buildings

If this policy covers Building, you may extend that insurance to apply to:

(a) Your new buildings while being built on the described premises; and

(b) Buildings you acquire at locations, other than the described premises, intended for:

(i) Similar use as the building described in the Declarations; or

(ii) Use as a warehouse.

The most we will pay for loss or damage under this Extension is $250,000 at each building.

(2) Your Business Personal Property

(a) If this policy covers Your Business Personal Property, you may extend that insurance to apply to:

(i) Business personal property, including such property that you newly acquire, at any location you acquire other than at fairs, trade shows or exhibitions;

(ii) Business personal property, including such property that you newly acquire, located at your newly constructed or acquired buildings at the location described in the Declarations; or

(iii) Business personal property that you newly acquire, located at the described premises.

The most we will pay for loss or damage under this Extension is $100,000 at each building.

(b) This Extension does not apply to:

(i) Personal property of others that is temporarily in your possession in the course of installing or performing work on such property; or

(ii) Personal property of others that is temporarily in your possession in the course of your manufacturing or wholesaling activities.

(3) Period Of Coverage

With respect to insurance on or at each newly acquired or constructed property, coverage will end when any of the following first occurs:

(a) This policy expires;

(b) 30 days expire after you acquire the property or begin construction of that part of the building that would qualify as covered property; or

(c) You report values to us.

We will charge you additional premium for values reported from the date you acquire the property or begin construction of that part of the building that would qualify as covered property.

b. Personal Effects And Property Of Others

You may extend the insurance that applies to Your Business Personal Property to apply to:

(1) Personal effects owned by you, your officers, your partners or members, your managers or your employees. This extension does not apply to loss or damage by theft.

(2) Personal property of others in your care, custody or control.

The most we will pay for loss or damage under this Extension is $2,500 at each described premises. Our payment for loss of or damage to personal property of others will only be for the account of the owner of the property.

c. Valuable Papers And Records ⊐ Cost Of Research

You may extend the insurance that applies to Your Business Personal Property to apply to your costs to research, replace or restore the lost information on lost or damaged valuable papers and records, including those which exist on electronic or magnetic media, for which duplicates do not exist. The most we will pay under this Extension is $2,500 at each described premises, unless a higher limit is shown in the Declarations.

d. Property Off-Premises

(1) You may extend the insurance provided by this Coverage Form to apply to your Covered Property while it is away from the described premises, if it is:

(a) Temporarily at a location you do not own, lease or operate;

(b) In storage at a location you lease, provided the lease was executed after the beginning of the current policy term; or

(c) At any fair, trade show or exhibition.

(2) This Extension does not apply to property:

(a) In or on a vehicle; or

(b) In the care, custody or control of your salespersons, unless the property is in such care, custody or control at a fair, trade show or exhibition.

(3) The most we will pay for loss or damage under this Extension is $10,000.

e. Outdoor Property

You may extend the insurance provided by this Coverage Form to apply to your outdoor fences, radio and television antennas (including satellite dishes), signs (other than signs attached to buildings), trees, shrubs and plants (other than "stock" of trees, shrubs or plants), including debris removal expense, caused by or resulting from any of the following causes of loss if they are Covered Causes of Loss:

(1) Fire;

(2) Lightning;

(3) Explosion;

(4) Riot or Civil Commotion; or

(5) Aircraft.

 Copyright, Insurance Services Office, Inc., 1999

The most we will pay for loss or damage under this Extension is $1,000, but not more than $250 for any one tree, shrub or plant. These limits apply to any one occurrence, regardless of the types or number of items lost or damaged in that occurrence.

f. Non-Owned Detached Trailers

(1) You may extend the insurance that applies to Your Business Personal Property to apply to loss or damage to trailers that you do not own, provided that:

(a) The trailer is used in your business;

(b) The trailer is in your care, custody or control at the premises described in the Declarations; and

(c) You have a contractual responsibility to pay for loss or damage to the trailer.

(2) We will not pay for any loss or damage that occurs:

(a) While the trailer is attached to any motor vehicle or motorized conveyance, whether or not the motor vehicle or motorized conveyance is in motion;

(b) During hitching or unhitching operations, or when a trailer becomes accidentally unhitched from a motor vehicle or motorized conveyance.

(3) The most we will pay for loss or damage under this Extension is $5,000, unless a higher limit is shown in the Declarations.

(4) This insurance is excess over the amount due (whether you can collect on it or not) from any other insurance covering such property.

Each of these Extensions is additional insurance. The Additional Condition, Coinsurance, does not apply to these Extensions.

B. Exclusions And Limitations

See applicable Causes of Loss Form as shown in the Declarations.

C. Limits Of Insurance

The most we will pay for loss or damage in any one occurrence is the applicable Limit of Insurance shown in the Declarations.

The most we will pay for loss or damage to outdoor signs attached to buildings is $1,000 per sign in any one occurrence.

The limits applicable to the Coverage Extensions and the Fire Department Service Charge and Pollutant Clean Up and Removal Additional Coverages are in addition to the Limits of Insurance.

Payments under the Preservation of Property Additional Coverage will not increase the applicable Limit of Insurance.

D. Deductible

In any one occurrence of loss or damage (hereinafter referred to as loss), we will first reduce the amount of loss if required by the Coinsurance Condition or the Agreed Value Optional Coverage. If the adjusted amount of loss is less than or equal to the Deductible, we will not pay for that loss. If the adjusted amount of loss exceeds the Deductible, we will then subtract the Deductible from the adjusted amount of loss, and will pay the resulting amount or the Limit of Insurance, whichever is less.

When the occurrence involves loss to more than one item of Covered Property and separate Limits of Insurance apply, the losses will not be combined in determining application of the Deductible. But the Deductible will be applied only once per occurrence.

Example No. 1:

(This example assumes there is no coinsurance penalty.)

Deductible:	$ 250
Limit of Insurance ▭ Bldg. 1:	$ 60,000
Limit of Insurance ▭ Bldg. 2:	$ 80,000
Loss to Bldg. 1:	$ 60,100
Loss to Bldg. 2:	$ 90,000

The amount of loss to Bldg. 1 ($60,100) is less than the sum ($60,250) of the Limit of Insurance applicable to Bldg. 1 plus the Deductible.

The Deductible will be subtracted from the amount of loss in calculating the loss payable for Bldg. 1:

$ 60,100

▭   250

$ 59,850 Loss Payable ▭ Bldg. 1

The Deductible applies once per occurrence and therefore is not subtracted in determining the amount of loss payable for Bldg. 2. Loss payable for Bldg. 2 is the Limit of Insurance of $80,000.

Total amount of loss payable: $59,850 + 80,000 = $139, 850

Example No. 2:

(This example, too, assumes there is no coinsurance penalty.)

The Deductible and Limits of Insurance are the same as those in Example No. 1.

Loss to Bldg. 1: $ 70,000

(exceeds Limit of Insurance plus Deductible)

Loss to Bldg. 2: $ 90,000

(exceeds Limit of Insurance plus Deductible)

Loss Payable ⊐ Bldg. 1: $60,000

(Limit of Insurance)

Loss Payable ⊐ Bldg. 2: $80,000

(Limit of Insurance)

Total amount of loss payable:

$140,000

E. Loss Conditions

The following conditions apply in addition to the Common Policy Conditions and the Commercial Property Conditions.

1. Abandonment

There can be no abandonment of any property to us.

2. Appraisal

If we and you disagree on the value of the property or the amount of loss, either may make written demand for an appraisal of the loss. In this event, each party will select a competent and impartial appraiser. The two appraisers will select an umpire. If they cannot agree, either may request that selection be made by a judge of a court having jurisdiction. The appraisers will state separately the value of the property and amount of loss. If they fail to agree, they will submit their differences to the umpire. A decision agreed to by any two will be binding. Each party will:

a. Pay its chosen appraiser; and

b. Bear the other expenses of the appraisal and umpire equally.

If there is an appraisal, we will still retain our right to deny the claim.

3. Duties In The Event Of Loss Or Damage

a. You must see that the following are done in the event of loss or damage to Covered Property:

(1) Notify the police if a law may have been broken.

(2) Give us prompt notice of the loss or damage. Include a description of the property involved.

(3) As soon as possible, give us a description of how, when and where the loss or damage occurred.

(4) Take all reasonable steps to protect the Covered Property from further damage, and keep a record of your expenses necessary to protect the Covered Property, for consideration in the settlement of the claim. This will not increase the Limit of Insurance. However, we will not pay for any subsequent loss or damage resulting from a cause of loss that is not a Covered Cause of Loss. Also, if feasible, set the damaged property aside and in the best possible order for examination.

(5) At our request, give us complete inventories of the damaged and undamaged property. Include quantities, costs, values and amount of loss claimed.

(6) As often as may be reasonably required, permit us to inspect the property proving the loss or damage and examine your books and records.

Also permit us to take samples of damaged and undamaged property for inspection, testing and analysis, and permit us to make copies from your books and records.

(7) Send us a signed, sworn proof of loss containing the information we request to investigate the claim. You must do this within 60 days after our request. We will supply you with the necessary forms.

(8) Cooperate with us in the investigation or settlement of the claim.

b. We may examine any insured under oath, while not in the presence of any other insured and at such times as may be reasonably required, about any matter relating to this insurance or the claim, including an insured's books and records. In the event of an examination, an insured's answers must be signed.

4. Loss Payment

a. In the event of loss or damage covered by this Coverage Form, at our option, we will either:

(1) Pay the value of lost or damaged property;

(2) Pay the cost of repairing or replacing the lost or damaged property, subject to **b.** below;

(3) Take all or any part of the property at an agreed or appraised value; or

(4) Repair, rebuild or replace the property with other property of like kind and quality, subject to **b.** below.

Copyright, Insurance Services Office, Inc., 1999   CP 00 10 10 00   ☐

We will determine the value of lost or damaged property, or the cost of its repair or replacement, in accordance with the applicable terms of the Valuation Condition in this Coverage Form or any applicable provision which amends or supersedes the Valuation Condition.

b. The cost to repair, rebuild or replace does not include the increased cost attributable to enforcement of any ordinance or law regulating the construction, use or repair of any property.

c. We will give notice of our intentions within 30 days after we receive the sworn proof of loss.

d. We will not pay you more than your financial interest in the Covered Property.

e. We may adjust losses with the owners of lost or damaged property if other than you. If we pay the owners, such payments will satisfy your claims against us for the owners' property. We will not pay the owners more than their financial interest in the Covered Property.

f. We may elect to defend you against suits arising from claims of owners of property. We will do this at our expense.

g. We will pay for covered loss or damage within 30 days after we receive the sworn proof of loss, if you have complied with all of the terms of this Coverage Part and:

(1) We have reached agreement with you on the amount of loss; or

(2) An appraisal award has been made.

5. Recovered Property

If either you or we recover any property after loss settlement, that party must give the other prompt notice. At your option, the property will be returned to you. You must then return to us the amount we paid to you for the property. We will pay recovery expenses and the expenses to repair the recovered property, subject to the Limit of Insurance.

6. Vacancy

a. Description Of Terms

(1) As used in this Vacancy Condition, the term building and the term vacant have the meanings set forth in **(1)(a)** and **(1)(b)** below:

(a) When this policy is issued to a tenant, and with respect to that tenant's interest in Covered Property, building means the unit or suite rented or leased to the tenant. Such building is vacant when it does not contain enough business personal property to conduct customary operations.

(b) When this policy is issued to the owner or general lessee of a building, building means the entire building. Such building is vacant unless at least 31% of its total square footage is:

(i) Rented to a lessee or sub-lessee and used by the lessee or sub-lessee to conduct its customary operations; and/or

(ii) Used by the building owner to conduct customary operations.

(2) Buildings under construction or renovation are not considered vacant.

b. Vacancy Provisions

If the building where loss or damage occurs has been vacant for more than 60 consecutive days before that loss or damage occurs:

(1) We will not pay for any loss or damage caused by any of the following even if they are Covered Causes of Loss:

(a) Vandalism;

(b) Sprinkler leakage, unless you have protected the system against freezing;

(c) Building glass breakage;

(d) Water damage;

(e) Theft; or

(f) Attempted theft.

(2) With respect to Covered Causes of Loss other than those listed in **b.(1)(a)** through **b.(1)(f)** above, we will reduce the amount we would otherwise pay for the loss or damage by 15%.

7. Valuation

We will determine the value of Covered Property in the event of loss or damage as follows:

a. At actual cash value as of the time of loss or damage, except as provided in **b., c., d., e.** and **f.** below.

b. If the Limit of Insurance for Building satisfies the Additional Condition, Coinsurance, and the cost to repair or replace the damaged building property is $2,500 or less, we will pay the cost of building repairs or replacement.

The cost of building repairs or replacement does not include the increased cost attributable to enforcement of any ordinance or law regulating the construction, use or repair of any property. However, the following property will be valued at the actual cash value even when attached to the building:

(1) Awnings or floor coverings;

(2) Appliances for refrigerating, ventilating, cooking, dishwashing or laundering; or

(3) Outdoor equipment or furniture.

c. "Stock" you have sold but not delivered at the selling price less discounts and expenses you otherwise would have had.

d. Glass at the cost of replacement with safety glazing material if required by law.

e. Tenant's Improvements and Betterments at:

(1) Actual cash value of the lost or damaged property if you make repairs promptly.

(2) A proportion of your original cost if you do not make repairs promptly. We will determine the proportionate value as follows:

(a) Multiply the original cost by the number of days from the loss or damage to the expiration of the lease; and

(b) Divide the amount determined in **(a)** above by the number of days from the installation of improvements to the expiration of the lease.

If your lease contains a renewal option, the expiration of the renewal option period will replace the expiration of the lease in this procedure.

(3) Nothing if others pay for repairs or replacement.

f. Valuable Papers and Records, including those which exist on electronic or magnetic media (other than prepackaged software programs), at the cost of:

(1) Blank materials for reproducing the records; and

(2) Labor to transcribe or copy the records when there is a duplicate.

F. Additional Conditions

The following conditions apply in addition to the Common Policy Conditions and the Commercial Property Conditions.

1. Coinsurance

If a Coinsurance percentage is shown in the Declarations, the following condition applies.

a. We will not pay the full amount of any loss if the value of Covered Property at the time of loss times the Coinsurance percentage shown for it in the Declarations is greater than the Limit of Insurance for the property.

Instead, we will determine the most we will pay using the following steps:

(1) Multiply the value of Covered Property at the time of loss by the Coinsurance percentage;

(2) Divide the Limit of Insurance of the property by the figure determined in Step **(1)**;

(3) Multiply the total amount of loss, before the application of any deductible, by the figure determined in Step **(2)**; and

(4) Subtract the deductible from the figure determined in Step **(3)**.

We will pay the amount determined in Step **(4)** or the limit of insurance, whichever is less. For the remainder, you will either have to rely on other insurance or absorb the loss yourself.

Example No. 1 (Underinsurance):

When:		
The value of the property is	$	250,000
The Coinsurance percentage for it is		80%
The Limit of Insurance for it is	$	100,000
The Deductible is	$	250
The amount of loss is	$	40,000

Step **(1)**: $250,000 x 80% = $200,000 (the minimum amount of insurance to meet your Coinsurance requirements)

Step **(2)**: $100,000 ÷ $200,000 = .50

Step **(3)**: $40,000 x .50 = $20,000

Step **(4)**: $20,000 ⊐ $250 = $19,750

We will pay no more than $19,750. The remaining $20,250 is not covered.

Example No. 2 (Adequate Insurance):

When:

The value of the property is	$	250,000
The Coinsurance percentage for it is		80%
The Limit of Insurance for it is	$	200,000
The Deductible is	$	250
The amount of loss is	$	40,000

The minimum amount of insurance to meet your Coinsurance requirement is $200,000 ($250,000 x 80%). Therefore, the Limit of Insurance in this Example is adequate and no penalty applies. We will pay no more than $39,750 ($40,000 amount of loss minus the deductible of $250).

b. If one Limit of Insurance applies to two or more separate items, this condition will apply to the total of all property to which the limit applies.

Example No. 3:

When:

The value of property is:		
Bldg. at Location No. 1	$	75,000
Bldg. at Location No. 2	$	100,000
Personal Property at Location No. 2	$	75,000
	$	250,000
The Coinsurance percentage for it is		90%
The Limit of Insurance for Buildings and Personal Property at Location Nos. 1 and 2 is	$	180,000
The Deductible is	$	1,000
The amount of loss is:		
Bldg. at Location No. 2	$	30,000
Personal Property at Location No. 2.	$	20,000
	$	50,000

Step **(1):** $250,000 x 90% = $225,000 (the minimum amount of insurance to meet your Coinsurance requirements and to avoid the penalty shown below)

Step **(2):** $180,000 ÷ $225,000 = .80

Step **(3):** $50,000 x .80 = $40,000

Step **(4):** $40,000 ☐ $1,000 = $39,000

We will pay no more than $39,000. The remaining $11,000 is not covered.

2. Mortgageholders

a. The term mortgageholder includes trustee.

b. We will pay for covered loss of or damage to buildings or structures to each mortgageholder shown in the Declarations in their order of precedence, as interests may appear.

c. The mortgageholder has the right to receive loss payment even if the mortgageholder has started foreclosure or similar action on the building or structure.

d. If we deny your claim because of your acts or because you have failed to comply with the terms of this Coverage Part, the mortgageholder will still have the right to receive loss payment if the mortgageholder:

(1) Pays any premium due under this Coverage Part at our request if you have failed to do so;

(2) Submits a signed, sworn proof of loss within 60 days after receiving notice from us of your failure to do so; and

(3) Has notified us of any change in ownership, occupancy or substantial change in risk known to the mortgageholder.

All of the terms of this Coverage Part will then apply directly to the mortgageholder.

e. If we pay the mortgageholder for any loss or damage and deny payment to you because of your acts or because you have failed to comply with the terms of this Coverage Part:

(1) The mortgageholder's rights under the mortgage will be transferred to us to the extent of the amount we pay; and

(2) The mortgageholder's right to recover the full amount of the mortgageholder's claim will not be impaired.

At our option, we may pay to the mortgageholder the whole principal on the mortgage plus any accrued interest. In this event, your mortgage and note will be transferred to us and you will pay your remaining mortgage debt to us.

f. If we cancel this policy, we will give written notice to the mortgageholder at least:

(1) 10 days before the effective date of cancellation if we cancel for your nonpayment of premium; or

(2) 30 days before the effective date of cancellation if we cancel for any other reason.

g. If we elect not to renew this policy, we will give written notice to the mortgageholder at least 10 days before the expiration date of this policy.

G. Optional Coverages

If shown as applicable in the Declarations, the following Optional Coverages apply separately to each item.

1. Agreed Value

a. The Additional Condition, Coinsurance, does not apply to Covered Property to which this Optional Coverage applies. We will pay no more for loss of or damage to that property than the proportion that the Limit of Insurance under this Coverage Part for the property bears to the Agreed Value shown for it in the Declarations.

b. If the expiration date for this Optional Coverage shown in the Declarations is not extended, the Additional Condition, Coinsurance, is reinstated and this Optional Coverage expires.

c. The terms of this Optional Coverage apply only to loss or damage that occurs:

(1) On or after the effective date of this Optional Coverage; and

(2) Before the Agreed Value expiration date shown in the Declarations or the policy expiration date, whichever occurs first.

2. Inflation Guard

a. The Limit of Insurance for property to which this Optional Coverage applied will automatically increase by the annual percentage shown in the Declarations.

b. The amount of increase will be:

(1) The Limit of Insurance that applied on the most recent of the policy inception date, the policy anniversary date, or any other policy change amending the Limit of Insurance, times

(2) The percentage of annual increase shown in the Declarations, expressed as a decimal (example: 8% is .08), times

(3) The number of days since the beginning of the current policy year or the effective date of the most recent policy change amending the Limit of Insurance, divided by 365.

Example:

If:

The applicable Limit of Insurance is	$	100,000
The annual percentage increase is		8%
The number of days since the beginning of the policy year (or last policy change) is		146
The amount of increase is $100,000 x .08 x 146 ÷ 365 =	$	3,200

3. Replacement Cost

a. Replacement Cost (without deduction for depreciation) replaces Actual Cash Value in the Loss Condition, Valuation, of this Coverage Form.

b. This Optional Coverage does not apply to:

(1) Personal property of others;

(2) Contents of a residence;

(3) Manuscripts;

(4) Works of art, antiques or rare articles, including etchings, pictures, statuary, marbles, bronzes, porcelains and bric-a-brac; or

(5) "Stock", unless the Including "Stock" option is shown in the Declarations.

Under the terms of this Replacement Cost Optional Coverage, tenants' improvements and betterments are not considered to be the personal property of others.

c. You may make a claim for loss or damage covered by this insurance on an actual cash value basis instead of on a replacement cost basis. In the event you elect to have loss or damage settled on an actual cash value basis, you may still make a claim for the additional coverage this Optional Coverage provides if you notify us of your intent to do so within 180 days after the loss or damage.

d. We will not pay on a replacement cost basis for any loss or damage:

(1) Until the lost or damaged property is actually repaired or replaced; and

     Copyright, Insurance Services Office, Inc., 1999   CP 00 10 10 00   □

(2) Unless the repairs or replacement are made as soon as reasonably possible after the loss or damage.

With respect to tenants' improvements and betterments, the following also apply:

(3) If the conditions in **d.(1)** and **d.(2)** above are not met, the value of tenants' improvements and betterments will be determined as a proportion of your original cost, as set forth in the Valuation Condition of this Coverage Form; and

(4) We will not pay for loss or damage to tenants' improvements and betterments if others pay for repairs or replacement.

e. We will not pay more for loss or damage on a replacement cost basis than the least of **(1)**, **(2)** or **(3)**, subject to **f.** below:

(1) The Limit of Insurance applicable to the lost or damaged property;

(2) The cost to replace the lost or damaged property with other property:

(a) Of comparable material and quality; and

(b) Used for the same purpose; or

(3) The amount actually spent that is necessary to repair or replace the lost or damaged property.

If a building is rebuilt at a new premises, the cost described in **e.(2)** above is limited to the cost which would have been incurred if the building had been rebuilt at the original premises.

f. The cost of repair or replacement does not include the increased cost attributable to enforcement of any ordinance or law regulating the construction, use or repair of any property.

4. Extension Of Replacement Cost To Personal Property Of Others

a. If the Replacement Cost Optional Coverage is shown as applicable in the Declarations, then this Extension may also be shown as applicable. If the Declarations show this Extension as applicable, then Paragraph **3.b.(1)** of the Replacement Cost Optional Coverage is deleted and all other provisions of the Replacement Cost Optional Coverage apply to replacement cost on personal property of others.

b. With respect to replacement cost on the personal property of others, the following limitation applies:

If an item(s) of personal property of others is subject to a written contract which governs your liability for loss or damage to that item(s), then valuation of that item(s) will be based on the amount for which you are liable under such contract, but not to exceed the lesser of the replacement cost of the property or the applicable Limit of Insurance.

H. Definitions

1. "Pollutants" means any solid, liquid, gaseous or thermal irritant or contaminant, including smoke, vapor, soot, fumes, acids, alkalis, chemicals and waste. Waste includes materials to be recycled, reconditioned or reclaimed.

2. "Stock" means merchandise held in storage or for sale, raw materials and in-process or finished goods, including supplies used in their packing or shipping.

 Copyright, Insurance Services Office, Inc., 1999

COMMERCIAL PROPERTY
CP 00 17 10 00

CONDOMINIUM ASSOCIATION COVERAGE FORM

Various provisions in this policy restrict coverage. Read the entire policy carefully to determine rights, duties and what is and is not covered.

Throughout this policy the words "you" and "your" refer to the Named Insured shown in the Declarations. The words "we", "us" and "our" refer to the Company providing this insurance.

Other words and phrases that appear in quotation marks have special meaning. Refer to Section **H. ⊐ Definitions.**

A. Coverage

We will pay for direct physical loss of or damage to Covered Property at the premises described in the Declarations caused by or resulting from any Covered Cause of Loss.

1. Covered Property

Covered Property, as used in this Coverage Part, means the type of property described in this Section, **A.1.**, and limited in **A.2.**, Property Not Covered, if a Limit of Insurance is shown in the Declarations for that type of property.

a. **Building,** meaning the building or structure described in the Declarations, including:

(1) Completed additions;

(2) Fixtures, outside of individual units, including outdoor fixtures;

(3) Permanently installed:

(a) Machinery and

(b) Equipment;

(4) Personal property owned by you that is used to maintain or service the building or structure or its premises, including:

(a) Fire extinguishing equipment;

(b) Outdoor furniture;

(c) Floor coverings; and

(d) Appliances used for refrigerating, ventilating, cooking, dishwashing or laundering that are not contained within individual units;

(5) If not covered by other insurance:

(a) Additions under construction, alterations and repairs to the building or structure;

(b) Materials, equipment, supplies, and temporary structures, on or within 100 feet of the described premises, used for making additions, alterations or repairs to the building or structure; and

(6) Any of the following types of property contained within a unit, regardless of ownership, if your Condominium Association Agreement requires you to insure it:

(a) Fixtures, improvements and alterations that are a part of the building or structure; and

(b) Appliances, such as those used for refrigerating, ventilating, cooking, dishwashing, laundering, security or housekeeping.

But Building does not include personal property owned by, used by or in the care, custody or control of a unit-owner except for personal property listed in Paragraph **A.1.a.(6)** above.

b. **Your Business Personal Property** located in or on the building described in the Declarations or in the open (or in a vehicle) within 100 feet of the described premises, consisting of the following:

(1) Personal property owned by you or owned indivisibly by all unit-owners;

(2) Your interest in the labor, materials or services furnished or arranged by you on personal property of others;

(3) Leased personal property for which you have a contractual responsibility to insure, unless otherwise provided for under Personal Property of Others.

But Your Business Personal Property does not include personal property owned only by a unit-owner.

c. **Personal Property Of Others** that is:

(1) In your care, custody or control; and

(2) Located in or on the building described in the Declarations or in the open (or in a vehicle) within 100 feet of the described premises.

However, our payment for loss of or damage to personal property of others will only be for the account of the owner of the property.

2. **Property Not Covered**

Covered Property does not include:

a. Accounts, bills, currency, deeds, food stamps or other evidences of debt, money, notes or securities. Lottery tickets held for sale are not securities;

b. Animals, unless owned by others and boarded by you;

c. Automobiles held for sale;

d. Bridges, roadways, walks, patios or other paved surfaces;

e. Contraband, or property in the course of illegal transportation or trade;

f. The cost of excavations, grading, back filling or filling;

g. Foundations of buildings, structures, machinery or boilers if their foundations are below:

(1) The lowest basement floor; or

(2) The surface of the ground if there is no basement.

h. Land (including land on which the property is located), water, growing crops or lawns;

i. Personal property while airborne or waterborne;

j. Bulkheads, pilings, piers, wharves or docks;

k. Property that is covered under this or any other policy in which it is more specifically described, except for the excess of the amount due (whether you can collect on it or not) from that other insurance;

l. Retaining walls that are not part of a building;

m. Underground pipes, flues or drains;

n. The cost to research, replace or restore the information on valuable papers and records, including those which exist on electronic or magnetic media, except as provided in the Coverage Extensions;

o. Vehicles or self-propelled machines (including aircraft or watercraft) that:

(1) Are licensed for use on public roads; or

(2) Are operated principally away from the described premises.

This paragraph does not apply to:

(a) Vehicles or self-propelled machines or autos you manufacture or warehouse;

(b) Vehicles or self-propelled machines, other than autos, you hold for sale;

(c) Rowboats or canoes out of water at the described premises; or

(d) Trailers, but only to the extent provided for in the Coverage Extension for Non-Owned Detached Trailers.

p. The following property while outside of buildings:

(1) Grain, hay, straw or other crops; or

(2) Fences, radio or television antennas (including satellite dishes) and their lead-in wiring, masts or towers, signs (other than signs attached to buildings), trees, shrubs, or plants (other than "stock" of trees, shrubs or plants), all except as provided in the Coverage Extensions.

3. **Covered Causes Of Loss**

See applicable Causes of Loss Form as shown in the Declarations.

4. **Additional Coverages**

a. **Debris Removal**

(1) Subject to Paragraphs **(3)** and **(4)**, we will pay your expense to remove debris of Covered Property caused by or resulting from a Covered Cause of Loss that occurs during the policy period. The expenses will be paid only if they are reported to us in writing within 180 days of the date of direct physical loss or damage.

(2) Debris Removal does not apply to costs to:

(a) Extract "pollutants" from land or water; or

(b) Remove, restore or replace polluted land or water.

(3) Subject to the exceptions in Paragraph **(4)**, the following provisions apply:

(a) The most we will pay for the total of direct physical loss or damage plus debris removal expense is the Limit of Insurance applicable to the Covered Property that has sustained loss or damage.

Copyright, Insurance Services Office, Inc., 1999   **CP 00 17 10 00**   □

(b) Subject to **(a)** above, the amount we will pay for debris removal expense is limited to 25% of the sum of the deductible plus the amount that we pay for direct physical loss or damage to the Covered Property that has sustained loss or damage.

(4) We will pay up to an additional $10,000 for debris removal expense, for each location, in any one occurrence of physical loss or damage to Covered Property, if one or both of the following circumstances apply:

(a) The total of the actual debris removal expense plus the amount we pay for direct physical loss or damage exceeds the Limit of Insurance on the Covered Property that has sustained loss or damage.

(b) The actual debris removal expense exceeds 25% of the sum of the deductible plus the amount that we pay for direct physical loss or damage to the Covered Property that has sustained loss or damage.

Therefore, if **(4)(a)** and/or **(4)(b)** apply, our total payment for direct physical loss or damage and debris removal expense may reach but will never exceed the Limit of Insurance on the Covered Property that has sustained loss or damage, plus $10,000.

(5) Examples

The following examples assume that there is no coinsurance penalty.

Example #1

Limit of Insurance	$ 90,000
Amount of Deductible	$ 500
Amount of Loss	$ 50,000
Amount of Loss Payable	$ 49,500
	($50,000 ⊐ $500)
Debris Removal Expense	$ 10,000
Debris Removal Expense Payable	$ 10,000

($10,000 is 20% of $50,000)

The debris removal expense is less than 25% of the sum of the loss payable plus the deductible. The sum of the loss payable and the debris removal expense ($49,500 + $10,000 = $59,500) is less than the Limit of Insurance. Therefore, the full amount of debris removal expense is payable in accordance with the terms of Paragraph **(3)**.

Example #2

Limit of Insurance	$ 90,000
Amount of Deductible	$ 500
Amount of Loss	$ 80,000
Amount of Loss Payable	$ 79,500
	($80,000 ⊐ $500)
Debris Removal Expense	$ 30,000
Debris Removal Expense Payable	
Basic Amount	$ 10,500
Additional Amount	$ 10,000

The basic amount payable for debris removal expense under the terms of Paragraph **(3)** is calculated as follows: $80,000 ($79,500 + $500) x .25 = $20,000; capped at $10,500. The cap applies because the sum of the loss payable ($79,500) and the basic amount payable for debris removal expense ($10,500) cannot exceed the Limit of Insurance ($90,000).

The additional amount payable for debris removal expense is provided in accordance with the terms of Paragraph **(4)**, because the debris removal expense ($30,000) exceeds 25% of the loss payable plus the deductible ($30,000 is 37.5% of $80,000), and because the sum of the loss payable and debris removal expense ($79,500 + $30,000 = $109,500) would exceed the Limit of Insurance ($90,000). The additional amount of covered debris removal expense is $10,000, the maximum payable under Paragraph **(4)**. Thus the total payable for debris removal expense in this example is $20,500; $9,500 of the debris removal expense is not covered.

b. Preservation Of Property

If it is necessary for you to move Covered Property from the described premises to preserve it from loss or damage by a Covered Cause of Loss, we will pay for any direct physical loss or damage to that property:

(1) While it is being moved or while temporarily stored at another location; and

(2) Only if the loss or damage occurs within 30 days after the property is first moved.

c. Fire Department Service Charge

When the fire department is called to save or protect Covered Property from a Covered Cause of Loss, we will pay up to $1,000 for your liability for fire department service charges:

(1) Assumed by contract or agreement prior to loss; or

(2) Required by local ordinance.

No Deductible applies to this Additional Coverage.

d. Pollutant Clean Up And Removal

We will pay your expense to extract "pollutants" from land or water at the described premises if the discharge, dispersal, seepage, migration, release or escape of the "pollutants" is caused by or results from a Covered Cause of Loss that occurs during the policy period. The expenses will be paid only if they are reported to us in writing within 180 days of the date on which the Covered Cause of Loss occurs.

This Additional Coverage does not apply to costs to test for, monitor or assess the existence, concentration or effects of "pollutants". But we will pay for testing which is performed in the course of extracting the "pollutants" from the land or water.

The most we will pay under this Additional Coverage for each described premises is $10,000 for the sum of all covered expenses arising out of Covered Causes of Loss occurring during each separate 12 month period of this policy.

e. Increased Cost Of Construction

(1) This Additional Coverage applies only to buildings to which the Replacement Cost Optional Coverage applies.

(2) In the event of damage by a Covered Cause of Loss to a building that is Covered Property, we will pay the increased costs incurred to comply with enforcement of an ordinance or law in the course of repair, rebuilding or replacement of damaged parts of that property, subject to the limitations stated in **e.(3)** through **e.(9)** of this Additional Coverage.

(3) The ordinance or law referred to in **e.(2)** of this Additional Coverage is an ordinance or law that regulates the construction or repair of buildings or establishes zoning or land use requirements at the described premises, and is in force at the time of loss.

(4) Under this Additional Coverage, we will not pay any costs due to an ordinance or law that:

(a) You were required to comply with before the loss, even when the building was undamaged; and

(b) You failed to comply with.

(5) Under this Additional Coverage, we will not pay any costs associated with the enforcement of an ordinance or law which requires any insured or others to test for, monitor, clean up, remove, contain, treat, detoxify or neutralize, or in any way respond to, or assess the effects of "pollutants".

(6) The most we will pay under this Additional Coverage, for each described building insured under this Coverage Form, is $10,000 or 5% of the Limit of Insurance applicable to that building, whichever is less. If a damaged building is covered under a blanket Limit of Insurance which applies to more than one building or item of property, then the most we will pay under this Additional Coverage, for that damaged building, is the lesser of: $10,000 or 5% times the value of the damaged building as of the time of loss times the applicable coinsurance percentage.

The amount payable under this Additional Coverage is additional insurance.

    Copyright, Insurance Services Office, Inc., 1999   CP 00 17 10 00   ▢

(7) With respect to this Additional Coverage:

(a) We will not pay for the Increased Cost of Construction:

(i) Until the property is actually repaired or replaced, at the same or another premises; and

(ii) Unless the repairs or replacement are made as soon as reasonably possible after the loss or damage, not to exceed two years. We may extend this period in writing during the two years.

(b) If the building is repaired or replaced at the same premises, or if you elect to rebuild at another premises, the most we will pay for the Increased Cost of Construction, subject to the provisions of **e.(6)** of this Additional Coverage, is the increased cost of construction at the same premises.

(c) If the ordinance or law requires relocation to another premises, the most we will pay for the Increased Cost of Construction, subject to the provisions of **e.(6)** of this Additional Coverage, is the increased cost of construction at the new premises.

(8) This Additional Coverage is not subject to the terms of the Ordinance or Law Exclusion, to the extent that such Exclusion would conflict with the provisions of this Additional Coverage.

(9) The costs addressed in the Loss Payment and Valuation Conditions, and the Replacement Cost Optional Coverage, in this Coverage Form, do not include the increased cost attributable to enforcement of an ordinance or law. The amount payable under this Additional Coverage, as stated in **e.(6)** of this Additional Coverage, is not subject to such limitation.

5. Coverage Extensions

Except as otherwise provided, the following Extensions apply to property located in or on the building described in the Declarations or in the open (or in a vehicle) within 100 feet of the described premises.

If a Coinsurance percentage of 80% or more is shown in the Declarations, you may extend the insurance provided by this Coverage Part as follows:

a. Newly Acquired Or Constructed Property

(1) Buildings

You may extend the insurance that applies to Building to apply to:

(a) Your new buildings while being built on the described premises; and

(b) Buildings you acquire at locations, other than the described premises, intended for:

(i) Similar use as the building described in the Declarations; or

(ii) Use as a warehouse.

The most we will pay for loss or damage under this Extension is $250,000 at each building.

(2) Your Business Personal Property

(a) If this policy covers Your Business Personal Property, you may extend that insurance to apply to:

(i) Business personal property, including such property that you newly acquire, at any location you acquire other than at fairs, trade shows or exhibitions;

(ii) Business personal property, including such property that you newly acquire, located at your newly constructed or acquired buildings at the location described in the Declarations; or

(iii) Business personal property that you newly acquire, located at the described premises.

The most we will pay for loss or damage under this Extension is $100,000 at each building.

(b) This Extension does not apply to:

(i) Personal property of others that is temporarily in your possession in the course of installing or performing work on such property; or

(ii) Personal property of others that is temporarily in your possession in the course of your manufacturing or wholesaling activities.

(3) Period Of Coverage

With respect to insurance on or at each newly acquired or constructed property, coverage will end when any of the following first occurs:

(a) This policy expires;

(b) 30 days expire after you acquire the property or begin construction of that part of the building that would qualify as covered property; or

(c) You report values to us.

We will charge you additional premium for values reported from the date you acquire the property or begin construction of that part of the building that would qualify as covered property.

b. Personal Effects And Property Of Others

You may extend the insurance that applies to Your Business Personal Property to apply to:

(1) Personal effects owned by you, your officers, your partners or members, your managers or your employees. This extension does not apply to loss or damage by theft.

(2) Personal property of others in your care, custody or control.

The most we will pay for loss or damage under this Extension is $2,500 at each described premises. Our payment for loss of or damage to personal property of others will only be for the account of the owner of the property.

c. Valuable Papers And Records ⊐ Cost Of Research

You may extend the insurance that applies to Your Business Personal Property to apply to your costs to research, replace or restore the lost information on lost or damaged valuable papers and records, including those which exist on electronic or magnetic media, for which duplicates do not exist. The most we will pay under this Extension is $2,500 at each described premises, unless a higher limit is shown in the Declarations.

d. Property Off-Premises

(1) You may extend the insurance provided by this Coverage Form to apply to your Covered Property while it is away from the described premises, if it is:

(a) Temporarily at a location you do not own, lease or operate;

(b) In storage at a location you lease, provided the lease was executed after the beginning of the current policy term; or

(c) At any fair, trade show or exhibition.

(2) This Extension does not apply to property:

(a) In or on a vehicle; or

(b) In the care, custody or control of your salespersons, unless the property is in such care, custody or control at a fair, trade show or exhibition.

(3) The most we will pay for loss or damage under this Extension is $10,000.

e. Outdoor Property

You may extend the insurance provided by this Coverage Form to apply to your outdoor fences, radio and television antennas (including satellite dishes), signs (other than signs attached to buildings), trees, shrubs and plants, (other than "stock" of trees, shrubs or plants), including debris removal expense, caused by or resulting from any of the following causes of loss if they are Covered Causes of Loss:

(1) Fire;

(2) Lightning;

(3) Explosion;

(4) Riot or Civil Commotion; or

(5) Aircraft.

The most we will pay for loss or damage under this Extension is $1,000, but not more than $250 for any one tree, shrub or plant. These limits apply to any one occurrence, regardless of the types or number of items lost or damaged in that occurrence.

f. Non-Owned Detached Trailers

(1) You may extend the insurance that applies to Your Business Personal Property to apply to loss or damage to trailers that you do not own, provided that:

(a) The trailer is used in your business;

(b) The trailer is in your care, custody or control at the premises described in the Declarations; and

(c) You have a contractual responsibility to pay for loss or damage to the trailer.

(2) We will not pay for any loss or damage that occurs:

(a) While the trailer is attached to any motor vehicle or motorized conveyance, whether or not the motor vehicle or motorized conveyance is in motion;

(b) During hitching or unhitching operations, or when a trailer becomes accidentally unhitched from a motor vehicle or motorized conveyance.

(3) The most we will pay for loss or damage under this Extension is $5,000, unless a higher limit is shown in the Declarations.

(4) This insurance is excess over the amount due (whether you can collect on it or not) from any other insurance covering such property.

Each of these Extensions is additional insurance. The Additional Condition, Coinsurance, does not apply to these Extensions.

B. Exclusions And Limitations

See applicable Causes of Loss Form as shown in the Declarations.

C. Limits Of Insurance

The most we will pay for loss or damage in any one occurrence is the applicable Limit of Insurance shown in the Declarations.

The most we will pay for loss or damage to outdoor signs attached to buildings is $1,000 per sign in any one occurrence.

The limits applicable to the Coverage Extensions and the Fire Department Service Charge and Pollutant Clean Up and Removal Additional Coverages are in addition to the Limits of Insurance.

Payments under the Preservation of Property Additional Coverage will not increase the applicable Limit of Insurance.

D. Deductible

In any one occurrence of loss or damage (hereinafter referred to as loss), we will first reduce the amount of loss if required by the Coinsurance Condition or the Agreed Value Optional Coverage. If the adjusted amount of loss is less than or equal to the Deductible, we will not pay for that loss. If the adjusted amount of loss exceeds the Deductible, we will then subtract the Deductible from the adjusted amount of loss, and will pay the resulting amount or the Limit of Insurance, whichever is less.

When the occurrence involves loss to more than one item of Covered Property and separate Limits of Insurance apply, the losses will not be combined in determining application of the Deductible. But the Deductible will be applied only once per occurrence.

Example No. 1:

(This example assumes there is no coinsurance penalty.)

Deductible:	$ 250
Limit of Insurance ▢ Bldg. 1:	$ 60,000
Limit of Insurance ▢ Bldg. 2:	$ 80,000
Loss to Bldg. 1:	$ 60,100
Loss to Bldg. 2:	$ 90,000

The amount of loss to Bldg. 1 ($60,100) is less than the sum ($60,250) of the Limit of Insurance applicable to Bldg. 1 plus the Deductible.

The Deductible will be subtracted from the amount of loss in calculating the loss payable for Bldg. 1:

$ 60,100
▢   250
$ 59,850 Loss Payable ▢ Bldg. 1

The Deductible applies once per occurrence and therefore is not subtracted in determining the amount of loss payable for Bldg. 2. Loss payable for Bldg. 2 is the Limit of Insurance of $80,000.

Total amount of loss payable: $59,850 + 80,000 = $139,850

Example No. 2:

(This example, too, assumes there is no coinsurance penalty.)

The Deductible and Limits of Insurance are the same as those in Example No. 1.

Loss to Bldg. 1: $70,000
(exceeds Limit of Insurance plus Deductible)
Loss to Bldg. 2: $90,000
(exceeds Limit of Insurance plus Deductible)
Loss Payable ▢ Bldg. 1: $60,000
(Limit of Insurance)
Loss Payable ▢ Bldg. 2: $80,000
(Limit of Insurance)
Total amount of loss payable: $140,000

E. Loss Conditions

The following conditions apply in addition to the Common Policy Conditions and the Commercial Property Conditions.

1. Abandonment

There can be no abandonment of any property to us.

2. Appraisal

If we and you disagree on the value of the property or the amount of loss, either may make written demand for an appraisal of the loss. In this event, each party will select a competent and impartial appraiser. The two appraisers will select an umpire. If they cannot agree, either may request that selection be made by a judge of a court having jurisdiction. The appraisers will state separately the value of the property and amount of loss. If they fail to agree, they will submit their differences to the umpire. A decision agreed to by any two will be binding. Each party will:

a. Pay its chosen appraiser; and

b. Bear the other expenses of the appraisal and umpire equally.

If there is an appraisal, we will still retain our right to deny the claim.

3. Duties In The Event Of Loss Or Damage

a. You must see that the following are done in the event of loss or damage to Covered Property:

(1) Notify the police if a law may have been broken.

(2) Give us prompt notice of the loss or damage. Include a description of the property involved.

(3) As soon as possible, give us a description of how, when and where the loss or damage occurred.

(4) Take all reasonable steps to protect the Covered Property from further damage, and keep a record of your expenses necessary to protect the Covered Property, for consideration in the settlement of the claim. This will not increase the Limit of Insurance. However, we will not pay for any subsequent loss or damage resulting from a cause of loss that is not a Covered Cause of Loss. Also, if feasible, set the damaged property aside and in the best possible order for examination.

(5) At our request, give us complete inventories of the damaged and undamaged property. Include quantities, costs, values and amount of loss claimed.

(6) As often as may be reasonably required, permit us to inspect the property proving the loss or damage and examine your books and records.

Also permit us to take samples of damaged and undamaged property for inspection, testing and analysis, and permit us to make copies from your books and records.

(7) Send us a signed, sworn proof of loss containing the information we request to investigate the claim. You must do this within 60 days after our request. We will supply you with the necessary forms.

(8) Cooperate with us in the investigation or settlement of the claim.

b. We may examine any insured under oath, while not in the presence of any other insured and at such times as may be reasonably required, about any matter relating to this insurance or the claim, including an insured's books and records. In the event of an examination, an insured's answers must be signed.

4. Loss Payment

a. In the event of loss or damage covered by this Coverage Form, at our option, we will either:

(1) Pay the value of lost or damaged property;

(2) Pay the cost of repairing or replacing the lost or damaged property, subject to **b.** below;

(3) Take all or any part of the property at an agreed or appraised value; or

(4) Repair, rebuild or replace the property with other property of like kind and quality, subject to **b.** below.

We will determine the value of lost or damaged property, or the cost of its repair or replacement, in accordance with the applicable terms of the Valuation Condition in this Coverage Form or any applicable provision which amends or supersedes the Valuation Condition.

b. The cost to repair, rebuild or replace does not include the increased cost attributable to enforcement of any ordinance or law regulating the construction, use or repair of any property.

c. We will give notice of our intentions within 30 days after we receive the sworn proof of loss.

d. We will not pay you more than your financial interest in the Covered Property.

e. We may adjust losses with the owners of lost or damaged property if other than you. If we pay the owners, such payments will satisfy your claims against us for the owners' property. We will not pay the owners more than their financial interest in the Covered Property.

f. We may elect to defend you against suits arising from claims of owners of property. We will do this at our expense.

     Copyright, Insurance Services Office, Inc., 1999   CP 00 17 10 00   □

g. We will pay for covered loss or damage to Covered Property within 30 days after we receive the sworn proof of loss, if you have complied with all of the terms of this Coverage Part and:

(1) We have reached agreement with you on the amount of loss; or

(2) An appraisal award has been made.

If you name an insurance trustee, we will adjust losses with you, but we will pay the insurance trustee. If we pay the trustee, the payments will satisfy your claims against us.

5. Recovered Property

If either you or we recover any property after loss settlement, that party must give the other prompt notice. At your option, the property will be returned to you. You must then return to us the amount we paid to you for the property. We will pay recovery expenses and the expenses to repair the recovered property, subject to the Limit of Insurance.

6. Unit-Owner's Insurance

A unit-owner may have other insurance covering the same property as this insurance. This insurance is intended to be primary, and not to contribute with such other insurance.

7. Vacancy

a. Description Of Terms

(1) As used in this Vacancy Condition, the term building and the term vacant have the meanings set forth in **(1)(a)** and **(1)(b)** below:

(a) When this policy is issued to a tenant, and with respect to that tenant's interest in Covered Property, building means the unit or suite rented or leased to the tenant. Such building is vacant when it does not contain enough business personal property to conduct customary operations.

(b) When this policy is issued to the owner or general lessee of a building, building means the entire building. Such building is vacant unless at least 31% of its total square footage is:

(i) Rented to a lessee or sub-lessee and used by the lessee or sub-lessee to conduct its customary operations; and/or

(ii) Used by the building owner to conduct customary operations.

(2) Buildings under construction or renovation are not considered vacant.

b. Vacancy Provisions

If the building where loss or damage occurs has been vacant for more than 60 consecutive days before that loss or damage occurs:

(1) We will not pay for any loss or damage caused by any of the following even if they are Covered Causes of Loss:

(a) Vandalism;

(b) Sprinkler leakage, unless you have protected the system against freezing;

(c) Building glass breakage;

(d) Water damage;

(e) Theft; or

(f) Attempted theft.

(2) With respect to Covered Causes of Loss other than those listed in **b.(1)(a)** through **b.(1)(f)** above, we will reduce the amount we would otherwise pay for the loss or damage by 15%.

8. Valuation

We will determine the value of Covered Property in the event of loss or damage as follows:

a. At actual cash value as of the time of loss or damage, except as provided in **b., c.** and **d.** below.

b. If the Limit of Insurance for Building satisfies the Additional Condition, Coinsurance, and the cost to repair or replace the damaged building property is $2,500 or less, we will pay the cost of building repairs or replacement.

The cost of building repairs or replacement does not include the increased cost attributable to enforcement of any ordinance or law regulating the construction, use or repair of any property. However, the following property will be valued at the actual cash value even when attached to the building:

(1) Awnings or floor coverings;

(2) Appliances for refrigerating, ventilating, cooking, dishwashing or laundering; or

(3) Outdoor equipment or furniture.

c. Glass at the cost of replacement with safety glazing material if required by law.

d. Valuable Papers and Records, including those which exist on electronic or magnetic media (other than prepackaged software programs), at the cost of:

(1) Blank materials for reproducing the records; and

(2) Labor to transcribe or copy the records when there is a duplicate.

9. Waiver Of Rights Of Recovery

We waive our rights to recover payment from any unit-owner of the condominium that is shown in the Declarations.

F. Additional Conditions

The following conditions apply in addition to the Common Policy Conditions and the Commercial Property Conditions.

1. Coinsurance

If a Coinsurance percentage is shown in the Declarations, the following condition applies.

a. We will not pay the full amount of any loss if the value of Covered Property at the time of loss times the Coinsurance percentage shown for it in the Declarations is greater than the Limit of Insurance for the property.

Instead, we will determine the most we will pay using the following steps:

(1) Multiply the value of Covered Property at the time of loss by the Coinsurance percentage;

(2) Divide the Limit of Insurance of the property by the figure determined in Step **(1)**;

(3) Multiply the total amount of loss, before the application of any deductible, by the figure determined in Step **(2)**; and

(4) Subtract the deductible from the figure determined in Step **(3)**.

We will pay the amount determined in Step **(4)** or the Limit of Insurance, whichever is less. For the remainder, you will either have to rely on other insurance or absorb the loss yourself.

Example No. 1 (Underinsurance):

When:	The value of the property is	$	250,000
	The Coinsurance percentage for it is		80%
	The Limit of Insurance for it is	$	100,000
	The Deductible is	$	250
	The amount of loss is	$	40,000

Step **(1):**	$250,000 x 80% = $200,000 (the minimum amount of insurance to meet your Coinsurance requirements)
Step **(2):**	$100,000 ÷ $200,000 = .50
Step **(3):**	$40,000 x .50 = $20,000
Step **(4):**	$20,000 - $250 = $19,750

We will pay no more than $19,750. The remaining $20,250 is not covered.

Example No. 2 (Adequate Insurance):

When:	The value of the property is	$	250,000
	The Coinsurance percentage for it is		80%
	The Limit of Insurance for it is	$	200,000
	The Deductible is	$	250
	The amount of loss is	$	40,000

The minimum amount of insurance to meet your Coinsurance requirement is $200,000 ($250,000 x 80%). Therefore, the Limit of Insurance in this Example is adequate and no penalty applies. We will pay no more than $39,750 ($40,000 amount of loss minus the deductible of $250).

b. If one Limit of Insurance applies to two or more separate items, this condition will apply to the total of all property to which the limit applies.

Example No. 3:

When:	The value of property is:		
	Bldg. at Location No. 1	$	75,000
	Bldg. at Location No. 2	$	100,000
	Personal Property at Location No. 2	$	75,000
		$	250,000
	The Coinsurance percentage for it is		90%
	The Limit of Insurance for Buildings and Personal Property at Location Nos. 1 and 2 is	$	180,000
	The Deductible is	$	1,000
	The amount of loss is:		
	Bldg. at Location No. 2	$	30,000
	Personal Property at Location No. 2	$	20,000
		$	50,000

Step **(1):**	$250,000 x 90% = $225,000 (the minimum amount of insurance to meet your Coinsurance requirements and to avoid the penalty shown below)
Step **(2):**	$180,000 ÷ $225,000 = .80
Step **(3):**	$50,000 x .80 = $40,000
Step **(4):**	$40,000 ⊐ $1,000 = $39,000

We will pay no more than $39,000. The remaining $11,000 is not covered.

Copyright, Insurance Services Office, Inc., 1999

2. Mortgageholders

a. The term mortgageholder includes trustee.

b. We will pay for covered loss of or damage to buildings or structures to each mortgageholder shown in the Declarations in their order of precedence, as interests may appear.

c. The mortgageholder has the right to receive loss payment even if the mortgageholder has started foreclosure or similar action on the building or structure.

d. If we deny your claim because of your acts or because you have failed to comply with the terms of this Coverage Part, the mortgageholder will still have the right to receive loss payment if the mortgageholder:

   (1) Pays any premium due under this Coverage Part at our request if you have failed to do so;

   (2) Submits a signed, sworn proof of loss within 60 days after receiving notice from us of your failure to do so; and

   (3) Has notified us of any change in ownership, occupancy or substantial change in risk known to the mortgageholder.

   All of the terms of this Coverage Part will then apply directly to the mortgageholder.

e. If we pay the mortgageholder for any loss or damage and deny payment to you because of your acts or because you have failed to comply with the terms of this Coverage Part:

   (1) The mortgageholder's rights under the mortgage will be transferred to us to the extent of the amount we pay; and

   (2) The mortgageholder's right to recover the full amount of the mortgageholder's claim will not be impaired.

   At our option, we may pay to the mortgageholder the whole principal on the mortgage plus any accrued interest. In this event, your mortgage and note will be transferred to us and you will pay your remaining mortgage debt to us.

f. If we cancel this policy, we will give written notice to the mortgageholder at least:

   (1) 10 days before the effective date of cancellation if we cancel for your non-payment of premium; or

   (2) 30 days before the effective date of cancellation if we cancel for any other reason.

g. If we elect not to renew this policy, we will give written notice to the mortgageholder at least 10 days before the expiration date of this policy.

G. Optional Coverages

If shown as applicable in the Declarations, the following Optional Coverages apply separately to each item.

1. Agreed Value

a. The Additional Condition, Coinsurance, does not apply to Covered Property to which this Optional Coverage applies. We will pay no more for loss of or damage to that property than the proportion that the Limit of Insurance under this Coverage Part for the property bears to the Agreed Value shown for it in the Declarations.

b. If the expiration date for this Optional Coverage shown in the Declarations is not extended, the Additional Condition, Coinsurance, is reinstated and this Optional Coverage expires.

c. The terms of this Optional Coverage apply only to loss or damage that occurs:

   (1) On or after the effective date of this Optional Coverage; and

   (2) Before the Agreed Value expiration date shown in the Declarations or the policy expiration date, whichever occurs first.

2. Inflation Guard

a. The Limit of Insurance for property to which this Optional Coverage applies will automatically increase by the annual percentage shown in the Declarations.

b. The amount of increase will be:

   (1) The Limit of Insurance that applied on the most recent of the policy inception date, the policy anniversary date, or any other policy change amending the Limit of Insurance, times

   (2) The percentage of annual increase shown in the Declarations, expressed as a decimal (example: 8% is .08), times

   (3) The number of days since the beginning of the current policy year or the effective date of the most recent policy change amending the Limit of Insurance, divided by 365.

Example:

If:		
The applicable Limit of Insurance is	$	100,000
The annual percentage increase is		8%
The number of days since the beginning of the policy year (or last policy change) is		146
The amount of increase is $100,000 x .08 x 146 ÷ 365 =	$	3,200

3. Replacement Cost

a. Replacement Cost (without deduction for depreciation) replaces Actual Cash Value in the Loss Condition, Valuation, of this Coverage Form.

b. This Optional Coverage does not apply to:

(1) Personal property of others;

(2) Contents of a residence;

(3) Manuscripts; or

(4) Works of art, antiques or rare articles, including etchings, pictures, statuary, marbles, bronzes, porcelains and bric-a-brac.

Under the terms of this Replacement Cost Optional Coverage, personal property owned indivisibly by all unit owners, and the property covered under Paragraph **A.1.a.(6)** of this Coverage Form, are not considered to be the personal property of others.

c. You may make a claim for loss or damage covered by this insurance on an actual cash value basis instead of on a replacement cost basis. In the event you elect to have loss or damage settled on an actual cash value basis, you may still make a claim for the additional coverage this Optional Coverage provides if you notify us of your intent to do so within 180 days after the loss or damage.

d. We will not pay on a replacement cost basis for any loss or damage:

(1) Until the lost or damaged property is actually repaired or replaced; and

(2) Unless the repairs or replacement are made as soon as reasonably possible after the loss or damage.

e. We will not pay more for loss or damage on a replacement cost basis than the least of **(1)**, **(2)** or **(3)**, subject to **f.** below:

(1) The Limit of Insurance applicable to the lost or damaged property;

(2) The cost to replace the lost or damaged property with other property:

(a) Of comparable material and quality; and

(b) Used for the same purpose; or

(3) The amount actually spent that is necessary to repair or replace the lost or damaged property.

If a building is rebuilt at a new premises, the cost described in **e.(2)** above is limited to the cost which would have been incurred if the building had been rebuilt at the original premises.

f. The cost of repair or replacement does not include the increased cost attributable to enforcement of any ordinance or law regulating the construction, use or repair of any property.

4. Extension Of Replacement Cost To Personal Property Of Others

a. If the Replacement Cost Optional Coverage is shown as applicable in the Declarations, then this Extension may also be shown as applicable. If the Declarations show this Extension as applicable, then Paragraph **3.b.(1)** of the Replacement Cost Optional Coverage is deleted and all other provisions of the Replacement Cost Optional Coverage apply to replacement cost on personal property of others.

b. With respect to replacement cost on the personal property of others, the following limitation applies:

If an item(s) of personal property of others is subject to a written contract which governs your liability for loss or damage to that item(s), then valuation of that item(s) will be based on the amount for which you are liable under such contract, but not to exceed the lesser of the replacement cost of the property or the applicable Limit of Insurance.

H. Definitions

"Pollutants" means any solid, liquid, gaseous or thermal irritant or contaminant, including smoke, vapor, soot, fumes, acids, alkalis, chemicals and waste. Waste includes materials to be recycled, reconditioned or reclaimed.

  Copyright, Insurance Services Office, Inc., 1999 CP 00 17 10 00   □

COMMERCIAL PROPERTY
CP 00 18 10 00

CONDOMINIUM COMMERCIAL UNIT-OWNERS COVERAGE FORM

Various provisions in this policy restrict coverage. Read the entire policy carefully to determine rights, duties and what is and is not covered.

Throughout this policy the words "you" and "your" refer to the Named Insured shown in the Declarations. The words "we", "us" and "our" refer to the Company providing this insurance.

Other words and phrases that appear in quotation marks have special meaning. Refer to Section **H.** ❑ **Definitions.**

A. Coverage

We will pay for direct physical loss of or damage to Covered Property at the premises described in the Declarations caused by or resulting from any Covered Cause of Loss.

1. Covered Property

Covered Property, as used in this Coverage Part, means the type of property described in this Section, **A.1.**, and limited in **A.2.**, Property Not Covered, if a Limit of Insurance is shown in the Declarations for that type of property.

a. Your Business Personal Property located in or on the building described in the Declarations or in the open (or in a vehicle) within 100 feet of the described premises, consisting of the following unless otherwise specified in the Declarations or on the Your Business Personal Property ❑ Separation of Coverage form:

(1) Furniture;

(2) Fixtures, improvements and alterations making up part of the building and owned by you;

(3) Machinery and equipment;

(4) "Stock";

(5) All other personal property owned by you and used in your business;

(6) Labor, materials or services furnished or arranged by you on personal property of others;

(7) Leased personal property for which you have a contractual responsibility to insure, unless otherwise provided for under Personal Property of Others.

b. Personal Property of Others, that is:

(1) In your care, custody or control; and

(2) Located in or on the building described in the Declarations or in the open (or in a vehicle) within 100 feet of the described premises.

However, our payment for loss of or damage to personal property of others will only be for the account of the owner of the property.

2. Property Not Covered

Covered Property does not include:

a. Accounts, bills, currency, deeds, food stamps or other evidences of debt, money, notes or securities. Lottery tickets held for sale are not securities;

b. Animals, unless owned by others and boarded by you, or if owned by you, only as "stock" while inside of buildings;

c. Automobiles held for sale;

d. Contraband, or property in the course of illegal transportation or trade;

e. Water, growing crops or lawns;

f. Personal property while airborne or waterborne;

g. Property that is covered under another coverage form of this or any other policy in which it is more specifically described, except for the excess of the amount due (whether you can collect on it or not) from that other insurance;

h. The cost to research, replace or restore the information on valuable papers and records, including those which exist on electronic or magnetic media, except as provided in the Coverage Extensions;

i. Vehicles or self-propelled machines (including aircraft or watercraft) that:

(1) Are licensed for use on public roads; or

(2) Are operated principally away from the described premises.

This paragraph does not apply to:

(a) Vehicles or self-propelled machines or autos you manufacture, process or warehouse;

(b) Vehicles or self-propelled machines, other than autos, you hold for sale;

(c) Rowboats or canoes out of water at the described premises; or

(d) Trailers, but only to the extent provided for in the Coverage Extension for Non-Owned Detached Trailers.

j. The following property while outside of buildings:

(1) Grain, hay, straw or other crops; or

(2) Fences, radio or television antennas (including satellite dishes) and their lead-in wiring, masts or towers, signs (other than signs attached to buildings), trees, shrubs, or plants (other than "stock" of trees, shrubs or plants), all except as provided in the Coverage Extensions;

k. Any of the following types of property contained within a unit, regardless of ownership, if your Condominium Association Agreement requires the Association to insure it:

(1) Fixtures, improvements and alterations that are a part of the building; and

(2) Appliances, such as those used for refrigerating, ventilating, cooking, dishwashing, laundering, security or housekeeping.

3. Covered Causes Of Loss

See applicable Causes of Loss Form as shown in the Declarations.

4. Additional Coverages

a. Debris Removal

(1) Subject to Paragraphs **(3)** and **(4)**, we will pay your expense to remove debris of Covered Property caused by or resulting from a Covered Cause of Loss that occurs during the policy period. The expenses will be paid only if they are reported to us in writing within 180 days of the date of direct physical loss or damage.

(2) Debris Removal does not apply to costs to:

(a) Extract "pollutants" from land or water; or

(b) Remove, restore or replace polluted land or water.

(3) Subject to the exceptions in Paragraph **(4)**, the following provisions apply:

(a) The most we will pay for the total of direct physical loss or damage plus debris removal expense is the Limit of Insurance applicable to the Covered Property that has sustained loss or damage.

(b) Subject to **(a)** above, the amount we will pay for debris removal expense is limited to 25% of the sum of the deductible plus the amount that we pay for direct physical loss or damage to the Covered Property that has sustained loss or damage.

(4) We will pay up to an additional $10,000 for debris removal expense, for each location, in any one occurrence of physical loss or damage to Covered Property, if one or both of the following circumstances apply:

(a) The total of the actual debris removal expense plus the amount we pay for direct physical loss or damage exceeds the Limit of Insurance on the Covered Property that has sustained loss or damage.

(b) The actual debris removal expense exceeds 25% of the sum of the deductible plus the amount that we pay for direct physical loss or damage to the Covered Property that has sustained loss or damage.

Therefore, if **(4)(a)** and/or **(4)(b)** apply, our total payment for direct physical loss or damage and debris removal expense may reach but will never exceed the Limit of Insurance on the Covered Property that has sustained loss or damage, plus $10,000.

(5) Examples

The following examples assume that there is no coinsurance penalty.

Example #1

Limit of Insurance	$ 90,000
Amount of Deductible	$ 500
Amount of Loss	$ 50,000
Amount of Loss Payable	$ 49,500
	($50,000 - $500)
Debris Removal Expense	$ 10,000
Debris Removal Expense Payable	$ 10,000
($10,000 is 20% of $50,000)	

The debris removal expense is less than 25% of the sum of the loss payable plus the deductible. The sum of the loss payable and the debris removal expense ($49,500 + $10,000 = $59,500) is less than the Limit of Insurance. Therefore the full amount of debris removal expense is payable in accordance with the terms of Paragraph **(3).**

Example #2

Limit of Insurance	$ 90,000
Amount of Deductible	$ 500
Amount of Loss	$ 80,000
Amount of Loss Payable	$ 79,500
	($80,000 - $500)
Debris Removal Expense	$ 30,000
Debris Removal Expense Payable	
Basic Amount	$ 10,500
Additional Amount	$ 10,000

The basic amount payable for debris removal expense under the terms of Paragraph **(3)** is calculated as follows: $80,000 ($79,500 + $500) x .25 = $20,000; capped at $10,500. The cap applies because the sum of the loss payable ($79,500) and the basic amount payable for debris removal expense ($10,500) cannot exceed the Limit of Insurance ($90,000).

The additional amount payable for debris removal expense is provided in accordance with the terms of Paragraph **(4),** because the debris removal expense ($30,000) exceeds 25% of the loss payable plus the deductible ($30,000 is 37.5% of $80,000), and because the sum of the loss payable and debris removal expense ($79,500 + $30,000 = $109,500) would exceed the Limit of Insurance ($90,000). The additional amount of covered debris removal expense is $10,000, the maximum payable under Paragraph **(4).** Thus the total payable for debris removal expense in this example is $20,500; $9,500 of the debris removal expense is not covered.

b. Preservation Of Property

If it is necessary to move Covered Property from the described premises to preserve it from loss or damage by a Covered Cause of Loss, we will pay for any direct physical loss or damage to that property:

(1) While it is being moved or while temporarily stored at another location; and

(2) Only if the loss or damage occurs within 30 days after the property is first moved.

c. Fire Department Service Charge

When the fire department is called to save or protect Covered Property from a Covered Cause of Loss, we will pay up to $1,000 for your liability for fire department service charges:

(1) Assumed by contract or agreement prior to loss; or

(2) Required by local ordinance.

No Deductible applies to this Additional Coverage.

d. Pollutant Clean Up And Removal

We will pay your expense to extract "pollutants" from land or water at the described premises if the discharge, dispersal, seepage, migration, release or escape of the "pollutants" is caused by or results from a Covered Cause of Loss that occurs during the policy period. The expenses will be paid only if they are reported to us in writing within 180 days of the date on which the Covered Cause of Loss occurs.

This Additional Coverage does not apply to costs to test for, monitor or assess the existence, concentration or effects of "pollutants". But we will pay for testing which is performed in the course of extracting the "pollutants" from the land or water.

The most we will pay under this Additional Coverage for each described premises is $10,000 for the sum of all covered expenses arising out of Covered Causes of Loss occurring during each separate 12 month period of this policy.

5. Coverage Extensions

Except as otherwise provided, the following Extensions apply to property located in or on the building described in the Declarations or in the open (or in a vehicle) within 100 feet of the described premises.

If a Coinsurance percentage of 80% or more or, a Value Reporting period symbol, is shown in the Declarations, you may extend the insurance provided by this Coverage Part as follows:

a. Newly Acquired Property

(1) You may extend the insurance that applies to Your Business Personal Property to apply to:

   (a) Business personal property, including such property that you newly acquire, at any location you acquire other than at fairs, trade shows or exhibitions;

   (b) Business personal property, including such property that you newly acquire, located at your newly constructed or acquired buildings at the location described in the Declarations; or

   (c) Business personal property that you newly acquire, located at the described premises.

The most we will pay for loss or damage under this Extension is $100,000 at each building.

(2) This Extension does not apply to:

   (a) Personal property of others that is temporarily in your possession in the course of installing or performing work on such property; or

   (b) Personal property of others that is temporarily in your possession in the course of your manufacturing or wholesaling activities.

(3) Insurance under this Extension for each newly acquired property will end when any of the following first occurs:

   (a) This policy expires;

   (b) 30 days expire after you acquire the property; or

   (c) You report values to us.

We will charge you additional premium for values reported from the date you acquire the property.

b. Personal Effects And Property Of Others

You may extend the insurance that applies to Your Business Personal Property to apply to:

(1) Personal effects owned by you, your officers, your partners or members, your managers or your employees. This extension does not apply to loss or damage by theft.

(2) Personal property of others, in your care, custody or control.

The most we will pay for loss or damage under this Extension is $2,500 at each described premises. Our payment for loss of or damage to personal property of others will only be for the account of the owner of the property.

c. Valuable Papers And Records □ Cost Of Research

You may extend the insurance that applies to Your Business Personal Property to apply to your costs to research, replace or restore the lost information on lost or damaged valuable papers and records, including those which exist on electronic or magnetic media, for which duplicates do not exist. The most we will pay under this Extension is $2,500 at each described premises, unless a higher limit is shown in the Declarations.

d. Property Off-Premises

(1) You may extend the insurance that applies to Your Business Personal Property, to apply to your business personal property while it is away from the described premises, if it is:

   (a) Temporarily at a location you do not own, lease or operate;

   (b) In storage at a location you lease, provided the lease was executed after the beginning of the current policy term; or

   (c) At any fair, trade show or exhibition.

(2) This Extension does not apply to property:

   (a) In or on a vehicle; or

(b) In the care, custody or control of your salespersons, unless the property is in such care, custody or control at a fair, trade show or exhibition.

(3) The most we will pay for loss or damage under this Extension is $10,000.

e. Outdoor Property

You may extend the insurance that applies to Your Business Personal Property to apply to your outdoor fences, radio and television antennas (including satellite dishes), signs (other than signs attached to buildings), trees, shrubs and plants (other than "stock" of trees, shrubs or plants), including debris removal expense, caused by or resulting from any of the following causes of loss if they are Covered Causes of Loss:

(1) Fire;

(2) Lightning;

(3) Explosion;

(4) Riot or Civil Commotion; or

(5) Aircraft.

The most we will pay for loss or damage under this Extension is $1,000, but not more than $250 for any one tree, shrub or plant. These limits apply to any one occurrence, regardless of the types or number of items lost or damaged in that occurrence.

f. Non-Owned Detached Trailers

(1) You may extend the insurance that applies to Your Business Personal Property to apply to loss or damage to trailers that you do not own, provided that:

(a) The trailer is used in your business;

(b) The trailer is in your care, custody or control at the premises described in the Declarations; and

(c) You have a contractual responsibility to pay for loss or damage to the trailer.

(2) We will not pay for any loss or damage that occurs:

(a) While the trailer is attached to any motor vehicle or motorized conveyance, whether or not the motor vehicle or motorized conveyance is in motion;

(b) During hitching or unhitching operations, or when a trailer becomes accidentally unhitched from a motor vehicle or motorized conveyance.

(3) The most we will pay for loss or damage under this Extension is $5,000, unless a higher limit is shown in the Declarations.

(4) This insurance is excess over the amount due (whether you can collect on it or not) from any other insurance covering such property.

Each of these Extensions is additional insurance. The Additional Condition, Coinsurance, does not apply to these Extensions.

B. Exclusions And Limitations

See applicable Causes of Loss Form as shown in the Declarations.

C. Limits Of Insurance

The most we will pay for loss or damage in any one occurrence is the applicable Limit of Insurance shown in the Declarations.

The most we will pay for loss or damage to outdoor signs attached to buildings is $1,000 per sign in any one occurrence.

The limits applicable to the Coverage Extensions and the Fire Department Service Charge and Pollutant Clean Up and Removal Additional Coverages are in addition to the Limits of Insurance.

Payments under the Preservation of Property Additional Coverage will not increase the applicable Limit of Insurance.

D. Deductible

In any one occurrence of loss or damage (hereinafter referred to as loss), we will first reduce the amount of loss if required by the Coinsurance Condition or the Agreed Value Optional Coverage. If the adjusted amount of loss is less than or equal to the Deductible, we will not pay for that loss. If the adjusted amount of loss exceeds the Deductible, we will then subtract the Deductible from the adjusted amount of loss, and will pay the resulting amount or the Limit of Insurance, whichever is less.

When the occurrence involves loss to more than one item of Covered Property and separate Limits of Insurance apply, the losses will not be combined in determining application of the Deductible. But the Deductible will be applied only once per occurrence.

Example No. 1:

(This example assumes there is no coinsurance penalty.)

Deductible:	$	250
Limit of Insurance ☐ Bldg. 1:	$	60,000
Limit of Insurance ☐ Bldg. 2:	$	80,000
Loss to Bldg. 1:	$	60,100
Loss to Bldg. 2:	$	90,000

The amount of loss to Bldg. 1 ($60,100) is less than the sum ($60,250) of the Limit of Insurance applicable to Bldg. 1 plus the Deductible.

The Deductible will be subtracted from the amount of loss in calculating the loss payable for Bldg. 1:

$ 60,100

☐ 250

$ 59,850 Loss Payable ☐ Bldg. 1

The Deductible applies once per occurrence and therefore is not subtracted in determining the amount of loss payable for Bldg. 2. Loss payable for Bldg. 2 is the Limit of Insurance of $80,000.

Total amount of loss payable:

$59,850 + $80,000 = $139,850

Example No. 2:

(This example, too, assumes there is no coinsurance penalty.)

The Deductible and Limits of Insurance are the same as those in Example No. 1.

Loss to Bldg. 1: $70,000
  (exceeds Limit of Insurance plus Deductible)

Loss to Bldg. 2: $90,000
  (exceeds Limit of Insurance plus Deductible)

Loss Payable - Bldg. 1: $60,000
  (Limit of Insurance)

Loss Payable - Bldg. 2: $80,000
  (Limit of Insurance)

Total amount of loss payable: $140,000

E. Loss Conditions

The following conditions apply in addition to the Common Policy Conditions and the Commercial Property Conditions.

1. Abandonment

There can be no abandonment of any property to us.

2. Appraisal

If we and you disagree on the value of the property or the amount of loss, either may make written demand for an appraisal of the loss. In this event, each party will select a competent and impartial appraiser. The two appraisers will select an umpire. If they cannot agree, either may request that selection be made by a judge of a court having jurisdiction. The appraisers will state separately the value of the property and amount of loss. If they fail to agree, they will submit their differences to the umpire. A decision agreed to by any two will be binding. Each party will:

a. Pay its chosen appraiser; and

b. Bear the other expenses of the appraisal and umpire equally.

If there is an appraisal, we will still retain our right to deny the claim.

3. Condominium Association Insurance

The Condominium Association may have other insurance covering the same property as this insurance. This insurance is intended to be excess, and not to contribute with that other insurance.

4. Duties In The Event Of Loss Or Damage

a. You must see that the following are done in the event of loss or damage to Covered Property:

(1) Notify the police if a law may have been broken.

(2) Give us prompt notice of the loss or damage. Include a description of the property involved.

(3) As soon as possible, give us a description of how, when and where the loss or damage occurred.

(4) Take all reasonable steps to protect the Covered Property from further damage, and keep a record of your expenses necessary to protect the Covered Property, for consideration in the settlement of the claim. This will not increase the Limit of Insurance. However, we will not pay for any subsequent loss or damage resulting from a cause of loss that is not a Covered Cause of Loss. Also, if feasible, set the damaged property aside and in the best possible order for examination.

(5) At our request, give us complete inventories of the damaged and undamaged property. Include quantities, costs, values and amount of loss claimed.

(6) As often as may be reasonably required, permit us to inspect the property proving the loss or damage and examine your books and records.

Also permit us to take samples of damaged and undamaged property for inspection, testing and analysis, and permit us to make copies from your books and records.

(7) Send us a signed, sworn proof of loss containing the information we request to investigate the claim. You must do this within 60 days after our request. We will supply you with the necessary forms.

(8) Cooperate with us in the investigation or settlement of the claim.

b. We may examine any insured under oath, while not in the presence of any other insured and at such times as may be reasonably required, about any matter relating to this insurance or the claim, including an insured's books and records. In the event of an examination, an insured's answers must be signed.

5. Loss Payment

a. In the event of loss or damage covered by this Coverage Form, at our option, we will either:

(1) Pay the value of lost or damaged property;

(2) Pay the cost of repairing or replacing the lost or damaged property, subject to **b.** below;

(3) Take all or any part of the property at an agreed or appraised value; or

(4) Repair, rebuild or replace the property with other property of like kind and quality, subject to **b.** below.

We will determine the value of lost or damaged property, or the cost of its repair or replacement, in accordance with the applicable terms of the Valuation Condition in this Coverage Form or any applicable provision which amends or supersedes the Valuation Condition.

b. The cost to repair, rebuild or replace does not include the increased cost attributable to enforcement of any ordinance or law regulating the construction, use or repair of any property.

c. We will give notice of our intentions within 30 days after we receive the sworn proof of loss.

d. We will not pay you more than your financial interest in the Covered Property.

e. We may adjust losses with the owners of lost or damaged property if other than you. If we pay the owners, such payments will satisfy your claims against us for the owners' property. We will not pay the owners more than their financial interest in the Covered Property.

f. We may elect to defend you against suits arising from claims of owners of property. We will do this at our expense.

g. We will pay for covered loss or damage within 30 days after we receive the sworn proof of loss, if you have complied with all of the terms of this Coverage Part and:

(1) We have reached agreement with you on the amount of loss; or

(2) An appraisal award has been made.

6. Recovered Property

If either you or we recover any property after loss settlement, that party must give the other prompt notice. At your option, the property will be returned to you. You must then return to us the amount we paid to you for the property. We will pay recovery expenses to repair the recovered property, subject to the Limit of Insurance.

7. Vacancy

a. Description Of Terms

(1) As used in this Vacancy Condition, the term building and the term vacant have the meanings set forth in **(1)(a)** and **(1)(b)** below:

(a) When this policy is issued to a tenant, and with respect to that tenant's interest in Covered Property, building means the unit or suite rented or leased to the tenant. Such building is vacant when it does not contain enough business personal property to conduct customary operations.

(b) When this policy is issued to the owner or general lessee of a building, building means the entire building. Such building is vacant unless at least 31% of its total square footage is:

(i) Rented to a lessee or sub-lessee and used by the lessee or sub-lessee to conduct its customary operations; and/or

ii) Used by the building owner to conduct customary operations.

(2) Buildings under construction or renovation are not considered vacant.

b. Vacancy Provisions

If the building where loss or damage occurs has been vacant for more than 60 consecutive days before that loss or damage occurs:

(1) We will not pay for any loss or damage caused by any of the following even if they are Covered Causes of Loss:

(a) Vandalism;

(b) Sprinkler leakage, unless you have protected the system against freezing;

(c) Building glass breakage;

(d) Water damage;

(e) Theft; or

(f) Attempted theft.

(2) With respect to Covered Causes of Loss other than those listed in **b.(1)(a)** through **b.(1)(f)** above, we will reduce the amount we would otherwise pay for the loss or damage by 15%.

8. Valuation

We will determine the value of Covered Property in the event of loss or damage as follows:

a. At actual cash value as of the time of loss or damage, except as provided in **b.**, **c.** and **d.** below.

b. "Stock" you have sold but not delivered at the selling price less discounts and expenses you otherwise would have had.

c. Glass at the cost of replacement with safety glazing material if required by law.

d. Valuable Papers and Records, including those which exist on electronic or magnetic media (other than pre-packaged software programs) at the cost of:

(1) Blank materials for reproducing the records; and

(2) Labor to transcribe or copy the records when there is a duplicate.

F. Additional Condition

COINSURANCE

If a Coinsurance percentage is shown in the Declarations, the following condition applies in addition to the Common Policy Conditions and the Commercial Property Conditions.

a. We will not pay the full amount of any loss if the value of Covered Property at the time of loss times the Coinsurance percentage shown for it in the Declarations is greater than the Limit of Insurance for the property.

Instead, we will determine the most we will pay using the following steps:

(1) Multiply the value of Covered Property at the time of loss by the Coinsurance percentage;

(2) Divide the Limit of Insurance of the property by the figure determined in Step **(1)**;

(3) Multiply the total amount of loss, before the application of any deductible, by the figure determined in Step **(2)**; and

(4) Subtract the deductible from the figure determined in Step **(3)**.

We will pay the amount determined in Step **(4)** or the limit of insurance, whichever is less. For the remainder, you will either have to rely on other insurance or absorb the loss yourself.

Example No. 1 (Underinsurance):

When:	The value of the property is	$	250,000
	The Coinsurance percentage for it is		80%
	The Limit of Insurance for it is	$	100,000
	The Deductible is	$	250
	The amount of loss is	$	40,000

Step **(1)**:	$250,000 x 80% = $200,000 (the minimum amount of insurance to meet your Coinsurance requirements)
Step **(2)**:	$100,000 ÷ $200,000 = .50
Step **(3)**:	$40,000 x .50 = $20,000
Step **(4)**:	$20,000 ▢ $250 = $19,750

We will pay no more than $19,750. The remaining $20,250 is not covered.

Example No. 2 (Adequate Insurance):

When:	The value of the property is	$	250,000
	The Coinsurance percentage for it is		80%
	The Limit of Insurance for it is	$	200,000
	The Deductible is	$	250
	The amount of loss is	$	40,000

The minimum amount of insurance to meet your Coinsurance requirement is $200,000 ($250,000 x 80%). Therefore, the Limit of Insurance in this Example is adequate and no penalty applies. We will pay no more than $39,750 ($40,000 amount of loss minus the deductible of $250).

b. If one Limit of Insurance applies to two or more separate items, this condition will apply to the total of all property to which the limit applies.

Example No. 3:

When:	The value of the property is:		
	Personal Property at Location No. 1	$	175,000
	Personal Property at Location No. 2	$	75,000
		$	250,000
	The Coinsurance percentage for it is		90%
	The Limit of Insurance for Personal Property at Location Nos. 1 and 2 is	$	180,000
	The Deductible is	$	1,000
	The amount of loss is:		
	Personal Property at Location No. 1	$	30,000
	Personal Property at Location No. 2	$	20,000
		$	50,000

Step **(1):** $250,000 x 90% = $225,000 (the minimum amount of insurance to meet your Coinsurance requirements and to avoid the penalty shown below)

Step **(2):** $180,000 ÷ $225,000 = .80

Step **(3):** $50,000 x .80 = $40,000

Step **(4):** $40,000 ⊐ $1,000 = $39,000

We will pay no more than $39,000. The remaining $11,000 is not covered.

G. Optional Coverages

If shown as applicable in the Declarations, the following Optional Coverages apply separately to each item:

1. Agreed Value

a. The Additional Condition, Coinsurance, does not apply to Covered Property to which this Optional Coverage applies. We will pay no more for loss of or damage to that property than the proportion that the Limit of Insurance under this Coverage Part for the property bears to the Agreed Value shown for it in the Declarations.

b. If the expiration date for this Optional Coverage shown in the Declarations is not extended, the Additional Condition, Coinsurance, is reinstated and this Optional Coverage expires.

c. The terms of this Optional Coverage apply only to loss or damage that occurs:

(1) On or after the effective date of this Optional Coverage; and

(2) Before the Agreed Value expiration date shown in the Declarations or the policy expiration date, whichever occurs first.

2. Inflation Guard

a. The Limit of Insurance for property to which this Optional Coverage applies will automatically increase by the annual percentage shown in the Declarations.

b. The amount of increase will be:

(1) The Limit of Insurance that applied on the most recent of the policy inception date, the policy anniversary date, or any other policy change amending the Limit of Insurance, times

(2) The percentage of annual increase shown in the Declarations, expressed as a decimal (example: 8% is .08), times

(3) The number of days since the beginning of the current policy year or the effective date of the most recent policy change amending the Limit of Insurance, divided by 365.

Example:

If:	The applicable Limit of Insurance is	$	100,000
	The annual percentage increase is		8%
	The number of days since the beginning of the policy year (or last policy change) is		146
	The amount of increase is $100,000 x .08 x 146 ÷ 365 = $3,200		

3. Replacement Cost

a. Replacement Cost (without deduction for depreciation) replaces Actual Cash Value in the Loss Condition, Valuation, of this Coverage Form.

b. This Optional Coverage does not apply to:

(1) Personal property of others;

(2) Contents of a residence;

(3) Manuscripts;

(4) Works of art, antiques or rare articles, including etchings, pictures, statuary, marbles, bronzes, porcelains and bric-a-brac; or

(5) "Stock", unless the Including "Stock" option is shown in the Declarations.

c. You may make a claim for loss or damage covered by this insurance on an actual cash value basis instead of on a replacement cost basis. In the event you elect to have loss or damage settled on an actual cash value basis, you may still make a claim for the additional coverage this Optional Coverage provides if you notify us of your intent to do so within 180 days after the loss or damage.

d. We will not pay on a replacement cost basis for any loss or damage:

   (1) Until the lost or damaged property is actually repaired or replaced; and

   (2) Unless the repairs or replacement are made as soon as reasonably possible after the loss or damage.

e. We will not pay more for loss or damage on a replacement cost basis than the least of **(1)**, **(2)** or **(3)**, subject to **f.** below:

   (1) The Limit of Insurance applicable to the lost or damaged property;

   (2) The cost to replace the lost or damaged property with other property:

      (a) Of comparable material and quality; and

      (b) Used for the same purpose; or

   (3) The amount actually spent that is necessary to repair or replace the lost or damaged property.

If a building is rebuilt at a new premises, the cost described in **e.(2)** above is limited to the cost which would have been incurred if the building had been rebuilt at the original premises.

f. The cost of repair or replacement does not include the increased cost attributable to enforcement of any ordinance or law regulating the construction, use or repair of any property.

4. Extension Of Replacement Cost To Personal Property Of Others

a. If the Replacement Cost Optional Coverage is shown as applicable in the Declarations, then this Extension may also be shown as applicable. If the Declarations show this Extension as applicable, then Paragraph **3.b.(1)** of the Replacement Cost Optional Coverage is deleted and all other provisions of the Replacement Cost Optional Coverage apply to replacement cost on personal property of others.

b. With respect to replacement cost on the personal property of others, the following limitation applies:

If an item(s) of personal property of others is subject to a written contract which governs your liability for loss or damage to that item(s), then valuation of that item(s) will be based on the amount for which you are liable under such contract, but not to exceed the lesser of the replacement cost of the property or the applicable Limit of Insurance.

H. Definitions

1. "Pollutants" means any solid, liquid, gaseous or thermal irritant or contaminant, including smoke, vapor, soot, fumes, acids, alkalis, chemicals and waste. Waste includes materials to be recycled, reconditioned or reclaimed.

2. "Stock" means merchandise held in storage or for sale, raw materials and in-process or finished goods, including supplies used in their packing or shipping.

 Copyright, Insurance Services Office, Inc., 1999 CP 00 18 10 00 ☐

BUILDERS RISK COVERAGE FORM

Various provisions in this policy restrict coverage. Read the entire policy carefully to determine rights, duties and what is and is not covered.

Throughout this policy the words "you" and "your" refer to the Named Insured shown in the Declarations. The words "we", "us" and "our" refer to the Company providing this insurance.

Other words and phrases that appear in quotation marks have special meaning. Refer to Section **G.** ⊐ **Definitions.**

A. Coverage

We will pay for direct physical loss of or damage to Covered Property at the premises described in the Declarations caused by or resulting from any Covered Cause of Loss.

1. Covered Property

Covered Property, as used in this Coverage Part, means the type of property described in this Section, **A.1.**, and limited in **A.2.**, Property Not Covered, if a Limit of Insurance is shown in the Declarations for that type of property.

Building Under Construction, meaning the building or structure described in the Declarations while in the course of construction, including:

a. Foundations;

b. The following property:

(1) Fixtures and machinery;

(2) Equipment used to service the building; and

(3) Your building materials and supplies used for construction;

provided such property is intended to be permanently located in or on the building or structure described in the Declarations or within 100 feet of its premises;

c. If not covered by other insurance, temporary structures built or assembled on site, including cribbing, scaffolding and construction forms.

2. Property Not Covered

Covered Property does not include:

a. Land (including land on which the property is located) or water;

b. The following property when outside of buildings:

(1) Lawns, trees, shrubs or plants;

(2) Radio or television antennas (including satellite dishes) and their lead-in wiring, masts or towers; or

(3) Signs (other than signs attached to buildings).

3. Covered Causes Of Loss

See applicable Causes of Loss Form as shown in the Declarations.

4. Additional Coverages

a. Debris Removal

(1) Subject to Paragraphs **(3)** and **(4),** we will pay your expense to remove debris of Covered Property caused by or resulting from a Covered Cause of Loss that occurs during the policy period. The expenses will be paid only if they are reported to us in writing within 180 days of the date of direct physical loss or damage.

(2) Debris Removal does not apply to costs to:

(a) Extract "pollutants" from land or water; or

(b) Remove, restore or replace polluted land or water.

(3) Subject to the exceptions in Paragraph **(4),** the following provisions apply:

(a) The most we will pay for the total of direct physical loss or damage plus debris removal expense is the Limit of Insurance applicable to the Covered Property that has sustained loss or damage.

(b) Subject to **(a)** above, the amount we will pay for debris removal expense is limited to 25% of the sum of the deductible plus the amount that we pay for direct physical loss or damage to the Covered Property that has sustained loss or damage.

(4) We will pay up to an additional $10,000 for debris removal expense, for each location, in any one occurrence of physical loss or damage to Covered Property, if one or both of the following circumstances apply:

(a) The total of the actual debris removal expense plus the amount we pay for direct physical loss or damage exceeds the Limit of Insurance on the Covered Property that has sustained loss or damage.

(b) The actual debris removal expense exceeds 25% of the sum of the deductible plus the amount that we pay for direct physical loss or damage to the Covered Property that has sustained loss or damage.

Therefore, if **(4)(a)** and/or **(4)(b)** apply, our total payment for direct physical loss or damage and debris removal expense may reach but will never exceed the Limit of Insurance on the Covered Property that has sustained loss or damage, plus $10,000.

(5) Examples

The following examples assume that there is no coinsurance penalty.

Example #1

Limit of Insurance	$ 90,000
Amount of Deductible	$ 500
Amount of Loss	$ 50,000
Amount of Loss Payable	$ 49,500
	($50,000 ⊐ $500)
Debris Removal Expense	$ 10,000
Debris Removal Expense	
Payable	$ 10,000
($10,000 is 20% of $50,000)	

The debris removal expense is less than 25% of the sum of the loss payable plus the deductible. The sum of the loss payable and the debris removal expense ($49,500 + $10,000 = $59,500) is less than the Limit of Insurance. Therefore, the full amount of debris removal expense is payable in accordance with the terms of Paragraph **(3)**.

Example #2

Limit of Insurance		$ 90,000
Amount of Deductible		$ 500
Amount of Loss		$ 80,000
Amount of Loss Payable		$ 79,500
		($80,000 ⊐ $500)
Debris Removal Expense		$ 30,000
Debris Removal Expense		
Payable		
	Basic Amount	$ 10,500
	Additional Amount	$ 10,000

The basic amount payable for debris removal expense under the terms of Paragraph **(3)** is calculated as follows: $80,000 ($79,500 + $500) x .25 = $20,000; capped at $10,500. The cap applies because the sum of the loss payable ($79,500) and the basic amount payable for debris removal expense ($10,500) cannot exceed the Limit of Insurance ($90,000).

The additional amount payable for debris removal expense is provided in accordance with the terms of Paragraph **(4)**, because the debris removal expense ($30,000) exceeds 25% of the loss payable plus the deductible ($30,000 is 37.5% of $80,000), and because the sum of the loss payable and debris removal expense ($79,500 + $30,000 = $109,500) would exceed the Limit of Insurance ($90,000). The additional amount of covered debris removal expense is $10,000, the maximum payable under Paragraph **(4)**. Thus the total payable for debris removal expense in this example is $20,500; $9,500 of the debris removal expense is not covered.

b. Preservation Of Property

If it is necessary to move Covered Property from the described premises to preserve it from loss or damage by a Covered Cause of Loss, we will pay for any direct physical loss or damage to that property:

(1) While it is being moved or while temporarily stored at another location; and

(2) Only if the loss or damage occurs within 30 days after the property is first moved.

c. Fire Department Service Charge

When the fire department is called to save or protect Covered Property from a Covered Cause of Loss, we will pay up to $1,000 for your liability for fire department service charges:

(1) Assumed by contract or agreement prior to loss; or

(2) Required by local ordinance.

No Deductible applies to this Additional Coverage.

d. Pollutant Clean Up And Removal

We will pay your expense to extract "pollutants" from land or water at the described premises if the discharge, dispersal, seepage, migration, release or escape of the "pollutants" is caused by or results from a Covered Cause of Loss that occurs during the policy period. The expenses will be paid only if they are reported to us in writing within 180 days of the date on which the Covered Cause of Loss occurs.

This Additional Coverage does not apply to costs to test for, monitor or assess the existence, concentration or effects of "pollutants". But we will pay for testing which is performed in the course of extracting the "pollutants" from the land or water.

The most we will pay under this Additional Coverage for each described premises is $10,000 for the sum of all covered expenses arising out of Covered Causes of Loss occurring during each separate 12 month period of this policy.

5. Coverage Extensions

a. Building Materials And Supplies Of Others

(1) You may extend the insurance provided by this Coverage Form to apply to building materials and supplies that are:

(a) Owned by others;

(b) In your care, custody or control;

(c) Located in or on the building described in the Declarations, or within 100 feet of its premises; and

(d) Intended to become a permanent part of the building.

(2) The most we will pay for loss or damage under this Extension is $5,000 at each described premises, unless a higher Limit of Insurance is specified in the Declarations. Our payment for loss of or damage to property of others will only be for the account of the owner of the property.

b. Sod, Trees, Shrubs And Plants

You may extend the insurance provided by this Coverage Form to apply to loss or damage to sod, trees, shrubs and plants outside of buildings on the described premises, if the loss or damage is caused by or results from any of the following causes of loss:

(1) Fire;

(2) Lightning;

(3) Explosion;

(4) Riot or Civil Commotion; or

(5) Aircraft.

The most we will pay for loss or damage under this Extension is $1,000, but not more than $250 for any one tree, shrub or plant. These limits apply to any one occurrence, regardless of the types or number of items lost or damaged in that occurrence.

B. Exclusions And Limitations

See applicable Causes of Loss Form as shown in the Declarations.

C. Limits Of Insurance

The most we will pay for loss or damage in any one occurrence is the applicable Limit of Insurance shown in the Declarations.

The most we will pay for loss or damage to outdoor signs attached to buildings is $1,000 per sign in any one occurrence.

The limits applicable to the Coverage Extensions and the Fire Department Service Charge and Pollutant Clean Up and Removal Additional Coverages are in addition to the Limits of Insurance.

Payments under the Preservation of Property Additional Coverage will not increase the applicable Limit of Insurance.

D. Deductible

In any one occurrence of loss or damage (hereinafter referred to as loss), we will first reduce the amount of loss if required by the Additional Condition ⬜ Need For Adequate Insurance. If the adjusted amount of loss is less than or equal to the Deductible, we will not pay for that loss. If the adjusted amount of loss exceeds the Deductible, we will then subtract the Deductible from the adjusted amount of loss, and will pay the resulting amount or the Limit of Insurance, whichever is less.

When the occurrence involves loss to more than one item of Covered Property and separate Limits of Insurance apply, the losses will not be combined in determining application of the Deductible. But the Deductible will be applied only once per occurrence.

Example No. 1:

(This example assumes there is no penalty for under-insurance.)

Deductible:	$	1,000
Limit of Insurance ⬚ Bldg. 1:	$	60,000
Limit of Insurance ⬚ Bldg. 2:	$	80,000
Loss to Bldg. 1:	$	60,100
Loss to Bldg. 2:	$	90,000

The amount of loss to Bldg. 1 ($60,100) is less than the sum ($61,000) of the Limit of Insurance applicable to Bldg. 1 plus the Deductible.

The Deductible will be subtracted from the amount of loss in calculating the loss payable for Bldg. 1:

$ 60,100
⬚ 1,000
$ 59,100 Loss Payable ⬚ Bldg. 1

The Deductible applies once per occurrence and therefore is not subtracted in determining the amount of loss payable for Bldg. 2. Loss payable for Bldg. 2 is the Limit of Insurance of $80,000.

Total amount of loss payable: $59,100 + 80,000 = $139,100.

Example No. 2:

(This example, too, assumes there is no penalty for underinsurance.)

The Deductible and Limits of Insurance are the same as those in Example No. 1.

Loss to Bldg. 1:	$	70,000

(exceeds Limit of Insurance plus Deductible)

Loss to Bldg. 2:	$	90,000

(exceeds Limit of Insurance plus Deductible)

Loss Payable ⬚ Bldg. 1: $60,000
(Limit of Insurance)

Loss Payable ⬚ Bldg. 2: $80,000
(Limit of Insurance)

Total amount of loss payable: $140,000

E. Loss Conditions

The following conditions apply in addition to the Common Policy Conditions and the Commercial Property Conditions.

1. Abandonment

There can be no abandonment of any property to us.

2. Appraisal

If we and you disagree on the value of the property or the amount of loss, either may make written demand for an appraisal of the loss. In this event, each party will select a competent and impartial appraiser. The two appraisers will select an umpire. If they cannot agree, either may request that selection be made by a judge of a court having jurisdiction. The appraisers will state separately the value of the property and amount of loss. If they fail to agree, they will submit their differences to the umpire. A decision agreed to by any two will be binding. Each party will:

a. Pay its chosen appraiser; and

b. Bear the other expenses of the appraisal and umpire equally.

If there is an appraisal, we will still retain our right to deny the claim.

3. Duties In The Event Of Loss Or Damage

a. You must see that the following are done in the event of loss or damage to Covered Property:

(1) Notify the police if a law may have been broken.

(2) Give us prompt notice of the loss or damage. Include a description of the property involved.

(3) As soon as possible, give us a description of how, when and where the loss or damage occurred.

(4) Take all reasonable steps to protect the Covered Property from further damage, and keep a record of your expenses necessary to protect the Covered Property, for consideration in the settlement of the claim. This will not increase the Limit of Insurance. However, we will not pay for any subsequent loss or damage resulting from a cause of loss that is not a Covered Cause of Loss. Also, if feasible, set the damaged property aside and in the best possible order for examination.

(5) At our request, give us complete inventories of the damaged and undamaged property. Include quantities, costs, values and amount of loss claimed.

(6) As often as may be reasonably required, permit us to inspect the property proving the loss or damage and examine your books and records.

 Copyright, Insurance Services Office, Inc., 1999   ▯

Also permit us to take samples of damaged and undamaged property for inspection, testing and analysis, and permit us to make copies from your books and records.

(7) Send us a signed, sworn proof of loss containing the information we request to investigate the claim. You must do this within 60 days after our request. We will supply you with the necessary forms.

(8) Cooperate with us in the investigation or settlement of the claim.

b. We may examine any insured under oath, while not in the presence of any other insured and at such times as may be reasonably required, about any matter relating to this insurance or the claim, including an insured's books and records. In the event of an examination, an insured's answers must be signed.

4. Loss Payment

a. In the event of loss or damage covered by this Coverage Form, at our option, we will either:

(1) Pay the value of lost or damaged property;

(2) Pay the cost of repairing or replacing the lost or damaged property, subject to **b.** below;

(3) Take all or any part of the property at an agreed or appraised value; or

(4) Repair, rebuild or replace the property with other property of like kind and quality, subject to **b.** below.

We will determine the value of lost or damaged property, or the cost of its repair or replacement, in accordance with the applicable terms of the Valuation Condition in this Coverage Form or any applicable provision which amends or supersedes the Valuation Condition.

b. The cost to repair, rebuild or replace does not include the increased cost attributable to enforcement of any ordinance or law regulating the construction, use or repair of any property.

c. We will give notice of our intentions within 30 days after we receive the sworn proof of loss.

d. We will not pay you more than your financial interest in the Covered Property.

e. We may adjust losses with the owners of lost or damaged property if other than you. If we pay the owners, such payments will satisfy your claims against us for the owners' property. We will not pay the owners more than their financial interest in the Covered Property.

f. We may elect to defend you against suits arising from claims of owners of property. We will do this at our expense.

g. We will pay for covered loss or damage within 30 days after we receive the sworn proof of loss, if you have complied with all of the terms of this Coverage Part and:

(1) We have reached agreement with you on the amount of loss; or

(2) An appraisal award has been made.

5. Recovered Property

If either you or we recover any property after loss settlement, that party must give the other prompt notice. At your option, the property will be returned to you. You must then return to us the amount we paid to you for the property. We will pay recovery expenses and the expenses to repair the recovered property, subject to the Limit of Insurance.

6. Valuation

We will determine the value of Covered Property at actual cash value as of the time of loss or damage.

F. Additional Conditions

The following conditions apply in addition to the Common Policy Conditions and the Commercial Property Conditions.

1. Mortgageholders

a. The term mortgageholder includes trustee.

b. We will pay for covered loss of or damage to buildings or structures to each mortgageholder shown in the Declarations in their order of precedence, as interests may appear.

c. The mortgageholder has the right to receive loss payment even if the mortgageholder has started foreclosure or similar action on the building or structure.

d. If we deny your claim because of your acts or because you have failed to comply with the terms of this Coverage Part, the mortgageholder will still have the right to receive loss payment if the mortgageholder:

(1) Pays any premium due under this Coverage Part at our request if you have failed to do so;

(2) Submits a signed, sworn proof of loss within 60 days after receiving notice from us of your failure to do so; and

(3) Has notified us of any change in ownership, occupancy or substantial change in risk known to the mortgageholder.

All of the terms of this Coverage Part will then apply directly to the mortgageholder.

e. If we pay the mortgageholder for any loss or damage and deny payment to you because of your acts or because you have failed to comply with the terms of this Coverage Part:

(1) The mortgageholder's rights under the mortgage will be transferred to us to the extent of the amount we pay; and

(2) The mortgageholder's right to recover the full amount of the mortgageholder's claim will not be impaired.

At our option, we may pay to the mortgageholder the whole principal on the mortgage plus any accrued interest. In this event, your mortgage and note will be transferred to us and you will pay your remaining mortgage debt to us.

f. If we cancel this policy, we will give written notice to the mortgageholder at least:

(1) 10 days before the effective date of cancellation if we cancel for your non-payment of premium; or

(2) 30 days before the effective date of cancellation if we cancel for any other reason.

g. If we elect not to renew this policy, we will give written notice to the mortgageholder at least 10 days before the expiration date of this policy.

2. Need For Adequate Insurance

We will not pay a greater share of any loss than the proportion that the Limit of Insurance bears to the value on the date of completion of the building described in the Declarations.

Example No. 1 (Underinsurance):

When:	The value of the building on the date of completion is	$	200,000
	The Limit of Insurance for it is	$	100,000
	The Deductible is	$	500
	The amount of loss is	$	80,000

Step **1:** $100,000 ÷ $200,000 = .50

Step **2:** $ 80,000 x .50 = $40,000

Step **3:** $ 40,000 ⊐ $500 = $39,500

We will pay no more than $39,500. The remaining $40,500 is not covered.

Example No. 2 (Adequate Insurance):

When:	The value of the building on the date of completion is	$	200,000
	The Limit of Insurance for it is	$	200,000
	The Deductible is	$	1,000
	The amount of loss is	$	80,000

The Limit of Insurance in this Example is adequate and therefore no penalty applies. We will pay no more than $79,000 ($80,000 amount of loss minus the deductible of $1,000).

3. Restriction Of Additional Coverage ⊐ Collapse

If the Causes Of Loss ⊐ Broad Form is applicable to this coverage form, Paragraph **C.1.b.(6)** of the Additional Coverage ⊐ Collapse does not apply to this coverage form.

If the Causes Of Loss ⊐ Special Form is applicable to this coverage form, Paragraph **D.2.f.** of the Additional Coverage ⊐ Collapse does not apply to this coverage form.

4. When Coverage Ceases

The insurance provided by this Coverage Form will end when one of the following first occurs:

a. This policy expires or is cancelled;

b. The property is accepted by the purchaser;

c. Your interest in the property ceases;

d. You abandon the construction with no intention to complete it;

     Copyright, Insurance Services Office, Inc., 1999   CP 00 20 10 00   □

e. Unless we specify otherwise in writing:

   (1) 90 days after construction is complete; or

   (2) 60 days after any building described in the Declarations is:

      (a) Occupied in whole or in part; or

      (b) Put to its intended use.

G. Definitions

"Pollutants" means any solid, liquid, gaseous or thermal irritant or contaminant, including smoke, vapor, soot, fumes, acids, alkalis, chemicals and waste. Waste includes materials to be recycled, reconditioned or reclaimed.

LEGAL LIABILITY COVERAGE FORM

Various provisions in this policy restrict coverage. Read the entire policy carefully to determine rights, duties and what is and is not covered.

Throughout this policy the words "you" and "your" refer to the Named Insured shown in the Declarations. The words "we", "us" and "our" refer to the Company providing this insurance.

Other words and phrases that appear in quotation marks have special meaning. Refer to Section **F. ⊐ Definitions.**

A. Coverage

We will pay those sums that you become legally obligated to pay as damages because of direct physical loss or damage, including loss of use, to Covered Property caused by accident and arising out of any Covered Cause of Loss. We will have the right and duty to defend any "suit" seeking those damages. However, we have no duty to defend you against a "suit" seeking damages for direct physical loss or damage to which this insurance does not apply. We may investigate and settle any claim or "suit" at our discretion. But:

(1) The amount we will pay for damages is limited as described in Section **C.** Limits Of Insurance; and

(2) Our right and duty to defend end when we have used up the Limit of Insurance in the payment of judgments or settlements.

1. Covered Property

Covered Property, as used in this Coverage Form, means tangible property of others in your care, custody or control that is described in the Declarations or on the Legal Liability Coverage Schedule.

2. Covered Causes Of Loss

See applicable Causes of Loss Form as shown in the Declarations.

3. Additional Coverage

SUPPLEMENTARY PAYMENTS

We will pay, with respect to any claim or any "suit" against you we defend:

a. All expenses we incur.

b. The cost of bonds to release attachments, but only for bond amounts within our Limit of Insurance. We do not have to furnish these bonds.

c. All reasonable expenses incurred by you at our request, including actual loss of earnings up to $250 a day because of time off from work.

d. All costs taxed against you in the "suit".

e. Prejudgment interest awarded against you on that part of the judgment we pay. If we make an offer to pay the Limit of Insurance, we will not pay any prejudgment interest based on that period of time after the offer.

f. All interest on the full amount of any judgment that accrues after entry of the judgment and before we have paid, offered to pay, or deposited in court the part of the judgment that is within our Limit of Insurance.

4. Coverage Extensions

a. Additional Insureds

If the Named Insured shown in the Declarations is a partnership, limited liability company or corporation, throughout this Coverage Form, the words "you" and "your" include:

(1) Partners, members, executive officers, trustees, directors and stockholders of such partnership, limited liability company or corporation, but only with respect to their duties as such; and

(2) Managers of a limited liability company, but only with respect to their duties as such.

b. Newly Acquired Organizations

Throughout this Coverage Form, the words "you" and "your" also include any organization (other than a partnership, joint venture or limited liability company) you newly acquire or form and over which you maintain ownership or majority interest if there is no other similar insurance available to that organization.

Copyright, Insurance Services Office, Inc., 1999

This Coverage Extension ends:

(1) 90 days after you acquire or form the organization; or

(2) At the end of the policy period shown in the Declarations;

whichever is earlier.

This Extension does not apply to direct physical loss or damage that occurred before you acquired or formed the organization.

c. Newly Acquired Property

(1) You may extend the insurance that applies to Covered Property, as used in this Coverage Form, to apply to your liability for tangible property of others that comes under your care, custody or control after the beginning of the current policy period. This Extension is subject to the following:

(a) All terms and Conditions of this Coverage Form.

(b) Buildings must be intended for:

(i) Similar use as the building described in the Declarations or on the Legal Liability Coverage Schedule; or

(ii) Use as a warehouse.

The most we will pay as the result of any one accident for loss or damage to buildings covered under this Extension is $250,000 at each building.

(c) Personal property must be at a location:

(i) That you own; or

(ii) That is or comes under your care, custody or control;

other than at fairs or exhibitions.

The most we will pay as the result of any one accident for loss or damage to personal property covered under this Extension is $100,000 at each building.

(2) Insurance under this Extension for each item of property of others will end when any of the following first occurs:

(a) This policy expires;

(b) 30 days expire after the property has come under your care, custody or control; or

(c) You report values to us.

We will charge you additional premium for values reported from the date the property comes under your care, custody or control.

This Extension does not apply to direct physical loss or damage that occurred before the property came under your care, custody or control.

B. Exclusions And Limitations

See applicable Causes of Loss Form as shown in the Declarations.

C. Limits Of Insurance

The most we will pay in damages as the result of any one accident is the applicable Limit of Insurance shown on the Legal Liability Coverage Schedule, or in the Declarations.

Payments under the Additional Coverage and the Newly Acquired Property Coverage Extension are in addition to the Limits of Insurance.

The existence of one or more:

1. Additional Insureds, or

2. Newly Acquired Organizations,

does not increase the Limit of Insurance.

D. Loss Conditions

The following conditions apply in addition to the Commercial Property Conditions:

1. Duties In The Event Of Accident, Claim Or Suit

a. You must see to it that we are notified promptly of any accident that may result in a claim. Notice should include:

(1) How, when and where the accident took place; and

(2) The names and addresses of any witnesses.

Notice of an accident is not notice of a claim.

b. If a claim is made or "suit" is brought against you, you must see to it that we receive prompt written notice of the claim or "suit".

c. You must:

(1) Immediately send us copies of any demands, notices, summonses or legal papers received in connection with the claim or "suit";

(2) Authorize us to obtain records and other information;

(3) Cooperate with us in the investigation, settlement or defense of the claim or "suit"; and

 Copyright, Insurance Services Office, Inc., 1999 **CP 00 40 10 00** ☐

(4) Assist us, upon our request, in the enforcement of any right against any person or organization that may be liable to you because of damage to which this insurance may also apply.

d. You will not, except at your own cost, voluntarily make a payment, assume any obligation, or incur any expense without our consent.

2. Legal Action Against Us

No person or organization has a right under this Coverage Form:

a. To join us as a party or otherwise bring us into a "suit" asking for damages from you; or

b. To sue us on this Coverage Form unless all of its terms have been fully complied with.

A person or organization may sue us to recover on an agreed settlement or on a final judgment against you obtained after an actual trial; but we will not be liable for damages that are not payable under the terms of this Coverage Form or that are in excess of the Limit of Insurance. An agreed settlement means a settlement and release of liability signed by us, you and the claimant or the claimant's legal representative.

3. Other Insurance

You may have other insurance covering the same loss as the insurance under this Coverage Form. If you do, we will pay our share of the covered loss. Our share is the proportion that the Limit of Insurance under this Coverage Form covering such loss bears to the Limits of Insurance of all insurance covering the loss.

4. Transfer Of Rights Of Recovery Against Others To Us

If you have rights to recover all or part of any payment we have made under this Coverage Form, those rights are transferred to us. You must do nothing after loss to impair them. At our request, you will bring "suit" or transfer those rights to us and help us enforce them.

E. Additional Conditions

The following conditions apply in addition to the Common Policy Conditions.

1. Amendment Of Commercial Property Conditions

None of the Commercial Property Conditions apply to this Coverage Form, except:

a. Condition **A.**, Concealment, Misrepresentation Or Fraud;

b. Condition **C.**, Insurance Under Two Or More Coverages; and

c. Condition **E.**, Liberalization.

2. Bankruptcy

Bankruptcy or insolvency of you or your estate will not relieve us of our obligations under this Coverage Form.

3. Policy Period, Coverage Territory

Under this Coverage Form:

a. We will pay for loss or damage caused by an accident that occurs:

(1) During the policy period shown in the Declarations; and

(2) Within the coverage territory.

b. The coverage territory is:

(1) The United States of America;

(2) Puerto Rico; and

(3) Canada.

4. Separation Of Insureds

The insurance under this Coverage Form applies separately to you and each additional insured, except with respect to the Limits of Insurance.

F. Definition

"Suit" includes an arbitration proceeding to which you must submit or submit with our consent.

COMMERCIAL PROPERTY
CP 00 60 06 95

LEASEHOLD INTEREST COVERAGE FORM

Throughout this policy the words "you" and "your" refer to the Named Insured shown in the Declarations. The words "we", "us" and "our" refer to the Company providing this insurance.

Other words and phrases that appear in quotation marks have special meaning. Refer to SECTION **F.** – DEFINITIONS.

A. COVERAGE

We will pay for loss of Covered Leasehold Interest you sustain due to the cancellation of your lease. The cancellation must result from direct physical loss of or damage to property at the premises described in the Declarations caused by or resulting from any Covered Cause of Loss.

1. Covered Leasehold Interest

Covered Leasehold Interest means the following for which an amount of "net leasehold interest" at inception is shown in the Leasehold Interest Coverage Schedule:

a. **Tenants' Lease Interest,** meaning the difference between the:

(1) Rent you pay at the described premises; and

(2) Rental value of the described premises that you lease.

b. **Bonus Payments,** meaning the unamortized portion of a cash bonus that will not be refunded to you. A cash bonus is money you paid to acquire your lease. It does not include:

(1) Rent, whether or not prepaid; or

(2) Security.

c. **Improvements and Betterments,** meaning the unamortized portion of payments made by you for improvements and betterments. It does not include the value of improvements and betterments recoverable under any other insurance, but only to the extent of such other insurance.

Improvements and betterments are fixtures, alterations, installations or additions:

(1) Made a part of the building or structure you occupy but do not own; and

(2) You acquired or made at your expense but cannot legally remove.

d. **Prepaid Rent,** meaning the unamortized portion of any amount of advance rent you paid that will not be refunded to you. This does not include the customary rent due at:

(1) The beginning of each month; or

(2) Any other rental period.

2. Covered Causes Of Loss

See applicable Causes of Loss Form as shown in the Declarations.

B. EXCLUSIONS AND LIMITATIONS

See applicable Causes of Loss Form as shown in the Declarations.

C. LIMITS OF INSURANCE

1. Applicable to Tenants' Lease Interest

a. The most we will pay for loss because of the cancellation of any one lease is your "net leasehold interest" at the time of loss.

But, if your lease is cancelled and your landlord lets you continue to use your premises under a new lease or other arrangement, the most we will pay for loss because of the cancellation of any one lease is the lesser of:

(1) The difference between the rent you now pay and the rent you will pay under the new lease or other arrangement; or

(2) Your "net leasehold interest" at the time of loss.

b. Your "net leasehold interest" decreases automatically each month. The amount of "net leasehold interest" at any time is your "gross leasehold interest" times the leasehold interest factor for the remaining months of your lease. A proportionate share applies for any period of time less than a month.

Refer to the end of this form for a table of leasehold interest factors.

2. Applicable to Bonus Payments, Improvements and Betterments and Prepaid Rent

a. The most we will pay for loss because of the cancellation of any one lease is your "net leasehold interest" at the time of loss.

But, if your lease is cancelled and your landlord lets you continue to use your premises under a new lease or other arrangement, the most we will pay for loss because of the cancellation of any one lease is the lesser of:

(1) The loss sustained by you; or

(2) Your "net leasehold interest" at the time of loss.

b. Your "net leasehold interest" decreases automatically each month. The amount of each decrease is your "monthly leasehold interest". A proportionate share applies for any period of time less than a month.

D. LOSS CONDITIONS

The following conditions apply in addition to the Common Policy Conditions and the Commercial Property Conditions.

1. Appraisal

If we and you disagree on the amount of loss, either may make written demand for an appraisal. In this event, each party will select a competent and impartial appraiser. The two appraisers will select an umpire. If they cannot agree, either may request that selection be made by a judge of a court having jurisdiction. The appraisers will state the amount of loss. If they fail to agree, they will submit their differences to the umpire. A decision agreed to by any two will be binding. Each party will:

a. Pay its chosen appraiser; and

b. Bear the other expenses of the appraisal and umpire equally.

If there is an appraisal, we will still retain our right to deny the claim.

2. Duties In The Event Of Loss Of Covered Leasehold Interest

a. You must see that the following are done in the event of loss of Covered Leasehold Interest:

(1) Notify the police if a law may have been broken.

(2) Give us prompt notice of the direct physical loss or damage. Include a description of the property involved.

(3) As soon as possible, give us a description of how, when and where the direct physical loss or damage occurred.

(4) Take all reasonable steps to protect the property at the described premises from further damage by a Covered Cause of Loss. However, we will not pay for any subsequent loss or damage resulting from a cause of loss that is not a Covered Cause of Loss. Also, if feasible, set the damaged property aside and in the best possible order for examination.

(5) As often as may be reasonably required, permit us to inspect the property proving the loss or damage and examine your books and records.

Also permit us to take samples of damaged and undamaged property for inspection, testing and analysis, and permit us to make copies from your books and records.

(6) Send us a signed, sworn proof of loss containing the information we request to investigate the claim. You must do this within 60 days after our request. We will supply you with the necessary forms.

(7) Cooperate with us in the investigation or settlement of the claim.

b. We may examine any insured under oath, while not in the presence of any other insured and at such times as may be reasonably required, about any matter relating to this insurance or the claim, including an insured's books and records. In the event of an examination, an insured's answers must be signed.

3. Loss Payment

We will pay for covered loss within 30 days after we receive the sworn proof of loss, if:

a. You have complied with all of the terms of this Coverage Part; and

b.(1) We have reached agreement with you on the amount of loss; or

(2) An appraisal award has been made.

4. Vacancy

a. Description of Terms

(1) As used in this Vacancy Condition, with respect to the tenant's interest in Covered Property, building means the unit or suite rented or leased to the tenant. Such building is vacant when it does not contain enough business personal property to conduct customary operations.

(2) Buildings under construction or renovation are not considered vacant.

b. Vacancy Provisions – Subleased Premises

The following provisions apply if the building where direct physical loss or damage occurs has been vacant for more than 60 consecutive days before that loss or damage occurs, provided you have entered into an agreement to sublease the described premises as of the time of loss or damage:

(1) We will not pay for any loss or damage caused by any of the following even if they are Covered Causes of Loss:

(a) Vandalism;

(b) Sprinkler leakage, unless you have protected the system against freezing;

(c) Building glass breakage;

(d) Water damage;

(e) Theft; or

(f) Attempted theft.

(2) With respect to a Covered Cause of Loss not listed in **(1)(a)** through **(1)(f)** above, we will reduce the amount we would otherwise pay for the loss or damage by 15%.

c. If you have not entered into an agreement to sublease the described premises as of the time of loss or damage, we will not pay for any loss of Covered Leasehold Interest.

E. ADDITIONAL CONDITION

The following condition replaces the Cancellation Common Policy Condition:

CANCELLATION

1. The first Named Insured shown in the Declarations may cancel this policy by mailing or delivering to us advance notice of cancellation.

2. We may cancel this policy by mailing or delivering to the first Named Insured written notice of cancellation at least:

a. 10 days before the effective date of cancellation if we cancel for nonpayment of premium; or

b. 30 days before the effective date of cancellation if we cancel for any other reason.

3. We will mail or deliver our notice to the first Named Insured's last mailing address known to us.

4. Notice of cancellation will state the effective date of cancellation. The policy will end on that date.

5. If this policy is cancelled, we will send the first Named Insured any premium refund due. The cancellation will be effective even if we have not made or offered a refund.

6. If this coverage is cancelled, we will calculate the earned premium by:

a. Computing the average of the "net leasehold interest" at the:

(1) Inception date, and

(2) Cancellation date,

of this coverage.

b. Multiplying the rate for the period of coverage by the average "net leasehold interest".

c. If we cancel, we will send you a premium refund based on the difference between the:

(1) Premium you originally paid us; and

(2) Proportion of the premium calculated by multiplying the amount in paragraph **a.** times the rate for the period of coverage for the expired term of the policy.

d. If you cancel, your refund may be less than the refund calculated in paragraph **c.**

7. If notice is mailed, proof of mailing will be sufficient proof of notice.

F. DEFINITIONS

1. **"Gross Leasehold Interest"** means the difference between the:

   a. Monthly rental value of the premises you lease; and

   b. Actual monthly rent you pay including taxes, insurance, janitorial or other service that you pay for as part of the rent.

   This amount is not changed:

   (1) Whether you occupy all or part of the premises; or

   (2) If you sublet the premises.

   Example:

Rental value of your leased premises	$5,000
Monthly rent including taxes, insurance, janitorial or other service that you pay for as part of the rent	−4,000
"Gross Leasehold Interest"	$1,000

2. **"Monthly Leasehold Interest"** means the monthly portion of covered Bonus Payments, Improvements and Betterments and Prepaid Rent. To find your "monthly leasehold interest", divide your original costs of Bonus Payments, Improvements and Betterments or Prepaid Rent by the number of months left in your lease at the time of the expenditure.

   Example:

Original cost of Bonus Payment	$12,000
With 24 months left in the lease at time of Bonus Payment	÷ 24
"Monthly Leasehold Interest"	$500

3. **"Net Leasehold Interest":**

   a. Applicable to Tenants' Lease Interest.

   "Net Leasehold Interest" means the present value of your "gross leasehold interest" for each remaining month of the term of the lease at the rate of interest shown in the Leasehold Interest Coverage Schedule.

   The "net leasehold interest" is the amount that, placed at the rate of interest shown in the Leasehold Interest Coverage Schedule, would be equivalent to your receiving the "Gross Leasehold Interest" for each separate month of the unexpired term of the lease.

   To find your "net leasehold interest" at any time, multiply your "gross leasehold interest" by the leasehold interest factor found in the table of leasehold interest factors attached to this form.

   Example:

   (20 months left in lease, 10% effective annual rate of interest)

"Gross Leasehold Interest"	$ 1,000
Leasehold Interest Factor	× 18.419
"Net Leasehold Interest"	$18,419

   b. Applicable to Bonus Payments, Improvements and Betterments or Prepaid Rent.

   "Net Leasehold Interest" means the unamortized amount shown in the Schedule. Your "net leasehold interest" at any time is your "monthly leasehold interest" times the number of months left in your lease.

   Example:

"Monthly Leasehold Interest"	$ 500
With 10 months left in lease	× 10
"Net Leasehold Interest"	$5,000

 Copyright, ISO Commercial Risk Services, Inc., 1994   CP 00 60 06 95   ☐

COMMERCIAL PROPERTY
CP 00 70 10 00

MORTGAGEHOLDERS ERRORS AND OMISSIONS COVERAGE FORM

Various provisions in this policy restrict coverage. Read the entire policy carefully to determine rights, duties and what is and is not covered.

Throughout this policy the words "you" and "your" refer to the Named Insured shown in the Declarations. The words "we", "us" and "our" refer to the Company providing this insurance.

Other words and phrases that appear in quotation marks have special meaning. Refer to Section I. ⬜ **Definitions** in this Coverage Form.

A. Coverage

1. Coverage A ⬜ Mortgageholder's Interest   .

We will pay for loss to your "mortgageholder's interest" in Covered Property due to error or accidental omission, by you or your representative, in the operation of your customary procedure in requiring, procuring and maintaining "valid insurance" payable to you as mortgageholder against the Covered Causes of Loss.

a. Covered Property

Covered Property means:

(1) Real property; and

(2) Personal property secured in connection with that real property.

It includes such property:

  (a) During and after your foreclosure; and

  (b) Sold under an agreement in which you retain title, such as a conditional sales agreement.

b. Property Not Covered

Covered Property does not include:

(1) Accounts, bills, currency, deeds, food stamps or other evidences of debt, money, notes or securities. Lottery tickets held for sale are not securities; or

(2) Land (including land on which the property is located), water, growing crops or lawns.

c. Covered Causes Of Loss

The Covered Causes of Loss are those causes of loss against which you customarily require mortgagors to provide insurance policies that protect your "mortgageholder's interest". They do not include:

(1) Causes of Loss excluded under Section **B.**, Exclusions; or

(2) Losses insured under mortgage guarantee insurance policies or programs, or title, life, health or accident insurance policies.

d. Coverage Extension ⬜ Mortgages Serviced For Others

We will cover loss arising from mortgages owned by others and serviced by you as if you owned the "mortgageholder's interest" in them. All such mortgages must be serviced under a written contract. We will make loss payment payable jointly to you and the mortgage owner.

2. Coverage B ⬜ Property Owned Or Held In Trust

We will pay for direct physical loss of or damage to Covered Property caused by or resulting from any Covered Cause of Loss; provided the loss is not otherwise insured due to error or accidental omission, by you or your representative, in the operation of your customary procedure in procuring and maintaining "valid insurance" payable to you as owner or trustee of the Covered Property.

a. Covered Property

Covered Property means real and personal property:

(1) You own; or

(2) In which you have a fiduciary interest as trustee or otherwise.

b. Property Not Covered

Covered Property does not include:

(1) Accounts, bills, currency, deeds, food stamps or other evidences of debt, money, notes or securities. Lottery tickets held for sale are not securities; or

(2) Land (including land on which the property is located), water, growing crops or lawns.

   Copyright, Insurance Services Office, Inc., 1999

c. Covered Causes Of Loss

The Covered Causes of Loss are:

(1) Fire.

(2) Lightning.

(3) Explosion, including the explosion of gases or fuel within the furnace of any fired vessel or within the flues or passages through which the gases of combustion pass. This cause of loss does not include loss or damage by:

   (a) Rupture, bursting or operation of pressure relief devices; or

   (b) Rupture or bursting due to expansion or swelling of the contents of any building or structure, caused by or resulting from water.

(4) Windstorm or Hail, but not including:

   (a) Frost or cold weather;

   (b) Ice (other than hail), snow or sleet, whether driven by wind or not; or

   (c) Loss or damage to the interior of any building or structure, or the property inside the building or structure, caused by rain, snow, sand or dust, whether driven by wind or not, unless the building or structure first sustains wind or hail damage to its roof or walls through which the rain, snow, sand or dust enters.

(5) Smoke causing sudden and accidental loss or damage. This cause of loss does not include smoke from agricultural smudging or industrial operations.

(6) Aircraft or Vehicles, meaning only physical contact of an aircraft, a spacecraft, a self-propelled missile, a vehicle or an object thrown up by a vehicle with the property or with the building or structure containing the property. This cause of loss includes loss or damage by objects falling from aircraft.

   We will not pay for loss or damage caused by or resulting from vehicles you own or operate.

(7) Riot or Civil Commotion, including:

   (a) Acts of striking employees while occupying the premises; and

   (b) Looting occurring at the time and place of a riot or civil commotion.

(8) Sinkhole Collapse, meaning loss or damage caused by the sudden sinking or collapse of land into underground empty spaces created by the action of water on limestone or dolomite. This cause of loss does not include:

   (a) The cost of filling sinkholes; or

   (b) Sinking or collapse of land into man-made underground cavities.

(9) Volcanic Action, meaning direct loss or damage resulting from the eruption of a volcano when the loss or damage is caused by:

   (a) Airborne volcanic blast or airborne shock waves;

   (b) Ash, dust or particulate matter; or

   (c) Lava flow.

   All volcanic eruptions that occur within any 168-hour period will constitute a single occurrence.

   This cause of loss does not include the cost to remove ash, dust or particulate matter that does not cause direct physical loss or damage to the property.

3. Coverage C □ Mortgageholder's Liability

We will pay those sums that you become legally obligated to pay as damages due to error or accidental omission in the operation of your customary procedure in processing and maintaining "valid insurance" against the Covered Causes of Loss for the benefit of the mortgagor in amounts, and under conditions, customarily accepted by the mortgagor. We will have the right and duty to defend any "suit" seeking those damages. However, we have no duty to defend you against a "suit" seeking damages to which this insurance does not apply. We may investigate and settle any claim or "suit" at our discretion. But:

(1) The amount we will pay for damages is limited as described in Section **C.** Limits Of Insurance; and

(2) Our right and duty to defend end when we have used up the Limit of Insurance in the payment of judgments or settlements.

The damages payable under this Coverage Form must arise out of your capacity as a mortgageholder, mortgage fiduciary or mortgage servicing agency.

     Copyright, Insurance Services Office, Inc., 1999   CP 00 70 10 00   □

a. **Covered Causes Of Loss**

The Covered Causes of Loss are those risks and causes of loss against which the mortgagor customarily obtains insurance policies.

They do not include:

(1) Causes of loss excluded under Section **B.**, Exclusions; or

(2) Losses insured under mortgage guarantee insurance policies or programs, or title, life, health or accident insurance policies.

b. **Additional Coverage ⬚ Supplementary Payments**

In addition to the Limit of Insurance, we will pay, with respect to any claim or any "suit" against you we defend:

(1) All expenses we incur.

(2) The cost of bonds to release attachments, but only for bond amounts within our Limit of Insurance. We do not have to furnish these bonds.

(3) All reasonable expenses incurred by you at our request, including actual loss of earnings up to $250 a day because of time off from work.

(4) All costs taxed against you in the "suit".

(5) Prejudgment interest awarded against you on that part of the judgment we pay. If we make an offer to pay the Limit of Insurance, we will not pay any prejudgment interest based on that period of time after the offer.

(6) All interest on the full amount of any judgment that accrues after entry of the judgment and before we have paid, offered to pay, or deposited in court the part of the judgment that is within our Limit of Insurance.

c. **Coverage Extensions**

(1) **Additional Insureds**

If the Named Insured shown in the Declarations is a partnership, limited liability company or corporation, under Coverage **C** ⬚ Mortgageholder's Liability, the words "you" and "your" are extended to include:

(a) Your partners, members, executive officers, trustees, directors and stockholders of such partnership, limited liability company or corporation, but only with respect to their duties as such; and

(b) Managers of a limited liability company, but only with respect to their duties as such.

The existence of one or more Additional Insureds does not increase the Limit of Insurance.

(2) **Newly Acquired Organizations**

Under Coverage **C** ⬚ Mortgageholder's Liability, the words "you" and "your" also include any organization (other than a partnership, joint venture or limited liability company) that you acquire or form and over which you maintain ownership or majority interest if there is no other similar insurance available to that organization.

This Coverage Extension ends:

(a) 90 days after you acquire or form the organization; or

(b) At the end of the policy period shown in the Declarations;

whichever is earlier.

This Extension does not apply to errors or accidental omissions that occurred before you acquired or formed the organization.

4. **Coverage D ⬚ Real Estate Tax Liability**

We will pay for damages for which you are legally liable due to error or accidental omission in paying real estate taxes, as agreed, on behalf of the mortgagor.

B. **Exclusions**

The following exclusions apply to Coverages **A, B, C** and **D.**

1. We will not pay for loss or damage caused directly or indirectly by any of the following. Such loss or damage is excluded regardless of any other cause or event that contributes concurrently or in any sequence to the loss.

a. Ordinance Or Law

The enforcement of any ordinance or law:

(1) Regulating the construction, use or repair of any property; or

(2) Requiring the tearing down of any property, including the cost of removing its debris.

This exclusion, Ordinance or Law, applies whether the loss results from:

(1) An ordinance or law that is enforced even if the property has not been damaged; or

(2) The increased costs incurred to comply with an ordinance or law in the course of construction, repair, renovation, remodeling or demolition of property, or removal of its debris, following a physical loss to that property.

b. Earth Movement

(1) Earthquake, including any earth sinking, rising or shifting related to such event;

(2) Landslide, including any earth sinking, rising or shifting related to such event;

(3) Mine subsidence, meaning subsidence of a man-made mine, whether or not mining activity has ceased;

(4) Earth sinking (other than sinkhole collapse), rising or shifting including soil conditions which cause settling, cracking or other disarrangement of foundations or other parts of realty. Soil conditions include contraction, expansion, freezing, thawing, erosion, improperly compacted soil and the action of water under the ground surface.

But if Earth Movement, as described in **b.(1)** through **b.(4)** above, results in fire or explosion, we will pay for the loss or damage caused by that fire or explosion.

(5) Volcanic eruption, explosion or effusion. But if volcanic eruption, explosion or effusion results in fire or Volcanic Action, we will pay for the loss or damage caused by that fire or Volcanic Action.

c. Governmental Action

Seizure or destruction of property by order of governmental authority.

But we will pay for loss or damage caused by or resulting from acts of destruction ordered by governmental authority and taken at the time of a fire to prevent its spread, if the fire would be covered by this Coverage Part.

d. Nuclear Hazard

Nuclear reaction or radiation, or radioactive contamination, however caused.

But if nuclear reaction or radiation, or radioactive contamination, results in fire, we will pay for the loss or damage caused by that fire.

e. Utility Services

The failure of power or other utility service supplied to the described premises, however caused, if the failure occurs away from the covered premises.

But if the failure of power or other utility service results in a Covered Cause of Loss, we will pay for the loss or damage caused by that Covered Cause of Loss.

f. War And Military Action

(1) War, including undeclared or civil war;

(2) Warlike action by a military force, including action in hindering or defending against an actual or expected attack, by any government, sovereign or other authority using military personnel or other agents; or

(3) Insurrection, rebellion, revolution, usurped power, or action taken by governmental authority in hindering or defending against any of these.

g. Water

(1) Flood, surface water, waves, tides, tidal waves, overflow of any body of water, or their spray, all whether driven by wind or not;

(2) Mudslide or mudflow;

(3) Water that backs up or overflows from a sewer, drain or sump; or

(4) Water under the ground surface pressing on, or flowing or seeping through:

(a) Foundations, walls, floors or paved surfaces;

(b) Basements, whether paved or not; or

(c) Doors, windows or other openings.

But if Water, as described in **g.(1)** through **g.(4)** above, results in fire or explosion, we will pay for the loss or damage caused by that fire or explosion.

Exclusions **B.1.a.** through **B.1.g.** apply whether or not the loss event results in widespread damage or affects a substantial area.

2. We will not pay for loss or damage caused by or resulting from:

a. Discharge, dispersal, seepage, migration, release or escape of "pollutants". If you customarily require mortgagors to provide insurance against causes of loss on a special form basis (covering any cause of loss not excluded or limited in the policy), this exclusion does not apply if the discharge, dispersal, seepage, migration, release or escape is itself caused by any of the "specified causes of loss".

If the discharge, dispersal, seepage, migration, release or escape of "pollutants" results in a "specified cause of loss", we will pay for the loss or damage caused by that "specified cause of loss".

b. Artificially generated electrical current, including electrical arcing, that disturbs electrical devices, appliances or wires.

But if artificially generated electrical current results in fire, we will pay for the loss or damage caused by that fire.

c. Any event that occurs more than 30 days after you know that an error or accidental omission may have occurred.

d. Your failure to obtain, maintain or properly handle the following types of insurance policies or programs:

(1) Title;

(2) Mortgage guarantee;

(3) Life; or

(4) Health or accident.

e. Neglect of an insured to use all reasonable means to save and preserve property from further damage at and after the time of loss.

3. We will not pay for loss or damage caused by or resulting from any of the following, **3.a.** through **3.d.** But if an excluded cause of loss that is listed in **3.a.** through **3.d.** results in a Covered Cause of Loss, we will pay for the loss or damage caused by that Covered Cause of Loss.

a. Collapse, except as provided below in the Additional Coverage for Collapse.

b. Weather conditions, if weather conditions contribute in any way with a cause or event excluded in Paragraph **1.** above to produce the loss or damage.

c. Acts or decisions, including the failure to act or decide, of any person, group, organization or governmental body.

d. Faulty, inadequate or defective:

(1) Planning, zoning, development, surveying, siting;

(2) Design, specifications, workmanship, repair, construction, renovation, remodeling, grading, compaction;

(3) Materials used in repair, construction, renovation or remodeling; or

(4) Maintenance;

of part or all of any property on or off the described premises.

C. Limits Of Insurance

The most we will pay under this Coverage Form for all loss arising from one error or accidental omission is the applicable Limit of Insurance shown in the Declarations, subject to the following additional limitations:

1. Under Coverage **A** ⊐ Mortgageholder's Interest, or Coverage **B** ⊐ Property Owned Or Held In Trust, we will not pay more than the least of:

a. The amount of direct physical loss or damage determined in accordance with the insurance policies that would have covered the loss or damage if no error or accidental omission occurred, less the amount of any other insurance recovery payable to you on the Covered Property;

b. The amount that would have been paid to you under insurance policies you would customarily have procured and maintained if the error or accidental omission had not occurred; or

c. The amount of your "mortgageholder's interest" under Coverage **A.**

2. Under Coverage **D** ⊐ Real Estate Tax Liability, we will not pay more than 15% of the Limit of Insurance shown in the Declarations as applicable to this Coverage Form, for damages due to error or accidental omission in paying real estate taxes in connection with any single mortgage.

D. Additional Coverage ⊐ Collapse

This Collapse Additional Coverage applies if collapse is a coverage for which you customarily require mortgagors to provide insurance.

The term Covered Cause of Loss includes the Collapse Additional Coverage as described and limited in **D.1.** through **D.4.** below.

1. With respect to buildings:

    a. Collapse means an abrupt falling down or caving in of a building or any part of a building with the result that the building or part of the building cannot be occupied for its intended purpose;

    b. A building or any part of a building that is in danger of falling down or caving in is not considered to be in a state of collapse;

    c. A part of a building that is standing is not considered to be in a state of collapse even if it has separated from another part of the building;

    d. A building that is standing or any part of a building that is standing is not considered to be in a state of collapse even if it shows evidence of cracking, bulging, sagging, bending, leaning, settling, shrinkage or expansion.

2. We will pay for direct physical loss or damage to Covered Property, caused by collapse of a building or any part of a building that is insured under this Coverage Form or that contains Covered Property insured under this Coverage Form, if the collapse is caused by one or more of the following:

    a. The "specified causes of loss" or breakage of building glass;

    b. Decay that is hidden from view, unless the presence of such decay is known to a mortgagor prior to collapse;

    c. Insect or vermin damage that is hidden from view, unless the presence of such damage is known to a mortgagor prior to collapse;

    d. Weight of people or personal property;

    e. Weight of rain that collects on a roof;

    f. Use of defective material or methods in construction, remodeling, or renovation if the collapse occurs during the course of the construction, remodeling, or renovation. However, if the collapse occurs after construction, remodeling, or renovation is complete and is caused in part by a cause of loss listed in **D.2.a.** through **D.2.e.**, we will pay for the loss or damage even if use of defective material or methods, in construction, remodeling, or renovation, contributes to the collapse.

The criteria set forth in **1.a.** through **1.d.** do not limit the coverage otherwise provided under this Coverage Form for the causes of loss listed in **2.a.**, **2.d.** and **2.e.**

3. If personal property abruptly falls down or caves in and such collapse is not the result of collapse of a building, we will pay for loss or damage to Covered Property caused by such collapse of personal property only if:

    a. The collapse was caused by a Cause of Loss listed in **2.a.** through **2.f.** above; and

    b. The personal property which collapses is inside a building.

The coverage stated in this Paragraph **3.** does not apply to personal property if marring and/or scratching is the only damage to that personal property caused by the collapse.

Collapse of personal property does not mean cracking, bulging, sagging, bending, leaning, settling, shrinkage or expansion.

4. This Additional Coverage, Collapse, will not increase the Limits of Insurance provided in this Coverage Part.

ADDITIONAL CONDITIONS

The following conditions apply in addition to the Common Policy Conditions.

E. Condition Applicable To Coverage A □ Mortgageholder's Interest

TRANSFER OF MORTGAGE □ COVERAGE A

We and all other insurance companies covering a loss, if in agreement, may pay you an amount equal to the outstanding balance on the mortgage, even if that amount is greater than the amount of loss. If so, we and the other insurance companies may demand and receive a full assignment of the mortgage, including all securities held as collateral for the debt, as interests may appear.

F. Conditions Applicable To Coverage B □ Property Owned Or Held In Trust

1. Our Options □ Coverage B

In the event of loss or damage covered under Coverage **B**, at our option, we will either:

a. Pay the value of lost or damaged property;

b. Pay the cost of repairing or replacing the lost or damaged property;

c. Take all or any part of the property at an agreed or appraised value; or

d. Repair, rebuild or replace the property with other property of like kind and quality.

We will give notice of our intentions within 30 days after we receive the sworn statement of loss.

We will not pay you more than your financial interest in the Covered Property.

2. Recovered Property ⬚ Coverage B

If either you or we recover any property after loss settlement, that party must give the other prompt notice. At your option, the property will be returned to you. You must then return to us the amount we paid to you for the property. We will pay recovery expenses and the expenses to repair the recovered property, subject to the Limit of Insurance.

3. Time Period ⬚ Coverage B

Coverage on each item of Covered Property applies only during the period of time that:

a. Begins on the day you acquire the property or your fiduciary interest in it begins; and

b. Ends on the earlier of:

(1) 90 days after the date in Paragraph **a.** above; or

(2) The day other insurance on the property is obtained.

4. Valuation ⬚ Coverage B

We will determine the value of Covered Property in the event of loss or damage at actual cash value as of the time of loss or damage.

G. Conditions Applicable To Coverage C ⬚ Mortgageholder's Liability And Coverage D ⬚ Real Estate Tax Liability

1. Bankruptcy ⬚ Coverages C And D

Bankruptcy or insolvency of you or your estate will not relieve us of our obligations under Coverages **C** and **D.**

2. Separation Of Insureds ⬚ Coverages C And D

The insurance under Coverages **C** and **D** applies separately to you and each additional insured, except with respect to the Limits of Insurance.

H. Conditions Applicable To All Coverages

1. Abandonment

There can be no abandonment of any property to us.

2. Appraisal ⬚ Coverages A And B Only

If we and you disagree on the amount of loss, either may make written demand for an appraisal of the loss. In this event, each party will select a competent and impartial appraiser. The two appraisers will select an umpire. If they cannot agree, either may request that selection be made by a judge of a court having jurisdiction. The appraisers will state separately the amount of loss. If they fail to agree, they will submit their differences to the umpire. A decision agreed to by any two will be binding. Each party will:

a. Pay its chosen appraiser; and

b. Bear the other expenses of the appraisal and umpire equally.

If there is an appraisal, we will still retain our right to deny the claim.

3. Duties In the Event Of Loss

a. Under Coverages **A** and **B:**

(1) You must see that the following are done in the event of loss or damage to Covered Property:

(a) Notify the police if a law may have been broken.

(b) Give us prompt notice of the loss or damage once you are aware of it. Include a description of the property involved.

(c) Take all reasonable steps to protect the Covered Property from further damage, and keep a record of your expenses necessary to protect the Covered Property, for consideration in the settlement of the claim. This will not increase the Limit of Insurance. However, we will not pay for any subsequent loss or damage resulting from a cause of loss that is not a Covered Cause of Loss. Also, if feasible, set the damaged property aside and in the best possible order for examination.

(d) At our request, give us complete inventories of the damaged and undamaged property. Include quantities, costs, values and amount of loss claimed.

(e) As often as may be reasonably required, permit us to inspect the property proving the loss or damage and examine your books and records.

Also permit us to take samples of damaged and undamaged property for inspection, testing and analysis, and permit us to make copies from your books and records.

(f) Send us a signed, sworn proof of loss containing the information we request to investigate the claim. You must do this within 60 days after our request. We will supply you with the necessary forms.

(g) Cooperate with us in the investigation or settlement of the claim.

(2) We may examine any insured under oath, while not in the presence of any other insured and at such times as may be reasonably required, about any matter relating to this insurance or the claim, including an insured's books and records. In the event of an examination, an insured's answers must be signed.

b. Under Coverages **C** and **D:**

(1) If a claim is made or "suit" is brought against you, you must see to it that we receive prompt written notice of the claim or "suit".

(2) You must:

(a) Immediately send us copies of any demands, notices, summonses or legal papers received in connection with the claim or "suit";

(b) Authorize us to obtain records and other information;

(c) Cooperate with us in the investigation, settlement or defense of the claim or "suit";

(d) Assist us, upon our request, in the enforcement of any right against any person or organization that may be liable to you because of damage to which this insurance may also apply; and

(e) If requested, give us a signed statement of facts containing the information we request to determine our rights and duties under this insurance.

(3) You will not, except at your own cost, voluntarily make a payment, assume any obligation, or incur any expense without our consent.

4. Insurance Under Two Or More Coverages

If two or more of this policy's coverages apply to the same loss or damage, we will not pay more than the actual amount of the loss or damage.

5. Legal Action Against Us

a. No one may bring a legal action against us under Coverages **A** and **B** unless:

(1) There has been full compliance with all of the terms of Coverages **A** and **B**; and

(2) The action is brought within 2 years after you discover the error or accidental omission.

b. No person or organization has a right under Coverages **C** and **D:**

(1) To join us as a party or otherwise bring us into a "suit" asking for damages from you; or

(2) To sue us on this Coverage Form unless all of its terms have been fully complied with.

A person or organization may sue us to recover on an agreed settlement or on a final judgment against you obtained after an actual trial; but we will not be liable for damages that are not payable under the terms of this Coverage Form or that are in excess of the Limit of Insurance. An agreed settlement means a settlement and release of liability signed by us, you and the claimant or the claimant's legal representative.

6. Liberalization

If we adopt any revision that would broaden the coverage under this Coverage Part without additional premium within 45 days prior to or during the policy period, the broadened coverage will immediately apply to this Coverage Part.

7. Loss Payment

We will pay for covered loss or damage to Covered Property within 30 days after we receive the sworn proof of loss, if you have complied with all of the terms of this Coverage Part and:

a. We have reached agreement with you on the amount of loss; or

b. An appraisal award has been made.

    Copyright, Insurance Services Office, Inc., 1999   CP 00 70 10 00   □

8. **Other Insurance**

   a. You may have other insurance subject to the same plan, terms, conditions and provisions as the insurance under this Coverage Part. If you do, we will pay our share of the covered loss or damage. Our share is the proportion that the applicable Limit of Insurance under this Coverage Part bears to the Limits of Insurance of all insurance covering on the same basis.

   b. If there is other insurance covering the same loss or damage, other than that described in **a.** above, we will pay only for the amount of covered loss or damage in excess of the amount due from that other insurance, whether you can collect on it or not. But we will not pay more than the applicable Limit of Insurance.

9. **Policy Period, Coverage Territory**

   Under this Coverage Form:

   a. These coverages only apply to:

   (1) Loss or damage, or

   (2) Claims or "suits" arising from an event,

   that occurs during the policy period shown in the Declarations. The date of error or accidental omission does not have to be within the policy period.

   b. We will pay for loss arising from errors or accidental omissions in connection with insurance policies or real estate tax payments on property located in:

   (1) The United States of America (including its territories and possessions); and

   (2) Puerto Rico.

10. **Transfer Of Rights Of Recovery Against Others To Us**

   a. Under Coverages **A** and **B,** if any person or organization to or for whom we make payment under this Coverage Form has rights to recover damages from another, those rights are transferred to us to the extent of our payment. That person or organization must do everything necessary to secure our rights and must do nothing after loss to impair them. But you may waive your rights against another party in writing:

   (1) Prior to a loss to your Covered Property.

   (2) After a loss to your Covered Property only if, at time of loss, that party is one of the following:

   (a) Someone insured by this insurance;

   (b) A business firm:

   (i) Owned or controlled by you; or

   (ii) That owns or controls you; or

   (c) Your tenant.

   This will not restrict your insurance.

   b. Under Coverages **C** and **D,** if you have rights to recover all or part of any payment we have made under this Coverage Form, those rights are transferred to us. You must do nothing after loss to impair them. At our request, you will bring "suit" or transfer those rights to us and help us enforce them.

11. **Vacancy**

   We will not pay for any loss or damage if the building where loss or damage occurs, or out of which a claim or "suit" arises, has been vacant for more than 60 days before that loss or damage, or the event that gives rise to the claim or "suit".

   A building is vacant unless at least 31% of its total square footage is:

   a. Rented to a lessee or sub-lessee and used by the lessee or sub-lessee to conduct its customary operations; and/or

   b. Used by the building owner to conduct customary operations.

12. **Your Duties**

   You must make every reasonable effort, with respect to:

   a. Coverage **A** ⊐ Mortgageholder's Interest, to require, procure and maintain "valid insurance", payable to you as mortgageholder, against the Covered Causes of Loss.

   b. Coverage **B** ⊐ Property Owned Or Held In Trust, to procure and maintain "valid insurance" against the Covered Causes of Loss in amounts, and under conditions, you customarily require to protect your interest as owner, fiduciary or trustee of the Covered Property.

   c. Coverage **C** ⊐ Mortgageholder's Liability, to maintain "valid insurance" against the Covered Causes of Loss in amounts, and under conditions, customarily accepted by the mortgagor, as agreed.

   d. Coverage **D** ⊐ Real Estate Tax Liability, to promptly pay real estate taxes, if agreed to, on behalf of the mortgagor.

I. **Definitions**

   1. "Mortgageholder's Interest" means your interest, as mortgageholder, in real or personal property, including your interest in any legal fiduciary capacity.

2. "Pollutants" means any solid, liquid, gaseous or thermal irritant or contaminant, including smoke, vapor, soot, fumes, acids, alkalis, chemicals and waste. Waste includes materials to be recycled, reconditioned or reclaimed.

3. "Specified Causes of Loss" means the following: Fire; lightning; explosion; windstorm or hail; smoke; aircraft or vehicles; riot or civil commotion; vandalism; leakage from fire extinguishing equipment; sinkhole collapse; volcanic action; falling objects; weight of snow, ice or sleet; water damage. Water damage means accidental discharge or leakage of water or steam as the direct result of the breaking apart or cracking of any part of a system or appliance (other than a sump system including its related equipment and parts) containing water or steam.

4. "Suit" includes an arbitration proceeding to which you must submit or submit with our consent.

5. "Valid Insurance" means a valid policy, or other evidence, of insurance.

COMMERCIAL PROPERTY
CP 00 80 10 00

TOBACCO SALES WAREHOUSES COVERAGE FORM

Various provisions in this policy restrict coverage. Read the entire policy carefully to determine rights, duties and what is and is not covered.

Throughout this policy the words "you" and "your" refer to the Named Insured shown in the Declarations. The words "we", "us" and "our" refer to the Company providing this insurance.

Other words and phrases that appear in quotation marks have special meaning. Refer to Section **G.** ⬝ **Definitions.**

A. Coverage

We will pay for direct physical loss of or damage to Covered Property at the premises described in the Declarations caused by or resulting from any Covered Cause of Loss.

1. Covered Property

Covered Property, as used in this Coverage Part, means the following type of property for which a Limit of Insurance is shown in the Declarations:

Tobacco in Sales Warehouses, meaning leaf, loose, scrap and stem tobacco located in the building or structure described in the Declarations:

a. That belongs to others and is in your care, custody or control for auction; or

b. On your leaf account for resale.

Coverage for Tobacco in Sales Warehouses applies only between:

(1) 12:01 A.M. of the 15th day before the opening of the regular auction season at the described premises; and

(2) 12:01 A.M. of the 15th day following the Official Closing Date of the regular auction season at the described premises.

2. Property Not Covered

Covered Property does not include:

a. Growing crops or water;

b. Tobacco that is insured under this or any other policy in which it is more specifically described, except for the excess of the amount due (whether you can collect on it or not) from that other insurance;

c. Tobacco while outside buildings or structures;

d. Tobacco while waterborne; and

e. Contraband, or property in the course of illegal transportation or trade.

3. Covered Causes Of Loss

See applicable Causes of Loss Form as shown in the Declarations.

4. Additional Coverages

a. Debris Removal

(1) Subject to Paragraphs **(3)** and **(4)**, we will pay your expense to remove debris of Covered Property caused by or resulting from a Covered Cause of Loss that occurs during the policy period. The expenses will be paid only if they are reported to us in writing within 180 days of the date of direct physical loss or damage.

(2) Debris Removal does not apply to costs to:

(a) Extract "pollutants" from land or water; or

(b) Remove, restore, or replace polluted land or water.

(3) Subject to the exceptions in Paragraph **(4)**, the following provisions apply:

(a) The most we will pay for the total of direct physical loss or damage plus debris removal expense is the Limit of Insurance applicable to the Covered Property that has sustained loss or damage.

(b) Subject to **(a)** above, the amount we will pay for debris removal expense is limited to 25% of the sum of the deductible plus the amount that we pay for direct physical loss or damage to the Covered Property that has sustained loss or damage.

    Copyright, Insurance Services Office, Inc., 1999   ▢

(4) We will pay up to an additional $10,000 for debris removal expense, for each location, in any one occurrence of physical loss or damage to Covered Property, if one or both of the following circumstances apply:

    (a) The total of the actual debris removal expense plus the amount we pay for direct physical loss or damage exceeds the Limit of Insurance on the Covered Property that has sustained loss or damage.

    (b) The actual debris removal expense exceeds 25% of the sum of the deductible plus the amount that we pay for direct physical loss or damage to the Covered Property that has sustained loss or damage.

    Therefore, if **(4)(a)** and/or **(4)(b)** apply, our total payment for direct physical loss or damage and debris removal expense may reach but will never exceed the Limit of Insurance on the Covered Property that has sustained loss or damage, plus $10,000.

(5) Examples

    The following examples assume that there is no coinsurance penalty.

Example #1

Limit of Insurance	$ 90,000
Amount of Deductible	500
Amount of Loss	$ 50,000
Amount of Loss Payable	$ 49,500
	($50,000 - $500)
Debris Removal Expense	$ 10,000
Debris Removal Expense Payable	$ 10,000

($10,000 is 20% of $50,000)

The debris removal expense is less than 25% of the sum of the loss payable plus the deductible. The sum of the loss payable and the debris removal expense ($49,500 + $10,000 = $59,500) is less than the Limit of Insurance. Therefore, the full amount of debris removal expense is payable in accordance with the terms of Paragraph **(3).**

Example #2

Limit of Insurance	$ 90,000
Amount of Deductible	$ 500
Amount of Loss	$ 80,000
Amount of Loss Payable	$ 79,500
	($80,000 - $500)
Debris Removal Expense	$ 30,000
Debris Removal Expense Payable	
Basic Amount	$ 10,500
Additional Amount	$ 10,000

The basic amount payable for debris removal expense under the terms of Paragraph **(3)** is calculated as follows: $80,000 ($79,500 + $500) x .25 = $20,000; capped at $10,500. The cap applies because the sum of the loss payable ($79,500) and the basic amount payable for debris removal expense ($10,500) cannot exceed the Limit of Insurance ($90,000).

The additional amount payable for debris removal expense is provided in accordance with the terms of Paragraph **(4),** because the debris removal expense ($30,000) exceeds 25% of the loss payable plus the deductible ($30,000 is 37.5% of $80,000), and because the sum of the loss payable and debris removal expense ($79,500 + $30,000 = $109,500) would exceed the Limit of Insurance ($90,000). The additional amount of covered debris removal expense is $10,000, the maximum payable under Paragraph **(4).** Thus, the total payable for debris removal expense in this example is $20,500; $9,500 of the debris removal expense is not covered.

b. Preservation Of Property

If it is necessary to move Covered Property from the described premises to preserve it from loss or damage by a Covered Cause of Loss, we will pay for any direct physical loss or damage to that property:

(1) While it is being moved or while temporarily stored at another location; and

(2) Only if the loss or damage occurs within 30 days after the property is first moved.

Copyright, Insurance Services Office, Inc., 1999

c. **Fire Department Service Charge**

When the fire department is called to save or protect Covered Property from a Covered Cause of Loss, we will pay up to $1,000 for your liability for fire department service charges:

(1) Assumed by contract or agreement prior to loss; or

(2) Required by local ordinance.

No deductible applies to this Additional Coverage.

d. **Pollutant Clean Up And Removal**

We will pay your expense to extract "pollutants" from land or water at the described premises if the discharge, dispersal, seepage, migration, release or escape of the "pollutants" is caused by or results from a Covered Cause of Loss that occurs during the policy period. The expenses will be paid only if they are reported to us in writing within 180 days of the date on which the Covered Cause of Loss occurs.

This Additional Coverage does not apply to costs to test for, monitor or assess the existence, concentration or effects of "pollutants". But we will pay for testing which is performed in the course of extracting the "pollutants" from the land or water.

The most we will pay under this Additional Coverage for each described premises is $10,000 for the sum of all covered expenses arising out of Covered Causes of Loss occurring during each separate 12 month period of this policy.

5. **Coverage Extension**

PROPERTY OFF-PREMISES

You may extend the insurance provided by this Coverage Form to apply to Covered Property that is temporarily located in a building or structure you do not own, lease or operate. This Extension does not apply to Covered Property:

a. In a vehicle;

b. In the care, custody or control of your salespersons; or

c. At any fair or exhibition.

The most we will pay for loss or damage under this Extension is $10,000.

This Extension is additional insurance. The Additional Condition, Need For Full Reports, does not apply to this Extension.

B. **Exclusions And Limitations**

See applicable Causes of Loss Form as shown in the Declarations.

C. **Limits Of Insurance**

The most we will pay for loss or damage in any one occurrence is the applicable Limit of Insurance shown in the Declarations.

The limits applicable to the Coverage Extension and the Fire Department Service Charge and Pollutant Clean Up and Removal Additional Coverages are in addition to the Limits of Insurance.

Payments under the Preservation Of Property Additional Coverage will not increase the applicable Limit of Insurance.

D. **Deductible**

In any one occurrence of loss or damage (hereinafter referred to as loss), we will first reduce the amount of loss if required by the Additional Condition ☐ Need For Full Reports. If the adjusted amount of loss is less than or equal to the Deductible, we will not pay for that loss. If the adjusted amount of loss exceeds the Deductible, we will then subtract the Deductible from the adjusted amount of loss, and will pay the resulting amount or the Limit of Insurance, whichever is less.

E. **Loss Conditions**

The following conditions apply in addition to the Common Policy Conditions and the Commercial Property Conditions.

1. **Abandonment**

There can be no abandonment of any property to us.

2. **Appraisal**

If we and you disagree on the value of the property or the amount of loss, either may make written demand for an appraisal of the loss. In this event, each party will select a competent and impartial appraiser. The two appraisers will select an umpire. If they cannot agree, either may request that selection be made by a judge of a court having jurisdiction. The appraisers will state separately the value of the property and amount of loss. If they fail to agree, they will submit their differences to the umpire. A decision agreed to by any two will be binding. Each party will:

a. Pay its chosen appraiser; and

b. Bear the other expenses of the appraisal and umpire equally.

If there is an appraisal, we will still retain our right to deny the claim.

3. Duties In The Event Of Loss Or Damage

a. You must see that the following are done in the event of loss or damage to Covered Property:

(1) Notify the police if a law may have been broken.

(2) Give us prompt notice of the loss or damage. Include a description of the property involved.

(3) As soon as possible, give us a description of how, when and where the loss or damage occurred.

(4) Take all reasonable steps to protect the Covered Property from further damage, and keep a record of your expenses necessary to protect the Covered Property, for consideration in the settlement of the claim. This will not increase the Limit of Insurance. However, we will not pay for any subsequent loss or damage resulting from a cause of loss that is not a Covered Cause of Loss. Also, if feasible, set the damaged property aside and in the best possible order for examination.

(5) At our request, give us complete inventories of the damaged and undamaged property. Include quantities, costs, values and amount of loss claimed.

(6) As often as may be reasonably required, permit us to inspect the property proving the loss or damage and examine your books and records.

Also permit us to take samples of damaged and undamaged property for inspection, testing and analysis, and permit us to make copies from your books and records.

(7) Send us a signed, sworn proof of loss containing the information we request to investigate the claim. You must do this within 60 days after our request. We will supply you with the necessary forms.

(8) Cooperate with us in the investigation or settlement of the claim.

b. We may examine any insured under oath, while not in the presence of any other insured and at such times as may be reasonably required, about any matter relating to this insurance or the claim, including an insured's books and records. In the event of an examination, an insured's answers must be signed.

4. Loss Payment

a. In the event of loss or damage covered by this Coverage Form, at our option, we will either:

(1) Pay the value of lost or damaged property;

(2) Pay the cost of repairing or replacing the lost or damaged property, subject to **b.** below;

(3) Take all or any part of the property at an agreed or appraised value; or

(4) Repair, rebuild or replace the property with other property of like kind and quality, subject to **b.** below.

We will determine the value of lost or damaged property, or the cost of its repair or replacement, in accordance with the applicable terms of the Valuation Condition in this Coverage Form or any applicable provision which amends or supersedes the Valuation Condition.

b. The cost to repair, rebuild or replace does not include the increased cost attributable to enforcement of any ordinance or law regulating the construction, use or repair of any property.

c. We will give notice of our intentions within 30 days after we receive the sworn proof of loss.

d. We will not pay you more than your financial interest in the Covered Property.

e. We may adjust losses with the owners of lost or damaged property if other than you. If we pay the owners, such payments will satisfy your claims against us for the owners' property. We will not pay the owners more than their financial interest in the Covered Property.

f. We may elect to defend you against suits arising from claims of owners of property. We will do this at our expense.

g. We will pay for covered loss or damage within 30 days after we receive the sworn proof of loss, if you have complied with all of the terms of this Coverage Part and:

(1) We have reached agreement with you on the amount of loss; or

(2) An appraisal award has been made.

5. Recovered Property

If either you or we recover any property after loss settlement, that party must give the other prompt notice. At your option, the property will be returned to you.

    Copyright, Insurance Services Office, Inc., 1999   **CP 00 80 10 00**   ☐

You must then return to us the amount we paid to you for the property. We will pay recovery expenses and the expenses to repair the recovered property, subject to the Limit of Insurance.

6. Valuation

a. We will determine the value of Tobacco in Sales Warehouses in the event of loss or damage at the average price on sales of tobacco of like grades and types:

(1) On the day loss occurs;

(2) On the two sales days immediately prior to the day loss occurs; and

(3) On the two sales days immediately following the day loss occurs.

b. Prices will be based on sales at the tobacco sales warehouse nearest the premises where loss or damage occurs. We will determine the average price as follows:

(1) Divide the total sales by the total number of pounds; and

(2) Deduct any unearned warehouse charges, unearned auction fees and unpaid government taxes at the time of the loss.

F. Additional Conditions

The following conditions apply in addition to the Common Policy Conditions and the Commercial Property Conditions.

1. Need For Full Reports

a. We will not pay a greater proportion of loss than:

(1) The values you reported, divided by

(2) The value of the Covered Property during the last auction season,

if your last report of values before loss or damage at any location shows less than the full value of the Covered Property at that location during the last auction season.

b. For locations you acquire after the last report of values, we will not pay a greater proportion of loss than:

(1) The values you reported for all locations, divided by

(2) The value of the Covered Property at all locations during the last auction season.

2. Premium Adjustment

a. The premium charged at the inception of each policy year is an advance premium. We will determine the final premium for this insurance after the policy year or expiration, based on your reports of value.

b. Based on the difference between the advance premium and the final premium, for each policy year, we will:

(1) Charge additional premium; or

(2) Return excess premium.

3. Reports Of Value

You must file with us a report, within 30 days of the official closing of the sales auction season, showing separately for each location listed in the Declarations:

a. The total number of pounds of tobacco sold and resold during the last sales auction season; and

b. The total price paid per pound.

G. Definitions

"Pollutants" means any solid, liquid, gaseous or thermal irritant or contaminant, including smoke, vapor, soot, fumes, acids, alkalis, chemicals and waste. Waste includes materials to be recycled, reconditioned or reclaimed.

COMMERCIAL PROPERTY CONDITIONS

This Coverage Part is subject to the following conditions, the Common Policy Conditions and applicable Loss Conditions and Additional Conditions in Commercial Property Coverage Forms.

A. CONCEALMENT, MISREPRESENTATION OR FRAUD

This Coverage Part is void in any case of fraud by you as it relates to this Coverage Part at any time. It is also void if you or any other insured, at any time, intentionally conceal or misrepresent a material fact concerning:

1. This Coverage Part;
2. The Covered Property;
3. Your interest in the Covered Property; or
4. A claim under this Coverage Part.

B. CONTROL OF PROPERTY

Any act or neglect of any person other than you beyond your direction or control will not affect this insurance.

The breach of any condition of this Coverage Part at any one or more locations will not affect coverage at any location where, at the time of loss or damage, the breach of condition does not exist.

C. INSURANCE UNDER TWO OR MORE COVERAGES

If two or more of this policy's coverages apply to the same loss or damage, we will not pay more than the actual amount of the loss or damage.

D. LEGAL ACTION AGAINST US

No one may bring a legal action against us under this Coverage Part unless:

1. There has been full compliance with all of the terms of this Coverage Part; and
2. The action is brought within 2 years after the date on which the direct physical loss or damage occurred.

E. LIBERALIZATION

If we adopt any revision that would broaden the coverage under this Coverage Part without additional premium within 45 days prior to or during the policy period, the broadened coverage will immediately apply to this Coverage Part.

F. NO BENEFIT TO BAILEE

No person or organization, other than you, having custody of Covered Property will benefit from this insurance.

G. OTHER INSURANCE

1. You may have other insurance subject to the same plan, terms, conditions and provisions as the insurance under this Coverage Part. If you do, we will pay our share of the covered loss or damage. Our share is the proportion that the applicable Limit of Insurance under this Coverage Part bears to the Limits of Insurance of all insurance covering on the same basis.
2. If there is other insurance covering the same loss or damage, other than that described in 1. above, we will pay only for the amount of covered loss or damage in excess of the amount due from that other insurance, whether you can collect on it or not. But we will not pay more than the applicable Limit of Insurance.

H. POLICY PERIOD, COVERAGE TERRITORY

Under this Coverage Part:

1. We cover loss or damage commencing:
   a. During the policy period shown in the Declarations; and
   b. Within the coverage territory.
2. The coverage territory is:
   a. The United States of America (including its territories and possessions);
   b. Puerto Rico; and
   c. Canada.

I. TRANSFER OF RIGHTS OF RECOVERY AGAINST OTHERS TO US

If any person or organization to or for whom we make payment under this Coverage Part has rights to recover damages from another, those rights are transferred to us to the extent of our payment. That person or organization must do everything necessary to secure our rights and must do nothing after loss to impair them. But you may waive your rights against another party in writing:

1. Prior to a loss to your Covered Property or Covered Income.

2. After a loss to your Covered Property or Covered Income only if, at time of loss, that party is one of the following:

   a. Someone insured by this insurance;

   b. A business firm:

      (1) Owned or controlled by you; or

      (2) That owns or controls you; or

   c. Your tenant.

This will not restrict your insurance.

 Copyright, ISO Commercial Risk Services, Inc., 1983, 1987 **CP 00 90 07 88** ☐

COMMERCIAL PROPERTY
CP 10 10 10 00

CAUSES OF LOSS – BASIC FORM

A. Covered Causes Of Loss

When Basic is shown in the Declarations, Covered Causes of Loss means the following:

1. Fire.

2. Lightning.

3. Explosion, including the explosion of gases or fuel within the furnace of any fired vessel or within the flues or passages through which the gases of combustion pass. This cause of loss does not include loss or damage by:

   a. Rupture, bursting or operation of pressure relief devices; or

   b. Rupture or bursting due to expansion or swelling of the contents of any building or structure, caused by or resulting from water.

4. Windstorm or Hail, but not including:

   a. Frost or cold weather;

   b. Ice (other than hail), snow or sleet, whether driven by wind or not; or

   c. Loss or damage to the interior of any building or structure, or the property inside the building or structure, caused by rain, snow, sand or dust, whether driven by wind or not, unless the building or structure first sustains wind or hail damage to its roof or walls through which the rain, snow, sand or dust enters.

5. Smoke causing sudden and accidental loss or damage. This cause of loss does not include smoke from agricultural smudging or industrial operations.

6. Aircraft or Vehicles, meaning only physical contact of an aircraft, a spacecraft, a self-propelled missile, a vehicle or an object thrown up by a vehicle with the described property or with the building or structure containing the described property. This cause of loss includes loss or damage by objects falling from aircraft.

   We will not pay for loss or damage caused by or resulting from vehicles you own or which are operated in the course of your business.

7. Riot or Civil Commotion, including:

   a. Acts of striking employees while occupying the described premises; and

   b. Looting occurring at the time and place of a riot or civil commotion.

8. Vandalism, meaning willful and malicious damage to, or destruction of, the described property.

   We will not pay for loss or damage caused by or resulting from theft, except for building damage caused by the breaking in or exiting of burglars.

9. Sprinkler Leakage, meaning leakage or discharge of any substance from an Automatic Sprinkler System, including collapse of a tank that is part of the system.

   If the building or structure containing the Automatic Sprinkler System is Covered Property, we will also pay the cost to:

   a. Repair or replace damaged parts of the Automatic Sprinkler System if the damage:

      (1) Results in sprinkler leakage; or

      (2) Is directly caused by freezing.

   b. Tear out and replace any part of the building or structure to repair damage to the Automatic Sprinkler System that has resulted in sprinkler leakage.

   Automatic Sprinkler System means:

   (1) Any automatic fire protective or extinguishing system, including connected:

      (a) Sprinklers and discharge nozzles;

      (b) Ducts, pipes, valves and fittings;

      (c) Tanks, their component parts and supports; and

      (d) Pumps and private fire protection mains.

(2) When supplied from an automatic fire protective system:

(a) Non-automatic fire protective systems; and

(b) Hydrants, standpipes and outlets.

10. Sinkhole Collapse, meaning loss or damage caused by the sudden sinking or collapse of land into underground empty spaces created by the action of water on limestone or dolomite. This cause of loss does not include:

a. The cost of filling sinkholes; or

b. Sinking or collapse of land into man-made underground cavities.

11. Volcanic Action, meaning direct loss or damage resulting from the eruption of a volcano when the loss or damage is caused by:

a. Airborne volcanic blast or airborne shock waves;

b. Ash, dust or particulate matter; or

c. Lava flow.

All volcanic eruptions that occur within any 168-hour period will constitute a single occurrence.

This cause of loss does not include the cost to remove ash, dust or particulate matter that does not cause direct physical loss or damage to the described property.

B. Exclusions

1. We will not pay for loss or damage caused directly or indirectly by any of the following. Such loss or damage is excluded regardless of any other cause or event that contributes concurrently or in any sequence to the loss.

a. Ordinance Or Law

The enforcement of any ordinance or law:

(1) Regulating the construction, use or repair of any property; or

(2) Requiring the tearing down of any property, including the cost of removing its debris.

This exclusion, Ordinance Or Law, applies whether the loss results from:

(1) An ordinance or law that is enforced even if the property has not been damaged; or

(2) The increased costs incurred to comply with an ordinance or law in the course of construction, repair, renovation, remodeling or demolition of property, or removal of its debris, following a physical loss to that property.

b. Earth Movement

(1) Earthquake, including any earth sinking, rising or shifting related to such event;

(2) Landslide, including any earth sinking, rising or shifting related to such event;

(3) Mine subsidence, meaning subsidence of a man-made mine, whether or not mining activity has ceased;

(4) Earth sinking (other than sinkhole collapse), rising or shifting including soil conditions which cause settling, cracking or other disarrangement of foundations or other parts of realty. Soil conditions include contraction, expansion, freezing, thawing, erosion, improperly compacted soil and the action of water under the ground surface.

But if Earth Movement, as described in **b.(1)** through **(4)** above, results in fire or explosion, we will pay for the loss or damage caused by that fire or explosion.

(5) Volcanic eruption, explosion or effusion. But if volcanic eruption, explosion or effusion results in fire or Volcanic Action, we will pay for the loss or damage caused by that fire or Volcanic Action.

c. Governmental Action

Seizure or destruction of property by order of governmental authority.

But we will pay for loss or damage caused by or resulting from acts of destruction ordered by governmental authority and taken at the time of a fire to prevent its spread, if the fire would be covered under this Coverage Part.

d. Nuclear Hazard

Nuclear reaction or radiation, or radioactive contamination, however caused.

But if nuclear reaction or radiation, or radioactive contamination, results in fire, we will pay for the loss or damage caused by that fire.

e. Utility Services

The failure of power or other utility service supplied to the described premises, however caused, if the failure occurs away from the described premises.

But if the failure of power or other utility service results in a Covered Cause of Loss, we will pay for the loss or damage caused by that Covered Cause of Loss.

This exclusion does not apply to the Business Income coverage or to Extra Expense coverage. Instead, the Special Exclusion in Paragraph **B.3.a.(1)** applies to these coverages.

f. War And Military Action

(1) War, including undeclared or civil war;

(2) Warlike action by a military force, including action in hindering or defending against an actual or expected attack, by any government, sovereign or other authority using military personnel or other agents; or

(3) Insurrection, rebellion, revolution, usurped power, or action taken by governmental authority in hindering or defending against any of these.

g. Water

(1) Flood, surface water, waves, tides, tidal waves, overflow of any body of water, or their spray, all whether driven by wind or not;

(2) Mudslide or mudflow;

(3) Water that backs up or overflows from a sewer, drain or sump; or

(4) Water under the ground surface pressing on, or flowing or seeping through:

(a) Foundations, walls, floors or paved surfaces;

(b) Basements, whether paved or not; or

(c) Doors, windows or other openings.

But if Water, as described in **g.(1)** through **(4)** above, results in fire, explosion or sprinkler leakage, we will pay for the loss or damage caused by that fire, explosion or sprinkler leakage.

Exclusions **B.1.a.** through **B.1.g.** apply whether or not the loss event results in widespread damage or affects a substantial area.

2. We will not pay for loss or damage caused by or resulting from:

a. Artificially generated electrical current, including electric arcing, that disturbs electrical devices, appliances or wires.

But if artificially generated electrical current results in fire, we will pay for the loss or damage caused by that fire.

b. Rupture or bursting of water pipes (other than Automatic Sprinkler Systems) unless caused by a Covered Cause of Loss.

c. Leakage or discharge of water or steam from any part of a system or appliance containing water or steam (other than an Automatic Sprinkler System), unless the leakage or discharge occurs because the system or appliance was damaged by a Covered Cause of Loss.

d. Explosion of steam boilers, steam pipes, steam engines or steam turbines owned or leased by you, or operated under your control.

But if explosion of steam boilers, steam pipes, steam engines or steam turbines results in fire or combustion explosion, we will pay for the loss or damage caused by that fire or combustion explosion.

e. Mechanical breakdown, including rupture or busting caused by centrifugal force.

But if mechanical breakdown results in a Covered Cause of Loss, we will pay for the loss or damage caused by that Covered Cause of Loss.

f. Neglect of an insured to use all reasonable means to save and preserve property from further damage at and after the time of loss.

3. **Special Exclusions**

The following provisions apply only to the specified Coverage Forms.

a. Business Income (And Extra Expense) Coverage Form, Business Income (Without Extra Expense) Coverage Form, or Extra Expense Coverage Form

We will not pay for:

(1) Any loss caused directly or indirectly by the failure of power or other utility service supplied to the described premises, however caused, if the failure occurs outside of a covered building.

But if the failure of power or other utility service results in a Covered Cause of Loss, we will pay for the loss resulting from that Covered Cause of Loss.

(2) Any loss caused by or resulting from:

(a) Damage or destruction of "finished stock"; or

(b) The time required to reproduce "finished stock".

This exclusion does not apply to Extra Expense.

(3) Any loss caused by or resulting from direct physical loss or damage to radio or television antennas (including satellite dishes) and their lead-in wiring, masts or towers.

(4) Any increase of loss caused by or resulting from:

(a) Delay in rebuilding, repairing or replacing the property or resuming "operations", due to interference at the location of the rebuilding, repair or replacement by strikers or other persons; or

(b) Suspension, lapse or cancellation of any license, lease or contract. But if the suspension, lapse or cancellation is directly caused by the "suspension" of "operations", we will cover such loss that affects your Business Income during the "period of restoration" and any extension of the "period of restoration" in accordance with the terms of the Extended Business Income Additional Coverage and the Extended Period of Indemnity Optional Coverage or any variation of these.

(5) Any Extra Expense caused by or resulting from suspension, lapse or cancellation of any license, lease or contract beyond the "period of restoration".

(6) Any other consequential loss.

b. Leasehold Interest Coverage Form

(1) Paragraph **B.1.a.**, Ordinance Or Law; does not apply to insurance under this Coverage Form.

(2) We will not pay for any loss caused by:

(a) Your cancelling the lease;

(b) The suspension, lapse or cancellation of any license; or

(c) Any other consequential loss.

c. Legal Liability Coverage Form

(1) The following Exclusions do not apply to insurance under this Coverage Form:

(a) Paragraph **B.1.a.**, Ordinance Or Law;

(b) Paragraph **B.1.c.**, Governmental Action;

(c) Paragraph **B.1.d.**, Nuclear Hazard;

(d) Paragraph **B.1.e.**, Utility Services; and

(e) Paragraph **B.1.f.**, War And Military Action.

(2) The following additional exclusions apply to insurance under this Coverage Form:

(a) Contractual Liability

We will not defend any claim or "suit", or pay damages that you are legally liable to pay, solely by reason of your assumption of liability in a contract or agreement. But this exclusion does not apply to a written lease agreement in which you have assumed liability for building damage resulting from an actual or attempted burglary or robbery, provided that:

(i) Your assumption of liability was executed prior to the accident; and

(ii) The building is Covered Property under this Coverage Form.

(b) Nuclear Hazard

We will not defend any claim or "suit", or pay any damages, loss, expense or obligation, resulting from nuclear reaction or radiation, or radioactive contamination, however caused.

C. Limitation

We will pay for loss of animals only if they are killed or their destruction is made necessary.

   Copyright, Insurance Services Office, Inc., 1999   CP 10 10 10 00   ☐

CAUSES OF LOSS – BROAD FORM

A. Covered Causes Of Loss

When Broad is shown in the Declarations, Covered Causes of Loss means the following:

1. Fire.

2. Lightning.

3. Explosion, including the explosion of gases or fuel within the furnace of any fired vessel or within the flues or passages through which the gases of combustion pass. This cause of loss does not include loss or damage by:

   a. Rupture, bursting or operation of pressure relief devices; or

   b. Rupture or bursting due to expansion or swelling of the contents of any building or structure, caused by or resulting from water.

4. Windstorm or Hail, but not including:

   a. Frost or cold weather;

   b. Ice (other than hail), snow or sleet, whether driven by wind or not; or

   c. Loss or damage to the interior of any building or structure, or the property inside the building or structure, caused by rain, snow, sand or dust, whether driven by wind or not, unless the building or structure first sustains wind or hail damage to its roof or walls through which the rain, snow, sand or dust enters.

5. Smoke causing sudden and accidental loss or damage. This cause of loss does not include smoke from agricultural smudging or industrial operations.

6. Aircraft or Vehicles, meaning only physical contact of an aircraft, a spacecraft, a self-propelled missile, a vehicle or an object thrown up by a vehicle with the described property or with the building or structure containing the described property. This cause of loss includes loss or damage by objects falling from aircraft.

   We will not pay for loss or damage caused by or resulting from vehicles you own or which are operated in the course of your business.

7. Riot or Civil Commotion, including:

   a. Acts of striking employees while occupying the described premises; and

   b. Looting occurring at the time and place of a riot or civil commotion.

8. Vandalism, meaning willful and malicious damage to, or destruction of, the described property.

   We will not pay for loss or damage caused by or resulting from theft, except for building damage caused by the breaking in or exiting of burglars.

9. Sprinkler Leakage, meaning leakage or discharge of any substance from an Automatic Sprinkler System, including collapse of a tank that is part of the system.

   If the building or structure containing the Automatic Sprinkler System is Covered Property, we will also pay the cost to:

   a. Repair or replace damaged parts of the Automatic Sprinkler System if the damage:

      (1) Results in sprinkler leakage; or

      (2) Is directly caused by freezing.

   b. Tear out and replace any part of the building or structure to repair damage to the Automatic Sprinkler System that has resulted in sprinkler leakage.

   Automatic Sprinkler System means:

      (1) Any automatic fire protective or extinguishing system, including connected:

         (a) Sprinklers and discharge nozzles;

         (b) Ducts, pipes, valves and fittings;

         (c) Tanks, their component parts and supports; and

         (d) Pumps and private fire protection mains.

(2) When supplied from an automatic fire protective system:

    (a) Non-automatic fire protective systems; and

    (b) Hydrants, standpipes and outlets.

10. Sinkhole Collapse, meaning loss or damage caused by the sudden sinking or collapse of land into underground empty spaces created by the action of water on limestone or dolomite. This cause of loss does not include:

    a. The cost of filling sinkholes; or

    b. Sinking or collapse of land into man-made underground cavities.

11. Volcanic Action, meaning direct loss or damage resulting from the eruption of a volcano when the loss or damage is caused by:

    a. Airborne volcanic blast or airborne shock waves;

    b. Ash, dust or particulate matter; or

    c. Lava flow.

All volcanic eruptions that occur within any 168-hour period will constitute a single occurrence.

This cause of loss does not include the cost to remove ash, dust or particulate matter that does not cause direct physical loss or damage to the described property.

12. **Falling Objects**

But we will not pay for loss or damage to:

    a. Personal property in the open; or

    b. The interior of a building or structure, or property inside a building or structure, unless the roof or an outside wall of the building or structure is first damaged by a falling object.

13. **Weight Of Snow, Ice Or Sleet**

But we will not pay for loss or damage to personal property outside of buildings or structures.

14. **Water Damage**

    a. Water Damage, meaning accidental discharge or leakage of water or steam as the direct result of the breaking apart or cracking of a plumbing, heating, air conditioning or other system or appliance, that is located on the described premises and contains water or steam.

However, Water Damage does not include:

    (1) Discharge or leakage from:

        (a) An Automatic Sprinkler System;

        (b) A sump or related equipment and parts, including overflow due to sump pump failure or excessive volume of water; or

        (c) Roof drains, gutters, downspouts or similar fixtures or equipment.

    (2) The cost to repair any defect that caused the loss or damage;

    (3) Loss or damage caused by or resulting from continuous or repeated seepage or leakage that occurs over a period of 14 days or more; or

    (4) Loss or damage caused by or resulting from freezing, unless:

        (a) You do your best to maintain heat in the building or structure; or

        (b) You drain the equipment and shut off the water supply if the heat is not maintained.

    b. If coverage applies subject to **a.** above, and the building or structure containing the system or appliance is Covered Property, we will also pay the cost to tear out and replace any part of the building or structure to repair damage to the system or appliance from which the water or steam escapes. But we will not pay the cost to repair any defect that caused the loss or damage.

B. Exclusions

1. We will not pay for loss or damage caused directly or indirectly by any of the following. Such loss or damage is excluded regardless of any other cause or event that contributes concurrently or in any sequence to the loss.

    a. Ordinance Or Law

    The enforcement of any ordinance or law:

    (1) Regulating the construction, use or repair of any property; or

    (2) Requiring the tearing down of any property including the cost of removing its debris.

    This Exclusion, Ordinance Or Law, applies whether the loss results from:

    (1) An ordinance or law that is enforced even if the property has not been damaged; or

Copyright, Insurance Services Office, Inc., 1999

(2) The increased costs incurred to comply with an ordinance or law in the course of construction, repair, renovation, remodeling or demolition of property, or removal of its debris, following a physical loss to that property.

b. Earth Movement

(1) Earthquake, including any earth sinking, rising or shifting related to such event;

(2) Landslide, including any earth sinking, rising or shifting related to such event;

(3) Mine subsidence, meaning subsidence of a man-made mine, whether or not mining activity has ceased;

(4) Earth sinking (other than sinkhole collapse), rising or shifting including soil conditions which cause settling, cracking or other disarrangement of foundations or other parts of realty. Soil conditions include contraction, expansion, freezing, thawing, erosion, improperly compacted soil and the action of water under the ground surface.

But if Earth Movement, as described in **b.(1)** through **(4)** above, results in fire or explosion, we will pay for the loss or damage caused by that fire or explosion.

(5) Volcanic eruption, explosion or effusion. But if volcanic eruption, explosion or effusion results in fire, building glass breakage or Volcanic Action, we will pay for the loss or damage caused by that fire, building glass breakage or Volcanic Action.

c. Governmental Action

Seizure or destruction of property by order of governmental authority.

But we will pay for loss or damage caused by or resulting from acts of destruction ordered by governmental authority and taken at the time of a fire to prevent its spread, if the fire would be covered under this Coverage Part.

d. Nuclear Hazard

Nuclear reaction or radiation, or radioactive contamination, however caused.

But if nuclear reaction or radiation, or radioactive contamination, results in fire, we will pay for the loss or damage caused by that fire.

e. Utility Services

The failure of power or other utility service supplied to the described premises, however caused, if the failure occurs away from the described premises.

But if the failure of power or other utility service results in a Covered Cause of Loss, we will pay for the loss or damage caused by that Covered Cause of Loss.

This exclusion does not apply to the Business Income coverage or to Extra Expense coverage. Instead, the Special Exclusion in Paragraph **B.3.a.(1)** applies to these coverages.

f. War And Military Action

(1) War, including undeclared or civil war;

(2) Warlike action by a military force, including action in hindering or defending against an actual or expected attack, by any government, sovereign or other authority using military personnel or other agents; or

(3) Insurrection, rebellion, revolution, usurped power, or action taken by governmental authority in hindering or defending against any of these.

g. Water

(1) Flood, surface water, waves, tides, tidal waves, overflow of any body of water, or their spray, all whether driven by wind or not;

(2) Mudslide or mudflow;

(3) Water that backs up or overflows from a sewer, drain or sump; or

(4) Water under the ground surface pressing on, or flowing or seeping through:

(a) Foundations, walls, floors or paved surfaces;

(b) Basements, whether paved or not; or

(c) Doors, windows or other openings.

But if Water, as described in **g.(1)** through **g.(4)** above, results in fire, explosion or sprinkler leakage, we will pay for the loss or damage caused by that fire, explosion or sprinkler leakage.

Exclusions **B.1.a.** through **B.1.g.** apply whether or not the loss event results in widespread damage or affects a substantial area.

2. We will not pay for loss or damage caused by or resulting from:

    a. Artificially generated electrical current, including electric arcing, that disturbs electrical devices, appliances or wires. But if artificially generated electrical current results in fire, we will pay for the loss or damage caused by that fire.

    b. Explosion of steam boilers, steam pipes, steam engines or steam turbines owned or leased by you, or operated under your control.

        But if explosion of steam boilers, steam pipes, steam engines or steam turbines results in fire or combustion explosion, we will pay for the loss or damage caused by that fire or combustion explosion.

    c. Mechanical breakdown, including rupture or bursting caused by centrifugal force.

        But if mechanical breakdown results in a Covered Cause of Loss, we will pay for the loss or damage caused by that Covered Cause of Loss.

    d. Neglect of an insured to use all reasonable means to save and preserve property from further damage at and after the time of loss.

3. **Special Exclusions**

    The following provisions apply only to the specified Coverage Forms.

    a. **Business Income (And Extra Expense) Coverage Form, Business Income (Without Extra Expense) Coverage Form, or Extra Expense Coverage Form**

        We will not pay for:

        (1) Any loss caused directly or indirectly by the failure of power or other utility service supplied to the described premises, however caused, if the failure occurs outside of a covered building.

            But if the failure of power or other utility service results in a Covered Cause of Loss, we will pay for the loss resulting from that Covered Cause of Loss.

        (2) Any loss caused by or resulting from:

            (a) Damage or destruction of "finished stock"; or

        (b) The time required to reproduce "finished stock".

        This exclusion does not apply to Extra Expense.

        (3) Any loss caused by or resulting from direct physical loss or damage to radio or television antennas (including satellite dishes) and their lead-in wiring, masts or towers.

        (4) Any increase of loss caused by or resulting from:

            (a) Delay in rebuilding, repairing or replacing the property or resuming "operations", due to interference at the location of the rebuilding, repair or replacement by strikers or other persons; or

            (b) Suspension, lapse or cancellation of any license, lease or contract. But if the suspension, lapse or cancellation is directly caused by the "suspension" of "operations", we will cover such loss that affects your Business Income during the "period of restoration" and any extension of the "period of restoration" in accordance with the terms of the Extended Business Income Additional Coverage and the Extended Period Of Indemnity Optional Coverage or any variation of these.

        (5) Any Extra Expense caused by or resulting from suspension, lapse or cancellation of any license, lease or contract beyond the "period of restoration".

        (6) Any other consequential loss.

    b. **Leasehold Interest Coverage Form**

        (1) Paragraph **B.1.a.**, Ordinance Or Law, does not apply to insurance under this Coverage Form.

        (2) We will not pay for any loss caused by:

            (a) Your cancelling the lease;

            (b) The suspension, lapse or cancellation of any license; or

            (c) Any other consequential loss.

    c. **Legal Liability Coverage Form**

        (1) The following Exclusions do not apply to insurance under this Coverage Form:

            (a) Paragraph **B.1.a.**, Ordinance Or Law;

Copyright, Insurance Services Office, Inc., 1999

CP 10 20 10 00 □

(b) Paragraph **B.1.c.,** Governmental Action;

(c) Paragraph **B.1.d.,** Nuclear Hazard;

(d) Paragraph **B.1.e.,** Utility Services; and

(e) Paragraph **B.1.f.,** War And Military Action.

(2) The following additional exclusions apply to insurance under this Coverage Form:

(a) Contractual Liability

We will not defend any claim or "suit", or pay damages that you are legally liable to pay, solely by reason of your assumption of liability in a contract or agreement. But this exclusion does not apply to a written lease agreement in which you have assumed liability for building damage resulting from an actual or attempted burglary or robbery, provided that:

(i) Your assumption of liability was executed prior to the accident; and

(ii) The building is Covered Property under this Coverage Form.

(b) Nuclear Hazard

We will not defend any claim or "suit", or pay any damages, loss, expense or obligation, resulting from nuclear reaction or radiation, or radioactive contamination, however caused.

C. Additional Coverage ⬜ Collapse

The term Covered Cause of Loss includes the Collapse Additional Coverage as described and limited in **1.** through **5.** below.

1. With respect to buildings:

a. Collapse means an abrupt falling down or caving in of a building or any part of a building with the result that the building or part of the building cannot be occupied for its intended purpose;

b. A building or any part of a building that is in danger of falling down or caving in is not considered to be in a state of collapse;

c. A part of a building that is standing is not considered to be in a state of collapse even if it has separated from another part of the building;

d. A building that is standing or any part of a building that is standing is not considered to be in a state of collapse even if it shows evidence of cracking, bulging, sagging, bending, leaning, settling, shrinkage or expansion.

2. We will pay for direct physical loss or damage to Covered Property, caused by collapse of a building or any part of a building that is insured under this Coverage Form or that contains Covered Property insured under this Coverage Form, if the collapse is caused by one or more of the following:

a. Fire; lightning; explosion; windstorm or hail; smoke; aircraft or vehicles; riot or civil commotion; vandalism; leakage from fire extinguishing equipment; sinkhole collapse; volcanic action; breakage of building glass; falling objects; weight of snow, ice or sleet; water damage, meaning accidental discharge or leakage of water or steam as the direct result of the breaking apart or cracking of a plumbing, heating, air conditioning or other system or appliance (other than a sump system including its related equipment and parts), that is located on the described premises and contains water or steam; all only as insured against in this Coverage Part;

b. Decay that is hidden from view, unless the presence of such decay is known to an insured prior to collapse;

c. Insect or vermin damage that is hidden from view, unless the presence of such damage is known to an insured prior to collapse;

d. Weight of people or personal property;

e. Weight of rain that collects on a roof;

f. Use of defective material or methods in construction, remodeling, or renovation if the collapse occurs during the course of the construction, remodeling, or renovation. However, if the collapse occurs after construction, remodeling, or renovation is complete and is caused in part by a cause of loss listed in **2.a.** through **2.e.,** we will pay for the loss or damage even if use of defective material or methods, in construction, remodeling, or renovation, contributes to the collapse.

The criteria set forth in **1.a.** through **1.d.** do not limit the coverage otherwise provided under this Causes of Loss Form for the causes of loss listed in **2.a.**

3. With respect to the following property:

   a. Outdoor radio or television antennas (including satellite dishes) and their lead-in wiring, masts or towers;

   b. Awnings, gutters and downspouts;

   c. Yard fixtures;

   d. Outdoor swimming pools;

   e. Fences;

   f. Piers, wharves and docks;

   g. Beach or diving platforms or appurtenances;

   h. Retaining walls; and

   i. Walks, roadways and other paved surfaces;

   if the collapse is caused by a cause of loss listed in **2.b.** through **2.f.** we will pay for loss or damage to that property only if:

   a. Such loss or damage is a direct result of the collapse of a building insured under this Coverage Form; and

   b. The property is Covered Property under this Coverage Form.

4. If personal property abruptly falls down or caves in and such collapse is not the result of collapse of a building, we will pay for loss or damage to Covered Property caused by such collapse of personal property only if:

   a. The collapse was caused by a Cause of Loss listed in **2.a.** through **2.f.** above;

   b. The personal property which collapses is inside a building; and

   c. The property which collapses is not of a kind listed in **3.** above, regardless of whether that kind of property is considered to be personal property or real property.

   The coverage stated in this Paragraph **4.** does not apply to personal property if marring and/or scratching is the only damage to that personal property caused by the collapse.

   Collapse of personal property does not mean cracking, bulging, sagging, bending, leaning, settling, shrinkage or expansion.

5. This Additional Coverage, Collapse, will not increase the Limits of Insurance provided in this Coverage Part.

D. Limitation

We will pay for loss of animals only if they are killed or their destruction is made necessary.

CAUSES OF LOSS – SPECIAL FORM

Words and phrases that appear in quotation marks have special meaning. Refer to Section **F.** ☐ Definitions.

A. Covered Causes Of Loss

When Special is shown in the Declarations, Covered Causes of Loss means Risks Of Direct Physical Loss unless the loss is:

1. Excluded in Section **B.**, Exclusions; or

2. Limited in Section **C.**, Limitations;

that follow.

B. Exclusions

1. We will not pay for loss or damage caused directly or indirectly by any of the following. Such loss or damage is excluded regardless of any other cause or event that contributes concurrently or in any sequence to the loss.

a. Ordinance Or Law

The enforcement of any ordinance or law:

(1) Regulating the construction, use or repair of any property; or

(2) Requiring the tearing down of any property, including the cost of removing its debris.

This exclusion, Ordinance Or Law, applies whether the loss results from:

(1) An ordinance or law that is enforced even if the property has not been damaged; or

(2) The increased costs incurred to comply with an ordinance or law in the course of construction, repair, renovation, remodeling or demolition of property, or removal of its debris, following a physical loss to that property.

b. Earth Movement

(1) Earthquake, including any earth sinking, rising or shifting related to such event;

(2) Landslide, including any earth sinking, rising or shifting related to such event;

(3) Mine subsidence, meaning subsidence of a man-made mine, whether or not mining activity has ceased;

(4) Earth sinking (other than sinkhole collapse), rising or shifting including soil conditions which cause settling, cracking or other disarrangement of foundations or other parts of realty. Soil conditions include contraction, expansion, freezing, thawing, erosion, improperly compacted soil and the action of water under the ground surface.

But if Earth Movement, as described in **b.(1)** through **(4)** above, results in fire or explosion, we will pay for the loss or damage caused by that fire or explosion.

(5) Volcanic eruption, explosion or effusion. But if volcanic eruption, explosion or effusion results in fire, building glass breakage or Volcanic Action, we will pay for the loss or damage caused by that fire, building glass breakage or Volcanic Action.

Volcanic action means direct loss or damage resulting from the eruption of a volcano when the loss or damage is caused by:

(a) Airborne volcanic blast or airborne shock waves;

(b) Ash, dust or particulate matter; or

(c) Lava flow.

All volcanic eruptions that occur within any 168 hour period will constitute a single occurrence.

Volcanic action does not include the cost to remove ash, dust or particulate matter that does not cause direct physical loss or damage to the described property.

c. Governmental Action

Seizure or destruction of property by order of governmental authority.

But we will pay for loss or damage caused by or resulting from acts of destruction ordered by governmental authority and taken at the time of a fire to prevent its spread, if the fire would be covered under this Coverage Part.

 Copyright, Insurance Services Office, Inc., 1999

d. Nuclear Hazard

Nuclear reaction or radiation, or radioactive contamination, however caused.

But if nuclear reaction or radiation, or radioactive contamination, results in fire, we will pay for the loss or damage caused by that fire.

e. Utility Services

The failure of power or other utility service supplied to the described premises, however caused, if the failure occurs away from the described premises.

But if the failure of power or other utility service results in a Covered Cause of Loss, we will pay for the loss or damage caused by that Covered Cause of Loss.

This exclusion does not apply to the Business Income coverage or to Extra Expense coverage. Instead, the Special Exclusion in Paragraph **B.4.a.(1)** applies to these coverages.

f. War And Military Action

(1) War, including undeclared or civil war;

(2) Warlike action by a military force, including action in hindering or defending against an actual or expected attack, by any government, sovereign or other authority using military personnel or other agents; or

(3) Insurrection, rebellion, revolution, usurped power, or action taken by governmental authority in hindering or defending against any of these.

g. Water

(1) Flood, surface water, waves, tides, tidal waves, overflow of any body of water, or their spray, all whether driven by wind or not;

(2) Mudslide or mudflow;

(3) Water that backs up or overflows from a sewer, drain or sump; or

(4) Water under the ground surface pressing on, or flowing or seeping through:

(a) Foundations, walls, floors or paved surfaces;

(b) Basements, whether paved or not; or

(c) Doors, windows or other openings.

But if Water, as described in **g.(1)** through **g.(4)** above, results in fire, explosion or sprinkler leakage, we will pay for the loss or damage caused by that fire, explosion or sprinkler leakage.

Exclusions **B.1.a.** through **B.1.g.** apply whether or not the loss event results in widespread damage or affects a substantial area.

2. We will not pay for loss or damage caused by or resulting from any of the following:

a. Artificially generated electrical current, including electric arcing, that disturbs electrical devices, appliances or wires.

But if artificially generated electrical current results in fire, we will pay for the loss or damage caused by that fire.

b. Delay, loss of use or loss of market.

c. Smoke, vapor or gas from agricultural smudging or industrial operations.

d. (1) Wear and tear;

(2) Rust, corrosion, fungus, decay, deterioration, hidden or latent defect or any quality in property that causes it to damage or destroy itself;

(3) Smog;

(4) Settling, cracking, shrinking or expansion;

(5) Nesting or infestation, or discharge or release of waste products or secretions, by insects, birds, rodents or other animals.

(6) Mechanical breakdown, including rupture or bursting caused by centrifugal force. But if mechanical breakdown results in elevator collision, we will pay for the loss or damage caused by that elevator collision.

(7) The following causes of loss to personal property:

(a) Dampness or dryness of atmosphere;

(b) Changes in or extremes of temperature; or

(c) Marring or scratching.

But if an excluded cause of loss that is listed in **2.d.(1)** through **(7)** results in a "specified cause of loss" or building glass breakage, we will pay for the loss or damage caused by that "specified cause of loss" or building glass breakage.

      Copyright, Insurance Services Office, Inc., 1999   CP 10 30 10 00   ◻

e. Explosion of steam boilers, steam pipes, steam engines or steam turbines owned or leased by you, or operated under your control. But if explosion of steam boilers, steam pipes, steam engines or steam turbines results in fire or combustion explosion, we will pay for the loss or damage caused by that fire or combustion explosion. We will also pay for loss or damage caused by or resulting from the explosion of gases or fuel within the furnace of any fired vessel or within the flues or passages through which the gases of combustion pass.

f. Continuous or repeated seepage or leakage of water that occurs over a period of 14 days or more.

g. Water, other liquids, powder or molten material that leaks or flows from plumbing, heating, air conditioning or other equipment (except fire protective systems) caused by or resulting from freezing, unless:

(1) You do your best to maintain heat in the building or structure; or

(2) You drain the equipment and shut off the supply if the heat is not maintained.

h. Dishonest or criminal act by you, any of your partners, members, officers, managers, employees (including leased employees), directors, trustees, authorized representatives or anyone to whom you entrust the property for any purpose:

(1) Acting alone or in collusion with others; or

(2) Whether or not occurring during the hours of employment.

This exclusion does not apply to acts of destruction by your employees (including leased employees); but theft by employees (including leased employees) is not covered.

i. Voluntary parting with any property by you or anyone else to whom you have entrusted the property if induced to do so by any fraudulent scheme, trick, device or false pretense.

j. Rain, snow, ice or sleet to personal property in the open.

k. Collapse, except as provided below in the Additional Coverage for Collapse. But if collapse results in a Covered Cause of Loss at the described premises, we will pay for the loss or damage caused by that Covered Cause of Loss.

l. Discharge, dispersal, seepage, migration, release or escape of "pollutants" unless the discharge, dispersal, seepage, migration, release or escape is itself caused by any of the "specified causes of loss". But if the discharge, dispersal, seepage, migration, release or escape of "pollutants" results in a "specified cause of loss", we will pay for the loss or damage caused by that "specified cause of loss".

This Exclusion, **l.**, does not apply to damage to glass caused by chemicals applied to the glass.

m. Neglect of an insured to use all reasonable means to save and preserve property from further damage at and after the time of loss.

3. We will not pay for loss or damage caused by or resulting from any of the following, **3.a.** through **3.c.** But if an excluded cause of loss that is listed in **3.a.** through **3.c.** results in a Covered Cause of Loss, we will pay for the loss or damage caused by that Covered Cause of Loss.

a. Weather conditions. But this exclusion only applies if weather conditions contribute in any way with a cause or event excluded in Paragraph **1.** above to produce the loss or damage.

b. Acts or decisions, including the failure to act or decide, of any person, group, organization or governmental body.

c. Faulty, inadequate or defective:

(1) Planning, zoning, development, surveying, siting;

(2) Design, specifications, workmanship, repair, construction, renovation, remodeling, grading, compaction;

(3) Materials used in repair, construction, renovation or remodeling; or

(4) Maintenance;

of part or all of any property on or off the described premises.

4. Special Exclusions

The following provisions apply only to the specified Coverage Forms.

a. Business Income (And Extra Expense) Coverage Form, Business Income (Without Extra Expense) Coverage Form, or Extra Expense Coverage Form

We will not pay for:

(1) Any loss caused directly or indirectly by the failure of power or other utility service supplied to the described premises, however caused, if the failure occurs outside of a covered building.

But if the failure of power or other utility service results in a Covered Cause of Loss, we will pay for the loss resulting from that Covered Cause of Loss.

(2) Any loss caused by or resulting from:

(a) Damage or destruction of "finished stock"; or

(b) The time required to reproduce "finished stock".

This exclusion does not apply to Extra Expense.

(3) Any loss caused by or resulting from direct physical loss or damage to radio or television antennas (including satellite dishes) and their lead-in wiring, masts or towers.

(4) Any increase of loss caused by or resulting from:

(a) Delay in rebuilding, repairing or replacing the property or resuming "operations", due to interference at the location of the rebuilding, repair or replacement by strikers or other persons; or

(b) Suspension, lapse or cancellation of any license, lease or contract. But if the suspension, lapse or cancellation is directly caused by the "suspension" of "operations", we will cover such loss that affects your Business Income during the "period of restoration" and any extension of the "period of restoration" in accordance with the terms of the Extended Business Income Additional Coverage and the Extended Period Of Indemnity Optional Coverage or any variation of these.

(5) Any Extra Expense caused by or resulting from suspension, lapse or cancellation of any license, lease or contract beyond the "period of restoration".

(6) Any other consequential loss.

b. Leasehold Interest Coverage Form

(1) Paragraph **B.1.a.** Ordinance Or Law, does not apply to insurance under this Coverage Form.

(2) We will not pay for any loss caused by:

(a) Your cancelling the lease;

(b) The suspension, lapse or cancellation of any license; or

(c) Any other consequential loss.

c. Legal Liability Coverage Form

(1) The following exclusions do not apply to insurance under this Coverage Form:

(a) Paragraph **B.1.a.**, Ordinance Or Law;

(b) Paragraph **B.1.c.**, Governmental Action;

(c) Paragraph **B.1.d.**, Nuclear Hazard;

(d) Paragraph **B.1.e.**, Utility Services; and

(e) Paragraph **B.1.f.**, War And Military Action.

(2) The following additional exclusions apply to insurance under this Coverage Form:

(a) Contractual Liability

We will not defend any claim or "suit", or pay damages that you are legally liable to pay, solely by reason of your assumption of liability in a contract or agreement. But this exclusion does not apply to a written lease agreement in which you have assumed liability for building damage resulting from an actual or attempted burglary or robbery, provided that:

(i) Your assumption of liability was executed prior to the accident; and

(ii) The building is Covered Property under this Coverage Form.

(b) Nuclear Hazard

We will not defend any claim or "suit", or pay any damages, loss, expense or obligation, resulting from nuclear reaction or radiation, or radioactive contamination, however caused.

C. Limitations

The following limitations apply to all policy forms and endorsements, unless otherwise stated.

1. We will not pay for loss of or damage to property, as described and limited in this section. In addition, we will not pay for any loss that is a consequence of loss or damage as described and limited in this section.

a. Steam boilers, steam pipes, steam engines or steam turbines caused by or resulting from any condition or event inside such equipment. But we will pay for loss of or damage to such equipment caused by or resulting from an explosion of gases or fuel within the furnace of any fired vessel or within the flues or passages through which the gases of combustion pass.

b. Hot water boilers or other water heating equipment caused by or resulting from any condition or event inside such boilers or equipment, other than an explosion.

c. The interior of any building or structure, or to personal property in the building or structure, caused by or resulting from rain, snow, sleet, ice, sand or dust, whether driven by wind or not, unless:

   (1) The building or structure first sustains damage by a Covered Cause of Loss to its roof or walls through which the rain, snow, sleet, ice, sand or dust enters; or

   (2) The loss or damage is caused by or results from thawing of snow, sleet or ice on the building or structure.

d. Building materials and supplies not attached as part of the building or structure, caused by or resulting from theft.

   However, this limitation does not apply to:

   (1) Building materials and supplies held for sale by you, unless they are insured under the Builders Risk Coverage Form; or

   (2) Business Income coverage or Extra Expense coverage.

e. Property that is missing, where the only evidence of the loss or damage is a shortage disclosed on taking inventory, or other instances where there is no physical evidence to show what happened to the property.

f. Property that has been transferred to a person or to a place outside the described premises on the basis of unauthorized instructions.

2. We will not pay for loss of or damage to the following types of property unless caused by the "specified causes of loss" or building glass breakage:

a. Valuable papers and records, such as books of account, manuscripts, abstracts, drawings and card index systems, including those which exist on film, tape, disc, drum, cell or other data processing, recording or storage media. Valuable papers and records do not include prepackaged software programs.

b. Animals, and then only if they are killed or their destruction is made necessary.

c. Fragile articles such as statuary, marbles, chinaware and porcelains, if broken. This restriction does not apply to:

   (1) Glass; or

   (2) Containers of property held for sale.

d. Builders' machinery, tools and equipment owned by you or entrusted to you, provided such property is Covered Property.

   However, this limitation does not apply:

   (1) If the property is located on or within 100 feet of the described premises, unless the premises is insured under the Builders Risk Coverage Form; or

   (2) To Business Income coverage or to Extra Expense coverage.

3. The special limit shown for each category, **a.** through **d.**, is the total limit for loss of or damage to all property in that category. The special limit applies to any one occurrence of theft, regardless of the types or number of articles that are lost or damaged in that occurrence. The special limits are:

a. $2,500 for furs, fur garments and garments trimmed with fur.

b. $2,500 for jewelry, watches, watch movements, jewels, pearls, precious and semiprecious stones, bullion, gold, silver, platinum and other precious alloys or metals. This limit does not apply to jewelry and watches worth $100 or less per item.

c. $2,500 for patterns, dies, molds and forms.

d. $250 for stamps, tickets, including lottery tickets held for sale, and letters of credit.

These special limits are part of, not in addition to, the Limit of Insurance applicable to the Covered Property.

This limitation, **C.3.**, does not apply to Business Income coverage or to Extra Expense coverage.

4. We will not pay the cost to repair any defect to a system or appliance from which water, other liquid, powder or molten material escapes. But we will pay the cost to repair or replace damaged parts of fire extinguishing equipment if the damage:

a. Results in discharge of any substance from an automatic fire protection system; or

b. Is directly caused by freezing.

However, this limitation does not apply to Business Income coverage or to Extra Expense coverage.

D. Additional Coverage ☐ Collapse

The term Covered Cause of Loss includes the Additional Coverage ☐ Collapse as described and limited in **D.1.** through **D.5.** below.

1. With respect to buildings:

    a. Collapse means an abrupt falling down or caving in of a building or any part of a building with the result that the building or part of the building cannot be occupied for its intended purpose;

    b. A building or any part of a building that is in danger of falling down or caving in is not considered to be in a state of collapse;

    c. A part of a building that is standing is not considered to be in a state of collapse even if it has separated from another part of the building;

    d. A building that is standing or any part of a building that is standing is not considered to be in a state of collapse even if it shows evidence of cracking, bulging, sagging, bending, leaning, settling, shrinkage or expansion.

2. We will pay for direct physical loss or damage to Covered Property, caused by collapse of a building or any part of a building that is insured under this Coverage Form or that contains Covered Property insured under this Coverage Form, if the collapse is caused by one or more of the following:

    a. The "specified causes of loss" or breakage of building glass, all only as insured against in this Coverage Part;

    b. Decay that is hidden from view, unless the presence of such decay is known to an insured prior to collapse;

    c. Insect or vermin damage that is hidden from view, unless the presence of such damage is known to an insured prior to collapse;

    d. Weight of people or personal property;

    e. Weight of rain that collects on a roof;

    f. Use of defective material or methods in construction, remodeling or renovation if the collapse occurs during the course of the construction, remodeling or renovation. However, if the collapse occurs after construction, remodeling or renovation is complete and is caused in part by a cause of loss listed in **2.a.** through **2.e.**, we will pay for the loss or damage even if use of defective material or methods, in construction, remodeling or renovation, contributes to the collapse.

The criteria set forth in **1.a.** through **1.d.** do not limit the coverage otherwise provided under this Causes of Loss Form for the causes of loss listed in **2.a.**, **2.d.** and **2.e.**

3. With respect to the following property:

    a. Outdoor radio or television antennas (including satellite dishes) and their lead-in wiring, masts or towers;

    b. Awnings, gutters and downspouts;

    c. Yard fixtures;

    d. Outdoor swimming pools;

    e. Fences;

    f. Piers, wharves and docks;

    g. Beach or diving platforms or appurtenances;

    h. Retaining walls; and

    i. Walks, roadways and other paved surfaces;

    if the collapse is caused by a cause of loss listed in **2.b.** through **2.f.**, we will pay for loss or damage to that property only if:

    a. Such loss or damage is a direct result of the collapse of a building insured under this Coverage Form; and

    b. The property is Covered Property under this Coverage Form.

4. If personal property abruptly falls down or caves in and such collapse is not the result of collapse of a building, we will pay for loss or damage to Covered Property caused by such collapse of personal property only if:

    a. The collapse was caused by a Cause of Loss listed in **2.a.** through **2.f.** above;

    b. The personal property which collapses is inside a building; and

    c. The property which collapses is not of a kind listed in **3.** above, regardless of whether that kind of property is considered to be personal property or real property.

The coverage stated in this Paragraph **4.** does not apply to personal property if marring and/or scratching is the only damage to that personal property caused by the collapse.

Collapse of personal property does not mean cracking, bulging, sagging, bending, leaning, settling, shrinkage or expansion.

5. This Additional Coverage, Collapse, will not increase the Limits of Insurance provided in this Coverage Part.

Copyright, Insurance Services Office, Inc., 1999 CP 10 30 10 00 ☐

E. Additional Coverage Extensions

1. Property In Transit

This Extension applies only to your personal property to which this form applies.

a. You may extend the insurance provided by this Coverage Part to apply to your personal property (other than property in the care, custody or control of your salespersons) in transit more than 100 feet from the described premises. Property must be in or on a motor vehicle you own, lease or operate while between points in the coverage territory.

b. Loss or damage must be caused by or result from one of the following causes of loss:

   (1) Fire, lightning, explosion, windstorm or hail, riot or civil commotion, or vandalism.

   (2) Vehicle collision, upset or overturn. Collision means accidental contact of your vehicle with another vehicle or object. It does not mean your vehicle's contact with the road bed.

   (3) Theft of an entire bale, case or package by forced entry into a securely locked body or compartment of the vehicle. There must be visible marks of the forced entry.

c. The most we will pay for loss or damage under this Extension is $5,000.

This Coverage Extension is additional insurance. The Additional Condition, Coinsurance, does not apply to this Extension.

2. Water Damage, Other Liquids, Powder Or Molten Material Damage

If loss or damage caused by or resulting from covered water or other liquid, powder or molten material damage loss occurs, we will also pay the cost to tear out and replace any part of the building or structure to repair damage to the system or appliance from which the water or other substance escapes. This Coverage Extension does not increase the Limit of Insurance.

3. Glass

a. We will pay for expenses incurred to put up temporary plates or board up openings if repair or replacement of damaged glass is delayed.

b. We will pay for expenses incurred to remove or replace obstructions when repairing or replacing glass that is part of a building. This does not include removing or replacing window displays.

This Coverage Extension, **E.3.**, does not increase the Limit of Insurance.

F. Definitions

"Specified Causes of Loss" means the following: Fire; lightning; explosion; windstorm or hail; smoke; aircraft or vehicles; riot or civil commotion; vandalism; leakage from fire extinguishing equipment; sinkhole collapse; volcanic action; falling objects; weight of snow, ice or sleet; water damage.

1. Sinkhole collapse means the sudden sinking or collapse of land into underground empty spaces created by the action of water on limestone or dolomite. This cause of loss does not include:

   a. The cost of filling sinkholes; or

   b. Sinking or collapse of land into man-made underground cavities.

2. Falling objects does not include loss or damage to:

   a. Personal property in the open; or

   b. The interior of a building or structure, or property inside a building or structure, unless the roof or an outside wall of the building or structure is first damaged by a falling object.

3. Water damage means accidental discharge or leakage of water or steam as the direct result of the breaking apart or cracking of a plumbing, heating, air conditioning or other system or appliance (other than a sump system including its related equipment and parts), that is located on the described premises and contains water or steam.

IL 00 17 11 98

COMMON POLICY CONDITIONS

All Coverage Parts included in this policy are subject to the following conditions.

A. Cancellation

1. The first Named Insured shown in the Declarations may cancel this policy by mailing or delivering to us advance written notice of cancellation.

2. We may cancel this policy by mailing or delivering to the first Named Insured written notice of cancellation at least:

   a. 10 days before the effective date of cancellation if we cancel for nonpayment of premium; or

   b. 30 days before the effective date of cancellation if we cancel for any other reason.

3. We will mail or deliver our notice to the first Named Insured's last mailing address known to us.

4. Notice of cancellation will state the effective date of cancellation. The policy period will end on that date.

5. If this policy is cancelled, we will send the first Named Insured any premium refund due. If we cancel, the refund will be pro rata. If the first Named Insured cancels, the refund may be less than pro rata. The cancellation will be effective even if we have not made or offered a refund.

6. If notice is mailed, proof of mailing will be sufficient proof of notice.

B. Changes

This policy contains all the agreements between you and us concerning the insurance afforded. The first Named Insured shown in the Declarations is authorized to make changes in the terms of this policy with our consent. This policy's terms can be amended or waived only by endorsement issued by us and made a part of this policy.

C. Examination Of Your Books And Records

We may examine and audit your books and records as they relate to this policy at any time during the policy period and up to three years afterward.

D. Inspections And Surveys

1. We have the right to:

   a. Make inspections and surveys at any time;

   b. Give you reports on the conditions we find; and

   c. Recommend changes.

2. We are not obligated to make any inspections, surveys, reports or recommendations and any such actions we do undertake relate only to insurability and the premiums to be charged. We do not make safety inspections. We do not undertake to perform the duty of any person or organization to provide for the health or safety of workers or the public. And we do not warrant that conditions:

   a. Are safe or healthful; or

   b. Comply with laws, regulations, codes or standards.

3. Paragraphs 1. and 2. of this condition apply not only to us, but also to any rating, advisory, rate service or similar organization which makes insurance inspections, surveys, reports or recommendations.

4. Paragraph 2. of this condition does not apply to any inspections, surveys, reports or recommendations we may make relative to certification, under state or municipal statutes, ordinances or regulations, of boilers, pressure vessels or elevators.

E. Premiums

The first Named Insured shown in the Declarations:

1. Is responsible for the payment of all premiums; and

2. Will be the payee for any return premiums we pay.

F. Transfer Of Your Rights And Duties Under This Policy

Your rights and duties under this policy may not be transferred without our written consent except in the case of death of an individual named insured.

If you die, your rights and duties will be transferred to your legal representative but only while acting within the scope of duties as your legal representative. Until your legal representative is appointed, anyone having proper temporary custody of your property will have your rights and duties but only with respect to that property.

Index

AAIS

additional coverages 198, 206

additional property excluded and limitations 205, 206

building and personal property coverage part 196

covered property 196

endorsements 207, 208

how much we pay 201

loss payment 202

other conditions 203

other coverage parts 206

property excluded and limitations 197. 198

special causes of loss form 204

supplemental coverages 198

valuation 201

what must be done in case of a loss 200

Abandonment 103

Acts or decisions exclusion 86

Actual cash value 106

broad evidence rule 106, 107

fair market value 106, 107

personal property 107

raw materials 108

replacement cost less depreciation 106

Additional conditions 112

coinsurance 112

mortgageholders 114

Additional conditions, builders risk 123

collapse and removal of one cause 124

mortgageholders 123

need for adequate insurance 123

when coverage ceases 124

Additional coverages 27

debris removal 28

fire department service charge 31

increased cost of construction 34

pollutant cleanup and removal 32

preservation of property 31

Additional coverage extensions, special form 92

business personal property in transit 92

cost to tear out system 93

glass, temporary plates 94

Agreed value 41
    building or contents 41
    coinsurance not applicable 41
    eligible property 41
    predetermined amount 41
    statement of values 41
Aircraft or vehicles 54
    physical contact with 54
    falling objects 54
    objects thrown up by a vehicle 54
American Association of Insurance Services (AAIS) 195
    building and personal property coverage part 196
    commercial properties program 195
    eligibility 195
Animals, exclusion of damage by 81
"Any other insured" 98
    court decisions 98, 99
Appraisal 103
    method to settle differences 103
Artificially generated current
    exclusion in named perils forms 69
    exclusion in special perils form 76
Basic causes of loss form 50
    aircraft or vehicles 54
    explosion 50
    explosion, definition 50
    explosions excluded 51
    fire 50
    friendly fire doctrine 50
    hostile fire 50
    lightning 50
    riot or civil commotion 55
    sinkhole collapse 59
    smoke 52
    sprinkler leakage 58
    vandalism 57
    volcanic action 60
    windstorm or hail 51
Beverly Hills Supper Club 96, 97
Broad form causes of loss 60
    additional 3 perils 60
    additional coverage of collapse 70
    falling objects 60
    water damage 61
    weight of ice, snow, or sleet 60

Builders Risk 117
    additional conditions 123
    additional coverages 121
    blanket coverage option 118
    completed value 118
    coverage extensions 121
    coverage options 124
    covered causes of loss 121
    covered property 119
    deductible 123
    limits of insurance 122
    loss conditions 123
    property not covered 120
Building coverage 7
    additions and alterations 10
    completed additions 8
    fixtures 8
    permanently installed machinery and equipment 9
    personal property used to maintain building 10
Building supplies and materials of others 121
    application of extension 121, 122
    basic amount, $5,000 121
    builders risk form 121
Business personal property 11
    furniture and fixtures 12
    labor or services of others 14
    leased personal property 21
    machinery and equipment 13
    property used in the insured's business 14
    stock 13
    tenant's use interest in improvements and betterments 15
Coinsurance 112
    and the deductible 112
    principle 112
Collapse 70, 92
    "abrupt falling down" 71
    covered causes of collapse 71
    hidden decay, new provision 71
    hidden insect damage, new provision 71
    personal property 72
    serious impairment to building 71
    significant change in 2000 form 71
    special form exclusion 84
    what is not collapse 71

Commercial condominium unit-owners form 153
    additional coverages and coverage extension 154
    property 154
    limits and deductible 154
    loss conditions 155
    other provisions 155
Commercial property conditions 2, 95, 97
    concealment, misrepresentation, or fraud 98
    control of property 99
    insurance under two or more coverages 100
    legal action against the insurer 100
    liberalization 100
    no benefit to bailee 100, 101
    other insurance 101
    policy period, coverage territory 101
    subrogation 102
Commercial property endorsements 163
    additional building property 163
    additional covered property 163
    additional locations special coinsurance provision 164
    additional property not covered 165
    agricultural products storage 166
    alcoholic beverage tax exclusion 167
    brands and labels 167
    broken or cracked glass 168
    burglary and robbery protective safeguards 168
    condominium commercial unit owners optional coverages 169
    contributing insurance 169
    debris removal additional insurance 170
    deductible limitation 170
    distilled spirits and wins market value 170
    earthquake and volcanic eruption 171
    earthquake inception endorsement 172
    electrical apparatus 172
    flood coverage endorsement 172
    functional building valuation 173, 174, 175
    functional personal property valuation, other than stock 175, 176
    grain properties 176
    household personal property coverage 176
    leased property 177
    legal liability 177
    loss payable provisions 177
    manufacturer's consequential loss assumption 178
    manufacturer's selling price, finished stock 178
    market value stock 178

molten material 179
multiple deductible 179
multiple location/premium and dispersion credit application 179
newly acquired/constructed property - increased limit 179
off-premises services, direct damage 180
ordinance or law coverage 180
outdoor trees, shrubs, and plants 182
outside signs 182
peak season limit of insurance 183
pier and wharf additional covered causes of loss 184
pollutant cleanup and removal additional aggregate limit 184
protective safeguards 185
radio or TV antennas 186
radioactive contamination 186
report of values 187
spoilage coverage 187
sprinkler leakage exclusion 188
sprinkler leakage - earthquake extension 188
storage or repairs limited liability 188
tentative rates 189
theft exclusion 189
utility services 189
vacancy changes 189
vacancy permit 190
value reporting form 190
vandalism exclusion 191
watercraft exclusion 191
windstorm or hail percentage deductible 191
windstorm or hail direct damage 192
windstorm or hail exclusion 192
your business personal property - separation of coverage 193
Common policy conditions 2, 95
cancellation 95
changes 96
examination of your books and records 96
inspections and surveys 96
premiums 97
transfer of rights and duties 97
Concealment, misrepresentation, or fraud 98
"any other insured" 98
definition of "void" 98
material facts 98
use of building 98
Concurrent causation exclusions 62, 63, 85
acts or decisions 86

inadequate planning, design, etc. 87

legal doctrine 85

weather conditions 86

Condominium associations form 150

business personal property 152

"if the agreement requires" 151

covered property, six classes 150, 151

other provisions 152, 153

Consequential loss 6

Construction types 3

Continuous or repeated seepage of water 81

Contributing insurance 3

Control of property 99

protection from the acts of others 99

Coverage extensions 27, 35

newly acquired or constructed property 35

nonowned detached trailers 40

outdoor property 40

personal effects and property of others 37

property off-premises 38

valuable papers and records, cost of research 38

Coverage extensions, builders risk 121

building supplies and materials of others 121, 122

sod, trees, shrubs, and plants 121, 122

Coverage options, builders risk 124

builders risk reporting form 125

building materials of others 127

building renovations 125

collapse during construction 126

separate or subcontractors interest 126

theft of building materials, etc. 126

Coverage part 2

Covered property 6

building 6

business personal property 6

property of others 6

Covered property, builders risk policy 119

building under construction 119

fixtures and machinery 119

building materials and supplies 119

meaning of "construction" 120

no coverage for business personal property 120

no coverage for property of others 120

temporary structures 120

Debris removal 28

additional amount 28, 29
example 28, 29
newer, longer definition 28
no requirement to repair or replace 29
pollutants 28
top limit 28
Defined terms 7
Direct loss or damage 5
Discharge of pollutants 84
new exception to the exclusion 85
Dishonest or criminal acts exclusion 82
coverage for destruction by employee 83
court decisions 83
limited liability companies 82
Duties of the insured in the event of a loss 104
eight duties 105
examination under oath 105
"E-issues" under the CP policy 209
current policy language 212
insuring intangible assets 210, 211, 212
newly developed policies 213
what today's businesses face 209
Earth movement exclusion 63
naturally occurring phenomena 63
Exclusions - named peril forms 62
artificially generated current 69
concurrent causation 62, 63
earth movement 63
governmental action 64
mechanical breakdown 69
nuclear hazard 65
ordinance or law 63
steam boiler explosion 69
utility services 65
war and military action 66
water 67
Exposure 4
Extension of replacement cost to personal property of others 47
Falling objects 60
property covered 60
property not covered 60
Fire department service charge 31
difference from homeowners policy 31, 32
Firewalls 3
Friendly fire doctrine 50

Governmental action exclusion 64
    example of when exclusion applies 64
    example of when exclusion does not apply 64
Hostile fire 50
Improvements and betterments 16
    different from trade fixtures 17
    recovery for loss under the CP 17, 18
    repairs made by a landlord 18
    repairs made by a tenant-insured 16, 17
    repairs not made 18, 19
    repairs not made, effect of lease 20
"In the open" 11
Inadequate planning, design, etc. exclusion 87
Increased cost of construction 34
    conditions 34
    example 34
    limit 34
    newly added coverage 34
Indirect loss 6
    spoilage 6
Inflation guard 42
    building or personal property 42
    example 42
Inspections and surveys condition 96
    Beverly Hills Supper Club 96, 97
    not a warranty by the insurer 96
Insuring agreement 5
ISO rules 2
Interstate accounts 3
Leasehold interest form 129
    cancellation 133
    causes of loss 130
    exclusions 130
    leasehold interest factors 135
    limitations 130
    limits of insurance 131
    loss conditions 132
    schedule form CP 19 60 134
    what is insured 129
Legal liability coverage form 155
    additional conditions 161
    amount of insurance 156
    coverage 157
    coverage extensions 158
    ineligible additional insureds 157

loss conditions 160, 161
    newly acquired property 158
    perils and exclusions 159, 160
    property of others 155
    rules 155, 156
Liberalization condition 100
    example of 100
Limitations under the special form 87
    boilers or water heating equipment 88
    building interiors 88
    building materials, theft of 89
    glass, limit removed 90
    gutters and downspouts, removed in 2000 version 90
    missing property 89
    personal property in a building 88
    steam boilers, pipes, engines, or turbines 87
    transferred property 90
Limitations under the special form, other types of property 91
    animals 91
    coverage for specified perils only 91
    fragile articles 91
    glass limitation removed 91
    owned builders equipment or tools 91
    photographic lenses 91
    valuable papers and records 91
Limits of insurance, builders risk 122
    sublimit on outdoor signs 122
Limits of insurance and deductible 102
    application of deductible 103
    coverage extensions, addition to the limit 102
    preservation of property, within the limit 102
Loss conditions 103
    abandonment and appraisal 103
    duties in the event of a loss 104
    loss payment 105
    recovered property 108
    vacancy 108
Loss conditions, leasehold interest form 132
    clauses removed 132
    similar to CP policy 132
Loss payment 105
    four options 105
    property of others 106
Losses that happen over a period of time 76
    coverage for resulting losses 77
    settling, cracking, shrinking, or expansion 79

specified causes of loss 77
wear and tear, etc. 76
wear and tear, example 77, 78
wear and tear, purpose of 78
Mechanical breakdown exclusion 69, 79
example of coverage 69
special form exclusion 79, 80
Modular format 2
Mortgageholders 114
denial of claim to insured 115
rights and duties 115
Mortgageholders E&O form 135
additional conditions 143
collapse 142, 143
conditions applicable to all forms 144
coverage agreements 136
coverage A - mortgageholder's interest 136
coverage B - property owned or held in trust 138
coverage C - mortgageholder's liability 139
coverage D - real estate tax liability 130
definitions 147
exclusions 140, 141
limits of insurance 131, 142
Mortgageholder's E&O - coverage A 136
causes of loss 137
covered property 137
error in obtaining or maintaining insurance 137
property not covered 137
Mortgageholder's E&O - coverage B 138
limited perils 138
property owned or held in trust 138
time limit on coverage 138, 139
Mortgageholder's E&O - coverage C 139
needed when purchasing own coverage 139
Mortgageholder's E&O - coverage D 139
real estate tax liability 140
Mortgageholders E&O form, conditions 144
abandonment 144
appraisal 144
duties in the event of loss 144
insurance under two or more coverages 145
legal action against the insurer 145
liberalization 146
loss payment 146
other insurance 146

policy period, territory 146
transfer of rights of recovery 146
vacancy 146
your duties 147
Multiple policies 3
Named perils causes of loss 49
basic form 49
broad form 49
Need for adequate insurance, builders risk 123
resembles coinsurance 123
Newly acquired or constructed property 35
business personal property 36
conditions 35
limit 35
time period 36
Nonowned detached trailers 40
limit 40
reason for new coverage 40
requirements for coverage 40, 41
Nuclear exclusion 65
Occupancy 4
Open perils exclusions 75
animals 81
artificially generated electric current 76
better covered elsewhere 75
collapse 79, 84
continuous or repeated seepage of water 81
delay, loss of use or market 76
dishonest or criminal acts 82
discharge of pollutants 84
historically uninsurable events 75
losses that happen over a period of time 76
mechanical breakdown 79
neglect 85
rain, snow, ice or sleet and property in the open 84
smoke, vapor, smudging 76
steam boiler explosion 81
trick or device 83
underwriting policy 75
water, other liquids, powder, molten material 82
Optional coverages 27, 41
agreed value 41
extension of replacement cost to personal property of others 47
inflation guard 42
replacement cost 42

Ordinance or law exclusion 63
    example of when applied 63
    limited additional coverage 63
Other coverage forms 129
    leasehold interest 129
    mortgageholders E&O 135
    tobacco in sales warehouses 147
    commercial condominium unit-owners 153
    condominium associations 150
    legal liability 155
Other insurance condition 101
    example of 101
Other relevant provisions of the CP policy 102
    limits of insurance and deductible 102
Outdoor property 40
    limit 40
    restores coverage 40
Permanently installed 9
Personal property of others 21
    account of the owner 21
    coverage extension 37
    need for bailees coverage 37
    personal effects 38
Policy term 2
Pollutant cleanup and removal 32
    annual aggregate amount 32, 33
    costs not covered 33
Premises, meaning of 11
Preservation of property 31
    any direct physical loss 31
Property not covered 22
    accounts, bills, etc. 22
    airborne personal property 25
    animals 22
    autos held for sale 22
    bridges, roadways, etc. 22
    bulkheads 25
    contraband 22
    cost of excavations, etc. 22
    fences 26
    foundations 24
    grain, hay, etc. 26
    growing crops 24
    land 24
    plants 26

  radio or TV antennas 26
  retaining walls 25
  research costs 26
  satellite dishes 26
  shrubs 26
  specifically described property 25
  trees 26
  underground pipes 25
  vehicles 26
  water 24
  waterborne personal property 25
Property off-premises 38
  limit 38
  stock 39
  where covered 38
Protection 4
Protection class codes 4
  definitions
Replacement cost 42
  amount payable 44
  claim procedure 43
  eligible property 42, 43
  ineligible property 43
  "on the same premises" 44
  tenants improvements and betterments 43
Riot or civil commotion 55
  "Black's Law Dictionary" definition 55
  common definition 55
  court decisions 56
  looting 57
  striking employees 57
Schedule form CP 19 60, leasehold interest 134
Settling, cracking, shrinking, or expansion 79
  decisions favoring insured and insurer 79
Sinkhole collapse 59
  cost of filling in 60
  definition 59
Smoke 52
  definition of 52
  excluded causes 52, 53
  product of combustion 53
  vapors as smoke 53
Sod, trees, shrubs, and plants 121, 122
Special covered causes of loss 73
  additional coverage extensions 92

"all risks", use of 73
assumption of coverage 74
difference from named perils 73
exclusions 75, 76
limitations 87
losses that happen over a period of time 76
open perils exclusions 75
similarities to named perils forms 74
special theft limits 92
Sprinkler leakage 58
automatic sprinkler system 58
cost to repair system 59
cost to tear out and replace structure 59
exclusion endorsement 58
vacancy - no coverage 59
Steam boiler explosion 69
named peril forms exclusion 69
special form exclusion 81
Structure, defined 7
Subrogation condition 102
waiver of 102
Theft   92
special limits 92
Tobacco in sales warehouses 147
additional conditions 149
additional coverages 148
coverage extension 148
covered property 148
deductible 149
definitions 150
exclusions and limitations 149
loss conditions 149
policy term 147
reports by insured 147
Transfer of rights and duties 97
death of the named insured 97
Trick or device exclusion 83
Underwriting 3
Utility services exclusion 65
applies regardless of cause of outage 65
lightning strike off-premises 66
resulting damage 66
Vacancy 58, 59, 108
definition of 108
exemptions 109

    handling of losses in vacant building 108, 109

    no coverage for sprinkler leakage 59

    no coverage for vandalism 58

Valuable papers and records, cost of research 38

    limit 38

Valuation 110

    exceptions to ACV 110, 111

    glass 110

    losses under $2,500 110

    stock 110

    tenants improvements and betterments 110

    valuable papers and records 111

Vandalism

    definition 57

    exclusion endorsement 58

    glass coverage 58

    vacancy 58

War exclusion 66

    court cases 67

    genuine warlike act 67

Water damage

Water exclusion 67

Water, other liquids, powder, molten material 82

    accidental discharge 61

    cost of tearing out and replacing structure 61

    hydrostatic water pressure 68

    narrowing of coverage in 2000 form 61

    repeated leakage 61, 81

    sprinkler system 61

    surface water 68

    sump pump overflow 61, 68

Weather conditions exclusion 86

Weight of ice, snow, or sleet 60

    gutters and downspouts 60

Windstorm or hail 51

    damage to building's interior 52

    direct loss from windstorm, court decisions 51

    frost or cold weather not covered 52

    not included as 51

    property in poor condition 52

    removal of peril via endorsement 52

Coverage Scenario Index .... **x**

Application of the Mechanical Breakdown Exclusion 70

Appraisal of a Loss 104

Carpeting in Condominiums 151

Coinsurance Application in a Total Loss 1213
Damage by Police Action 64
Debris Removal—Is Repair or Replacement Required? 29
Debris Removal Coverage and Coinsurance Provision 30
Debris Removal—Volunteer Expense
Earth Movement Exclusion 64
Equipment Damaged by a Covered Peril—Spoilage Loss Consequential . 6
Excavation of Broken Water Pipe Covered? 23
Fire Department Service Charge Covered? 32
Foundations as Property Not Covered 24
Gunshot as Explosion 50
Heavy Construction and the Earth Movement Exclusion 75
Improvements and Betterments—Coverage Dependent
      on Term of Lease? 15
Lawn Tent as a Fixture 9
Leasehold Interest—Terms in a Lease 131
Loss During Foreclosure 115
May the Exclusion of Excavation Costs be Applied to Debris Removal? 22
Marble Slab as Fragile Article 91
Meaning of locations You "Own, Lease, or Operate" 39
Mechanical Breakdown Exclusion and Concurrent Causation 80
Missing Property—No Physical Evidence 89
Modular Office System as Fixture 12
Need for Builders Risk on Renovations to Existing Buildings 127
Newly Acquired Location 37
Nonfunctioning Water Tower as Covered Property 7
Outdoor Sprinkler System as Underground Pipes? 25
Pollution Cleanup 32
Power Failure vs. Power Surge 66
Property in Transit 93
Remodeling as "Vandalism" 57
Repeated Seepage or Leakage 82
Replacement by Substitution—Commercial Property 44
Replacement Cost—Reconditioned Property 45, 46
Sinkhole Collapse under CP Form 59
Steam Boilers—Condition or Event Inside 88
Tractor Falling off Trailer—Falling Object or Vehicle Damage? 55
Valuation and Selling Price 111
Value of the Building on the Completion Date 118
Water Damage and Boarded-Up Windows 88
Water Damage—Costs to Repair Leak Even if Building is Undamaged . 62
Wear and Tear Exclusion—Damage to Shower Stall 78

Call **1-800-543-0874**
to order and ask for
operator BB or fax
your order to
1-800-874-1916.
Ask about our complete
line of Coverage Guides.

PAYMENT INFORMATION

Add shipping & handling charges to
all orders as indicated. If your order
exceeds total amount listed in chart,
call 1-800-543-0874 for shipping &
handling charge. Any order
of 10 or more or $250.00 or over
will be billed for shipping by actual
weight, plus a handling fee.
Unconditional 30 day guarantee.

Shipping & Handling (Additional)

Order Total	Shipping & handling
$20.00 to $39.99	$6.00
40.00 to 59.99	7.00
60.00 to 79.99	9.00
80.00 to 109.99	10.00
110.00 to 149.99	12.00
150.00 to 199.99	13.00
200.00 to 249.99	15.50

Any order of 10 or more items or over $250 will be
billed by actual weight, plus a handling fee.

SALES TAX (Additional)

Sales tax is required for
residents of the following
states: CA, DC, FL, GA, IL,
KY, NJ, NY, OH, PA, WA.

The
NATIONAL
UNDERWRITER
Company

The National Underwriter Co.
Orders Dept #2-BB
P.O. Box 14448
Cincinnati, OH 45250-9786

2-BB

_____ Copies of *Commercial Property Coverage Guide*, 2nd Edition (#4380002) $34.99
_____ Copies of *Commercial Property Coverage Guide*, 2nd Edition CD-ROM (#4389002) $40.00
_____ Copies of *Commercial Property Coverage Guide*, 2nd Edition Internet (#4389102) $40.00
_____ Copies of *Commercial Property Coverage Guide*, 2nd Edition Print CE Exam** (#4386102) $25.00
_____ Copies of *Commercial Property Coverage Guide*, 2nd Edition Online CE Exam** (#4386702) $25.00

❑ Check enclosed*   ❑ Charge my VISA/MC/AmEx (circle one)   ❑ Bill me
*Make check payable to The National Underwriter Company.
Please include the appropriate shipping & handling charges and any applicable sales tax. (see charts at left)

Signature _____

Card # _____ *Exp. Date* _____

Name _____ *Title* _____

Company _____

Street Address _____

City _____ *State* _____ *Zip+4* _____

Business Phone (_____) _____ *Business Fax* (_____) _____

Email _____

** Visit our website at www.nationalunderwriter.com or call 1-800-543-0874 for state availability. CE exams are non-refundable once
package is opened or online exam is started. CE exam available only with print publication for an additional $25. Proof of purchase of
current edition is required.

The
NATIONAL
UNDERWRITER
Company

The National Underwriter Co.
Orders Dept #2-BB
P.O. Box 14448
Cincinnati, OH 45250-9786

2-BB

_____ Copies of *Commercial Property Coverage Guide*, 2nd Edition (#4380002) $34.99
_____ Copies of *Commercial Property Coverage Guide*, 2nd Edition CD-ROM (#4389002) $40.00
_____ Copies of *Commercial Property Coverage Guide*, 2nd Edition Internet (#4389102) $40.00
_____ Copies of *Commercial Property Coverage Guide*, 2nd Edition Print CE Exam** (#4386102) $25.00
_____ Copies of *Commercial Property Coverage Guide*, 2nd Edition Online CE Exam** (#4386702) $25.00

❑ Check enclosed*   ❑ Charge my VISA/MC/AmEx (circle one)   ❑ Bill me
*Make check payable to The National Underwriter Company.
Please include the appropriate shipping & handling charges and any applicable sales tax. (see charts at left)

Signature _____

Card # _____ *Exp. Date* _____

Name _____ *Title* _____

Company _____

Street Address _____

City _____ *State* _____ *Zip+4* _____

Business Phone (_____) _____ *Business Fax* (_____) _____

Email _____

** Visit our website at www.nationalunderwriter.com or call 1-800-543-0874 for state availability. CE exams are non-refundable once
package is opened or online exam is started. CE exam available only with print publication for an additional $25. Proof of purchase of
current edition is required.

The
NATIONAL
UNDERWRITER
Company

The National Underwriter Co.
Orders Dept #2-BB
P.O. Box 14448
Cincinnati, OH 45250-9786

Commercial Property Coverage Guide, 2nd Edition has been filed
in many states for continuing education. Call 1-800-543-0874 for
information or visit www.nationalunderwriter.com.

NO POSTAGE
NECESSARY
IF MAILED
IN THE
UNITED STATES

BUSINESS REPLY MAIL

FIRST CLASS MAIL   PERMIT NO 68   CINCINNATI, OH

POSTAGE WILL BE PAID BY ADDRESSEE

The National Underwriter Co.
Orders Department #2-BB
P.O. Box 14448
Cincinnati, OH 45250-9786

NO POSTAGE
NECESSARY
IF MAILED
IN THE
UNITED STATES

BUSINESS REPLY MAIL

FIRST CLASS MAIL   PERMIT NO 68   CINCINNATI, OH

POSTAGE WILL BE PAID BY ADDRESSEE

The National Underwriter Co.
Orders Department #2-BB
P.O. Box 14448
Cincinnati, OH 45250-9786